THE AUTOBIOGRAPHY OF
MARTIN LUTHER KING, JR.

EDITED BY
CLAYBORNE CARSON

IPM

INTELLECTUAL PROPERTIES MANAGEMENT, INC.

IN ASSOCIATION WITH

It gives me great pleasure to finally see my husband's words in autobiographical form. During the Civil Rights Movement a number of publishers and news organizations showed remarkable courage in bringing Martin's views to the public. Without these media outlets, the bits and pieces of which this autobiography is made would have been lost to posterity. Hence, my gratitude goes to Harper Collins, William Morrow, Pocket Books, Henry Holt, Pitman, University of California Press, Harper & Row, Random House, New American Library, Kennedy Presidential Library, *Albany Herald, Atlanta Journal, Christian Century, Ebony, Hindustan Times, Jet, Look, Massachusetts Review, McCall's, Montgomery Adviser, Nashville Tennessean, The Nation, New York Amsterdam News, New York Post, New York Times, Playboy, Progressive, Redbook, Saturday Review, Southern Courier, TIME*, ABC, BBC, CBC, *The Merv Griffin Show*, NBC, and WAII-TV, as well as others too numerous to mention.

Intellectual Properties Management (IPM) has made extensive efforts to identify the original source of all the material that appears in this autobiography, and to seek appropriate permission. But as with any endeavor, errors can take place. If an oversight is noted, please contact IPM so that proper credit can be made in future editions.

– Coretta Scott King, September 1998

ABACUS

First published in Great Britain by Little, Brown and Company in 1999
This paperback edition published by Abacus in 2000
Reprinted 2001, 2002, 2003, 2004, 2005, 2006, 2007, 2008

Published by arrangement with Warner Books, Inc., New York, USA

A CIP catalogue record for this book is available from the British Library

ISBN 978-0-349-11298-5

Printed and bound in Great Britain by Clays Ltd, St Ives plc

Abacus
An imprint of
Little, Brown Book Group
100 Victoria Embankment
London EC4Y 0DY

An Hachette Livre UK Company
www.hachettelivre.co.uk

www.littlebrown.co.uk

CONTENTS

EDITOR'S PREFACE

I first saw Martin Luther King, Jr., from a distance. He was up on the platform in front of the Lincoln Memorial, the concluding speaker at the 1963 March on Washington for Jobs and Freedom. I was below in the vast crowd of listeners around the reflecting pool, a nineteen-year-old college student attending my first civil rights demonstration. He would become a Man of the Year, a Nobel Prize laureate, and a national icon. I would become a foot soldier in the movement he symbolized and would walk through doors of opportunity made possible by that movement.

More than two decades later, after I became a historian at Stanford University, Mrs. Coretta Scott King unexpectedly called me to offer the opportunity to edit the papers of her late husband. Since accepting her offer to become director of the King Papers Project, I have immersed myself in the documents recording his life and have gradually come to know a man I never met. The study of King has become the central focus of my scholarly life, and this project is the culmination of my career as a documentary editor. The March on Washington started me on the path to *The Autobiography of Martin Luther King, Jr.* This book is a product of King's intellectual legacy, just as I am a beneficiary of his social justice legacy.

The following narrative of King's life is based entirely on his own words. These are his thoughts about the events in his life as he expressed them at different times in various ways. Although he never wrote a comprehensive autobiography, King published three major books as well as numerous articles and essays focusing on specific periods of his life. In addition, many of his speeches, sermons, letters, and unpublished manuscripts provide revealing information. Taken together, these materials provide the basis for this approximation of the autobiography that King might have written had his life not suddenly ended.

For the most part, this book consists of autobiographical writings that were published during King's lifetime and were personally edited by him. In many instances King was assisted by others, since he made considerable use of collaborators. Nevertheless, King's papers provide ample evidence of his active involvement in the editorial processes that resulted in his most significant publications. Indeed, the preparation for this autobiography involved examining preliminary drafts (several handwritten) of King's published writings in order to determine his authorial intentions. I have included passages from such drafts when they contain revealing or clarifying information that does not appear in the published version.

Although King's published autobiographical writings provide the basic structure of this book, they constitute an incomplete narrative. In order to fill out the narrative and to include King's accounts of events that are not discussed in his published writings, I have incorporated passages from hundreds of documents and recordings, including many statements that were not intended for publication or even intended as autobiography. These passages augment the published accounts and serve as transitions between more extended narratives. In some instances, I have made editorial changes, which are explained below, in order to construct a narrative that is readable and comprehensible. This exercise of editorial craft is intended to provide readers with a readily accessible assemblage of King's writings and recorded statements that would otherwise be available only to a handful of King scholars.

I trust that readers will recognize and appreciate the fact that this narrative can never approach the coherence and comprehensiveness that would have been possible if King had been able to write a complete account of his life. Thus, this narrative understates the importance in King's life of his family. Although King often acknowledged the centrality of his wife, Coretta Scott King, in his public and private life, his extant papers rarely noted the degree to which she participated in protest activities and other public events. Similarly, King's close ties to his parents, his children, his sister Christine King Farris, and his brother A. D. King are insufficiently reflected in his papers, despite the fact that these relatives played crucial roles in his life.

The Autobiography of Martin Luther King, Jr., is, therefore, largely a religious and political autobiography rather than an exploration of a private life. It is necessarily limited to those aspects of King's life that he chose to reveal in his papers, but King was never garrulous about his private life and was unlikely to have chosen his autobiography as an opportunity to reveal intimate details of his life. In his personal papers, however, King sometimes overcame his reticence to expose his private feelings to public view. He left behind documents that offer information that has never previously been published and that collectively defines his character. Although King may have selected or utilized these materials differently than I have, he (or researchers and co-authors working with him) would certainly have recognized them as essential starting points for understanding his life.

This book is an extension of my charge from the King estate to assemble and edit King's papers. I have benefited from the long-term, collective effort of dozens of staff members and student researchers who assisted in the search for autobiographical passages amidst the several hundred thousand King-related documents that the King Papers Project has identified (see Acknowledgments section). *The Autobiography of Martin Luther King, Jr.,* is one by-product of the project's continuing effort to publish a definitive, annotated fourteen-volume scholarly edition of *The Papers of Martin Luther King, Jr.*

The fact that *The Autobiography of Martin Luther King, Jr.,* has been compiled and edited after King's death warrants an explanation of how it was constructed. Although many autobiographies are written with some editorial assistance—from minor copyediting to extensive rewriting of raw information (often tape-recorded recollections) supplied by the subject—readers are rarely made aware of the significance of such assistance. The role of Alex Haley in the production of *The Autobiography of Malcolm X* is a well-known demonstration of the value of behind-the-scenes editorial assistance for a subject who lacks the time or the ability to write an autobiographical narrative that is compelling and of literary value. Autobiographical editing succeeds when the resulting narrative convinces readers that it accurately represents the thoughts of the subject.

The authenticity of this autobiography of Martin Luther King,

Jr., derives from the fact that I have followed a consistent methodology to preserve the integrity of King's statements and writing while also merging these texts into a single narrative. Although great care has been taken to insure that this account of King's life is based on his own words, it is also the result of many challenging editorial judgments. Among these was the decision to construct a narrative that traced King's life to its end by combining source texts of many different periods in his life. The comprehensiveness of this narrative implies that King wrote it, with considerable editorial and research assistance, at the very end of his life. Although many of the source texts present King's attitudes and perspectives at earlier points in his life, King's viewpoints on major issues remained quite stable during his adult years; I feel justified in believing that King's final recounting of his beliefs would not have differed in any significant way from his earlier recollections.

The materials used to construct this narrative are the types of documentary materials that King (or those assisting him) would undoubtedly have consulted while preparing an autobiography. These source texts, which constitute the raw materials for this work, include sections and passages taken from the following types of sources:

- major autobiographical books (and draft manuscripts): *Stride Toward Freedom: The Montgomery Story* (1958), *Why We Can't Wait* (1964), and *Where Do We Go from Here: Chaos or Community?* (1967);
- articles and essays (both published and unpublished) describing specific periods and events;
- speeches, sermons, and other public statements containing autobiographical passages;
- autobiographical statements in King's published or recorded interviews;
- letters from King;
- comments by King in official documents, meeting transcripts, and various audiovisual materials.

I have tried whenever possible to track down the original publishers of these materials, but in a few instances this was virtually impossible.

To insure that this narrative accurately reflects King's autobiographical thoughts, editorial interventions have been limited to those necessary to produce a narrative that is readable, internally coherent, and lucid. I have preserved the integrity and immediacy of certain texts by inserting italicized verbatim passages into the edited narrative. Other quotations from King-authored documents have been placed in boxes at appropriate places in the autobiographical narrative.

King's recollections of episodes in his life, like all autobiographical writings, were distorted by the passage of time and the vagaries of memory. Thus I have not attempted to correct historical inaccuracies in King's account. Rather, when multiple source texts are available for a particular event, I have sought to determine which of these represent King's most vivid and reliable recollection. The resulting narrative balances several considerations in the selection of source texts, including a preference for accounts that are near to the time of the event rather than later recollections and a preference for more precise descriptions over more general, abstract ones.

After source texts were selected and placed in rough chronological order, I constructed chapter-long narratives that cover periods in King's life. In this process, I condensed some of King's source texts by removing words and details that were redundant or superfluous in the context of a comprehensive narrative. Additional editorial interventions include the following: tenses have been changed (usually from present to past or past perfect); words or brief phrases have been added to indicate or clarify time, location, or name (such as "In June"); conjunctions and other transitional words have been provided when necessary; pronouns have been replaced with proper nouns when referents are unclear ("Ralph Abernathy" rather than "he"), and vice versa when context requires; spellings have been regularized; punctuation and sentence construction have been modified in order to clarify meaning and enhance readability.

CLAYBORNE CARSON
Stanford, California
August 1, 1998

THE AUTOBIOGRAPHY OF

MARTIN LUTHER KING, JR.

1

EARLY YEARS

Of course I was religious. I grew up in the church. My father is a preacher, my grandfather was a preacher, my great-grandfather was a preacher, my only brother is a preacher, my daddy's brother is a preacher. So I didn't have much choice.

NOVEMBER 25, 1926
Michael (later Martin) Luther King, Sr., marries Alberta Williams, daughter of A. D. Williams, pastor of Ebenezer Baptist Church

JANUARY 15, 1929
Michael (later Martin) Luther King, Jr., born at Williams/King family home at 501 Auburn Avenue in Atlanta

MARCH 21, 1931
A. D. Williams dies and is succeeded as pastor of Ebenezer by King Sr.

MAY 18, 1941
King Jr.'s grandmother Jennie Celeste Williams dies and family moves to 193 Boulevard in Atlanta

APRIL 17, 1944
King Jr. travels to Dublin, Georgia, to deliver "The Negro and the Constitution" in oratory contest

I was born in the late twenties on the verge of the Great Depression, which was to spread its disastrous arms into every corner of this nation for over a decade. I was much too young to remember the beginning of this depression, but I do recall, when I was about five years of age, how I questioned my parents about the numerous people standing in breadlines. I can see the effects of this early childhood experience on my present anticapitalistic feelings.

My birthplace was Atlanta, Georgia, the capital of the state and the so-called "gateway to the South." Atlanta is home for me. I was born on Auburn Avenue. Our church, Ebenezer Baptist, is on Auburn Avenue. I'm now co-pastor of that church, and my office in the Southern Christian Leadership Conference is on Auburn Avenue.

I went through the public schools of Atlanta for a period, and then I went to what was then known as the Atlanta University Laboratory High School for two years. After that school closed, I went to Booker T. Washington High School.

The community in which I was born was quite ordinary in terms of social status. No one in our community had attained any great wealth. Most of the Negroes in my hometown who had attained wealth lived in a section of town known as "Hunter Hills." The community was characterized with a sort of unsophisticated simplicity. No one was in the extremely poor class. It is probably fair to class the people of this community as those of average income. It was a wholesome community, notwithstanding the fact that none of us were ever considered members of the "upper-upper class." Crime was at a minimum, and most of our neighbors were deeply religious.

From the very beginning I was an extraordinarily healthy child. It is said that at my birth the doctors pronounced me a one hundred percent perfect child, from a physical point of view. I hardly know how an ill moment feels. I guess the same thing would apply to my mental life. I have always been somewhat precocious, both physically and mentally. So it seems that from a hereditary point of view, nature was very kind to me.

My home situation was very congenial. I have a marvelous mother and father. I can hardly remember a time that they ever argued (my father happens to be the kind who just won't argue) or had any great falling out. These factors were highly significant in determining my religious attitudes. It is quite easy for me to think of a God of love mainly because I grew up in a family where love was central and where lovely relationships were ever present. It is quite easy for me to think of the universe as basically friendly mainly because of my uplifting hereditary and environmental circumstances. It is quite easy for me to lean more toward optimism than pessimism about human nature mainly because of my childhood experiences.

In my own life and in the life of a person who is seeking to be strong, you combine in your character antitheses strongly marked. You are both militant and moderate; you are both idealistic and realistic. And I think that my strong determination for justice comes from the very strong, dynamic personality of my father, and I would hope that the gentle aspect comes from a mother who is very gentle and sweet.

"Mother Dear"

My mother, Alberta Williams King, has been behind the scene setting forth those motherly cares, the lack of which leaves a missing link in life. She is a very devout person with a deep commitment to the Christian faith. Unlike my father, she is soft-spoken and easygoing. Although possessed of a rather recessive personality, she is warm and easily approachable.

The daughter of A. D. Williams, a successful minister, Alberta Williams grew up in comparative comfort. She was sent to the best available schools and college and was, in general, protected from the worst blights of discrimination. An only child, she was provided with all of the conveniences that any high school and college student could expect. In spite of her relatively comfortable circumstances, my mother never complacently adjusted herself to the system of segregation. She instilled a sense of self-respect in all of her children from the very beginning.

My mother confronted the age-old problem of the Negro parent in America: how to explain discrimination and segregation to a small child. She taught me that I should feel a sense of "somebodiness" but that on the other hand I had to go out and face a system that stared me in the face every day saying you are "less than," you are "not equal to." She told me about slavery and how it ended with the Civil War. She tried to explain the divided system of the South—the segregated schools, restaurants, theaters, housing; the white and colored signs on drinking fountains, waiting rooms, lavatories—as a social condition rather than a natural order. She made it clear that she opposed this system and that I must never allow it to make me feel inferior. Then she said the words that almost every Negro hears before he can yet understand the injustice that makes them necessary: "You are as good as anyone." At this time Mother had no idea that the little boy in her arms would years later be involved in a struggle against the system she was speaking of.

"Daddy"

Martin Luther King, Sr., is as strong in his will as he is in his body. He has a dynamic personality, and his very physical presence (weighing about 220 pounds) commands attention. He has always been a very strong and self-confident person. I have rarely ever met a person more fearless and courageous than my father, notwithstanding the fact that he feared for me. He never feared the autocratic and brutal person in the white community. If they said something to him that was insulting, he made it clear in no uncertain terms that he didn't like it.

A sharecropper's son, he had met brutalities at firsthand, and had begun to strike back at an early age. His family lived in a little town named Stockbridge, Georgia, about eighteen miles from Atlanta. One day, while working on the plantation, he keenly observed that the boss was cheating his father out of some hard-earned money. He revealed this to his father right in the presence of the plantation owner. When his happened the boss angrily and furiously shouted, "Jim, if you don't keep this nigger boy of yours in his place, I am going to slap him down." Grandfather, being almost totally dependent on the boss for economic security, urged Dad to keep quiet.

My dad, looking back over that experience, says that at that moment he became determined to leave the farm. He often says humorously, "I ain't going to plough a mule anymore." After a few months he left Stockbridge and went to Atlanta determined to get an education. Although he was then eighteen—a year older than most persons finishing high school—he started out getting a high school education and did not stop until he had finished Atlanta's Morehouse College.

The thing that I admire most about my dad is his genuine Christian character. He is a man of real integrity, deeply committed to moral and ethical principles. He is conscientious in all of his undertakings. Even the person who disagrees with his frankness has to admit that his motives and actions are sincere. He never hesitates to tell the truth and speak his mind, however cutting it may be. This quality of frankness has often caused people to actually fear him. I have had young and old alike say to me, "I'm scared to death of your dad." Indeed, he is stern at many points.

My father has always had quite an interest in civil rights. He has been president of the NAACP in Atlanta, and he always stood out in social reform. From before I was born, he had refused to ride the city buses after witnessing a brutal attack on a load of Negro passengers. He led the fight in Atlanta to equalize teachers' salaries and was instrumental in the elimination of Jim Crow elevators in the courthouse.

As pastor of the Ebenezer Baptist Church, my father wielded great influence in the Negro community and perhaps won the grudging respect of the whites. At any rate, they never attacked him physically, a fact that filled my brother and sister and me with wonder as we grew up in this tension-packed atmosphere. With this heritage, it is not surprising that I also learned to abhor segregation, considering it both rationally inexplicable and morally unjustifiable.

I have never experienced the feeling of not having the basic necessities of life. These things were always provided by a father who always put his family first. My father never made more than an ordinary salary, but the secret was that he knew the art of saving and budgeting. He has always had sense enough not to live beyond his means. So for this reason he was able to provide us with the basic necessities of life with little strain. I went right on through school and never had to drop out to work or anything.

The first twenty-five years of my life were very comfortable years. If I had a problem I could always call Daddy. Things were solved. Life had been wrapped up for me in a Christmas package. This is not to say that I was born with a silver spoon in my mouth; far from it. I always had a desire to work, and I would spend my summers working.

"Doubts spring forth unrelentingly"

I joined the church at the age of five. I well remember how this event occurred. Our church was in the midst of the spring revival, and a guest evangelist had come down from Virginia. On Sunday morning the evangelist came into our Sunday school to talk to us about salvation, and after a short talk on this point he extended an invitation to any of us who wanted to join the church. My sister was the first one to join the church that morning, and after seeing her join I decided that I would not let her get ahead of me, so I was the next. I had never given this matter a thought, and even at the time of my baptism I was unaware of what was taking place. From this it seems quite clear that I joined the church not out of any dynamic conviction, but out of a childhood desire to keep up with my sister.

The church has always been a second home for me. As far back as I can remember I was in church every Sunday. My best friends were in Sunday school, and it was the Sunday school that helped me to build the capacity for getting along with people. I guess this was inevitable since my father was the pastor of my church, but I never regretted going to church until I passed through a state of skepticism in my second year of college.

The lessons which I was taught in Sunday school were quite in the fundamentalist line. None of my teachers ever doubted the infallibility of the Scriptures. Most of them were unlettered and had never heard of biblical criticism. Naturally, I accepted the teachings as they were being given to me. I never felt any need to doubt them—at least at that time I didn't. I guess I accepted biblical studies uncritically until I was about twelve years old. But this uncritical attitude could not last long, for it was contrary to the very nature of my being. I had always been the questioning and precocious type. At the age of thirteen, I shocked my Sunday school class by denying the bodily resurrection of Jesus. Doubts began to spring forth unrelentingly.

"How could I love a race of people who hated me?"

Two incidents happened in my late childhood and early adolescence that had a tremendous effect on my development. The first was the death of my grandmother. She was very dear to each of us, but especially to me. I sometimes think I was her favorite grandchild. I was particularly hurt by her death mainly because of the extreme love I had for her. She assisted greatly in raising all of us. It was after this incident that for the first time I talked at any length on the doctrine of immortality. My parents attempted to explain it to me, and I was assured that somehow my grandmother still lived. I guess this is why today I am such a strong believer in personal immortality.

The second incident happened when I was about six years of age. From the age of three I had a white playmate who was about my age. We always felt free to play our childhood games together. He did not live in our community, but he was usually around every day; his father owned a store across the street from our home. At the age of six we both entered school—separate schools, of course. I remember how our friendship began to break as soon as we entered school; this was not my desire but his. The climax came when he told me one day that his father had demanded that he would play with me no more. I never will forget what a great shock this was to me. I immediately asked my parents about the motive behind such a statement.

We were at the dinner table when the situation was discussed, and here for the first time I was made aware of the existence of a race problem. I had never been conscious of it before. As my parents discussed some of the tragedies that had resulted from this problem and some of the insults they themselves had confronted on account of it, I was greatly shocked, and from that moment on I was determined to hate every white person. As I grew older and older this feeling continued to grow.

My parents would always tell me that I should not hate the white man, but that it was my duty as a Christian to love him. The question arose in my mind: How could I love a race of people who hated me and who had been responsible for breaking me up with one of my best childhood friends? This was a great question in my mind for a number of years.

I always had a resentment towards the system of segregation and felt that it was a grave injustice. I remember a trip to a downtown shoe store with Father when I was still small. We had sat down in the first empty seats at the front of the store. A young white clerk came up and murmured politely:

"I'll be happy to wait on you if you'll just move to those seats in the rear."

Dad immediately retorted, "There's nothing wrong with these seats. We're quite comfortable here."

"Sorry," said the clerk, "but you'll have to move."

"We'll either buy shoes sitting here," my father retorted, "or we won't buy shoes at all."

Whereupon he took me by the hand and walked out of the store. This was the first time I had seen Dad so furious. That experience revealed to me at a very early age that my father had not adjusted to the system, and he played a great part in shaping my conscience. I still remember walking down the street beside him as he muttered, "I don't care how long I have to live with this system, I will never accept it."

And he never has. I remember riding with him another day when he accidentally drove past a stop sign. A policeman pulled up to the car and said:

"All right, boy, pull over and let me see your license."

My father instantly retorted: "Let me make it clear to you that you aren't talking to a boy. If you persist in referring to me as boy, I will be forced to act as if I don't hear a word you are saying."

The policeman was so shocked in hearing a Negro talk to him so forthrightly that he didn't quite know how to respond. He nervously wrote the ticket and left the scene as quickly as possible.

"The angriest I have ever been"

There was a pretty strict system of segregation in Atlanta. For a long, long time I could not go swimming, until there was a Negro YMCA. A Negro child in Atlanta could not go to any public park. I could not go to the so-called white schools. In many of the stores downtown, I couldn't go to a lunch counter to buy a hamburger or a cup of coffee. I could not attend any of the theaters. There were one or two Negro theaters, but they didn't get any of the main pictures. If they did get them, they got them two or three years later.

When I was about eight years old, I was in one of the downtown stores of Atlanta and all of a sudden someone slapped me, and the only thing I heard was somebody saying, "You are that nigger that stepped on my foot." And it turned out to be a white lady. Of course I didn't retaliate at any point; I wouldn't dare retaliate when a white person was involved. I think some of it was part of my native structure—that is, that I have never been one to hit back. I finally told my mother what had happened, and she was very upset about it. But the lady who slapped me had gone, and my mother and I left the store almost immediately.

I remember another experience I used to have in Atlanta. I went to high school on the other side of town—to the Booker T. Washington High School. I had to get the bus in what was known as the Fourth Ward and ride over to the West Side. In those days, rigid patterns of segregation existed on the buses, so that Negroes had to sit in the backs of buses. Whites were seated in the front, and often if whites didn't get on the buses, those seats were still reserved for whites only, so Negroes had to stand over empty seats. I would end up having to go to the back of that bus with my body, but every time I got on that bus I left my mind up on the front seat. And I said to myself, "One of these days, I'm going to put my body up there where my mind is."

When I was fourteen, I traveled from Atlanta to Dublin, Georgia, with a dear teacher of mine, Mrs. Bradley. I participated in an oratorical contest there and I succeeded in winning the contest. My subject, ironically enough, was "The Negro and the Constitution."

We cannot have an enlightened democracy with one great group living in ignorance. We cannot have a healthy nation with one-tenth of the people ill-nourished, sick, harboring germs of disease which recognize no color lines—obey no Jim Crow laws. We cannot have a nation orderly and sound with one group so ground down and thwarted that it is almost forced into unsocial attitudes and crime. We cannot be truly Christian people so long as we flout the central teachings of Jesus: brotherly love and the Golden Rule. We cannot come to full prosperity with one great group so ill-delayed that it cannot buy goods. So as we gird ourselves to defend democracy from foreign attack, let us see to it that increasingly at home we give fair play and free opportunity for all people.

Today thirteen million black sons and daughters of our forefathers continue the fight for the translation of the Thirteenth, Fourteenth, and Fifteenth Amendments from writing on the printed page to an actuality. We believe with them that "if freedom is good for any it is good for all," that we may conquer Southern armies by the sword, but it is another thing to conquer Southern hate, that if the franchise is given to Negroes, they will be vigilant and defend, even with their arms, the ark of federal liberty from treason and destruction by her enemies.

That night, Mrs. Bradley and I were on a bus returning to Atlanta. Along the way, some white passengers boarded the bus, and the white driver ordered us to get up and give the whites our seats. We didn't move quickly enough to suit him, so he began cursing us. I intended to stay right in that seat, but Mrs. Bradley urged me up, saying we had to obey the law. We stood up in the aisle for ninety miles to Atlanta. That night will never leave my memory. It was the angriest I have ever been in my life.

I had grown up abhorring not only segregation but also the oppressive and barbarous acts that grew out of it. I had seen police brutality with my own eyes, and watched Negroes receive the most tragic injustice in the courts. I can remember the organization known as the Ku Klux Klan. It stands on white supremacy, and it was an organization that in those days even used violent methods to preserve segregation and to keep the Negro in his place, so to speak. I remember seeing the Klan actually beat a Negro. I had passed spots where Negroes had been savagely lynched. All of these things did something to my growing personality.

I had also learned that the inseparable twin of racial injustice was economic injustice. Although I came from a home of economic security and relative comfort, I could never get out of my mind the economic insecurity of many of my playmates and the tragic poverty of those living around me. During my late teens I worked two summers (against my father's wishes—he never wanted my brother and me to work around white people because of the oppressive conditions) in a plant that hired both Negroes and whites. Here I saw economic injustice firsthand, and realized that the poor white was exploited just as much as the Negro. Through these early experiences I grew up deeply conscious of the varieties of injustice in our society.

"As if the curtain had been dropped on my selfhood"

Just before going to college I went to Simsbury, Connecticut, and worked for a whole summer on a tobacco farm to earn a little school money to supplement what my parents were doing. One Sunday, we went to church in Simsbury, and we were the only Negroes there. On Sunday mornings I was the religious leader and spoke on any text I wanted to 107 boys. I had never thought that a person of my race could eat anywhere, but we ate in one of the finest restaurants in Hartford.

After that summer in Connecticut, it was a bitter feeling going back to segregation. It was hard to understand why I could ride wherever I pleased on the train from New York to Washington and then had to change to a Jim Crow car at the nation's capital in order

---

LETTER TO MARTIN LUTHER KING, SR.

15 June 1944
Simsbury, Conn.

Dear Father:

I am very sorry I am so long about writing but I have been working most of the time. We are really having a fine time here and the work is very easy. We have to get up every day at 6:00. We have very good food. And I am working kitchen so you see I get better food.

We have service here every Sunday about 8:00 and I am the religious leader we have a Boys choir here and we are going to sing on the air soon. Sunday I went to church in Simsbury it was a white church. I could not get to Hartford to church but I am going next week. On our way here we saw some things I had never anticipated to see. After we passed Washington there was no discrimination at all the white people here are very nice. We go to any place we want to and sit any where we want to.

Tell everybody I said hello and I am still thinking of the church and reading my bible. And I am not doing any thing that I would not do in front of you.

Your Son

---

to continue the trip to Atlanta. The first time that I was seated behind a curtain in a dining car, I felt as if the curtain had been dropped on my selfhood. I could never adjust to the separate waiting rooms, separate eating places, separate rest rooms, partly because the separate was always unequal, and partly because the very idea of separation did something to my sense of dignity and self-respect.

2

MOREHOUSE COLLEGE

My call to the ministry was not a miraculous or supernatural something. On the contrary it was an inner urge calling me to serve humanity.

SEPTEMBER 20, 1944
King begins freshman year at Morehouse College

FEBRUARY 25, 1948
Is ordained at Ebenezer

JUNE 8
Receives bachelor of arts degree in sociology from Morehouse

At the age of fifteen, I entered Morehouse College. My father and my maternal grandfather had also attended, so Morehouse has had three generations of Kings.

I shall never forget the hardships that I had upon entering college, for though I had been one of the top students in high school, I was still reading at only an eighth-grade level. I went to college from the eleventh grade. I never went to the twelfth grade, and skipped another grade earlier, so I was a pretty young fellow at Morehouse.

My days in college were very exciting ones. There was a free atmosphere at Morehouse, and it was there I had my first frank discussion on race. The professors were not caught up in the clutches of state funds and could teach what they wanted with academic freedom. They encouraged us in a positive quest for a solution to racial ills. I realized that nobody there was afraid. Important people came in to discuss the race problem rationally with us.

When I went to Morehouse as a freshman in 1944, my concern for racial and economic justice was already substantial. During my student days I read Henry David Thoreau's essay "On Civil Disobedience" for the first time. Here, in this courageous New Englander's refusal to pay his taxes and his choice of jail rather than support a war that would spread slavery's territory into Mexico, I made my first contact with the theory of nonviolent resistance. Fascinated by the idea of refusing to cooperate with an evil system, I was so deeply moved that I reread the work several times.

I became convinced that noncooperation with evil is as much a moral obligation as is cooperation with good. No other person has been more eloquent and passionate in getting this idea across than Henry David Thoreau. As a result of his writings and personal witness, we are the heirs of a legacy of creative protest. The teachings of Thoreau came alive in our civil rights movement; indeed, they are more alive than ever before. Whether expressed in a sit-in at lunch counters, a freedom ride into Mississippi, a peaceful protest in Albany, Georgia, a bus boycott in Montgomery, Alabama, these are outgrowths of Thoreau's insistence that evil must be resisted and that no moral man can patiently adjust to injustice.

As soon as I entered college, I started working with the organizations that were trying to make racial justice a reality. The wholesome relations we had in the Intercollegiate Council convinced me that we had many white persons as allies, particularly among the younger generation. I had been ready to resent the whole white race, but as I got to see more of white people, my resentment was softened, and a spirit of cooperation took its place. I was at the point where I was deeply interested in political matters and social ills. I could envision myself playing a part in breaking down the legal barriers to Negro rights.

"An inner urge calling me to serve society"

Because of the influence of my mother and father, I guess I always had a deep urge to serve humanity, but I didn't start out with an interest to enter the ministry. I thought I could probably do it better as a lawyer or doctor. One of my closest friends at Morehouse, Walter McCall, was clear about his intention of going into the ministry,

---

"KICK UP DUST"

I often find when decent treatment for the Negro is urged, a certain class of people hurry to raise the scarecrow of social mingling and intermarriage. These questions have nothing to do with the case. And most people who kick up this kind of dust know that it is simple dust to obscure the real question of rights and opportunities. It is fair to remember that almost the total of race mixture in America has come, not at Negro initiative, but by the acts of those very white men who talk loudest of race purity. We aren't eager to marry white girls, and we would like to have our own girls left alone by both white toughs and white aristocrats.

We want and are entitled to the basic rights and opportunities of American citizens: The right to earn a living at work for which we are fitted by training and ability; equal opportunities in education, health, recreation, and similar public services; the right to vote; equality before the law; some of the same courtesy and good manners that we ourselves bring to all human relations.

Letter to the Editor, *Atlanta Constitution*, August 6, 1946

---

but I was slow to make up my mind. I did serve as assistant to my father for six months.

As stated above, my college training, especially the first two years, brought many doubts into my mind. It was then that the shackles of fundamentalism were removed from my body. More and more I could see a gap between what I had learned in Sunday school and what I was learning in college. My studies had made me skeptical, and I could not see how many of the facts of science could be squared with religion.

I revolted, too, against the emotionalism of much Negro religion, the shouting and stamping. I didn't understand it, and it embarrassed me. I often say that if we, as a people, had as much religion in our hearts and souls as we have in our legs and feet, we could change the world.

I had seen that most Negro ministers were unlettered, not trained in seminaries, and that gave me pause. I had been brought up in the church and knew about religion, but I wondered whether it could serve as a vehicle to modern thinking, whether religion could be intellectually respectable as well as emotionally satisfying.

This conflict continued until I studied a course in Bible in which I came to see that behind the legends and myths of the Book were many profound truths which one could not escape. Two men—Dr. Mays, president of Morehouse College and one of the great influences in my life, and Dr. George Kelsey, a professor of philosophy and religion—made me stop and think. Both were ministers, both deeply religious, and yet both were learned men, aware of all the trends of modern thinking. I could see in their lives the ideal of what I wanted a minister to be.

It was in my senior year of college that I entered the ministry. I had felt the urge to enter the ministry from my high school days, but accumulated doubts had somewhat blocked the urge. Now it appeared again with an inescapable drive. I felt a sense of responsibility which I could not escape.

I guess the influence of my father had a great deal to do with my going into the ministry. This is not to say that he ever spoke to me in terms of being a minister but that my admiration for him was the great moving factor. He set forth a noble example that I didn't mind following. I still feel the effects of the noble moral and ethical ideals that I grew up under. They have been real and precious to me, and even in moments of theological doubt I could never turn away from them.

At the age of nineteen I finished college and was ready to enter seminary.

3

CROZER SEMINARY

I was well aware of the typical white stereotype of the Negro, that he is always late, that he's loud and always laughing, that he's dirty and messy, and for a while I was terribly conscious of trying to avoid identification with it. If I were a minute late to class, I was almost morbidly conscious of it and sure that everyone else noticed it. Rather than be thought of as always laughing, I'm afraid I was grimly serious for a time. I had a tendency to overdress, to keep my room spotless, my shoes perfectly shined, and my clothes immaculately pressed.

SEPTEMBER 14, 1948
King enters Crozer Theological Seminary

SPRING 1950
Hears Howard University president Mordecai Johnson lecture on Gandhi

MAY 8, 1951
Receives bachelor of divinity degree from Crozer

Not until 1948, when I entered Crozer Theological Seminary in Chester, Pennsylvania, did I begin a serious intellectual quest for a method to eliminate social evil. I turned to a serious study of the social and ethical theories of the great philosophers, from Plato and Aristotle down to Rousseau, Hobbes, Bentham, Mill, and Locke. All of these masters stimulated my thinking—such as it was—and, while finding things to question in each of them, I nevertheless learned a great deal from their study.

I spent a great deal of time reading the works of the great social philosophers. I came early to Walter Rauschenbusch's *Christianity and the Social Crisis,* which left an indelible imprint on my thinking by giving me a theological basis for the social concern which had already grown up in me as a result of my early experiences. Of course there were points at which I differed with Rauschenbusch. I felt that he had fallen victim to the nineteenth-century "cult of inevitable progress" which led him to a superficial optimism concerning man's nature. Moreover, he came perilously close to identifying the Kingdom of God with a particular social and economic system—a tendency which should never befall the Church. But in spite of these shortcomings Rauschenbusch had done a great service for the Christian Church by insisting that the gospel deals with the whole man—not only his soul but his body; not only his spiritual well-being but his material well-being.

"The preaching ministry"

It has been my conviction ever since reading Rauschenbusch that any religion that professes concern for the souls of men and is not equally concerned about the slums that damn them, the economic conditions that strangle them, and the social conditions that cripple them is a spiritually moribund religion only waiting for the day to be buried. It well has been said: "A religion that ends with the individual, ends."

I feel that preaching is one of the most vital needs of our society, if it is used correctly. There is a great paradox in preaching: on the one hand it may be very helpful and on the other it may be very pernicious. It is my opinion that sincerity is not enough for the preaching ministry. The minister must be both sincere and intelligent. . . . I also think that the minister should possess profundity of conviction. We have too many minsters in the pulpit who are great spellbinders and too few who possess spiritual power. It is my profound conviction that I, as an aspirant for the ministry, should possess these powers.

I think that preaching should grow out of the experiences of the people. Therefore, I, as a minister, must know the problems of the people that I am pastoring. Too often do educated ministers leave the people lost in the fog of theological abstraction, rather than presenting that theology in the light of the people's experiences. It is my conviction that the minister must somehow take profound theological and philosophical

---

LETTER TO ALBERTA WILLIAMS KING

Dear Mother,

Your letter was received this morning. I often tell the boys around the campus I have the best mother in the world. You will never know how I appreciate the many kind things you and daddy are doing for me. So far I have gotten the money (5 dollars) every week.

As to my wanting some clippings from the newspapers, I must answer yes. I wondered why you hadn't sent many, especially the Atlanta World.

You stated that my letters aren't newsy enough. Well I don't have much news. I never go anywhere much but in these books. Some times the professor comes in class and tells us to read our assignments in Hebrew, and that is really hard.

Do you know the girl I used to date at Spelman (Gloria Royster). She is in school at Temple and I have been to see her twice. Also I met a fine chick in Phila who has gone wild over the old boy. Since Barbor told the members of his church that my family was rich, the girls are running me down. Of course, I don't ever think about them. I am too busy studying.

I hear from Christine every week. I try to answer her as regularly as possible.

Well I guess I must go back to studying. Give everybody my Regards.
Your son,
M.L.

October 1948

---

views and place them in a concrete framework. I must forever make the complex the simple.

Above all, I see the preaching ministry as a dual process. On the one hand I must attempt to change the soul of individuals so that their societies may be changed. On the other I must attempt to change the societies so that the individual soul will have a change. Therefore, I must be concerned about unemployment, slums, and economic insecurity. I am a profound advocate of the social gospel.

"Truth is found neither in Marxism nor in traditional capitalism"

During the Christmas holidays of 1949 I decided to spend my spare time reading Karl Marx to try to understand the appeal of communism for many people. For the first time I carefully scrutinized *Das Kapital* and *The Communist Manifesto*. I also read some interpretive works on the thinking of Marx and Lenin. In reading such Communist writings I drew certain conclusions that have remained with me as convictions to this day.

First, I rejected their materialistic interpretation of history. Communism, avowedly secularistic and materialistic, has no place for God. This I could never accept, for as a Christian I believe that there is a creative personal power in this universe who is the ground and essence of all reality—a power that cannot be explained in materialistic terms. History is ultimately guided by spirit, not matter.

Second, I strongly disagreed with communism's ethical relativism. Since for the Community there is no divine government, no absolute moral order, there are no fixed, immutable principles; consequently almost anything—force, violence, murder, lying—is a justifiable means to the "millennial" end. This type of relativism was abhorrent to me. Constructive ends can never give absolute moral justification to destructive means, because in the final analysis the end is preexistent in the means.

Third, I opposed communism's political totalitarianism. In communism the individual ends up in subjection to the state. True, the Marxist would argue that the state is an "interim" reality which is to be eliminated when the classless society emerges; but the state is the end while it lasts, and man only a means to that end. And if any man's so-called rights or liberties stand in the way of that end, they are simply swept aside. His liberties of expression, his freedom to vote, his freedom to listen to what news he likes or to choose his books are all restricted. Man becomes hardly more, in communism, than a depersonalized cog in the turning wheel of the state.

This deprecation of individual freedom was objectionable to me. I am convinced now, as I was then, that man is an end because he is a child of God. Man is not made for the state; the state is made for man. To deprive man of freedom is to relegate him to the status of a thing, rather than elevate him to the status of a person. Man must never be treated as a means to the end of the state, but always as an end within himself.

Yet, in spite of the fact that my response to communism was and is negative, and I consider it basically evil, there were points at which

I found it challenging. With all of its false assumptions and evil methods, communism grew as a protest against the hardships of the underprivileged. Communism in theory emphasized a classless society, and a concern for social justice, though the world knows from sad experience that in practice it created new classes and a new lexicon of injustice. The Christian ought always to be challenged by any protest against unfair treatment of the poor.

I also sought systematic answers to Marx's critique of modern bourgeois culture. He presented capitalism as essentially a struggle between the owners of the productive resources and the workers, whom Marx regarded as the real producers. Marx interpreted economic forces as the dialectical process by which society moved from feudalism through capitalism to socialism, with the primary mechanism of this historical movement being the struggle between economic classes whose interests were irreconcilable. Obviously this theory left out the numerous and significant complexities—political, economic, moral, religious, and psychological—which played a vital role in shaping the constellation of institutions and ideas known today as Western civilization. Moreover, it was dated in the sense that the capitalism Marx wrote about bore only a partial resemblance to the capitalism we know in this country.

But in spite of the shortcomings of his analysis, Marx had raised some basic questions. I was deeply concerned from my early teen days about the gulf between superfluous wealth and abject poverty, and my reading of Marx made me ever more conscious of this gulf. Although modern American capitalism had greatly reduced the gap through social reforms, there was still need for a better distribution of wealth. Moreover, Marx had revealed the danger of the profit motive as the sole basis of an economic system: capitalism is always in danger of inspiring men to be more concerned about making a living than making a life. We are prone to judge success by the index of our salaries or the size of our automobiles, rather than by the quality of our service and relationship to humanity. Thus capitalism can lead to a practical materialism that is as pernicious as the materialism taught by communism.

In short, I read Marx as I read all of the influential historical thinkers—from a dialectical point of view, combining a partial yes and a partial no. Insofar as Marx posited a metaphysical materialism, an ethical relativism, and a strangulating totalitarianism, I responded with an unambiguous no; but insofar as he pointed to weaknesses of traditional capitalism, contributed to the growth of a definite self-consciousness in the masses, and challenged the social conscience of the Christian churches, I responded with a definite yes.

My reading of Marx also convinced me that truth is found neither in Marxism nor in traditional capitalism. Each represents a partial truth. Historically capitalism failed to see the truth in collective enterprise and Marxism failed to see the truth in individual enterprise. Nineteenth-century capitalism failed to see that life is social and Marxism failed and still fails to see that life is individual and personal. The Kingdom of God is neither the thesis of individual enterprise nor the antithesis of collective enterprise, but a synthesis which reconciles the truths of both.

"The only morally and practically sound method open to oppressed people"

During my stay at Crozer, I was also exposed for the first time to the pacifist position in a lecture by Dr. A. J. Muste. I was deeply moved by Dr. Muste's talk, but far from convinced of the practicability of his position. Like most of the students of Crozer, I felt that while

---

"THE SIGNIFICANT CONTRIBUTIONS OF JEREMIAH TO RELIGIOUS THOUGHT"

Again Jeremiah is a shining example of the truth that religion should never sanction the status quo. This more than anything else should be inculcated into the minds of modern religionists, for the worst disservice that we as individuals or churches can do to Christianity is to become sponsors and supporters of the status quo. How often has religion gone down, chained to a status quo it allied itself with. Therefore, we must admit that men like Jeremiah are valuable to any religion. Religion, in a sense, through men like Jeremiah, provides for its own advancement, and carries within it the promise of progress and renewed power. But what is society's reaction to such men? It has reacted, and always will react, in the only way open to it. It destroys such men. Jeremiah died a martyr.

Course paper submitted at Crozer Seminary, November 1948

---

war could never be a positive or absolute good, it could serve as a negative good in the sense of preventing the spread and growth of an evil force. War, horrible as it is, might be preferable to surrender to a totalitarian system—Nazi, Fascist, or Communist.

During this period I had about despaired of the power of love in solving social problems. I thought the only way we could solve our problem of segregation was an armed revolt. I felt that the Christian ethic of love was confined to individual relationships. I could not see how it could work in social conflict.

Perhaps my faith in love was temporarily shaken by the philosophy of Nietzsche. I had been reading parts of *The Genealogy of Morals* and the whole of *The Will to Power*. Nietzsche's glorification of power—in his theory, all life expressed the will to power—was an outgrowth of his contempt for ordinary mortals. He attacked the whole of the Hebraic-Christian morality—with its virtues of piety and humility, its otherworldliness, and its attitude toward suffering—as the glorification of weakness, as making virtues out of necessity and impotence. He looked to the development of a superman who would surpass man as man surpassed the ape.

Then one Sunday afternoon I traveled to Philadelphia to hear a sermon by Dr. Mordecai Johnson, president of Howard University. He was there to preach for the Fellowship House of Philadelphia. Dr. Johnson had just returned from a trip to India, and, to my great interest, he spoke of the life and teachings of Mahatma Gandhi. His message was so profound and electrifying that I left the meeting and bought a half-dozen books on Gandhi's life and works.

Like most people, I had heard of Gandhi, but I had never studied him seriously. As I read I became deeply fascinated by his campaigns of nonviolent resistance. I was particularly moved by his Salt March to the Sea and his numerous fasts. The whole concept of *Satyagraha* (*Satya* is truth which equals love, and *agraha* is force; *Satyagraha*, therefore, means truth force or love force) was profoundly significant to me. As I delved deeper into the philosophy of Gandhi, my skepticism concerning the power of love gradually diminished, and I came to see for the first time its potency in the area of social reform. Prior to reading Gandhi, I had about concluded that the ethics of Jesus were only effective in individual relationships. The "turn the other cheek" philosophy and the "love your enemies" philosophy were only valid, I felt, when individuals were in conflict with other individuals; when racial groups and nations were in conflict a more realistic approach seemed necessary. But after reading Gandhi, I saw how utterly mistaken I was.

Gandhi was probably the first person in history to lift the love ethic of Jesus above mere interaction between individuals to a powerful and effective social force on a large scale. Love for Gandhi was a potent instrument for social and collective transformation. It was in this Gandhian emphasis on love and nonviolence that I discovered the method for social reform that I had been seeking. The intellectual and moral satisfaction that I failed to gain from the utilitarianism of Bentham and Mill, the revolutionary methods of Marx and Lenin, the social contracts theory of Hobbes, the "back to nature" optimism of Rousseau, the superman philosophy of Nietzsche, I found in the nonviolent resistance philosophy of Gandhi.

"The liberal doctrine of man"

But my intellectual odyssey to nonviolence did not end here. During my senior year in theological seminary, I engaged in the exciting reading of various theological theories. Having been raised in a rather strict fundamentalist tradition, I was occasionally shocked when my intellectual journey carried me through new and sometimes complex doctrinal lands, but the pilgrimage was always stimulating; it gave me a new appreciation for objective appraisal and critical analysis, and knocked me out of my dogmatic slumber.

When I came to Crozer, I could accept the liberal interpretation of Christianity with relative ease. Liberalism provided me with an intellectual satisfaction that I had never found in fundamentalism. I became so enamored of the insights of liberalism that I almost fell into the trap of accepting uncritically everything that came under its name. I was absolutely convinced of the natural goodness of man and the natural power of human reason.

The basic change in my thinking came when I began to question the liberal doctrine of man. My thinking went through a state of transition. At one time I found myself leaning toward a mild neo-orthodox view of man, and at other times I found myself leaning toward a liberal view of man. The former leaning may root back to certain experiences that I had in the South, with its vicious race problem, that made it very difficult for me to believe in the essential goodness of man. The more I observed the tragedies of history and man's shameful inclination to choose the low road, the more I came to see the depths and strength of sin. Liberalism's superficial optimism concerning human nature caused it to overlook the fact that reason is darkened by sin. The more I thought about human nature, the more I saw how our tragic inclination for sin causes us to use our minds to rationalize our actions. Liberalism failed to see that reason by itself is little more than an instrument to justify man's defensive ways of thinking. Moreover, I came to recognize the complexity of man's social involvement and the glaring reality of collective evil. I came to feel that liberalism had been all too sentimental concerning human nature and that it leaned toward a false idealism. Reason, devoid of the purifying power of faith, can never free itself from distortions and rationalizations.

On the other hand, part of my liberal leaning had its source in another branch of the same root. In noticing the gradual improvements of this same race problem, I came to see some noble possibilities in human nature. Also my liberal leaning may have rooted back to the great imprint that many liberal theologians have left upon me and to my ever-present desire to be optimistic about human nature. Of course there is one phase of liberalism that I hope to cherish always: its devotion to the search for truth, its insistence on an open and analytical mind, its refusal to abandon the best light of reason. Its contribution to the philological-historical criticism of biblical literature has been of immeasurable value.

"A courageous confrontation of evil by the power of love"

During my last year in theological school, I began to read the works of Reinhold Niebuhr. The prophetic and realistic elements in Niebuhr's passionate style and profound thought were appealing to me, and made me aware of the complexity of human motives and the reality of sin on every level of man's existence. I became so enamored of his social ethics that I almost fell into the trap of accepting uncritically everything he wrote.

I read Niebuhr's critique of the pacifist position. Niebuhr had himself once been a member of the pacifist ranks. For several years, he had been national chairman of the Fellowship of Reconciliation. His break with pacifism came in the early thirties, and the first full statement of his criticism of pacifism was in *Moral Man and Immoral Society*. Here he argued that there was no intrinsic moral difference between violent and nonviolent resistance. The social consequences of the two methods were different, he contended, but the differences were in degree rather than kind. Later Niebuhr began emphasizing the irresponsibility of relying on nonviolent resistance when there was no ground for believing that it would be successful in preventing the spread of totalitarian tyranny. It could only be successful, he argued, if the groups against whom the resistance was taking place had some degree of moral conscience, as was the case in Gandhi's struggle against the British. Niebuhr's ultimate rejection of pacifism was based primarily on the doctrine of man. He argued that pacifism failed to do justice to the reformation doctrine of justification by faith, substituting for it a sectarian perfectionism which believes "that divine grace actually lifts man out of the sinful contradictions of history and establishes him above the sins of the world."

At first, Niebuhr's critique of pacifism left me in a state of confusion. As I continued to read, however, I came to see more and more the shortcomings of his position. For instance, many of his statements revealed that he interpreted pacifism as a sort of passive nonresistance to evil expressing naive trust in the power of love. But this was a serious distortion. My study of Gandhi convinced me that true pacifism is not nonresistance to evil, but nonviolent resistance to evil. Between the two positions, there is a world of difference. Gandhi resisted evil with as much vigor and power as the violent resister, but he resisted with love instead of hate. True pacifism is not unrealistic submission to evil power, as Niebuhr contends. It is rather a courageous confrontation of evil by the power of love, in the faith that it is better to be the recipient of violence than the inflicter of it, since the latter only multiplies the existence of violence and bitterness in the universe, while the former may develop a sense of shame in the opponent, and thereby bring about a transformation and change of heart.

In spite of the fact that I found many things to be desired in Niebuhr's philosophy, there were several points at which he constructively influenced my thinking. Niebuhr's great contribution to theology is that he has refuted the false optimism characteristic of a great segment of Protestant liberalism. Moreover, Niebuhr has extraordinary insight into human nature, especially the behavior of nations and social groups. He is keenly aware of the complexity of human motives and of the relation between morality and power. His theology is a persistent reminder of the reality of sin on every level of man's existence. These elements in Niebuhr's thinking helped me to recognize the illusions of a superficial optimism concerning human nature and the dangers of a false idealism. While I still believed in man's potential for good, Niebuhr made me realize his potential for evil as well. Moreover, Niebuhr helped me to recognize the complexity of man's social involvement and the glaring reality of collective evil.

Many pacifists, I felt, failed to see this. All too many had an unwarranted optimism concerning man and leaned unconsciously toward self-righteousness. After reading Niebuhr, I tried to arrive at a realistic pacifism. In other words, I came to see the pacifist position not as sinless but as the lesser evil in the circumstances. I do not claim to be free from the moral dilemmas that the Christian non-pacifist confronts, but I am convinced that the church cannot be silent while mankind faces the threat of nuclear annihilation. I felt that the pacifist would have a greater appeal if he did not claim to be free from the moral dilemmas that the Christian non-pacifist confronts.

I anticipated graduating from Crozer in May 1951. For a number of years I had been desirous of teaching in a college or a school of religion. Realizing the necessity for scholastic attainment in the teaching profession, I felt that graduate work would give me a better grasp of my field. I had a general knowledge of my field, but I had not done adequate research to meet the scholarly issues which I would confront in this area. I felt that a few years of intensified study in a graduate school would give me a thorough grasp of knowledge in my field.

My particular interest in Boston University could be summed up in two statements. First, my thinking in philosophical areas had been greatly influenced by some of the faculty members there, particularly

"A CONCEPTION AND IMPRESSION OF RELIGION DRAWN FROM DR. EDGAR S. BRIGHTMAN'S BOOK ENTITLED *A PHILOSOPHY OF RELIGION*"

It is religion that gives meaning to life. It is religion that gives meaning to the Universe. It is religion that is the greatest incentive for the good life. It is religion which gives us the assurance that all that is high noble and valuable will be conserved. Such fruits of religion I find to be its greatest virtues, and certainly they cannot be ignored by any sane man. I must now conclude that any atheistic view is both philosophically unsound and practically disadvantageous. How long now for that religious experience which Dr. Brightman so cogently speaks of throughout his book. It seems to be an experience, the lack of which life becomes dull and meaningless. As I reflect on the matter, however, I do remember moments that I have been awe awakened; there have been times that I have been carried out of myself by something greater than myself and to that something I gave myself. Has this great something been God? Maybe after all I have been religious for a number of years, and am now only becoming aware of it.

From a course paper submitted at Crozer Seminary, March 28, 1951

Dr. Edgar S. Brightman. For this reason, I longed for the possibility of studying under him. Secondly, one of my professors at Crozer was a graduate of Boston University, and his great influence over me turned my eyes toward his former school. I had gotten some valuable information about Boston University from him, and I was convinced that there were definite advantages there for me.

"O THAT I KNEW WHERE I MIGHT FIND HIM"

I can remember very vividly how in my recent seminary days, I was able to strengthen my spiritual life through communing with nature. The seminary campus is a beautiful sight, particularly so in the spring. And it was at this time of year that I made it a practice to go out to the edge of the campus every afternoon for at least an hour to commune with nature. On the side of the campus ran a little tributary from the Delaware river. Every day I would sit on the edge of the campus by the side of the river and watch the beauties of nature. My friend, in this experience, I saw God. I saw him in birds of the air, the leaves of the tree, the movement of the rippling waves. . . . Sometimes I go out at night and look up at the stars as they bedeck the heavens like shining silver pins sticking in a magnificent blue pin cushion. There is God. Sometimes I watch the sun as it gets up in the morning and paints its technicolor across the eastern horizon. There is God. Sometimes I watch the moon as it walks across the sky as a queen walks across her masterly mansion. There is God. Henry Ward Beecher was right: "Nature is God's tongue."

Reminiscence about Crozer years, ca. 1953

4

BOSTON UNIVERSITY

As a young man with most of my life ahead of me, I decided early to give my life to something eternal and absolute. Not to these little gods that are here today and gone tomorrow. But to God who is the same yesterday, today, and forever.

SEPTEMBER 13, 1951
King enters Boston University's School of Theology

FEBRUARY 25, 1953
Academic advisor Edgar S. Brightman dies; Harold DeWolf becomes new advisor

JUNE 5, 1955
Receives doctorate in systematic theology from Boston University

The next stage of my intellectual pilgrimage to nonviolence came during my doctoral studies at Boston University. Here I had the opportunity to talk to many exponents of nonviolence, both students and visitors at the campus.

Boston University School of Theology, under the influence of Dean Walter Muelder and Professor Allen Knight Chalmers, had a deep sympathy for the pacifist position. Both Dean Muelder and Dr. Chalmers had a passion for social justice. One never got the impression that this passion stemmed from a superficial optimism concerning human nature, but from a deep faith in the possibilities of human beings when they allowed themselves to become co-workers with God. My association with men like that also caused me to deepen my concern, and of course many of the studies I continued to make concerning the philosophy and theory of nonviolence naturally influenced my thinking.

Theologically I found myself still holding to the liberal position. I had come to see more than ever before that there were certain enduring qualities in liberalism which all of the vociferous noises of fundamentalism and neo-orthodoxy could never destroy. However, while at Boston, I became much more sympathetic towards the neo-orthodox position than I had been in previous years. I do not mean that I accept neo-orthodoxy as a set of doctrines, but I did see in it a necessary corrective for a liberalism that had become all too shallow and that too easily capitulated to modern culture. Neo-orthodoxy certainly had the merit of calling us back to the depths of Christian faith.

I also came to see that Reinhold Niebuhr had overemphasized the corruption of human nature. His pessimism concerning human nature was not balanced by an optimism concerning divine nature. He was so involved in diagnosing man's sickness of sin that he overlooked the cure of grace.

I studied philosophy and theology at Boston University under Edgar S. Brightman and L. Harold DeWolf. I did most of my work under Dr. DeWolf, who is a very dear friend of mine, and, of course, I was greatly influenced by him and by Dr. Brightman, whom I had the privilege to study with before he passed on. It was mainly under these teachers that I studied Personalistic philosophy—the theory that the clue to the meaning of ultimate reality is found in personality. This personal idealism remains today my basic philosophical position. Personalism's insistence that only personality—finite and infinite—is ultimately real strengthened me in two convictions: it

---

MEMORIES OF HOUSING BIAS WHILE IN GRADUATE SCHOOL

I remember very well trying to find a place to live. I went into place after place where there were signs that rooms were for rent. They were for rent until they found out I was a Negro, and suddenly they had just been rented.

Quoted in *Boston Globe*, April 23, 1965

gave me metaphysical and philosophical grounding for the idea of a personal God, and it gave me a metaphysical basis for the dignity and worth of all human personality.

Just before Dr. Brightman's death, I began studying the philosophy of Hegel with him. This course proved to be both rewarding and stimulating. Although the course was mainly a study of Hegel's monumental work, *Phenomenology of Mind,* I spent my spare time reading his *Philosophy of History* and *Philosphy of Right.* There were points in Hegel's philosophy that I strongly disagreed with. For instance, his absolute idealism was rationally unsound to me because it tended to swallow up the many in the one. But there were other aspects of his thinking that I found stimulating. His contention that "truth is the whole" led me to a philosophical method of rational coherence. His analysis of the dialectical process, in spite of its shortcomings, helped me to see that growth comes through struggle.

My work at Boston University progressed very well. Both Dr. DeWolf and Dr. Brightman were quite impressed. I completed my residence work and began the process of writing my dissertation. My dissertation title was "A Comparison of the Conception of God in the Thinking of Paul Tillich and Henry Nelson Wieman." The concept of God was chosen because of the central place which it occupies in any religion and because of the ever-present need to interpret and clarify the God concept. Tillich and Wieman were chosen because they represent different types of theology and because each of them had an increasing influence upon theological and philosophical thought.

In 1954 I ended my formal training with divergent intellectual forces converging into a positive social philosophy. One of the main tenets of this philosophy was the conviction that nonviolent resistance was one of the most potent weapons available to oppressed people in their quest for social justice. Interestingly enough, at this time I had merely an intellectual understanding and appreciation of the position, with no firm determination to organize it in a socially effective situation.

"Rediscovering Lost Values"

The thing that we need in the world today, is a group of men and women who will stand up for right and be opposed to wrong, wherever it is. A group of people who have come to see that some things are wrong, whether they're never caught up with. Some things are right, whether nobody sees you doing them or not.

All I'm trying to say is, our world hinges on moral foundations. God has made it so! God has made the universe to be based on a moral law. . . .

This universe hinges on moral foundations. There is something in this universe that justifies Carlyle in saying,

"No lie can live forever."

There is something in this universe that justifies William Cullen Bryant in saying,

"Truth, crushed to earth, will rise again."

There is something in this universe that justifies James Russell Lowell in saying,

"Truth forever on the scaffold,

Wrong forever on the throne.

With that scaffold sways the future.

Behind the dim unknown stands God,

Within the shadow keeping watch above his own."

There is something in this universe that justifies the biblical writer in saying,

"You shall reap what you sow."

As a young man with most of my life ahead of me, I decided early to give my life to something eternal and absolute. Not to these little gods that are here today and gone tomorrow. But to God who is the same yesterday, today, and forever.

I'm not going to put my ultimate faith in the little gods that can be destroyed in an atomic age, but the God who has been our help in ages past, and our hope for years to come, and our shelter in the time of storm, and our eternal home. That's the God that I'm putting my ultimate faith in. . . . The God that I'm talking about this morning is the God of the universe and the God that will last through the ages. If we are to go forward this morning, we've got to go back and find that God. That is the God that demands and commands our ultimate allegiance.

If we are to go forward, we must go back and rediscover these precious values—that all reality hinges on moral foundations and that all reality has spiritual control.

5

CORETTA

I am indebted to my wife Coretta, without whose love, sacrifices, and loyalty neither life nor work would bring fulfillment. She has given me words of consolation when I needed them and a well-ordered home where Christian love is a reality.

APRIL 27, 1927
Coretta Scott born in Heiberger, Alabama

JANUARY 1952
Coretta and Martin meet in Boston

JUNE 18, 1953
King Sr. performs marriage in Marion, Alabama

It was in Boston that I met and fell in love with the attractive singer Coretta Scott, whose gentle manner and air of repose did not disguise her lively spirit. I had met quite a few girls in Boston, but none that I was particularly fond of.

I was about to get cynical. So I asked Mary Powell, a friend from Atlanta who was also a student at the New England Conservatory of Music, "Do you know any nice, attractive young ladies?"

Mary Powell introduced us and I was fortunate enough to get Coretta's telephone number. We met over the telephone: "This is M. L. King, Jr. A mutual friend of ours told me about you and gave me your telephone number. She said some very wonderful things about you, and I'd like very much to meet you and talk to you."

We talked awhile. "You know every Napoleon has his Waterloo. I'm like Napoleon. I'm at my Waterloo, and I'm on my knees. I'd like to meet you and talk some more. Perhaps we could have lunch tomorrow or something like that."

She agreed to see me. "I'll come over and pick you up. I have a green Chevy that usually takes ten minutes to make the trip from B.U., but tomorrow I'll do it in seven."

She talked about things other than music. I never will forget, the first discussion we had was about the question of racial and economic injustice and the question of peace. She had been actively engaged in movements dealing with these problems.

After an hour, my mind was made up. I said, "So you can do something else besides sing? You've got a good mind also. You have everything I ever wanted in a woman. We ought to get married someday."

I didn't want a wife I couldn't communicate with. I had to have a wife who would be as dedicated as I was. I wish I could say that I led her down this path, but I must say we went down it together because she was as actively involved and concerned when we met as she is now.

I told my mother, "Coretta is going to be my wife." On June 18, 1953, we were married. Although we had returned to Marion to be married by my father on the Scotts' spacious lawn, it was in Boston that we began our married life together.

"Corrie"

Coretta Scott is a native of the South. She is from Marion, Alabama, and she went to college in Ohio, Antioch College. Having inherited a talent for music from her mother, Bernice Scott, as well as the strength of quiet determination, she had then gone on with the aid of a scholarship to work her way through the New England Conservatory in Boston. She wanted to be a concert singer. She was a mezzo-soprano and I'm sure she would have gone on into this area if a Baptist preacher hadn't interrupted her life.

Coretta's father, Obie Scott, a short, stocky man of dark complexion, is a strong and courageous man. People are strongly attracted to him because of his warm personality. He loves people and is always ready to help someone in need. Although reared on a farm, Obie Scott was always concerned about going into business for him-

LETTER TO CORETTA

Darling, I miss you so much. In fact, much too much for my own good. I never realized that you were such an intimate part of my life. My life without you is like a year without a spring time which comes to give illumination and heat to the atmosphere saturated by the dark cold breeze of winter. . . . O excuse me, my darling. I didn't mean to go off on such a poetical and romantic flight. But how else can we express the deep emotions of life other than in poetry? Isn't love too ineffable to be grasped by the cold calculating hands of intellect?

By the way (to turn to something more intellectual) I have just completed Bellamy's *Looking Backward*. It was both stimulating and fascinating. There can be no doubt about it. Bellamy had the insight of a social prophet as well as the fact finding mind of the social scientist. I welcomed the book because much of its content is in line with my basic ideas. I imagine you already know that I am much more socialistic in my economic theory than capitalistic. And yet I am not so opposed to capitalism that I have failed to see its relative merits. It started out with a noble and high motive, viz., to block the trade monopolies of nobles, but like most human systems it fell victim to the very thing it was revolting against. So today capitalism has out-lived its usefulness. It has brought about a system that takes necessities from the masses to give luxuries to the classes. So I think Bellamy is right in seeing the gradual decline of capitalism.

I think you noticed that Bellamy emphasized that the change would be evolutionary rather than revolutionary. This, it seems to me, is the most sane and ethical way for social change to take place.

Eternally Yours,
Martin

Atlanta, July 18, 1952

self. He finally succeeded and operated a trucking business, a combination filling station and grocery store, and a chicken farm. Despite the reprisals and physical threats of his white competitors, he attempted to get ahead in these various businesses and dared to make a decent living for his family. He has never been an Uncle Tom, but he had to suffer certain insults and even humiliation in order to survive in his community. The amazing thing is that he came through all of this with his courage undaunted, without becoming bitter. Coretta often made comparison between me and her father. Even in the early days of our courtship, she used to say, "You remind me so much of my father." I don't suppose any compliment could be more inflating to the male ago.

Coretta's mother, Bernice Scott, is quite different from her father in many respects. In contrast to his overflowing personality she is rather shy. She is an attractive woman, fair in complexion, possessing narrow features and long black straight hair. In knowing her, one soon detects that she is a person of courage, determination, and amazing internal strength. She is deeply devoted to her family, always willing to sacrifice her needs to those of her children. More than anyone else, she taught Coretta her moral and ethical values, not by what she said alone, but also by her example.

"Staying with the struggle to the end"

My devoted wife has been a constant source of consolation to me through all the difficulties. In the midst of the most tragic experiences, she never became panicky or overemotional. I have come to see the real meaning of that rather trite statement: a wife can either make or break a husband. My wife was always stronger than I was through the struggle. While she had certain natural fears and anxieties concerning my welfare, she never allowed them to hamper my active participation in the movement. Corrie proved to be that type of wife with qualities to make a husband when he could have been so easily broken. In the darkest moments, she always brought the light of hope. I am convinced that if I had not had a wife with the fortitude, strength, and calmness of Corrie, I could not have withstood the ordeals and tensions surrounding the movement.

She saw the greatness of the movement and had a unique willingness to sacrifice herself for its continuation. If I have done anything in this struggle, it is because I have had behind me and at my side a devoted, understanding, dedicated, patient companion in the person of my wife. I can remember times when I sent her away for safety. I would look up a few days later, and she was back home, because she wanted to be there.

LETTER TO CORETTA

July 23, 1954
Boston

Darling,

How goes everything? I received your special and naturally I was over-joyed to hear from you. I was happy to know that the Women's Day went over in a big way. Your analysis of Gardner's sermon was very good. I see you are a very keen observer.

I am doing quite well, and studying hard as usual. I have plenty of privacy here and nobody to bother me.

All of your friends that I have seen are doing fine. Everybody asks about you.

We had our Philosophy Club Monday night and it was well attended. Brother Satterwhite did the paper.

How are all of the folks?

I will be arriving in Atlanta by plane at 1:25 A.M. Friday night or rather Saturday morning. You all be sure to meet me at the airport. We will leave for Montgomery sometime Saturday morning, that is, if you can go.

Give everybody my regards and let me hear from you soon. Let me know how you are doing.

Be sweet and I will see you soon.

Your Darling,
Martin

Coretta was never satisfied in being away from me, but she could not always be with me because she had to stay home with our four rather young children. She did join me on some occasions, and she was always a deep consolation to me, supporting my every move. I didn't have the problem of having a wife who was afraid and trying to run from the situation. And that was a great help in all of the difficulties that I confronted.

Coretta had to settle down to a few concerts here and there. Basically she has been a pastor's wife and mother of our four children, Martin Luther III, Dexter Scott, Yolanda Denise, and Bernice Albertine.

When I thought of my future, I also thought of my family. I had to think of what's best for them also. One of the frustrating aspects of my life has been the great demands that come as a result of my involvement in the civil rights movement and the struggle for justice and peace. I have to be away from home a great deal and that takes me away from the family so much. It's just impossible to carry out the responsibilities of a father and husband when you have these kinds of demands. But fortunately I have a most understanding wife who has tried to explain to the children why I have to be absent so much. I think in some way they understand, even though it's pretty hard on them.

6

DEXTER AVENUE
BAPTIST CHURCH

You the people of Dexter Avenue Baptist Church have called me to serve as pastor of your historic church; and I have gladly accepted the call. It is with more than perfunctory gratitude that I offer my appreciation to you for bestowing upon me this great honor. I accept the pastorate dreadfully aware of the tremendous responsibilities accompanying it. Contrary to some shallow thinking, the responsibilities of the pastorate both stagger and astound the imagination. They tax the whole man.

JANUARY 24, 1954
King delivers trial sermon at Dexter Avenue Baptist Church in Montgomery, Alabama

FEBRUARY 28
Delivers guest sermon at Second Baptist Church in Detroit, Michigan

APRIL 14
Accepts call to Dexter's pastorate

MAY 2
Delivers first sermon as Dexter's minister

OCTOBER 31
Offically becomes pastor of Dexter; King Sr. delivers installation sermon

AUGUST 26, 1955
Rosa Parks, secretary of Montgomery NAACP chapter, informs King of his election to executive committee

NOVEMBER 17
First child, Yolanda Denise, is born

Afterbeing in school twenty-one years without a break, I reached the satisfying moment of completing the residential requirements for the Ph.D. degree. The major job that remained was to write my doctoral thesis. In the meantime I felt that it would be wise to start considering a job. I was not sure what area of the ministry I wanted to settle down in. I had had a great deal of satisfaction in the pastorate and had almost come to the point of feeling that I could best render my service in this area. I never could quite get the idea out of my mind that I should do some teaching, yet I felt a great deal of satisfaction with the pastorate.

Two churches in the East—one in Massachusetts and one in New York—had expressed an interest in calling me. Three colleges had offered attractive and challenging posts—one a teaching post, one a deanship, and the other an administrative position. In the midst of thinking about each of these positions, I received a letter from the officers of the Dexter Avenue Baptist Church of Montgomery, saying that they were without a pastor and that they would be glad to have me preach when I was again in that section of the country. They had heard of me through my father in Atlanta. I wrote immediately saying that I would be home in Atlanta for the Christmas holidays, and that I would be happy to come to Montgomery to preach one Sunday in January.

The Dexter Avenue Baptist Church had a rich history. Many outstanding ministers served there, including Dr. Vernon Johns. It was a very fine church with even greater possibilities.

"Asking for God's guidance"

On a cool Saturday afternoon in January 1954, I set out to drive from Atlanta, Georgia, to Montgomery, Alabama. It was one of those clear wintry days when the sun bedecked the skies with all of its radiant beauty. After starting out on the highway, I happened to have turned on the radio. Fortunately, the Metropolitan Opera was on the air with a performance of one of my favorite operas— Donizetti's *Lucia di Lammermoor*. So with the captivating beauty of the countryside, the inspiration of Donizetti's inimitable music, and the matchless splendor of the skies, the usual monotony that accompanies a relatively long drive—especially when one is alone—was absorbed into meaningful diversions.

After about a four-hour drive, I arrived in Montgomery. Although I had passed through the city before, I had never been there on a real visit. Now I would have the opportunity to spend a few days in this beautiful little town, which has the distinction of being one of the oldest cities in the United States. It occupies an undulating site around a sharp bend in the Alabama River in the midst of rich and fertile farmland.

Not long after I arrived a friend was gracious enough to take me by the Dexter Avenue Baptist Church where I was to preach the following morning. A solid brick structure erected in Reconstruction days, it stood at one corner of a handsome square not far from the center of town. As we drove up, I noticed diagonally across the square a stately white building of impressive proportions and arresting beauty, the State Capitol—one of the finest examples of classical Georgian architecture in America. Here on January 7, 1861, Alabama voted to secede from the Union, and on February 18, on the steps of the portico, Jefferson Davis took his oath of office as President of the Confederate States. For this reason, Montgomery has been known across the years as the Cradle of the Confederacy. Here the first Confederate flag was made and unfurled. I was to see this imposing reminder of the Confederacy from the steps of the Dexter Avenue Baptist Church many times in the following years.

Saturday evening, as I began going over my sermon, I was aware of a certain anxiety. Although I had preached many times before—having served as associate pastor of my father's church in Atlanta for four years, and actually doing all of the preaching there for three straight summers—I had never preached in a situation in which I was being considered for the pastorate of a church. In such a situation one cannot but be conscious of the fact that he is on trial. Many questions came to my mind. How could I best impress the congregation? Should I attempt to interest it with a display of scholarship? Or should I preach just as I had always done, depending finally on the inspiration of the spirit of God? I decided to follow the latter course. I said to myself over and over again, "Keep Martin Luther King in the background and God in the foreground and everything will be all right. Remember you are a channel of the gospel and not the source." With these words on my lips I knelt and prayed my regular evening prayer. I closed the prayer by asking for God's guidance and His abiding presence as I confronted the congregation of His people on the next morning. With the assurance that always comes to me after sincere prayer, I rose from my knees to the comfortable bed, and in almost an instant I fell asleep.

I arose early on Sunday morning—a custom I follow every Sunday in order to have an hour of quiet meditation. It was a beautiful morning. From my window I watched the sun rise in the eastern horizon and move out as if to point its Technicolor across the lofty blue. I went over my sermon one more time.

Eleven o'clock soon came around and I found myself in the pulpit of Dexter Avenue Baptist Church. A large congregation turned out that morning. My sermon topic was "The Three Dimensions of a Complete Life." The congregation was receptive, and I left with the feeling that God had used me well. I was also greatly impressed with Dexter and its vast possibilities. Later in the day the pulpit committee asked me if I would accept the pastorate in the event they saw fit to call me. I answered that I would give such a call my most prayerful and serious consideration. After this meeting, I left Montgomery for Atlanta, and then took a flight back to Boston.

About a month later I received an air-mail, special-delivery letter from Montgomery, telling me that I had been unanimously called to

---

"THE THREE DIMENSIONS OF A COMPLETE LIFE"

The Length of Life, as we shall use it, is not its duration, not its longevity. It is rather the push of a life forward to its personal ends and ambitions. It is the inward concern for one's personal welfare. The Breadth of Life is the outward concern for the welfare of others. The Height of Life is the upward reach toward God. These are the three dimensions of life, and, without the due development of all, no life becomes complete. Life at its best is a great triangle. At one angle stands the individual person, at the other angle stands other persons, and at the tip top stands God. Unless these three are concatenated, working harmoniously together in a single life, that life is incomplete.

From sermon delivered at Dexter, January 24, 1954

the pastorate of the Dexter Avenue Baptist Church. I was very happy to have this offer, but I did not answer immediately. Now I had to face up to the problem of what to do about the several offers that had come my way. It so happened that I was to take a flight to Detroit, Michigan, the next day, where I was to preach the following Sunday. I thought about this important matter all the way to Detroit. It was one of those turbulent days in which the clouds were hovering very low, but as the plane lifted itself above the clouds, the choppiness of the flight soon passed away. As I sailed along noticing the shining silvery sheets of the clouds below and the dark deep shadow of the blue above, several things came to my mind.

At this time I was torn in two directions. On the one hand I was inclined toward the pastorate; on the other hand, toward educational work. Which way should I go? And if I accepted a church, should it be one in the South, with all the tragic implications of segregation, or one of the two available pulpits in the North? Now, I thought, as the plane carried me toward Detroit, I had a chance to escape from the long night of segregation. Could I return to a society that condoned a system I had abhorred since childhood?

These questions were still unanswered when I returned to Boston. I discussed them with my wife, Coretta (we had been married less than a year), to find that she too was hesitant about returning south. We discussed the all-important question of raising children in the bonds of segregation. We reviewed our own growth in the South, and the many advantages that we had been deprived of as a result of segregation. The question of my wife's musical career came up. She was certain that a Northern city would afford a greater opportunity for continued study than any city in the deep South. For several days we talked and thought and prayed over each of these matters.

Finally we agreed that, in spite of the disadvantages and inevitable sacrifices, our greatest service could be rendered in our native South. We came to the conclusion that we had something of a moral obligation to return—at least for a few years.

The South, after all, was our home. Despite its shortcomings, we had a real desire to do something about the problems that we had felt so keenly as youngsters. We never wanted to be considered detached spectators. Since racial discrimination was most intense in the South, we felt that some of the Negroes who had received a portion of their training in other sections of the country should return to share their broader contacts and educational experience. Moreover, despite having to sacrifice much of the cultural life we loved, despite the existence of Jim Crow, which kept reminding us at all times of the color of our skin, we had the feeling that something remarkable was unfolding in the South, and we wanted to be on hand to witness it.

With this decision my inclination toward the pastorate temporarily won out over my desire to teach, and I decided to accept the call to Dexter for a few years and satisfy my fondness for scholarship later by turning to the teaching field.

So I went back to Montgomery. Because of my desire to spend at least four more months of intensive work on my doctoral thesis, I asked for and was granted the condition that I would not be required to take up the full-time pastorate until September 1, 1954. I agreed, however, to come at least once a month to keep things running smoothly during this interim period. For the next four months I commuted by plane between Boston and Montgomery.

On a Sunday in May 1954 I preached my first sermon as minister of the Dexter Avenue Baptist Church:

It is a significant fact that I come to the pastorate of Dexter at a most crucial hour of our world's history; at a time when the flame of war might arise at any time to redden the skies of our dark and dreary world; at a time when men know all too well that without the proper guidance the whole of civilization can be plunged across the abyss of destruction; at a time when men are experiencing in all realms of life disruption and conflict, self-destruction, and meaningless despair and anxiety. Today men who were but yesterday ridiculing the Church of Christ are now asking the Church the way to the paradise of peace and happiness. We must somehow give our generation an answer. Dexter, like all other churches, must somehow lead men and women of a decadent generation to the high mountain of peace and salvation. We must give men and women, who are all but on the brink of despair, a new bent on life. I pray God that I will be able to lead Dexter in this urgent mission.

I come to you with nothing so special to offer. I have no pretense to

*being a great preacher or even a profound scholar. I certainly have no
pretense to infallibility—that is reserved for the height of the Divine,
rather than the depth of the human. At every moment, I am conscious
of my finiteness, knowing so clearly that I have never been bathed in
the sunshine of omniscience or baptized in the waters of omnipotence.
I come to you with only the claim of being a servant of Christ, and a
feeling of dependence on his grace for my leadership. I come with a
feeling that I have been called to preach and to lead God's people. I
have felt like Jeremiah, "The word of God is in my heart like burning
fire shut up in my bones." I have felt with Amos that when God speaks
who can but prophesy? I have felt with Jesus that the spirit of the Lord
is upon me, because he hath anointed me to preach the gospel to the
poor, to heal the brokenhearted, to preach deliverance to the captives
and to set at liberty those that are bruised.*

"I began my full-time pastorate"

Montgomery was not unfamiliar to Coretta, for her home was just
eighty miles away. (I teased her that she had better be thankful. If she
hadn't married me, she'd still be back in Marion, Alabama, picking
cotton.) Since her teens she had breathed the free air of unsegregated
colleges, and stayed as a welcome guest in white homes. Now in
preparation for our long-term return to the South, she visited the
Negro section of town where we would be living without choice. She
saw the Negroes crowded into the backs of segregated buses and
knew that she would be riding there too. But on the same visit she
was introduced to the church and cordially received by its fine congregation. And with her sense of optimism and balance, which were
to be my constant support in the days to come, she placed her faith
on the side of the opportunities and the challenge for Christian service that were offered by Dexter and the Montgomery community.

The church work was stimulating from the beginning. The first
few weeks of the autumn of 1954 were spent formulating a program
that would be meaningful to this particular congregation. I was anx-
ious to change the impression in the community that Dexter was a
sort of silk-stocking church catering only to a certain class. Often it
was referred to as the "big folk church." Revolting against this idea,
I was convinced that worship at its best is a social experience with

people of all levels of life coming together to realize their oneness and unity under God. Whenever the church, consciously or unconsciously, caters to one class it loses the spiritual force of the "whosoever will, let him come" doctrine, and is in danger of becoming little more than a social club with a thin veneer of religiosity.

For several months I had to divide my efforts between completing my thesis and carrying out my duties with the church. I continued to study hard as usual. I rose every morning at five-thirty and spent three hours writing the thesis, returning to it late at night for another three hours. The remainder of the day was given to church work, including, besides the weekly service, marriages, funerals, and personal conferences. One day each week was given over to visiting and praying with members who were either sick or otherwise confined to their homes.

On September 1, 1954, we moved into the parsonage and I began my full-time pastorate. The first months were busy with the usual chores of getting to know a new house, a new job, a new city. There were old friendships to pick up and new ones to be made, and little time to look beyond our private lives to the general community around us.

My installation at Dexter was held on October 31. Daddy came down to preach the sermon and brought about a hundred people. It was a great success. Members of Ebenezer Baptist were present and contributed. Their presence in large numbers meant much to me at the beginning of my pastorate. Their generosity and bigheartedness were in the forefront and continued to prove to me that there was but one Ebenezer. I felt greatly indebted. I would remember that occasion so long as the cords of memory would lengthen.

I took an active part in current social problems. I insisted that every church member become a registered voter and a member of the NAACP and organized within the church a social and political action committee—designed to keep the congregation intelligently informed on the social, political, and economic situations. The duties of the Social and Political Action Committee were, among others, to keep before the congregation the importance of the NAACP and the necessity of being registered voters, and—during state and national elections—to sponsor forums and mass meetings to discuss the major issues. Two members of the Social and Political Action

"LOOKING BEYOND YOUR CIRCUMSTANCES"

The Negro who experiences bitter and agonizing circumstances as a result of some ungodly white person is tempted to look upon all white persons as evil, if he fails to look beyond his circumstances. But the minute he looks beyond his circumstances and sees the whole of the situation, he discovers that some of the most implacable and vehement advocates of racial equality are consecrated white persons. We must never forget that such a noble organization as the National Association for the Advancement of Colored People was organized by whites, and even to this day gains a great deal of support from Northern and Southern white persons.

Sermon delivered at Dexter, 1955

Committee—Jo Ann Robinson and Rufus Lewis—were among the first people to become prominent in the bus boycott that was soon to mobilize the latent strength of Montgomery's Negro community.

I joined the local branch of the NAACP and began to take an active interest in implementing its program in the community itself. By attending most of the monthly meetings I was brought face-to-face with some of the racial problems that plagued the community, especially those involving the courts.

Around the time that I started working with the NAACP, the Alabama Council on Human Relations also caught my attention. This interracial group was concerned with human relations in Alabama and employed educational methods to achieve its purpose. It sought to attain, through research and action, equal opportunity for all the people of Alabama. After working with the Council for a few months, I was elected to the office of vice-president. Although the Council never had a large membership, it played an important role. As the only truly interracial group in Montgomery, it served to keep the desperately needed channels of communication open between the races.

I was surprised to learn that many people found my dual interest in the NAACP and the Council inconsistent. Many Negroes felt that integration could come only through legislation and court action—

the chief emphases of the NAACP. Many white people felt that integration could come only through education—the chief emphasis of the Council on Human Relations. How could one give his allegiance to two organizations whose approaches and methods seemed so diametrically opposed?

This question betrayed an assumption that there was only one approach to the solution of the race problem. On the contrary, I felt that both approaches were necessary. Through education we seek to change attitudes and internal feelings (prejudice, hate, etc.); through legislation and court orders we seek to regulate behavior. Anyone who starts out with the conviction that the road to racial justice is only one lane wide will inevitably create a traffic jam and make the journey infinitely longer.

After I lived in Montgomery about a year, I became the proud father of a little daughter—Yolanda Denise. "Yoki." was a big little girl—she weighed nine pounds and eleven ounces. She kept her father quite busy walking the floor.

And then, the bus boycott began.

7

MONTGOMERY MOVEMENT BEGINS

While the nature of this account causes me to make frequent use of the pronoun "I," in every important part of the story it should be "we." This is not a drama with only one actor. More precisely it is the chronicle of fifty thousand Negroes who took to heart the principles of nonviolence, who learned to fight for their rights with the weapon of love, and who, in the process, acquired a new estimate of their own human worth.

DECEMBER 1, 1955
Rosa Parks arrested for violating segregation laws

DECEMBER 5
King elected head of newly formed protest group, the Montgomery Improvement Association (MIA)

On December 1, 1955, Mrs. Rosa Parks refused to move when she was asked to get up and move back by the bus operator. Mrs. Parks was sitting in the first seat in the unreserved section. All of the seats were taken, and if Mrs. Parks had followed the command of the bus operator she would have stood up and given up her seat for a *male* white passenger, who had just boarded the bus. In a quiet, calm, dignified manner, so characteristic of the radiant personality of Mrs. Parks, she refused to move. The result was her arrest.

One can never understand the action of Mrs. Parks until one realizes that eventually the cup of endurance runs over, and the human personality cries out, "I can't take it no longer." Mrs. Parks's refusal to move back was her intrepid and courageous affirmation to the world that she had had enough. (No, she was not planted there by the NAACP or any other organization; she was planted there by her sense of dignity and self-respect.) She was a victim of both the forces of history and the forces of destiny. Mrs. Parks was ideal for the role assigned to her by history. Her character was impeccable and her dedication deep-rooted. All of these traits made her one of the most respected people in the Negro community.

Her trial was set for Monday, December 5.

Only E. D. Nixon—the signer of Mrs. Parks's bond—and one or two other persons were aware of the arrest when it occurred early Thursday evening. Nixon had always been a foe of injustice. You could look at the face of this tall, dark-skinned, graying man and tell that he was a fighter. In his work as a Pullman porter, he was in close contact with organized labor. He had served as state president of the NAACP and also as president of the Montgomery branch. Through each of these mediums E. D. Nixon worked fearlessly to achieve the rights of his people, and to rouse the Negroes from their apathy.

Early Friday morning, December 2, Nixon called me. He was so caught up in what he was about to say that he forgot to greet me with the usual hello but plunged immediately into the story of what had happened to Mrs. Parks the night before. I listened, deeply shocked, as he described the humiliating incident. "We have taken this type of thing too long already," Nixon concluded, his voice trembling. "I feel that the time has come to boycott the buses. Only through a boycott can we make it clear to the white folks that we will not accept this type of treatment any longer."

I agreed that some protest was necessary and that the boycott method would be an effective one.

Just before calling me Nixon had discussed the idea with Rev. Ralph Abernathy, the young minister of Montgomery's First Baptist Church who was to become one of the central figures in the protest. Abernathy also felt a bus boycott was our best course of action. So for thirty or forty minutes the three of us telephoned back and forth concerning plans and strategy. Nixon suggested that we call a meeting of all the ministers and civic leaders that same evening in order to get their thinking on the proposal, and I offered my church as the meeting place.

As the hour for the meeting arrived, I approached the church with some apprehension, wondering how many of the leaders would respond to our call. More than forty people, from every segment of Negro life, were crowded into the large church meeting room. The largest number there was from the Christian ministry. I was filled with joy when I found so many of them there; for then I knew that something unusual was about to happen.

Rev. L. Roy Bennett, president of Montgomery's Interdenominational Alliance and minister of the Mt. Zion A.M.E. Church, presented the proposal that the Negro citizens of Montgomery should boycott the buses on Monday in protest. "Now is the time to move," he concluded. "This is no time to talk; it is time to act." He appointed a committee, including myself, to prepare the statement. Our final message read as follows:

> Don't ride the bus to work, to town, to school, or any place Monday, December 5. Another Negro woman has been arrested and put in jail because she refused to give up her bus seat. Don't ride the buses to work, to town, to school, or anywhere on Monday. If you work, take a cab, or share a ride, or walk. Come to a mass meeting, Monday at 7:00 P.M., at the Holt Street Baptist Church for further instruction.

I was so excited that I slept very little that night, and early the next morning I was on my way to the church to get the leaflets out. By eleven o'clock an army of women and young people had taken the seven thousand leaflets off to distribute by hand.

"Put justice in business"

The bus situation was one of the sore spots of Montgomery. If a visitor had come to Montgomery before the bus boycott, he would have heard bus operators referring to Negro passengers as "niggers," "black apes," and "black cows." He would have frequently noticed Negro passengers getting on at the front door and paying their fares, and then being forced to get off and go to the back doors to board the bus, and often he would have noticed that before the Negro passenger could get to the back door, the bus rode off with his fare in the box. But even more, that visitor would have noticed Negro passengers standing over empty seats. No matter if a white person never got on the bus and the bus was filled up with Negro passengers, these Negro passengers were prohibited from sitting in the first four seats because they were only for white passengers. It even went beyond this. If the reserved section for whites was filled up with white persons, and additional white persons boarded the bus, then Negro passengers sitting in the unreserved section were often asked to stand up and give their seats to white persons. If they refused to do this, they were arrested.

After a heavy day of work, I went home late Sunday afternoon and sat down to read the morning paper. There was a long article on the proposed boycott. Implicit throughout the article, I noticed, was the idea that the Negroes were preparing to use the same approach to their problem as the White Citizens Councils used.

As a result of reading that article, I was forced for the first time to think seriously on the nature of the boycott method. Up to this time I had uncritically accepted this method as our best course of action. Now certain doubts began to bother me. Were we following an ethical course of action? Is the boycott method basically unchristian? Isn't it a negative approach to the solution of a problem? Was it true that we would be following the course of some of the White Citizens Councils? Even if lasting practical results came from such a boycott, would immoral means justify moral ends? Each of these questions demanded honest answers.

I had to recognize that the boycott method could be used to unethical and unchristian ends. I had to concede, further, that this was the method used so often by White Citizens Councils to deprive many Negroes, as well as white persons of goodwill, of the basic necessities of life. But certainly, I said to myself, our pending actions could not be interpreted in this light. Our purposes were altogether different. We would use this method to give birth to justice and freedom, and also to urge men to comply with the law of the land. Our concern would not be to put the bus company out of business, but to put justice in business.

As I thought further, I came to see that what we were really doing was withdrawing our cooperation from an evil system, rather than merely withdrawing our support from the bus company. The bus company, being an external expression of the system, would naturally suffer, but the basic aim was to refuse to cooperate with evil. At this point I began to think about Thoreau's "Essay on Civil Disobedience." I became convinced that what we were preparing to do in Montgomery was related to what Thoreau had expressed. We were simply saying to the white community, "We can no longer lend our cooperation to an evil system." From this moment on I conceived of our movement as an act of massive noncooperation. From then on I rarely used the word "boycott."

"A miracle had taken place"

Wearied, but no longer doubtful about the morality of our proposed protest, I prepared to retire early. But, soon after I was in bed, two-week-old Yolanda Denise began crying and the telephone started ringing. Clearly condemned to stay awake for some time longer, I used the time to think about other things. My wife and I discussed the possible success of the protest. Coretta and I agreed that if we could get 60 percent cooperation the protest would be a success.

Around midnight a call from one of the committee members informed me that every Negro taxi company in Montgomery had agreed to support the protest on Monday morning. After midnight the phone stopped ringing and Yoki stopped crying. Wearily, I said good night to Coretta, and with a strange mixture of hope and anxiety, I fell asleep.

My wife and I awoke earlier than usual on Monday morning. We were up and fully dressed by five-thirty. The day for the protest had arrived, and we were determined to see the first act of this unfolding drama.

Fortunately, a bus stop was just five feet from our house. We could observe the opening stages from our front window. And so we waited through an interminable half hour. I was in the kitchen drinking my coffee when I heard Coretta cry, "Martin, Martin, come quickly!" I put down my cup and ran toward the living room. As I approached the front window Coretta pointed joyfully to a slowly moving bus: "Darling, it's empty!" I could hardly believe what I saw. I knew that the South Jackson line, which ran past our house, carried more Negro passengers than any other line in Montgomery, and that this first bus was usually filled with domestic workers going to their jobs. Would all of the other buses follow the pattern that had been set by the first? Eagerly we waited for the next bus. In fifteen minutes it rolled down the street, and, like the first, it was empty. A third bus appeared, and it too was empty of all but two white passengers.

I jumped in my car and for almost an hour I cruised down every major street and examined every passing bus. At the peak of the morning traffic, I saw no more than eight Negro passengers riding the buses. Instead of the 60 percent cooperation we had hoped for, it was becoming apparent that we had reached almost 100 percent. A miracle had taken place. The once dormant and quiescent Negro community was now fully awake.

All day long it continued. At the afternoon peak the buses were still as empty of Negro passengers as they had been in the morning. Students of Alabama State College were cheerfully walking or thumbing rides. Job holders had either found other means of transportation or made their way on foot. Men were seen riding mules to work, and more than one horse-drawn buggy drove the streets of Montgomery that day.

During the rush hours the sidewalks were crowded with laborers and domestic workers trudging patiently to their jobs and home again, sometimes as much as twelve miles. They knew why they walked, and the knowledge was evident in the way they carried themselves. And as I watched them I knew that there is nothing more majestic than the determined courage of individuals willing to suffer and sacrifice for their freedom and dignity.

Around nine-thirty in the morning I tore myself from the action of the city streets and headed for the crowded police court. Here Mrs. Parks was being tried for disobeying the city segregation ordinance. After the judge heard the arguments, he found Mrs. Parks guilty and fined her $10.00 and court costs (a total of $14.00). She appealed the case. This was one of the first clear-cut instances in which a Negro had been convicted for disobeying the segregation law. In the past, either cases like this had been dismissed or the people involved had been charged with disorderly conduct. So in a real sense the arrest and conviction of Mrs. Parks had a twofold impact: it was a precipitating factor to arouse the Negroes to positive action; and it was a test of the validity of the segregation law itself. I am sure that supporters of such prosecutions would have acted otherwise if they had had the prescience to look beyond the moment.

Leaving Mrs. Parks's trial, Ralph Abernathy, E. D. Nixon, and Rev. E. N. French—then minister of the Hilliard Chapel A.M.E. Zion Church—discussed the need for some organization to guide and direct the protest. Up to this time things had moved forward more or less spontaneously. These men were wise enough to see that the moment had now come for a clearer order and direction.

Meanwhile Roy Bennett had called several people together at three o'clock to make plans for the evening mass meeting. Everyone present was elated by the tremendous success that had already attended the protest. But beneath this feeling was the question, where do we go from here? When E. D. Nixon reported on his discussion with Abernathy and French earlier in the day, and their suggestions for an ad hoc organization, the group responded enthusiastically. The new organization needed a name, and several were suggested. Someone proposed the Negro Citizens Committee; but this was rejected because it resembled too closely the White Citizens Councils. Other suggestions were made and dismissed until finally Ralph Abernathy offered a name that was agreeable to all—the Montgomery Improvement Association (MIA). The next job was to elect the officers.

As soon as Bennett had opened the nominations for president, Rufus Lewis spoke from the far corner of the room: "Mr. Chairman, I would like to nominate Reverend M. L. King for president." The motion was seconded and carried, and in a matter of minutes I was unanimously elected.

The action had caught me unawares. It had happened so quickly that I did not even have time to think it through. It is probable that if I had, I would have declined the nomination. They probably picked me because I had not been in town long enough to be identified with any particular group or clique. Just three weeks before, several members of the local chapter of the NAACP had urged me to run for the presidency of that organization, assuring me that I was certain of election. After my wife and I discussed the matter, we agreed that I should not then take on any heavy community responsibilities, since I had so recently finished my thesis, and needed to give more attention to my church work. Coretta's opposition probably resulted in one of the luckiest decisions of my life. For when the bus protest movement broke out, I would hardly have been able to accept the presidency of the Montgomery Improvement Association without lending weight to the oft-made white contention that the whole thing was an NAACP conspiracy.

With these organizational matters behind us, we turned to a discussion of the evening meeting. Several people, not wanting the reporters to know our future moves, suggested that we just sing and pray; if there were specific recommendations to be made to the people, these could be mimeographed and passed out secretly during the meeting. This, they felt, would leave the reporters in the dark. Others urged that something should be done to conceal the true identity of the leaders, feeling that if no particular name was revealed it would be safer for all involved. After a rather lengthy discussion, E. D. Nixon rose impatiently:

"We are acting like little boys," he said. "Somebody's name will have to be known, and if we are afraid we might just as well fold up right now. We must also be men enough to discuss our recommendations in the open; this idea of secretly passing something around on paper is a lot of bunk. The white folks are eventually going to find it out anyway. We'd better decide now if we are going to be fearless men or scared boys."

With this forthright statement the air was cleared. Nobody would again suggest that we try to conceal our identity or avoid facing the issue head-on. Nixon's courageous affirmation had given new heart to those who were about to be crippled by fear.

It was unanimously agreed that the protest should continue until certain demands were met, and that a committee under the chairmanship of Ralph Abernathy would draw up these demands in the form of a resolution and present them to the evening mass meeting for approval. Someone suggested that perhaps we should reconsider our decision to continue the protest. "Would it not be better," said the speaker, "to call off the protest while it is still a success rather than let it go on a few more days and fizzle out? We have already proved our united strength to the white community. If we stop now we can get anything we want from the bus company, simply because they will have the feeling that we can do it again. But if we continue, and most of the people return to the buses tomorrow or the next day, the white people will laugh at us, and we will end up getting nothing." This argument was so convincing that we almost resolved to end the protest. But we finally agreed to let the mass meeting—which was only about an hour off—be our guide. If the meeting was well attended and the people were enthusiastic, we would continue; otherwise we would call off the protest that night.

"The most decisive speech of my life"

I went home for the first time since seven that morning, and found Coretta relaxing from a long day of telephone calls and general excitement. After we had brought each other up to date on the day's developments, I told her, somewhat hesitantly—not knowing what her reaction would be—that I had been elected president of the new association. I need not have worried. Naturally surprised, she still saw that since the responsibility had fallen on me, I had no alternative but to accept it. She did not need to be told that we would now have even less time together, and she seemed undisturbed at the possible danger to all of us in my new position. "You know," she said quietly, "that whatever you do, you have my backing."

Reassured, I went to my study and closed the door. The minutes were passing fast. I had only twenty minutes to prepare the most decisive speech of my life. I became possessed by fear. Now I was faced with the inescapable task of preparing, in almost no time at all, a speech that was expected to give a sense of direction to a people imbued with a new and still unplumbed passion for justice. I was also conscious that reporters and television men would be there with their pencils and sound cameras poised to record my words and send them across the nation.

I was now almost overcome, obsessed by a feeling of inadequacy. In this state of anxiety, I wasted five minutes of the original twenty. With nothing left but faith in a power whose matchless strength stands over against the frailties and inadequacies of human nature, I turned to God in prayer. My words were brief and simple, asking God to restore my balance and to be with me in a time when I needed His guidance more than ever.

With less than fifteen minutes left, I began preparing an outline.

In the midst of this, however, I faced a new and sobering dilemma: how could I make a speech that would be militant enough to keep my people aroused to positive action and yet moderate enough to keep this fervor within controllable and Christian bounds? I knew that many of the Negro people were victims of bitterness that could easily rise to flood proportions. What could I say to keep them courageous and prepared for positive action and yet devoid of hate and resentment? Could the militant and the moderate be combined in a single speech?

I decided that I had to face the challenge head-on, and attempt to combine two apparent irreconcilables. I would seek to arouse the group to action by insisting that their self-respect was at stake and that if they accepted such injustices without protesting, they would betray their own sense of dignity and the eternal edicts of God Himself. But I would balance this with a strong affirmation of the Christian doctrine of love. By the time I had sketched an outline of the speech in my mind, my time was up. Without stopping to eat supper (I had not eaten since morning) I said good-bye to Coretta and drove to the Holt Street Church. Within five blocks of the church I noticed a traffic jam. Cars were lined up as far as I could see on both sides of the street.

It took fully fifteen minutes to push my way through to the pastor's study. By now my doubts concerning the continued success of our venture were dispelled. The question of calling off the protest was now academic. The enthusiasm of these thousands of people swept everything along like an onrushing tidal wave.

It was some time before the remaining speakers could push their way to the rostrum through the tightly packed church. When the meeting began it was almost half an hour late. The opening hymn was the old familiar "Onward Christian Soldiers," and when that mammoth audience stood to sing, the voices outside swelling the chorus in the church, there was a mighty ring like the glad echo of heaven itself.

The chairman introduced me. I rose and stood before the pulpit. Television cameras began to shoot from all sides. The crowd grew quiet.

Without manuscript or notes, I told the story of what had happened to Mrs. Parks. Then I reviewed the long history of abuses and insults that Negro citizens had experienced on the city buses:

We are here this evening for serious business. We are here in a general sense because first and foremost we are American citizens and we are determined to apply our citizenship to the fullness of its meaning. We are here also because of our love for democracy, because of our deep-seated belief that democracy transformed from thin paper to thick action is the greatest form of government on earth. . . .

You know, my friends, there comes a time when people get tired of being trampled over by the iron feet of oppression. There comes a time, my friends, when people get tired of being plunged across the abyss of humiliation, where they experience the bleakness of nagging despair. There comes a time when people get tired of being pushed out of the glittering sunlight of life's July, and left standing amid the piercing chill of an alpine November.

And we are not wrong. We are not wrong in what we are doing. If we are wrong, the Supreme Court of this nation is wrong. If we are wrong, the Constitution of the United States is wrong. If we are wrong, God Almighty is wrong. If we are wrong, Jesus of Nazareth was merely a utopian dreamer that never came down to earth. And we are determined here in Montgomery to work and fight until justice runs down like water and righteousness like a mighty stream.

I want to say that in all of our actions we must stick together. Unity is the great need of the hour, and if we are united we can get many of the things that we not only desire but which we justly deserve. And don't let anybody frighten you. We are not afraid of what we are doing, because we are doing it within the law. There is never a time in our American democracy that we must ever think we're wrong when we protest. We reserve that right.

We, the disinherited of this land, we who have been oppressed so long, are tired of going through the long night of captivity. And now we are reaching out for the daybreak of freedom and justice and equality. May I say to you, my friends, as I come to a close . . . that we must keep . . . God in the forefront. Let us be Christian in all of our actions. But I want to tell you this evening that it is not enough for us to talk about love. Love is one of the pivotal points of the Christian faith. There is another side called justice.

Standing beside love is always justice and we are only using the

*tools of justice. Not only are we using the tools of persuasion but we've
come to see that we've got to use the tools of coercion. Not only is this
thing a process of education but it is also a process of legislation.*

*As we stand and sit here this evening and as we prepare ourselves
for what lies ahead, let us go out with a grim and bold determination
that we are going to stick together. We are going to work together. Right
here in Montgomery, when the history books are written in the future,
somebody will have to say, "There lived a race of people, a black people,
'fleecy locks and black complexion,' a people who had the moral courage
to stand up for their rights. And thereby they injected a new meaning
into the veins of history and of civilization."*

As I took my seat the people rose to their feet and applauded. I
was thankful to God that the message had gotten over and that the
task of combining the militant and the moderate had been at least
partially accomplished. The people had been as enthusiastic when I
urged them to love as they were when I urged them to protest.

As I sat listening to the continued applause I realized that this
speech had evoked more response than any speech or sermon I had
ever delivered, and yet it was virtually unprepared. I came to see for
the first time what the older preachers meant when they said, "Open
your mouth and God will speak for you." While I would not let this
experience tempt me to overlook the need for continued preparation, it would always remind me that God can transform man's
weakness into his glorious opportunity.

Now the time had come for the all-important resolution. Ralph
Abernathy read the words slowly and forcefully. The resolution
called upon the Negroes not to resume riding the buses until (1)
courteous treatment by the bus operators was guaranteed; (2) passengers were seated on a first-come, first-served basis—Negroes
seating from the back of the bus toward the front, whites from the
front toward the back; (3) Negro bus operators were employed on
predominantly Negro routes. At the words, "All in favor of the motion stand," every person to a man stood up, and those who were
already standing raised their hands. Cheers began to ring out from
both inside and outside.

As I drove away my heart was full. I had never seen such enthusiasm for freedom. And yet this enthusiasm was tempered by amazing

REFLECTIONS ON FIRST BOYCOTT MEETING

The deliberations of that brisk and cold night in December will long be stenciled on the mental sheets of succeeding generations. Little did we know on that night that we were starting a movement that would rise to international proportions; a movement whose lofty echos would ring in the ears of people of every nation; a movement that would stagger and astound the imagination of the oppressor, while leaving a glittering star of hope etched in the midnight skies of the oppressed. Little did we know that night that we were starting a movement that would gain the admiration of men of goodwill all over the world. But God still has a mysterious way to perform His wonders. It seems that God decided to use Montgomery as the proving ground for the struggle and triumph of freedom and justice in America. It is one of the ironies of our day that Montgomery, the Cradle of the Confederacy, is being transformed into Montgomery, the cradle of freedom and justice.

Address at First Institute for Nonviolence and Social Change, December 3, 1956

self-discipline. The unity of purpose and esprit de corps of these people had been indescribably moving. No historian would ever be able fully to describe this meeting and no sociologist would ever be able to interpret it adequately. One had to be a part of the experience really to understand it.

The day of days, December 5, 1955, was drawing to a close. We all prepared to go to our homes, not yet fully aware of what had happened. I said to myself, the victory is already won, no matter how long we struggle to attain the three points of the resolution. It is a victory infinitely larger than the bus situation. The real victory was in the mass meeting, where thousands of black people stood revealed with a new sense of dignity and destiny. That night we were starting a movement that would gain national recognition; whose echoes would ring in the ears of people of every nation; a movement that would astound the oppressor, and bring new hope to the oppressed. That night was Montgomery's moment in history.

8

THE VIOLENCE OF
DESPERATE MEN

*Along the way of life, someone must have sense enough and morality
enough to cut off the chain of hate and evil. The greatest way to do
that is through love. I believe firmly that love is a transforming power
than can lift a whole community to new horizons of fair play, goodwill, and justice.*

DECEMBER 17, 1955
King and other MIA leaders meet with white representatives in
unsuccessful attempt to resolve bus dispute

JANUARY 26, 1956
During "Get Tough" campaign, King is arrested and jailed for
speeding

JANUARY 28
Receives $14 fine for speeding

JANUARY 30
After his home is bombed, King pleads for nonviolence

After ascending the mountain on Monday night, I woke up Tuesday morning urgently aware that I had to leave the heights and
come back to earth. I was faced with a number of organizational
decisions. The movement could no longer continue without careful
planning.

I began to think of the various committees necessary to give the
movement guidance and direction. First we needed a more permanent transportation committee, since the problem of getting the ex–

bus riders about the city was paramount. We would also need to raise money to carry on the protest. Therefore, a finance committee was necessary. Since we would be having regular mass meetings, there must be a program committee for these occasions. And then, I reasoned, from time to time strategic decisions would have to be made; we needed the best minds of the association to think them through and then make recommendations to the executive board. So I felt that a strategy committee was essential.

"The response was tremendous"

From the beginning of the protest Ralph Abernathy was my closest associate and most trusted friend. We prayed together and made important decisions together. His ready good humor lightened many tense moments. Whenever I went out of town I always left him in charge of the important business of the association, knowing that it was in safe hands. After Roy Bennett left Montgomery, Ralph became first vice president of the MIA, and has held that position ever since with dignity and efficiency.

In the early stages of the protest the problem of transportation demanded most of our attention. The labor and ingenuity that went into that task is one of the most interesting sides of the Montgomery story. For the first few days we had depended on the Negro taxi companies who had agreed to transport the people for the same ten-cent fare that they paid on the buses. But during the first "negotiation meeting" that we held with the city commission on Thursday, December 8, Police Commissioner Sellers mentioned in passing that there was a law that limited the taxis to a minimum fare. I caught this hint and realized that Commissioner Sellers would probably use this point to stop the taxis from assisting in the protest.

At that moment I remembered that some time previously my good friend the Reverend Theodore Jemison had led a bus boycott in Baton Rouge, Louisiana. Knowing that Jemison and his associates had set up an effective private car pool, I put in a long-distance call to ask him for suggestions for a similar pool in Montgomery. As I expected, his painstaking description of the Baton Rouge experience was invaluable. I passed on word of Sellers's remark and Jemison's advice to the transportation committee and suggested that we immediately begin setting up a pool in order to offset the confusion which could come if the taxis were eliminated from service.

Fortunately, a mass meeting was being held that night. There I asked all those who were willing to offer their cars to give us their names, addresses, telephone numbers, and the hours that they could drive, before leaving the meeting. The response was tremendous. More than a hundred and fifty signed slips volunteering their automobiles. Some who were not working offered to drive in the car pool all day; others volunteered a few hours before and after work. Practically all of the ministers offered to drive whenever they were needed.

On Friday afternoon, as I had predicted, the police commissioner issued an order to all of the cab companies reminding them that by law they had to charge a minimum fare of forty-five cents, and that failure to comply would be a legal offense. This brought an end to the cheap taxi service.

Our answer was to call hastily on our volunteers, who responded immediately. They started out simply by cruising the streets of Montgomery with no particular system. On Saturday the ministers agreed to go to their pulpits the following day and seek additional recruits. Again the response was tremendous. With the new additions, the number of cars swelled to about three hundred.

Thousands of mimeographed leaflets were distributed throughout the Negro community with a list of the forty-eight dispatch and the forty-two pick-up stations. In a few days this system was working astonishingly well. The white opposition was so impressed at this miracle of quick organization that they had to admit in a White Citizens Council meeting that the pool moved with "military precision." The MIA had worked out in a few nights a transportation problem that the bus company had grappled with for many years.

Despite this success, so profoundly had the spirit of the protest become a part of the people's lives that sometimes they even preferred to walk when a ride was available. The act of walking, for many, had become of symbolic importance. Once a pool driver stopped beside an elderly woman who was trudging along with obvious difficulty.

"Jump in, Grandmother," he said. "You don't need to walk."

She waved him on. "I'm not walking for myself," she explained.

"I'm walking for my children and my grandchildren." And she continued toward home on foot.

While the largest number of drivers were ministers, their ranks were augmented by housewives, teachers, businessmen, and unskilled laborers. At least three white men from the air bases drove in the pool during their off-duty hours. One of the most faithful drivers was Mrs. A. W. West, who had early shown her enthusiasm for the protest idea by helping to call the civic leaders to the first organizing meeting. Every morning she drove her large green Cadillac to her assigned dispatch station, and for several hours in the morning and again in the afternoon one could see this distinguished and handsome gray-haired chauffeur driving people to work and home again.

Another loyal driver was Jo Ann Robinson. Attractive, fairskinned, and still youthful, Jo Ann came by her goodness naturally. She did not need to learn her nonviolence from any book. Apparently indefatigable, she, perhaps more than any other person, was active on every level of the protest. She took part in both the executive board and the strategy committee meetings. When the MIA newsletter was inaugurated a few months after the protest began, she became its editor. She was sure to be present whenever negotiations were in progress. And although she carried a full teaching load at Alabama State, she still found time to drive both morning and afternoon.

The ranks of our drivers were further swelled from an unforeseen source. Many white housewives, whatever their commitment to segregation, had no intention of being without their maids. And so every day they drove to the Negro sections to pick up their servants and return them at night. Certainly, if selfishness was a part of the motive, in many cases affection for a faithful servant also played its part. There was some humor in the tacit understandings—and sometimes mutually accepted misunderstandings—between these white employers and their Negro servants. One old domestic, an influential matriarch to many young relatives in Montgomery, was asked by her wealthy employer, "Isn't this bus boycott terrible?"

The old lady responded: "Yes, ma'am, it sure is. And I just told all my young'uns that this kind of thing is white folks' business and we just stay off the buses till they get this whole thing settled."

"The inspiration of Mahatma Gandhi"

From the beginning a basic philosophy guided the movement. This guiding principle has since been referred to variously as nonviolent resistance, noncooperation, and passive resistance. But in the first days of the protest none of these expressions was mentioned; the phrase most often heard was "Christian love." It was the Sermon on the Mount, rather than a doctrine of passive resistance, that initially inspired the Negroes of Montgomery to dignified social action. It was Jesus of Nazareth that stirred the Negroes to protest with the creative weapon of love.

As the days unfolded, however, the inspiration of Mahatma Gandhi began to exert its influence. I had come to see early that the Christian doctrine of love operating through the Gandhian method of nonviolence was one of the most potent weapons available to the Negro in his struggle for freedom. About a week after the protest started, a white woman who understood and sympathized with the Negroes' efforts wrote a letter to the editor of the *Montgomery Advertiser* comparing the bus protest with the Gandhian movement in India. Miss Juliette Morgan, sensitive and frail, did not long survive the rejection and condemnation of the white community, but long before she died in the summer of 1957 the name of Mahatma Gandhi was well known in Montgomery. People who had never heard of the little brown saint of India were now saying his name with an air of familiarity. Nonviolent resistance had emerged as the technique of the movement, while love stood as the regulating ideal. In other words, Christ furnished the spirit and motivation while Gandhi furnished the method.

People responded to this philosophy with amazing ardor. To be sure, there were some who were slow to concur. Occasionally members of the executive board would say to me in private that we needed a more militant approach. They looked upon nonviolence as weak and compromising. Others felt that at least a modicum of violence would convince the white people that the Negroes meant business and were not afraid. A member of my church came to me one day and solemnly suggested that it would be to our advantage to "kill off" eight or ten white people. "This is the only language these white folks will understand," he said. "If we fail to do this they will think we're afraid. We must show them we're not afraid any longer." Besides, he thought, if a few white persons were killed the federal government would inevitably intervene and this, he was certain, would benefit us.

Still others felt that they could be nonviolent only if they were not attacked personally. They would say: "If nobody bothers me, I will bother nobody. If nobody hits me, I will hit nobody. But if I am hit I will hit back." They thus drew a moral line between aggressive and retaliatory violence. But in spite of these honest disagreements, the vast majority were willing to try the experiment.

In a real sense, Montgomery's Negroes showed themselves willing to grapple with a new approach to the crisis in race relations. It is probably true that most of them did not believe in nonviolence as a philosophy of life, but because of their confidence in their leaders and because nonviolence was presented to them as a simple expression of Christianity in action, they were willing to use it as a technique. Admittedly, nonviolence in the truest sense is not a strategy that one uses simply because it is expedient at the moment; nonviolence is ultimately a way of life that men live by because of the sheer morality of its claim. But even granting this, the willingness to use nonviolence as a technique is a step forward. For he who goes this far is more likely to adopt nonviolence later as a way of life.

"I almost broke down under the continual battering"

In spite of the fact that the bus protest had been an immediate success, the city fathers and the bus officials felt that it would fizzle out in a few days. They were certain that the first rainy day would find the Negroes back on the buses. But the first rainy day came and passed and the buses remained empty.

In the meantime, the city fathers and the bus officials had expressed their first willingness to negotiate. At a special session of the MIA executive board a negotiating committee of twelve was appointed and I was chosen to serve as their spokesman. It was agreed that we would present three proposals: (1) a guarantee of courteous treatment; (2) passengers to be seated on a first-come first-served basis, the Negroes seating from the back; and (3) employment of Negro bus operators on predominantly Negro routes. The aim of these proposals was frankly no more than a temporary alleviation of the problem that we confronted. We never felt that the first-come first-served seating arrangement would provide a final solution, since this would eventually have to depend on a change in the law. We were sure, however, that the Rosa Parks case, which was by then in the courts, would be the test that would ultimately bring about the defeat of bus segregation itself.

We arrived at the city hall and were directed to the Commissioners' Chamber. We sat down near the front. The mayor then turned to the Negro delegation and demanded: "Who is the spokesman?" When all eyes turned toward me, the mayor said: "All right, come forward and make your statement." In the glare of the television lights, I walked slowly toward the front of the room and took a seat at the opposite end.

I opened by stating briefly why we found it necessary to "boycott" the buses. I made it clear that the arrest of Mrs. Parks was not the cause of the protest, but merely the precipitating factor. "Our action," I said, "is the culmination of a series of injustices and indignities that have existed over the years."

As soon as I finished the mayor opened the meeting to general discussion. The commissioners and the attorney for the bus company began raising questions. They challenged the legality of the seating arrangement that we were proposing. They contended that the Negroes were demanding something that would violate the law. We answered by reiterating our previous argument that a first-come first-served seating arrangement could exist entirely within the segregation law, as it did in many Southern cities.

It soon became clear that Jack Crenshaw, the attorney for the bus company, was our most stubborn opponent. Doggedly he sought to convince the group that there was no way to grant the suggested seating proposal without violating the city ordinance. The more Crenshaw talked, the more he won the city fathers to his position. Eventually I saw that the meeting was getting nowhere, and suggested that we bring it to a close.

I soon saw that I was the victim of an unwarranted pessimism because I had started out with an unwarranted optimism. I had gone to the meeting with a great illusion. I had believed that the privileged would give up their privileges on request. This experience, however, taught me a lesson. I came to see that no one gives up his privileges without strong resistance. I saw further that the underlying purpose of segregation was to oppress and exploit the segregated, not simply to keep them apart. Even when we asked for justice *within* the segregation laws, the "powers that be" were not willing to grant it. Justice and equality, I saw, would never come while segregation remained, because the basic purpose of segregation was to perpetuate injustice and inequality.

Shortly after this first negotiating conference, I called a meeting of the executive board of the MIA to report the results. The members were disappointed, but agreed that we should stand firm on our three proposals. In the meantime, the mayor sent word that he was calling a citizens committee to meet with the bus officials and Negro leaders on the morning of December 17. Over a week had passed since the first conference and the protest had still shown no signs of faltering.

White members of the committee began to lash out against me. They contended that I was the chief stumbling block to a real solution of the problem. For a moment it appeared that I was alone. Nobody came to my rescue, until suddenly Ralph Abernathy was on the floor in my defense. He pointed out that, since I was the spokesman for the group, I naturally had to do most of the talking, but this did not mean that I did not have the support of the rest of the committee. By trying to convince the Negroes that I was the main obstacle to a solution, the white committee members had hoped to divide us among ourselves. But Ralph's statement left no doubt. From this moment on, the white group saw the futility of attempting to negotiate us into a compromise.

That Monday I went home with a heavy heart. I was weighted down by a terrible sense of guilt, remembering that on two or three occasions I had allowed myself to become angry and indignant. I had spoken hastily and resentfully. Yet I knew that this was no way to solve a problem. "You must not harbor anger," I admonished myself. "You must be willing to suffer the anger of the opponent, and yet not return anger. You must not become bitter. No matter how emotional your opponents are, you must be calm."

After the opposition had failed to negotiate us into a compromise, it turned to subtler means for blocking the protest; namely, to conquer by dividing. False rumors were spread concerning the leaders of the movement. During this period the rumor was spread that I had purchased a brand-new Cadillac for myself and a Buick station wagon for my wife. Of course none of this was true.

Not only was there a conscious attempt to raise questions about the integrity of the Negro leaders, and thereby cause their followers to lose faith in them, there was also an attempt to divide the leaders among themselves. Prominent white citizens went to many of the older Negro ministers and said: "If there has to be a protest, you should be the leaders. It is a shame for you, who have been in the community for so many years, to have your own people overlook you and choose these young upstarts to lead them." Certain members of the white community tried to convince several of the other protest leaders that the problem could be solved if I were out of the picture. "If one of you," they would say, "took over the leadership, things would change overnight."

I almost broke down under the continual battering of this argument. I began to think that there might be some truth in it, and I also feared that some were being influenced by this argument. After two or three troubled days and nights of little sleep, I called a meeting of the executive board and offered my resignation. I told them that I would be the last person to want to stand in the way of a solution to the problem which plagued our community, and that maybe a more mature person could bring about a speedier conclusion. I further assured the board that I would be as active in the background as I had been in the position of spokesman. But I had barely finished talking before board members began to urge me from every side to forget the idea of resignation. With a unanimous vote of confidence, they made it clear that they were well pleased with the way I was handling things, and that they would follow my leadership to the end.

Afterward, as I drove up to the parsonage, more at peace than I had been in some time, I could hear Coretta's high, true soprano through the living room window. In the back bedroom Yoki, now more than a month old, was wide awake and busy discovering her fingers. I picked her up and walked to the front room, bouncing her in time to Coretta's song.

Such moments together had become rare. We could never plan them, for I seldom knew from one hour to the next when I would be home. Many times Coretta saw her good meals grow dry in the oven when a sudden emergency kept me away. Yet she never complained, and she was always there when I needed her. Yoki and Beethoven, she said, kept her company when she was alone. Calm and unruffled, Coretta moved quietly about the business of keeping the household going. When I needed to talk things out, she was ready to listen, or to offer suggestions when I asked for them.

"Conquer by dividing"

The height of the attempt to conquer by dividing came on Sunday, January 22, when the city commissioners shocked the Negro community by announcing in the local newspaper that they had met with a group of prominent Negro ministers and worked out a settlement. Many people were convinced the boycott was over. It was soon clear that this announcement was a calculated design to get the Negroes back on the buses Sunday morning. The city commission felt certain that once a sizable number of Negroes began riding the buses, the boycott would end.

I began to wonder whether any of my associates had betrayed me and made an agreement in my absence. I needed to find out if a group of Negro ministers had actually met with the city commission. After about an hour of calling here and there we were able to identify the "three prominent Negro ministers." They were neither prominent nor were they members of the MIA.

It was now about eleven o'clock on Saturday night. Something had to be done to let the people know that the article they would read the next morning was false. I asked one group to call all the Negro ministers of the city and urge them to announce in church Sunday morning that the protest was still on. Another group joined me on a tour of the Negro nightclubs and taverns to inform those present of the false statement. For the first time I had a chance to see the inside of most of Montgomery's night spots. As a result of our fast maneuvering, the word got around so well that the next day the buses were empty as usual.

With the failure of the attempted hoax, the city fathers lost face.

They were now desperate. Their answer was to embark on a "get-tough" policy. The mayor went on television and denounced the boycott. The vast majority of white Montgomerians, he declared, did not care if a Negro ever rode the buses again, and he called upon the white employers to stop driving Negro employees to and from work. During this period all three city commissioners let it be known that they had joined the White Citizens Council.

The "get-tough" policy turned out to be a series of arrests for minor and often imaginary traffic violations. Faced with these difficulties, the volunteer car pool began to weaken. Some drivers became afraid that their licenses would be revoked or their insurance canceled. Many of the drivers quietly dropped out of the pool. It became more and more difficult to catch a ride. Complaints began to rise. From early morning to late at night my telephone rang and my doorbell was seldom silent. I began to have doubts about the ability of the Negro community to continue the struggle.

"Going to jail"

I did not suspect that I myself was soon to face arrest as a result of the "get-tough" operation. One afternoon in the middle of January, after several hours of work at my church office, I started driving home with a friend, Robert Williams, and the church secretary, Mrs. Lilie Thomas. Before leaving the downtown district, I decided to make a quick trip to the parking lot to pick up a few people going in my direction. As we entered the lot, I noticed four or five policemen questioning the drivers. I picked up three passengers and drove to the edge of the lot, where I was stopped by one of these officers. While he asked to see my license and questioned me concerning the ownership of the car, I heard a policeman across the street say, "That's that damn King fellow."

Leaving the lot, I noticed two motorcycle policemen behind me. One was still following three blocks later. When I told Bob Williams that we were being trailed, he said, "Be sure that you follow every traffic regulation." Slowly and meticulously I drove toward home, with the motorcycle behind me. Finally, as I stopped to let my passengers out, the policeman pulled up and said, "Get out, King; you are under arrest for speeding thirty miles an hour in a twenty-five mile zone." Without a question I got out of the car, telling Bob Williams and Mrs. Thomas to drive on and notify my wife. Soon a patrol car came. Two policemen got out and searched me from top to bottom, put me in the car, and drove off.

As we drove off, presumably to the city jail, a feeling of panic began to come over me. The jail was in the downtown section of Montgomery. Yet we were going in a different direction. The more we rode, the farther we were from the center of town. In a few minutes we turned into a dark and dingy street that I had never seen and headed under a desolate old bridge. By this time I was convinced that these men were carrying me to some faraway spot to dump me off. "But this couldn't be," I said to myself. "These men are officers of the law." Then I began to wonder whether they were driving me out to some waiting mob, planning to use the excuse later on that they had been overpowered. I found myself trembling within and without. Silently, I asked God to give me the strength to endure whatever came.

By this time we were passing under the bridge. I was sure now that I was going to meet my fateful hour on the other side. But as I looked up I noticed a glaring light in the distance, and soon I saw the words "Montgomery City Jail." I was so relieved that it was some time before I realized the irony of my position: going to jail at that moment seemed like going to some safe haven!

A policeman ushered me in. After depositing my things and giving the jailer the desired information, I was led to a dingy and odorous cell. As the big iron door swung open the jailer said to me: "All right, get on in there with all the others." For the moment strange gusts of emotion swept through me like cold winds on an open prairie. For the first time in my life I was thrown behind bars.

As I entered the crowded cell, I recognized two acquaintances, one a teacher, who had also been arrested on pretexts connected with the protest. In the democracy of the jail they were packed together with vagrants and drunks and serious lawbreakers. But democracy did not go so far as to break the rules of segregation. Here whites and Negroes languished in separate enclosures.

When I began to look around I was so appalled at the conditions I saw that I soon forgot my own predicament. I saw men lying on hard wood slats, and others resting on cots with torn-up mattresses.

The toilet was in one corner of the cell without a semblance of an enclosure. I said to myself that no matter what these men had done, they shouldn't be treated like this.

They all gathered around to find out why I was there, and showed some surprise that the city had gone so far as to arrest me. Soon one man after another began talking to me about his reason for being in jail and asking if I could help him out. I turned to the group and said: "Fellows, before I can assist in getting any of you out, I've got to get my ownself out." At this they laughed.

Shortly after, the jailer came to get me. As I left the cell, wondering where he was going to take me, one of the men called after me: "Don't forget us when you get out." I assured them that I would not forget. The jailer led me down a long corridor into a little room in the front of the jail. He ordered me to be seated, and began rubbing my fingers on an ink pad. I was about to be fingerprinted like a criminal.

By this time the news of my arrest had spread over Montgomery, and a number of people had headed for the city jail. The first to arrive was my good friend Ralph Abernathy. He immediately sought to sign my bond, but the officials told him that he had to bring a certified statement from the court asserting that he owned a sufficient amount of property to sign a bond. Ralph pointed out that since it was almost six-thirty at night, the courthouse was already closed.

Indifferently, the official retorted: "Well, you will just have to wait till tomorrow morning."

Ralph then asked if he could see me.

The jailer replied: "No, you can't see him until ten o'clock tomorrow."

"Well, is it possible," said Abernathy, "to pay a cash bond?"

The jailer reluctantly answered yes. Ralph rushed to call someone who could produce the cash.

Meanwhile a number of people had assembled in front of the jail. Soon the crowd had become so large that the jailer began to panic. Rushing into the fingerprinting room he said, "King, you can go now," and before I could half get my coat on, he was ushering me out, released on my own bond.

As I walked out and noticed the host of friends and well-wishers,

I regained the courage that I had temporarily lost. I knew that I did not stand alone. After a brief statement to the crowd, I was driven home. My wife greeted me with a kiss. Many members of my church were waiting anxiously to hear the outcome. Their words of encouragement gave me further assurance that I was not alone.

From that night on my commitment to the struggle for freedom was stronger than ever before. Before retiring I talked with Coretta, and, as usual, she gave me the reassurance that can only come from one who is as close to you as your own heartbeat. Yes, the night of injustice was dark: the "get-tough" policy was taking its toll. But in the darkness I could see a radiant star of unity.

"I heard the voice of Jesus saying still to fight on"

Almost immediately after the protest started we had begun to receive threatening telephone calls and letters. They increased as time went on. By the middle of January, they had risen to thirty and forty a day.

From the beginning of the protest both my parents and Coretta's parents always had the unconscious, and often conscious, fear that something fatal might befall us. They never had any doubt about the rightness of our actions but they were concerned about what might happen to us. My father made a beaten path between Atlanta and Montgomery throughout the days of the protest. Every time I saw him I went through a deep feeling of anxiety, because I knew that my every move was driving him deeper and deeper into a state of worry. During those days he could hardly mention the many harassments that Coretta, the baby, and I were subjected to without shedding tears.

As the weeks passed, I began to see that many of the threats were in earnest. Soon I felt myself faltering and growing in fear. One day, a white friend told me that he had heard from reliable sources that plans were being made to take my life. For the first time I realized that something could happen to me.

One night at a mass meeting, I found myself saying: "If one day you find me sprawled out dead, I do not want you to retaliate with a single act of violence. I urge you to continue protesting with the same dignity and discipline you have shown so far." A strange silence came over the audience.

One night toward the end of January I settled into bed late, after a strenuous day. Coretta had already fallen asleep and just as I was about to doze off the telephone rang. An angry voice said, "Listen, nigger, we've taken all we want from you; before next week you'll be sorry you ever came to Montgomery." I hung up, but I couldn't sleep. It seemed that all of my fears had come down on me at once. I had reached the saturation point.

I got out of bed and began to walk the floor. I had heard these things before, but for some reason that night it got to me. I turned over and I tried to go to sleep, but I couldn't sleep. I was frustrated, bewildered, and then I got up. Finally I went to the kitchen and heated a pot of coffee. I was ready to give up. With my cup of coffee sitting untouched before me I tried to think of a way to move out of the picture without appearing a coward. I sat there and thought about a beautiful little daughter who had just been born. I'd come in night after night and see that little gentle smile. I started thinking about a dedicated and loyal wife, who was over there asleep. And she could be taken from me, or I could be taken from her. And I got to the point that I couldn't take it any longer. I was weak. Something said to me, "You can't call on Daddy now, you can't even call on Mama. You've got to call on that something in that person that your Daddy used to tell you about, that power that can make a way out of no way." With my head in my hands, I bowed over the kitchen table and prayed aloud. The words I spoke to God that midnight are still vivid in my memory: "Lord, I'm down here trying to do what's right. I think I'm right. I am here taking a stand for what I believe is right. But Lord, I must confess that I'm weak now, I'm faltering. I'm losing my courage. Now, I am afraid. And I can't let the people see me like this because if they see me weak and losing my courage, they will begin to get weak. The people are looking to me for leadership, and if I stand before them without strength and courage, they too will falter. I am at the end of my powers. I have nothing left. I've come to the point where I can't face it alone."

It seemed as though I could hear the quiet assurance of an inner voice saying: "Martin Luther, stand up for righteousness. Stand up for justice. Stand up for truth. And lo, I will be with you. Even until the end of the world."

I tell you I've seen the lightning flash. I've heard the thunder roar. I've felt sin breakers dashing trying to conquer my soul. But I heard the voice of Jesus saying still to fight on. He promised never to leave me alone. At that moment I experienced the presence of the Divine as I had never experienced Him before. Almost at once my fears began to go. My uncertainty disappeared. I was ready to face anything.

"The bombing"

Three nights later, on January 30, I left home a little before seven to attend our Monday evening mass meeting at the First Baptist Church. A member of my congregation had come to the parsonage to keep my wife company in my absence. About nine-thirty they heard a noise in front that sounded as though someone had thrown a brick. In a matter of seconds an explosion rocked the house. A bomb had gone off on the porch.

After word of the bombing reached the mass meeting, everybody attempted to keep it from me. People looked at me and then away; one or two seemed about to approach me and then changed their minds. Soon I noticed several of my fellow ministers going in and out of the church in a rather unusual manner, and from this I surmised that something had happened. Unable to restrain my curiosity any longer, I called three of my closest associates and urged them to tell me what had happened. I assured them that I was prepared for whatever it was. Ralph Abernathy said hesitantly, "Your house has been bombed."

STATEMENT AT MIA MASS MEETING

I want you to know that if M. L. King had never been born this movement would have taken place. I just happened to be here. You know there comes a time when time itself is ready for change. That time has come in Montgomery, and I had nothing to do with it.

Statement at MIA Mass Meeting, January 30, 1956

I asked if my wife and baby were all right.

They said, "We are checking on that now."

Strangely enough, I accepted the word of the bombing calmly. My religious experience a few nights before had given me the strength to face it. I urged each person to go straight home after the meeting and adhere strictly to our philosophy of nonviolence. I admonished them not to become panicky and lose their heads. "Let us keep moving," I urged them, "with the faith that what we are doing is right, and with the even greater faith that God is with us in the struggle."

I was immediately driven home. As we neared the scene I noticed hundreds of people with angry faces in front of the house. The policemen were trying, in their usual rough manner, to clear the streets, but they were ignored by the crowd. One Negro was saying to a policeman, who was attempting to push him aside: "I ain't gonna move nowhere. That's the trouble now; you white folks is always pushin' us around. Now you got your .38 and I got mine; so let's battle it out." As I walked toward the front porch, I realized that many people were armed. Nonviolent resistance was on the verge of being transformed into violence.

I rushed into the house to see if Coretta and Yoki were safe. When I walked into the bedroom and saw my wife and daughter uninjured, I drew my first full breath in many minutes. Coretta was neither bitter nor panicky. She had accepted the whole thing with unbelievable composure. As I noticed her calmness I became more calm myself.

The mayor, the police commissioner, and several white reporters had reached the house before I did and were standing in the dining room. After reassuring myself about my family's safety, I went to speak to them. They expressed their regret that "this unfortunate incident has taken place in our city." One of the trustees of my church turned to the mayor and said: "You may express your regrets, but you must face the fact that your public statements created the atmosphere for this bombing. This is the end result of your 'get-tough' policy."

By this time the crowd outside was getting out of hand. The policemen had failed to disperse them, and throngs of additional people were arriving every minute. The white reporters were afraid to face the angry crowd. The mayor and police commissioner, though they might not have admitted it, were very pale.

In this atmosphere I walked out to the porch and asked the crowd to come to order. In less than a moment there was complete silence. Quietly I told them that I was all right and that my wife and baby were all right.

We believe in law and order. Don't get panicky. Don't do anything panicky at all. Don't get your weapons. He who lives by the sword will perish by the sword. Remember that is what God said. We are not advocating violence. We want to love our enemies. I want you to love our enemies. Be good to them. Love them and let them know you love them.

I did not start this boycott. I was asked by you to serve as your spokesman. I want it known the length and breadth of this land that if I am stopped this movement will not stop. If I am stopped our work will not stop. For what we are doing is right. What we are doing is just. And God is with us.

As I finished speaking there were shouts of "Amen" and "God bless you." I could hear voices saying: "We are with you all the way, Reverend." I looked out over that vast throng of people and noticed tears on many faces.

After our many friends left the house late that evening, Coretta, Yoki, and I were driven to the home of one of our church members to spend the night. I could not get to sleep. While I lay in that quiet front bedroom, with a distant street lamp throwing a reassuring glow through the curtained window, I began to think of the viciousness of people who would bomb my home. I could feel the anger rising when I realized that my wife and baby could have been killed. I thought about the city commissioners and all the statements that they had made about me and the Negro generally. I was once more on the verge of corroding hatred. And once more I caught myself and said: "You must not allow yourself to become bitter."

Midnight had long since passed. Coretta and the baby were sound asleep. I turned over in bed and fell into a dazed slumber. But the night was not yet over. Some time later Coretta and I were awakened by a slow, steady knocking at the front door. Through the window we could see the dark outline of a figure on the front porch. I

MEANING OF THE BOYCOTT

There are those who would try to make of this a hate campaign. This is not war between the white and the Negro but a conflict between justice and injustice. This is bigger than the Negro race revolting against the white. We are seeking to improve not the Negro of Montgomery but the whole of Montgomery.

If we are arrested every day, if we are exploited every day, if we are trampled over every day, don't ever let anyone pull you so low as to hate them. We must use the weapon of love. We must have compassion and understanding for those who hate us. We must realize so many people are taught to hate us that they are not totally responsible for their hate. But we stand in life at midnight, we are always on the threshold of a new dawn.

Quoted in the *New York Times,* February 24, 1956

---

pulled myself out of bed, peered through the curtains, and recognized the stocky, reassuring back of Coretta's father.

Obie Scott had heard the news of the bombing over the radio and had driven to Montgomery. He came in the house with an obvious sign of distress on his face. After talking with us a while he turned and said: "Coretta, I came to take you and the baby back home with me until this tension cools off." In a calm but positive manner Coretta answered: "I'm sorry, Dad, but I can't leave Martin now. I must stay here with him through this whole struggle." And so Obie Scott drove back to Marion alone.

Just two nights later, a stick of dynamite was thrown on the lawn of E. D. Nixon. Fortunately, again no one was hurt. Once more a large crowd of Negroes assembled, but they did not lose control. And so nonviolence had won its first and its second tests.

After the bombings, many of the officers of my church and other trusted friends urged me to hire a bodyguard and armed watchmen for my house. When my father came to town, he concurred with both of these suggestions. I tried to tell them that I had no fears now and consequently needed no weapons for protection. This they would not hear. They insisted that I protect the house and family, even if I didn't want to protect myself. In order to satisfy the wishes of these close friends and associates, I decided to consider the question of an armed guard. I went down to the sheriff's office and applied for a license to carry a gun in the car; but this was refused.

Meanwhile I reconsidered. How could I serve as one of the leaders of a nonviolent movement and at the same time use weapons of violence for my personal protection? Coretta and I talked the matter over for several days and finally agreed that arms were no solution. We decided then to get rid of the one weapon we owned. We tried to satisfy our friends by having floodlights mounted around the house, and hiring unarmed watchmen around the clock. I also promised that I would not travel around the city alone.

I was much more afraid in Montgomery when I had a gun in my house. When I decided that I couldn't keep a gun, I came face-to-face with the question of death and I dealt with it. From that point on, I no longer needed a gun nor have I been afraid. Had we become distracted by the question of my safety we would have lost the moral offensive and sunk to the level of our oppressors.

9

DESEGREGATION AT LAST

We came to see that, in the long run, it is more honorable to walk in dignity than ride in humiliation. So in a quiet dignified manner, we decided to substitute tired feet for tired souls, and walk the streets of Montgomery until the sagging walls of injustice had been crushed by the battering rams of surging justice.

FEBRUARY 21, 1956
Montgomery grand jury indicts King and other MIA leaders for violating antiboycott law

MARCH 22
King is found guilty of leading illegal boycott and sentenced to $500 fine or 386 days in jail; the case is appealed

NOVEMBER 13
U.S. Supreme Court declares bus segregation laws unconstitutional

DECEMBER 21
After MIA votes to end boycott, King is one of first passengers to ride desegregated buses

When the opposition discovered that violence could not block the protest, they resorted to mass arrests. As early as January 9, a Montgomery attorney had called the attention of the press to an old state law against boycotts. On February 13 the Montgomery County Grand Jury was called to determine whether Negroes who were boycotting the buses were violating this law. After about a week of deliberations, the jury, composed of seventeen whites and one Negro, found the boycott illegal and indicted more than one hundred persons. My name, of course, was on the list.

At the time of the indictments I was at Fisk University in Nashville, giving a series of lectures. During this period I was talking to Montgomery on the phone at least three times a day in order to keep abreast of developments. Thus I heard of the indictments first in a telephone call from Ralph Abernathy, late Tuesday night, February 21. He said that the arrests were scheduled to begin the following morning. Knowing that he would be one of the first to be arrested, I assured him that I would be with him and the others in my prayers. As usual he was unperturbed.

All night long I thought of the people in Montgomery. Would these mass arrests so frighten them that they would urge us to call off the protest? I knew how hard-pressed they had been. For more than thirteen weeks they had walked, and sacrificed, and worn down their cars. They had been harassed and intimidated on every hand. And now they faced arrest on top of all this. Would they become battle-weary, I wondered. Would they give up in despair? Would this be the end of our movement?

"The point of no return"

I arose early Wednesday morning and flew to Atlanta to pick up my wife and daughter, whom I had left at my parents' home while I was in Nashville. My wife, my mother and father met me at the airport. I had told them about the indictments over the phone, and they had gotten additional information from a radio broadcast. Coretta showed her usual composure, but my parents' faces wore signs of deep perturbation.

My father, so unafraid for himself, had fallen into a constant state of worry for me and my family. Many times he sat in on our councils and had never shown any doubt about the justice of our actions. Yet this stern and courageous man had reached the point where he could scarcely mention the protest without tears. My mother too had suffered. Like all parents, she was afraid for her son and his family. After the bombing she had had to take to bed under doctor's orders, and she was often ill later. During this period I piled up high long distance telephone bills calling between Atlanta and Montgomery—knowing that if Mother could hear my voice on the telephone she would be temporarily consoled. My parents' expressions—even the way they walked as they came toward me at the airport—had begun to show the strain.

As we drove toward my parents' home, my father said that he thought it would be unwise for me to return to Montgomery now. "Although many others have been indicted," he said, "their main concern is to get you. They might even put you in jail without a bond." He went on to tell me that the law enforcement agencies in Montgomery had been trying to find something on my record in Atlanta that would make it possible to have me deported from Alabama. They had gone to the Atlanta police department, and were disappointed when they learned that I did not have even a minor police record. "All of this shows," my father concluded, "that they are out to get you."

I listened to him attentively, and yet I knew that I could not follow his suggestion and stay in Atlanta. I was profoundly concerned about my parents. I was worried about their worry. These were difficult days for me. On the one hand I had to be concerned about keeping my emotional and psychological balance; on the other hand I was deeply concerned about my mother's worrying. But if I eased out now I would be plagued by my own conscience, reminding me that I lacked the moral courage to stand by a cause to the end. No one can understand my conflict who has not looked into the eyes of those he loves, knowing that he has no alternative but to take a dangerous stand that leaves them tormented.

We continued our drive from the airport and soon arrived at my parents' house. I went directly upstairs to see my daughter, Yoki, now three months old. The innocence of her smile and the warmth of her affection brought temporary relief to my tension.

My father asked several trusted friends to come to the house in the early afternoon to discuss the whole issue. Feeling that this exchange of ideas might help to relieve his worries, I readily agreed to stay over and talk to them. Among those who came were A. T. Walden, distinguished attorney; C. R. Yates and T. M. Alexander, both prominent businessmen; C. A. Scott, editor of the *Atlanta Daily World*; Bishop Sherman L. Green of A.M.E. Church; Benjamin E.

Mays, president of Morehouse College; and Rufus E. Clement, president of Atlanta University. Coretta and my mother joined us.

My father explained to the group that because of his respect for their judgment he was calling on them for advice on whether I should return to Montgomery. He gave them a brief history of the attempts that had been made to get me out of Montgomery. He admitted that the fear of what might happen to me caused him and my mother many restless nights. He concluded by saying that he had talked to a liberal white attorney a few hours earlier, who had confirmed his feeling that I should not go back at this time.

There were murmurs of agreement in the room, and I listened as sympathetically and objectively as I could while two of the men gave their reasons for concurring. These were my elders, leaders among my people. Their words commanded respect. But soon I could not restrain myself any longer. "I must go back to Montgomery," I protested. "My friends and associates are being arrested. It would be the height of cowardice for me to stay away. I would rather be in jail ten years than desert my people now. I have begun the struggle, and I can't turn back. I have reached the point of no return." In the moment of silence that followed I heard my father break into tears. I looked at Dr. Mays, one of the great influences in my life. Perhaps he heard my unspoken plea. At any rate, he was soon defending my position strongly. Then others joined him in supporting me. They assured my father that things were not so bad as they seemed. Mr. Walden put through two calls on the spot to Thurgood Marshall, general counsel of the NAACP, and Arthur Shores, NAACP counsel in Alabama, both of whom assured him that I would have the best legal protection. In the face of all of these persuasions, my father began to be reconciled to my return to Montgomery.

Characteristically, my father, having withdrawn his objections to our return to Montgomery, decided to go along with us, unconcerned with any possible danger or unpleasantness to himself. Ralph Abernathy, released on bail after his arrest the previous day, came to the house. With Ralph and my father, I set out for the county jail, several of my church members following after.

"I was proud of my crime"

At the jail, an almost holiday atmosphere prevailed. People had rushed down to get arrested. No one had been frightened. No one had tried to evade arrest. Many Negroes had gone voluntarily to the sheriff's office to see if their names were on the list, and were even disappointed when they were not. A once fear-ridden people had been transformed. Those who had previously trembled before the law were now proud to be arrested for the cause of freedom. With this feeling of solidarity around me, I walked with firm steps toward the rear of the jail. After I had been photographed and fingerprinted, one of my church members paid my bond and I left for home.

The trial was set for March 19. Friends from all over the country came to Montgomery to be with us during the proceedings. Judge Eugene Carter brought the court to order, and after the necessary preliminaries the state called me up as the first defendant. For four days I sat in court listening to arguments and waiting for a verdict. On Thursday afternoon, March 22, both sides rested. All eyes were turned toward Judge Carter, as with barely a pause he rendered his verdict: "I declare the defendant guilty of violating the state's anti-boycott law." The penalty was a fine of $500 and court costs, or 386 days at hard labor in the county of Montgomery. Then Judge Carter announced that he was giving a minimum penalty because of what I had done to prevent violence. In the cases of the other Negroes charged with the same violation, Judge Carter entered a continuance until a final appeal was complete in my case.

In a few minutes several friends had come up to sign my bond, and the lawyers had notified the judge that the case would be appealed. I left the courtroom with my wife at my side and a host of friends following. In front of the courthouse hundreds of Negroes and whites, including television cameramen and photographers, were waiting. As I waved my hand, they began to sing, "We ain't gonna ride the buses no more."

Ordinarily, a person leaving a courtroom with a conviction behind him would wear a somber face. But I left with a smile. I knew that I was a convicted criminal, but I was proud of my crime. It was the crime of joining my people in a nonviolent protest against injustice. It was the crime of seeking to instill within my people a sense of dignity and self-respect. It was the crime of desiring for my people the unalienable rights of life, liberty, and the pursuit of happiness. It was above all the crime of seeking to convince my people that noncooperation with evil is just as much a moral duty as is cooperation with good.

So ended another effort to halt the protest. I had faith that as the case was appealed and went up through the higher courts, the decision would be reversed. Instead of stopping the movement, the opposition's tactics had only served to give it greater momentum, and to draw us closer together. On that cloudy afternoon in March, Judge Carter had convicted more than Martin Luther King, Jr., Case No. 7399; he had convicted every Negro in Montgomery. It is no wonder that the movement couldn't be stopped. It was too large to be stopped. Its links were too well bound together in a powerfully effective chain. There is amazing power in unity. Where there is true unity, every effort to disunite only serves to strengthen the unity. What the opposition failed to see was that our mutual sufferings had wrapped us all in a single garment of destiny. What happened to one happened to all.

The members of the opposition had also revealed that they did not know the Negroes with whom they were dealing. They thought they were dealing with a group who could be cajoled or forced to do whatever the white man wanted them to do. They were not aware that they were dealing with Negroes who had been freed from fear. And so every move they made proved to be a mistake. It could not be otherwise, because their methods were geared to the "old Negro," and they were dealing with a "new Negro."

I have always felt that ultimately along the way of life an individual must stand up and be counted and be willing to face the consequences whatever they are. And if he is filled with fear he cannot do it. My great prayer is always for God to save me from the paralysis of crippling fear, because I think when a person lives with the fears of the consequences for his personal life he can never do anything in terms of lifting the whole of humanity and solving many of the social problems which we confront in every age and every generation.

In this crisis the members of my church were always nearby to lend their encouragement and active support. As I gradually lost my role as husband and father, having to be away from home for hours and sometimes days at a time, women came into the house to keep Coretta company. Many of the men took turns as watchmen. My day-to-day contact with my parishioners had almost ceased. I had become no more than a Sunday preacher. But my church willingly shared me with the community, and threw their own considerable resources of time and money into the struggle.

White friends, too, came forward with their support. Often they called to say an encouraging word, and when the house was bombed several of them, known and unknown to us, came by to express their regret.

Through all of these trying and difficult days, Coretta remained amazingly calm and even-tempered. In the midst of the most tragic experiences, she never became panicky or overemotional. She was always strong and courageous. While she had certain natural fears and anxieties concerning my welfare, she never allowed them to hamper my active participation in the movement. And she seemed to have no fear for herself. She was always a deep consolation to me and supported my every move. Occasionally, I would send Coretta and Yoki to Atlanta to stay with my parents or to Marion to stay with hers in order to give them some relief from the heat of the struggle. However, she was never satisfied being away from me. She always insisted on coming back and staying with the struggle to the end. I am convinced that if I had not had a wife with the fortitude, strength, and calmness of Coretta, I could not have stood up amid the ordeals and tensions surrounding the Montgomery movement. In the darkest moments, she always brought the light of hope.

"Segregation must die"

Let's not fool ourselves, we haven't reached the promised land, North or South. We still confront segregation in the South in its glaring and conspicuous forms. We still confront it in the North in its subtle and hidden forms. Segregation is still a fact. Now it might be true that old man segregation is on its deathbed. But history has proven that social systems have a great last-minute breathing power. And the guardians of the status-quo are always on hand with their oxygen tents to keep the old order alive. But if democracy is to live, segregation must die.

The underlying philosophy of democracy is diametrically opposed to the underlying philosophy of segregation, and all of the dialectics of the logicians cannot make them lie down together. Segregation is an evil, segregation is a cancer in the body politic which must be removed before our democratic health can be realized.

There was a time that we attempted to live with segregation. There were those who felt that we could live by a doctrine of separate but equal and so back in 1896, the Supreme Court of this nation through the Plessy v. Ferguson *decision established the doctrine of separate but equal as the law of the land. But we all know what happened as a result of that doctrine; there was always a strict enforcement of the separate without the slightest intention to abide by the equal. And so as a result of the old* Plessy *doctrine, we ended up being plunged across the abyss of exploitation, where we experienced the bleakness of nagging injustice.*

But even if it had been possible to provide the Negro with equal facilities in terms of external construction and quantitative distribution we would have still confronted inequality. If it had been possible to give Negro children the same number of schools proportionately and the same type of buildings as white children, the Negro children would have still confronted inequality in the sense that they would not have had the opportunity of communicating with all children. You see, equality is not only a matter of mathematics and geometry, but it's a matter of psychology. It's not only a quantitative something but it is a qualitative something; and it is possible to have quantitative equality and qualitative inequality. The doctrine of separate but equal can never be.

I experienced this the other day. I left Montgomery, Alabama, Thursday morning, September 27, via Eastern Air Lines en route to Virginia. In Atlanta I changed from Eastern to Capitol Air Lines. Just as we were about to take off we discovered that we had generator trouble which necessitated our deplaning and going back in the waiting room. We were to have lunch on the flight and so while we were waiting they gave all of us tickets to go in the Dobbs House in the Atlanta airport and have lunch. I was the only Negro passenger on the plane, and I followed everybody else going into the Dobbs House to get lunch. When I got there one of the waiters ushered me back and I thought they were giving me a very nice comfortable seat with everybody else and I discovered they were leading me to a compartment in the back. And this compartment was around you, you were completely closed in, cut off from everybody else, so I immediately said that I couldn't afford to eat there. I went on back and took a seat out in the main dining room with everybody else and I waited there, and nobody served me. I waited a long time, everybody else was being served. So finally I asked for the manager and he came out and started talking, and I told him the situation and he talked in very sympathetic terms. And I never will forget what he said to me.

He said, "Now Reverend, this is the law; this is the state law and the city ordinance and we have to do it. We can't serve you out here but now everything is the same. Everything is equal back there; you will get the same food; you will be served out of the same dishes and everything else; you will get the same service as everybody out here."

And I looked at him and started wondering if he really believed that. And I started talking with him. I said, "I don't see how I can get the same service. Number one, I confront aesthetic inequality. I can't see all these beautiful pictures that you have around the walls here. We don't have them back there. But not only that, I just don't like sitting back there and it does something to me. It makes me almost angry. I know that I shouldn't get angry. I know that I shouldn't become bitter, but when you put me back there something happens to my soul, so that I confront inequality in the sense that I have a greater potential for the accumulation of bitterness because you put me back there. And then not only that, I met a young man from Mobile who was my seat mate, a white fellow from Mobile, Alabama, and we were discussing some very interesting things. And when we got in the dining room, if we followed what you're saying, we would have to be separated. And this means that I can't communicate with this young man. I am completely cut off from communication. So I confront inequality on three levels: I confront aesthetic inequality; I confront inequality in the sense of a greater potential for the accumulation of bitterness; and I confront inequality in the sense that I can't communicate with the person who was my seat mate."

And I came to see what the Supreme Court meant when they came out saying that separate facilities are inherently unequal. There is no such thing as separate but equal.

"A glorious daybreak"

The battle was not yet won. We would have to walk and sacrifice for several more months, while the city appealed the case. But at least we could walk with new hope. Now it was only a matter of time. The summer days gave way to the shorter cooler days of an Alabama autumn. The Supreme Court decision on our appeal was still pending. Meanwhile we were facing continued attempts to block the car pool. Insurance agents decided, almost overnight, to refuse to insure our station wagons, contending that the risk was too high. Finally the company that held our liability insurance notified us that all the policies would be canceled as of September 15. A Northern friend who had read of our trouble wrote suggesting that we contact Lloyds of London. A few days later I talked to T. M. Alexander, an insurance broker in Atlanta, who approved of the idea and agreed to make the contact for us. In a few days he was able to tell us that Lloyds of London would take the insurance.

But we were in for even greater difficulties. The city decided to take legal action against the car pool itself. We tried to block this maneuver by filing a request in the federal court for an order restraining the city from interfering with the pool. But U.S. District Judge Frank M. Johnson refused to grant the request. Soon several of us received subpoenas; the city had filed the petition. The hearing was set for Tuesday, November 13.

The night before the hearing I had to go before the mass meeting to warn the people that the car pool would probably be enjoined. I knew that they had willingly suffered for nearly twelve months, but how could they function at all with the car pool destroyed? Could we ask them to walk back and forth every day to their jobs? And if not, would we then be forced to admit that the protest had failed in the end? For the first time in our long struggle together, I almost shrank from appearing before them.

The evening came, and I mustered up enough courage to tell them the truth. I tried, however, to end on a note of hope. "This may well be," I said, "the darkest hour just before dawn. We have moved all of these months with the daring faith that God was with us in our struggle. The many experiences of days gone by have vindicated that faith in a most unexpected manner. We must go out with the same faith, the same conviction. We must believe that a way will be made out of no way." But in spite of these words, I could feel the cold breeze of pessimism passing through the audience. It was a dark night—darker than a thousand midnights. It was a night in which the light of hope was about to fade away and the lamp of faith about to flicker. We went home with nothing before us but a cloud of uncertainty.

Tuesday morning found us in court, once again before Judge Carter. The city's petition was directed against the MIA and several churches and individuals. It asked the court to grant the city compensation for damages growing out of the car pool operation. As chief defendant I sat at the front table with the prosecuting and defense attorneys.

Around twelve o'clock—during a brief recess—I noticed unusual commotion in the courtroom. Both Commissioner Sellers and Mayor Gayle were called to a back room, followed by two of the city attorneys. Several reporters moved excitedly in and out of the room.

I turned to my attorneys, Fred Gray and Peter Hall, and said: "Something is wrong."

Before I could fully get these words out, Rex Thomas—a reporter for Associated Press—came up to me with a paper in his hand.

"Here is the decision that you have been waiting for. Read this release."

Quickly, with a mixture of anxiety and hope, I read these words: "The United States Supreme Court today affirmed a decision of a special three-judge U.S. District Court in declaring Alabama's state and local laws requiring segregation on buses unconstitutional. The Supreme Court acted without listening to any argument; it simply said 'the motion to affirm is granted and the judgment is affirmed.'"

At this moment my heart began to throb with an inexpressible joy. At once I told the news to the attorneys at the table. Then I rushed to the back of the room to tell my wife, Ralph Abernathy, and E. D. Nixon. Soon the word had spread to the whole courtroom. The faces of the Negroes showed that they had heard. "God Almighty has spoken from Washington, D.C.," said one joyful bystander.

After a few minutes Judge Carter called the court to order again, and we settled down to the case at hand for the remainder of the day. About five o'clock both sides rested, and the judge's decision came in a matter of minutes: As we had all expected, the city was granted a temporary injunction to halt the motor pool. But the decision was an anticlimax. Tuesday, November 13, 1956, will always remain an important and ironic date in the history of the Montgomery bus protest. On that day two historic decisions were rendered— one to do away with the pool; the other to remove the underlying conditions that made it necessary. The darkest hour of our struggle had become the hour of victory. Disappointment, sorrow, and despair are born at midnight, but morning follows.

I rushed home and notified the press that I was calling the Negro citizens together on Wednesday night, November 14, to decide whether to call off the protest. In order to accommodate as many people as possible, two simultaneous meetings were scheduled, one on each side of town, with the speakers traveling from one meeting to the other. In the meantime, the executive board decided, on the advice of counsel, to recommend that the official protest be ended immediately, but that the return to the buses be delayed until the mandatory order arrived from the Supreme Court in Washington. It was expected in a few days.

The eight thousand men and women who crowded in and around the two churches were in high spirits. At the first meeting it was clear that the news of the decision had spread fast. Each of the meetings accepted the recommendations of the executive board to call off the protest but refrain from riding the buses until the mandate reached Alabama. It was a glorious daybreak to end a long night of enforced segregation.

That night the Ku Klux Klan rode. The radio had announced their plan to demonstrate throughout the Negro community, and threats of violence and new bombings were in the air. For a short period during the late summer and early fall, there had been a decline in harassments, but they started again when the Supreme Court rendered its verdict. The evening after the decision my telephone rang almost every five minutes. One caller said to me, "If you allow the niggers to go back to the buses and sit on the front seat, we are going to burn down more than fifty nigger houses in one night, including yours." I said to him very calmly that that wasn't the way to solve the problem. Before I could complete my sentence, he said,

"Shut up your mouth, nigger, or we will come out there and blow you up right now." Another caller spent his time cursing the Supreme Court. He told me that he had evidence that all the Supreme Court justices were Communists. He closed his bitter statement by saying: "We are just waiting for that damn Hugo Black to come back to Alabama, and we are going to hang you and him on the same tree."

Ordinarily, threats of Klan action were a signal to the Negroes to go into their houses, close the doors, pull the shades, or turn off the lights. Fearing death, they played dead. But this time they had prepared a surprise. When the Klan arrived—according to the newspapers "about forty carloads of robed and hooded members"—porch lights were on and doors open. As the Klan drove by, the Negroes behaved as though they were watching a circus parade. Concealing the effort it cost them, many walked about as usual; some simply watched from their steps; a few waved at the passing cars. After a few blocks, the Klan, nonplussed, turned off into a side street and disappeared into the night.

Meanwhile we went to work to prepare the people for integrated buses. In mass meeting after mass meeting we stressed nonviolence. The prevailing theme was that "we must not take this as a victory over the white man, but as a victory for justice and democracy." We hammered away at the point that "we must not go back on the buses and push people around unnecessarily, boasting of our rights. We must simply sit where there is a vacant seat."

In spite of all of our efforts to prepare the Negroes for integrated buses, not a single white group would take the responsibility of preparing the white community. We tried to get the white ministerial alliance to make a simple statement calling for courtesy and Christian brotherhood, but in spite of the favorable response of a few ministers, the majority "dared not get involved in such a controversial issue." This was a deep disappointment.

"Our faith seems to be vindicated"

On December 20, 1956, the bus integration order finally reached Montgomery. A mass meeting was immediately scheduled for that evening, to give the people final instructions before returning to the buses the following day. I called and asked the manager of the bus company to be sure to have service restored on all of the major lines. With evident relief, he agreed.

To the overflow crowd at the St. John A.M.E. Church I read the following message that I had carefully prepared in the afternoon:

These twelve months have not at all been easy. Our feet have often been tired. We have struggled against tremendous odds to maintain alternative transportation. There have been moments when roaring waters of disappointment poured upon us in staggering torrents. We can remember days when unfavorable court decisions came upon us like tidal waves, leaving us treading in the deep and confused waters of despair. But amid all of this we have kept going with the faith that as we struggle, God struggles with us, and that the arc of the moral universe, although long, is bending toward justice. We have lived under the agony and darkness of Good Friday with the conviction that one day the heightening glow of Easter would emerge on the horizon. We have seen truth crucified and goodness buried, but we have kept going with the conviction that truth crushed to earth will rise again.

Now our faith seems to be vindicated. This morning the long awaited mandate from the United States Supreme Court concerning bus segregation came to Montgomery. Our experience and growth during this past year of united nonviolent protest has been of such that we cannot be satisfied with a court "victory" over our white brothers. We must respond to the decision with an understanding of those who have oppressed us and with an appreciation of the new adjustments that the court order poses for them. We must be able to face up honestly to our own shortcomings. We must act in such a way as to make possible a coming together of white people and colored people on the basis of a real harmony of interests and understanding. We seek an integration based on mutual respect.

This is the time that we must evince calm dignity and wise restraint. Emotions must not run wild. Violence must not come from any of us, for if we become victimized with violent intents, we will have walked in vain, and our twelve months of glorious dignity will be transformed into an eve of gloomy catastrophe. As we go back to the buses let us be loving enough to turn an enemy into a friend. We must now move from protest to reconciliation. It is my firm conviction that God is working in Montgomery. Let all men of goodwill, both Negro and white, con-

tinue to work with Him. With this dedication we will be able to emerge
from the bleak and desolate midnight of man's inhumanity to man to
the bright and glittering daybreak of freedom and justice.

The audience stood and cheered loudly. This was the moment
toward which they had pressed for more than a year. The return to
the buses, on an integrated basis, was a new beginning. But it was a
conclusion too, the end of an effort that had drawn Montgomery's
Negroes together as never before. It had been gratifying to know
how the idea of nonviolence had gradually seeped into the hearts
and souls of the people. There had been an amazing amount of discipline on the part of our people. I felt that the whole struggle had
given the Negro a new sense of dignity and destiny. To many of
those present the joy was not unmixed. Some perhaps feared what
might happen when they began to ride the buses again the next day.
Others had found a spiritual strength in sacrifice to a cause; now the
sacrifice was no longer necessary. Like many consummations, this
one left a slight aftertaste of sadness.

I had decided that after many months of struggling with my people for the goal of justice I should not sit back and watch, but should
lead them back to the buses myself. I asked Ralph Abernathy, E. D.
Nixon, and Glenn Smiley to join me in riding on the first integrated
bus. They reached my house around 5:45 on Friday morning. Television cameras, photographers, and news reporters were hovering outside the door. At 5:55 we walked toward the bus stop, the cameras
shooting, the reporters bombarding us with questions. Soon the bus
appeared; the door opened, and I stepped on. The bus driver greeted
me with a cordial smile. As I put my fare in the box he said:

"I believe you are Reverend King, aren't you?"

I answered: "Yes I am."

"We are glad to have you this morning," he said.

I thanked him and took my seat, smiling now too. Abernathy,
Nixon, and Smiley followed, with several reporters and television
men behind them. Glenn Smiley sat next to me. So I rode the first
integrated bus in Montgomery with a white minister, and a native
Southerner, as my seat mate.

Downtown we transferred to one of the buses that serviced the
white residential section. As the white people boarded, many took
seats as if nothing were going on. Others looked amazed to see Ne-

groes sitting in front, and some appeared peeved to know that they either had to sit behind Negroes or stand. One elderly man stood up by the conductor, despite the fact that there were several vacant seats in the rear. When someone suggested to him that he sit in back, he responded: "I would rather die and go to hell than sit behind a nigger." A white woman unknowingly took a seat by a Negro. When she noticed her neighbor, she jumped up and said in a tone of obvious anger: "What are these niggers gonna do next?"

But despite such signs of hostility there were no major incidents on the first day. Many of the whites responded to the new system calmly. Several deliberately and with friendly smiles took seats beside Negroes. True, one Negro woman was slapped by a white man as she alighted, but she refused to retaliate. Later she said: "I could have broken that little fellow's neck all by myself, but I left the mass meeting last night determined to do what Reverend King asked." The *Montgomery Advertiser* reported at the end of the first day: "The calm but cautious acceptance of this significant change in Montgomery's way of life came without any major disturbance."

"A courageous new Negro"

Montgomery marked the first flash of organized, sustained, mass action and nonviolent revolt against the Southern way of life. In Montgomery, there emerged courageous and collective challenge to and protest against the American order, which promised so much for all, while perpetuating indignities and brutalities on the oppressed minority.

Montgomery marked the psychological turning point for the American Negro in his struggle against segregation. The revolution birthed in Montgomery was unlike the isolated, futile, and violent slave revolts. It was also unlike the many sporadic incidents of revolt against segregation by individuals, resisting in their own way the forces of oppression pinning them down. In Montgomery, all across the board, at one and the same time, the rank and file rose up and revolted, by refusing to ride the buses. By walking instead, and by brilliant use of car pools and improvising, the boycotters sustained their revolt all the way to victory.

Also, Montgomery contributed a new weapon to the Negro revolution. This was the social tool of nonviolent resistance. It was a weapon first applied on the American scene and in a collective way in Montgomery. In that city too, it was honed well for future use. It was effective in that it had a way of disarming the opponent. It exposed his moral defenses. It weakened his morale, and at the same time it worked on his conscience. It also provided a method for Negroes to struggle to secure moral ends through moral means. Thus, it provided a creative force through which men could channel their discontent.

Ultimately, victory in Montgomery came with the United States Supreme Court's decision; however, in a real sense, the victory had already come to the boycotters, who had proven to themselves, the community, and the world that Negroes could join in concert and sustain collective action against segregation, carrying it through until the desired objective was reached. In conclusion, then, Montgomery gave forth, for all the world to see, a courageous new Negro. He emerged, etched in sharpest relief, a person whom whites had to confront and even grudgingly respect, and one whom Negroes admired and, then, emulated. He had thrust off his stagnant passivity and deadening complacency, and emerged with a new sense of dignity and destiny. The Montgomery Negro had acquired a new sense of somebodiness and self-respect, and had a new determination to achieve freedom and human dignity no matter what the cost.

10

THE EXPANDING
STRUGGLE

History has thrust upon our generation an indescribably important destiny—to complete a process of democratization which our nation has too long developed too slowly, but which is our most powerful weapon for world respect and emulation. How we deal with this crucial situation will determine our moral health as individuals, our cultural health as a region, our political health as a nation, and our prestige as a leader of the free world.

FEBRUARY 14, 1957
King becomes head of Southern Leaders Conference (later SCLC)

MAY 17
Delivers address at Prayer Pilgrimage for Freedom in Washington, D.C.

SEPTEMBER 25
Applauds President Eisenhower's decision to use force to integrate Little Rock's Central High School

OCTOBER 23
Martin Luther King III is born

JUNE 23, 1958
King and other civil rights leaders meet with Eisenhower

On January 9, 1957, Ralph Abernathy and I went to Atlanta to prepare for a meeting of Negro leaders that I had called for the following day. In the middle of the night we were awakened by a telephone call from Ralph's wife, Juanita. I knew that only some new disaster would make her rouse us at two in the morning. When Ralph came back, his sober face told part of the story. "My home has been bombed," he said, "and three or four other explosions have been heard in the city, but Juanita doesn't know where yet." I asked about Juanita and their daughter. "Thank God, they are safe." Before we could talk any more, the telephone rang a second time. It was Juanita again, saying that the First Baptist Church had been hit. Ralph's home and his church had been bombed in one night. I knew no words to comfort him. There in the early morning hours we prayed to God together, asking for the power of endurance, the strength to carry on.

Ralph and I arranged to fly back, leaving the meeting of Southern leaders to begin without us. From the Montgomery airport we drove directly to Ralph's house. The street was roped off, and hundreds of people stood staring at the ruins. The front porch had been almost completely destroyed, and things inside the house were scattered from top to bottom. Juanita, though shocked and pale, was fairly composed.

The rest of the morning was spent in a grim tour of the other bombings. The Bell Street and Mt. Olive Baptist churches had been almost completely destroyed. The other two churches were less severely damaged, but nevertheless faced great losses.

That afternoon, I returned to Atlanta to make at least an appearance at the meeting of Negro leaders. There I found an enthusiastic group of almost a hundred men from all over the South, committed to the idea of a Southern movement to implement the Supreme Court's decision against bus segregation through nonviolent means. We wired President Dwight D. Eisenhower, asking him to come south immediately, to make a major speech in a major Southern city urging all Southerners to accept and to abide by the Supreme Court's decisions as the law of the land. We further urged him to use the weight of his great office to point out to the South the moral nature of the problems posed at home and abroad by the unsolved civil rights issue. Before adjourning they voted to form the Southern Leaders Conference (later the Southern Christian Leadership Conference or SCLC), a permanent organization to facilitate coordinated action of local protest groups. I became the group's president, a position I still hold.

"Wave of terror"

When I returned to Montgomery over the weekend I found the Negro community in low spirits. After the bombings the city commission had ordered all buses off the streets; and it now appeared that the city fathers would use this reign of violence as an excuse to cancel the bus company's franchise. As a result, many were coming to feel that all our gains had been lost; I myself started to fear that we were in for another long struggle to get bus service renewed. I was also beginning to wonder whether the virulent leaflets that were bombarding the Negro community might be having their effect. Discouraged, and still revolted by the bombings, for some strange reason I began to feel a personal sense of guilt for everything that was happening.

In this mood I went to the mass meeting on Monday night. There for the first time, I broke down in public. I had invited the audience to join me in prayer, and had begun by asking God's guidance and direction in all our activities. Then, in the grip of an emotion I could not control, I said, "Lord, I hope no one will have to die as a result of our struggle for freedom in Montgomery. Certainly I don't want to die. But if anyone has to die, let it be me." The audience was in an uproar. Shouts and cries of "no, no" came from all sides. So intense was the reaction, that I could not go on with my prayer. Two of my fellow ministers came to the pulpit and suggested that I take a seat. For a few minutes I stood with their arms around me, unable to move. Finally, with the help of my friends, I sat down. It was this scene that caused the press to report mistakenly that I had collapsed.

Unexpectedly, this episode brought me great relief. Many people came up to me after the meeting and many called the following day to assure me that we were all together until the end. For the next few days, the city was fairly quiet. Bus service was soon resumed, though still on a daytime schedule only.

Then another wave of terror hit. Early in the morning of January 28, the People's Service Station and Cab Stand was bombed, and

LETTER TO MRS. FANNIE E. SCOTT [CORETTA'S GRANDMOTHER]

Dear Mrs. Scott:

Thanks for your very kind letter of recent date. I am very happy to know of your interest here in Montgomery. May I assure you that things are going very well with me and the family. Coretta and the baby are doing fine. We are determined as ever before to continue to struggle for freedom and justice here in Montgomery. The impression that the paper gave a few days ago was totally false. I neither collapsed nor broke down in tears. I am still as strong and healthy as ever before. Be sure to keep us in your prayers.

January 28, 1957

another bomb fell at the home of a sixty-year-old Negro hospital worker. The same morning an unexploded bomb, crudely assembled from twelve sticks of dynamite, was found still smoldering on my porch.

I was staying with friends on the other side of town, and Coretta and Yoki were in Atlanta. So once more I heard the news first on the telephone. On my way home, I visited the other scenes of disaster nearby, and found to my relief that no one had been hurt.

At home I addressed the crowd from my porch, where the mark of the bomb was clear. "We must not return violence under any condition. I know this is difficult advice to follow, especially since we have been the victims of no less than ten bombings. But this is the way of Christ; it is the way of the cross. We must somehow believe that unearned suffering is redemptive." Then, since it was Sunday morning, I urged the people to go home and get ready for church. Gradually they dispersed.

With these bombings the community came to see that Montgomery was fast being plunged into anarchy. Finally, the city began to investigate in earnest. Rewards of $4,000 were offered for information leading to the arrest and conviction of the bombers. On January 31, the Negro community was surprised to hear that seven white men had been arrested in connection with the bombings.

The defense attorneys spent two days attempting to prove the innocence of their clients, arguing that the bombings had been carried out by the MIA in order to inspire new outside donations for their dwindling treasury. At the end of the second day I was called to the witness stand by the defense. For more than an hour I was questioned on things which had no relevance to the bombing case. The lawyers lifted statements of mine out of context to give the impression that I was a perpetrator of hate and violence. At many points they invented derogatory statements concerning white people, and attributed them to me. The men had signed confessions. But in spite of all the evidence, the jury returned a verdict of not guilty.

Justice had once more miscarried. But the diehards had made their last stand. The disturbances ceased abruptly. Desegregation on the buses proceeded smoothly. In a few weeks transportation was back to normal, and people of both races rode together wherever they pleased. The skies did not fall when integrated buses finally traveled the streets of Montgomery.

"A symbol of a movement"

After *Time* magazine published a cover story on our movement in February 1957, I thought I observed a lessening of tensions and feelings against me and the movement itself.

TO CORETTA SCOTT KING

14 February 1957
New Orleans, La.

MRS CORETTA KING =
309 SOUTH JACKSON ST MONTGOMERY ALA =

MY DARLING IT IS A PLEASURE FOR ME TO PAUSE WHILE ATTENDING TO IMPORTANT BUSINESS WHICH AFFECTS THE WELFARE OF THIS NATION AND ATTEND TO THE MOST IMPORTANT BUSINESS IN THE WORLD NAMELY CHOOSING AS MY VALENTINE THE SWEETEST AND MOST LOVELY WIFE AND MOTHER IN ALL THE WORLD AS THE DAYS GO BY MY LOVE GROWS EVEN GREATER FOR YOU WILL ALWAYS BE MY VALENTINE =

MARTIN =

During this period, I could hardly go into any city or any town in this nation where I was not lavished with hospitality by peoples of all races and of all creeds. I could hardly go anywhere to speak in this nation where hundreds and thousands of people were not turned away because of lack of space. And then after speaking, I often had to be rushed out to get away from the crowd rushing for autographs. I could hardly walk the street in any city of this nation where I was not confronted with people running up the street: "Isn't this Reverend King of Alabama?" And living under this it was easy to feel that I was something special.

When you are aware that you are a symbol, it causes you to search your soul constantly—to go through this job of self-analysis, to see if you live up to the high and noble principles that people surround you with, and to try at all times to keep the gulf between the public self and the private self at a minimum.

One of the prayers that I prayed to God every day was: "Oh God, help me to see myself in my true perspective. Help me, oh God, to see that I'm just a symbol of a movement. Help me to see that I'm the victim of what the Germans call a *Zeitgeist* and that something was getting ready to happen in history. And that a boycott would have taken place in Montgomery, Alabama, if I had never come to Alabama. Help me to realize that I'm where I am because of the forces of history and because of the fifty thousand Negroes of Alabama who will never get their names in the papers and in the headlines. Oh, God, help me to see that where I stand today, I stand because others helped me to stand there and because the forces of history projected me there."

"New Negro in the South"

It was clear that things were much better than they were before December 5, 1955, but Montgomery's racial problems were still far from solved. The problem in Montgomery was merely symptomatic of the larger national problem. Forces maturing for years had given rise to a crisis in race relations. The social upheavals of the two world wars, the Great Depression, and the spread of the automobile had made it both possible and necessary for the Negro to move away from his former isolation on the rural plantation. The decline of

THE CONSEQUENCES OF FAME

One of the frustrations of any young man is to approach the heights at such an early age. The average man reaches this point maybe in his late forties or early fifties. But when you reach it so young, your life becomes a kind of decrescendo. You feel yourself fading from the screen at a time you should just be starting to work toward your goal.

Frankly, I'm worried to death. A man who hits the peak at twenty-seven has a tough job ahead. People will be expecting me to pull rabbits out of the hat for the rest of my life. If I don't or there are no rabbits to be pulled, then they'll say I'm no good.

Quoted in the *New York Post*, April 14, 1957

agriculture and the parallel growth of industry had drawn large numbers of Negroes to urban centers and brought about a gradual improvement in their economic status. New contacts had led to a broadened outlook and new possibilities for educational advance.

All of these factors conjoined to cause the Negro to take a fresh look at himself. His expanding life experiences had created within him a consciousness that he was an equal element in a larger social compound and accordingly should be given rights and privileges commensurate with his new responsibilities. Once plagued with a tragic sense of inferiority resulting from the crippling effects of slavery and segregation, the Negro was driven to reevaluate himself. He had come to feel that he was somebody.

This growing self-respect has inspired the Negro with a new determination to struggle and sacrifice until first-class citizenship becomes a reality. This is the true meaning of the Montgomery Story. One can never understand the bus protest in Montgomery without understanding that there is a new Negro in the South, with a new sense of dignity and destiny.

Along with the Negro's changing image of himself has come an awakening moral consciousness on the part of millions of white Americans concerning segregation. Ever since the signing of the Declaration of Independence, America has manifested a schizophrenic personality on the question of race. She has been torn between selves—a self in which she has proudly professed democracy and a self in which she has sadly practiced the antithesis of democracy. The reality of segregation, like slavery, has always had to confront the ideals of democracy and Christianity. Indeed, segregation and discrimination are strange paradoxes in a nation founded on the principle that all men are created equal.

Climaxing this process was the Supreme Court's decision outlawing segregation in the public schools. For all men of goodwill May 17, 1954, marked a joyous end to the long night of enforced segregation. In unequivocal language the Court affirmed that "separate but equal" facilities are inherently unequal, and that to segregate a child on the basis of his race is to deny that child equal protection of the law. This decision brought hope to millions of disinherited Negroes who had formerly dared only to dream of freedom. It further enhanced the Negro's sense of dignity and gave him even greater determination to achieve justice.

This determination of Negro Americans to win freedom from all forms of oppression springs from the same deep longing that motivates oppressed peoples all over the world. The rumblings of discontent in Asia and Africa are expressions of a quest for freedom and human dignity by people who have long been the victims of colonialism and imperialism. So, in a real sense, the racial crisis in America is a part of the larger world crisis.

"Give us the ballot!"

On the seventeenth of May, 1957, civil rights advocates commemorated the third anniversary of the Supreme Court's momentous decision outlawing segregation by leading a Prayer Pilgrimage to Washington, D.C. On that day thousands of Negroes and white persons of goodwill from all over the country assembled at the Lincoln Memorial and had a service about two hours in length. We received strong and powerful support from organized labor. Walter Reuther, for instance, sent letters to all of his locals requesting them to send delegations and also money. The overall purpose of this pilgrimage was to arouse the conscience of the nation in favor of racial justice. The more specific purposes were to demonstrate the unity of the Negro in the struggle for freedom, the violence and terror which we suffer in the southland at this time, and to appeal to Congress to pass the Civil Rights Bill, which was being bottled up in committees by Southern congressmen.

In the midst of these prevailing conditions, we came to Washington to say to the men in the forefront of our government, that the civil rights issue was not an ephemeral, evanescent domestic issue that could be kicked about by reactionary guardians of the status quo; it was rather an eternal moral issue which may well determine the destiny of our nation in the ideological struggle with Communism.

Our most urgent request to the President of the United States and every member of Congress is to give us the right to vote. Give us the ballot and we will no longer have to worry the federal government about our basic rights. Give us the ballot and we will no longer plead to the federal government for passage of an anti-lynching law; we will by the power of our vote write the law on the statute books of the South and bring an end to the dastardly acts of the hooded perpetrators of violence. Give us the ballot and we will transform the salient misdeeds of bloodthirsty mobs into the calculated good deeds of orderly citizens. Give us the ballot and we will fill our legislative halls with men of goodwill and send to the sacred halls of Congress men who will not sign a Southern manifesto because of their devotion to the manifesto of justice. Give us the ballot and we will place judges on the benches of the South who will do justly and love mercy, and we will place at the head of the Southern states governors who will, who have felt not only the tang of the human, but the glow of the Divine. Give us the ballot and we will quietly and nonviolently, without rancor or bitterness, implement the Supreme Court's Decision of May 17, 1954. . . .

If the executive and legislative branches of the government were as concerned about the protection of our citizenship rights as the federal courts have been, then the transition from a segregated to an integrated society would be infinitely smoother. But we so often look to Washington in vain for this concern. In the midst of the tragic breakdown of law and order, the executive branch of the government is all too silent and apathetic. In the midst of the desperate need for civil rights legislation, the legislative branch of the government is all too stagnant and hypocritical.

This dearth of positive leadership from the federal government is not confined to one particular political party. Both political parties have betrayed the cause of justice. The Democrats have betrayed it by capitulating to the prejudices and undemocratic practices of the southern Dixiecrats. The Republicans have betrayed it by capitulating to the blatant hypocrisy of right wing, reactionary Northerners. These men so often have a high blood pressure of words and an anemia of deeds.

"Crusade for Citizenship"

During the summer of 1957 the SCLC made plans for a Crusade for Citizenship, a new Southwide educational and action campaign for the enforcement of Negro voting rights. The recently enacted Civil Rights law would be meaningless unless it was translated into action by Negroes exercising their right to vote. The main purpose of the Crusade for Citizenship was to get Negroes throughout the South to exercise that right.

It was my firm conviction that if the Negro achieved the ballot throughout the South, many of the problems which we faced would be solved. Once we gained the ballot, we would see a new day in the South. I had come to see that one of the most decisive steps that the Negro could take was a short walk to the voting booth. Until we gained the ballot and placed proper public officials in office, this condition would continue to exist.

In September 1957 I thought it was quite regrettable and unfortunate that young high school students in Little Rock, Arkansas, had to go to school under the protection of federal troops. But I thought it was even more unfortunate that Arkansas Governor Orval Faubus, through irresponsible actions, left the president of the United States with no other alternative. I believe firmly in nonviolence, but, at the same time, I am not an anarchist. I believe in the intelligent use of police force. And I thought that was all we had in Little Rock. It wasn't an army fighting against a nation or a race of people. It was just police force, seeking to enforce the law of the land. It was high time that a man as popular in the world as Eisenhower—a man with his moral influence—speak out and take a stand against what was happening all over the South. So I backed the President, and I sent him a telegram commending him for the positive and forthright stand that he took in the Little Rock school situation. He showed the nation and the world that the United States was a nation dedicated to law and order rather than mob rule.

Nevertheless, it was strange to me that the federal government was more concerned about what happened in Budapest than what happened in Birmingham. I thought Eisenhower believed that integration would be a fine thing. But I thought he felt that the more you push it, the more tension it would create, so, just wait a few more years and it will work itself out. I didn't think that Eisenhower felt like being a crusader for integration. President Eisenhower was a man of integrity and goodwill, but I am afraid that on the question of integration he didn't understand the dimensions of social change involved nor how the problem was to be worked out.

11

BIRTH OF A NEW NATION

Ghana has something to say to us. It says to us first that the oppressor never voluntarily gives freedom to the oppressed. You have to work for it. Freedom is never given to anybody. Privileged classes never give up their privileges without strong resistance.

MARCH 4, 1957
King party arrives in Gold Coast for independence celebration

MARCH 6
Attends midnight ceremony marking Ghana's independence

MARCH 12
Departs from Accra to Rome, by way of Nigeria

MARCH 26
Returns to New York after stays in Paris and London

The minute I knew I was coming to Ghana I had a very deep emotional feeling. A new nation was being born. It symbolized the fact that a new order was coming into being and an old order was passing away. So I was deeply concerned about it. I wanted to be involved in it, be a part of it, and notice the birth of this new nation with my own eyes. The trip, which included visits to other countries of Africa and several stops in Europe, was of tremendous cultural value and made possible many contacts of lasting significance.

Struggling had been going on in Ghana for years. The British

Empire saw that it could no longer rule the Gold Coast and agreed that on the sixth of March, 1957, it would release the nation. All of this was because of the persistent protest, the continual agitation, of Prime Minister Kwame Nkrumah and the other leaders who worked along with him and the masses of people who were willing to follow.

"A new age coming into being"

So that day finally came. About midnight on a dark night in 1957, a new nation came into being. That was a great hour. As we walked out, we noticed all over the polo grounds almost a half million people. They had waited for this hour and this moment for years.

People came from all over the world—seventy nations—to say to this new nation: "We greet you and give you our moral support. We hope for you God's guidance as you move now into the realm of independence." It was a beautiful experience to see some of the leading persons on the scene of civil rights in America on hand: to my left was Charles Diggs, to my right were Adam Powell and Ralph Bunche. All of these people from America: Mordecai Johnson, Horace Mann Bond, A. Philip Randolph; then you looked out and saw the vice-president of the United States.

A handsome black man walked out on the platform, and he was followed by eight or ten other men. He stood there and said, "We are no longer a British colony. We are a free and sovereign people." When he uttered those words, we looked back and saw an old flag coming down and a new flag going up. And I said to myself, "That old flag coming down doesn't represent the meaning of this drama taking place on the stage of history, for it is the symbol of an old order passing away. That new flag going up is the symbol of a new age coming into being." I could hear people shouting all over that vast audience, "Freedom! Freedom! Freedom!"

Before I knew it, I started weeping. I was crying for joy. And I knew about all of the struggles, all of the pain, and all of the agony that these people had gone through for this moment.

After Nkrumah made that final speech, we walked away, and we could hear little children six years old and old people eighty and ninety years old walking the streets of Accra crying: "Freedom! Freedom!" They were crying it in a sense that they had never heard it

---

SERMON ON GHANA

It seems this morning that I can hear God speaking. I can hear him speaking throughout the universe, saying, "Be still and know that I am God. And if you don't stop, if you don't straighten up, if you don't stop exploiting people, I'm going to rise up and break the backbone of your power. And your power will be no more!" And the power of Great Britain is no more. I looked at France. I looked at Britain. And I thought about the Britain that could boast, "The sun never sets on our great Empire." And I say now she had gone to the level that the sun hardly rises on the British Empire.

April 7, 1957

---

before. And I could hear that old Negro spiritual once more crying out: "Free at last, free at last, Great God Almighty, I'm free at last." They were experiencing that in their very souls. And everywhere we turned, we could hear it ringing out from the housetops. We could hear it from every corner, every nook and crook of the community. "Freedom! Freedom!" This was the breaking loose from Egypt.

The thing that impressed me more than anything else that night was when Nkrumah and his other ministers who had been in prison with him walked in. They didn't come in with the crowns and all of the garments of kings. They walked in with prison caps. Nkrumah stood up and made his closing speech to Parliament with the little cap that he wore in prison for several months and the coat that he wore in prison for several months. Often the path to freedom will carry you through prison.

Nkrumah had started out in a humble way. His mother and father were illiterate, not chiefs at all, but humble people. He went to school for a while in Africa and then he decided to work his way to America. He went to the Lincoln University in Pennsylvania, and took his theology degree there. He preached a while in Philadelphia. He went to the University of Pennsylvania and took a master's degree there in philosophy and sociology.

He always realized that colonialism was made for domination and exploitation. It was made to keep a certain group down and exploit that group economically for the advantage of another. He studied and thought about all of this, and one day he decided to go back to Africa.

He was immediately elected the executive secretary of the United Party of the Gold Coast, and he worked hard getting a following. And the people in this party—the old, the people who had had their hands on the plow for a long time—thought he was pushing a little too fast, and they got a little jealous of his influence. So finally he had to break from the United Party of the Gold Coast, and in 1949 he organized the Convention People's Party. It was this party that started out working for the independence of the Gold Coast.

He urged his people to unite for freedom and urged the officials of the British Empire to give them freedom. The officials were slow to respond, but the masses of people were with him, and they had united to become the most powerful and influential party that had ever been organized in that section of Africa.

Nkrumah himself was finally placed in jail for several years. He was an agitator. He was imprisoned on the basis of sedition, but he had inspired some people outside of prison. They got together just a few months after he had been in prison and elected him the prime minister. The British Empire saw that they had better let him out. He was placed there for fifteen years, but he only served eight or nine months. He came out the prime minister of the Gold Coast.

"A symbol of hope"

I thought that this event, the birth of this new nation, would give impetus to oppressed peoples all over the world. I thought it would have worldwide implications and repercussions—not only for Asia and Africa, but also for America. Just as in 1776, when America received its independence, the harbor of New York became sort of a beacon of hope for thousands of oppressed people of Europe, I thought Ghana would become a symbol of hope for hundreds and thousands of oppressed peoples all over the world as they struggled for freedom.

The birth of this new nation renewed my conviction in the ultimate triumph of justice. And it seemed to me, this was fit testimony to the fact that eventually the forces of justice triumph in the universe, and somehow the universe itself is on the side of freedom and justice. This gave new hope to me in the struggle for freedom.

Wednesday morning the official opening of Parliament was held, and we were able to get on the inside. There Nkrumah, now the Prime Minister of the Gold Coast, with no superior, made his first speech. The Duchess of Kent, who represented the Queen of England, walked in. She was just a passing visitor now—like M. L. King and Ralph Bunche and Coretta King and everybody else—because this was a new nation. After Parliament was open, and Nkrumah drove out, the people standing around the streets of the city cried out: "All hail, Nkrumah!" Everybody was crying his name because they knew he had suffered for them, he had sacrificed for them, he'd gone to jail for them.

This nation was now out of Egypt and had crossed the Red Sea. Now it would confront its wilderness. Nkrumah realized that. For instance, Ghana was a one-crop country, cocoa mainly. In order to make the economic system more stable, it would be necessary to industrialize. Nkrumah said to me that one of the first things that he would do would be to work toward industrialization.

Ninety percent of the people were illiterate, and it was necessary to lift the whole cultural standard of the community in order to make it possible to stand up in the free world. It was my hope that even people from America would go to Africa as immigrants. American Negroes could lend their technical assistance to a growing new nation. I was very happy to see people who had moved in. A doctor from Brooklyn, New York, had just come in that week. His wife was a dentist, and they were living there, and the people loved them. Nkrumah made it very clear to me that he would welcome any persons coming there as immigrants.

I realized that there would be difficulties. Whenever you have a transition, whenever you are moving from one system to another there will be definite difficulties, but I thought that there was enough brainpower, enough determination, enough courage and faith to meet the difficulties as they developed.

When I hear, "People aren't ready," that's like telling a person who is trying to swim, "Don't jump in that water until you learn how to swim." When actually you will never learn how to swim until you get in the water. People have to have an opportunity to develop themselves and govern themselves.

I am often reminded of the statement made by Nkrumah: "I prefer self-government with danger to servitude with tranquility." I think that's a great statement. They were willing to face the dangers and difficulties, but I thought that Ghana would be able to profit by the mistakes of other nations that had existed over so many years and develop into a great nation.

After meeting Kwame Nkrumah, we stopped in Nigeria for a day or so. Then we went to Europe and then back to America to deal with the problems there.

12

BRUSH WITH DEATH

This was a rather difficult year for me. I have had to confront the brutality of police officers, an unwarranted arrest, and a near fatal stab wound by a mentally deranged woman. These things were poured upon me like staggering torrents on a cold, wintry day.

SEPTEMBER 3, 1958
King is arrested in Montgomery

SEPTEMBER 4
After his conviction for failing to obey an officer, King's fine is paid by Montgomery police commissioner

SEPTEMBER 20
Is stabbed in Harlem

OCTOBER 3
After release from Harlem Hospital, begins convalescing at the home of the Reverend Sandy F. Ray

OCTOBER 24
Returns to Montgomery to continue recuperation

On a Saturday afternoon in 1958, I sat in a Harlem department store, surrounded by hundreds of people. I was autographing copies of *Stride Toward Freedom*, my book about the Montgomery bus boycott. And while sitting there, a demented black woman came up. The only question I heard from her was, "Are you Martin Luther King?"

I was looking down writing, and I said "Yes." And the next minute, I felt something sharp plunge forcefully into my chest. Before I knew it, I had been stabbed with a letter opener by a woman who would later be judged insane, Mrs. Izola Ware Curry.

Rushed by ambulance to Harlem Hospital, I lay in a bed for hours while preparations were made to remove the keen-edged knife from my body. Days later, when I was well enough to talk with Dr. Aubrey Maynard, the chief of the surgeons who performed the delicate, dangerous operation, I learned the reason for the long delay that preceded surgery. He told me that the razor tip of the instrument had been touching my aorta and that my whole chest had to be opened to extract it.

"If you had sneezed during all those hours of waiting," Dr. Maynard said, "your aorta would have been punctured and you would have drowned in your own blood."

It came out in the *New York Times* the next morning that, if I had sneezed, I would have died.

About four days later, after the operation, after my chest had been opened, and the blade had been taken out, they allowed me to move around in the wheelchair in the hospital and read some of the kind letters that came from all over the States, and the world. I read a few, but one of them I will never forget. There was a letter from a young girl who was a student at the White Plains High School. It said simply, "Dear Dr. King: I am a ninth-grade student at the White Plains High School." She said, "While it should not matter, I would like to mention that I am a white girl. I read in the paper of your misfortune, and of your suffering. And I read that if you had sneezed, you would have died. And I'm simply writing you to say that I'm so happy that you didn't sneeze."

"Uncertain but promising future"

If I demonstrated unusual calm during the recent attempt on my life, it was certainly not due to any extraordinary powers that I possess. Rather, it was due to the power of God working through me. Throughout this struggle for racial justice I have constantly asked God to remove all bitterness from my heart and to give me the strength and courage to face any disaster that came my way. This constant prayer life and feeling of dependence on God have given me the feeling that I have divine

---

TO THE MASS MEETING OF THE MONTGOMERY IMPROVEMENT ASSOCIATION

My Dear Friends and Co-Workers of the MIA:

While convalescing here in New York from an act of violence which was inflicted upon me two weeks ago, my mind inevitably turns toward you. Over and over again during these difficult days I have thought of you and our long association together.

First, let me relieve your minds by saying that I am doing quite well. The five physicians who have been at my side from the moment of the operation have all agreed that I have made an amazing recovery. I am gradually regaining my strength and the natural pain that follows an operation is gradually passing away. . . .

May I urge you to continue in the noble struggle for freedom and justice that has been so courageously started in the Cradle of the Confederacy. Fortunately, God has given Montgomery several marvelous leaders and my absence does not in any way have to impede the program of our movement. . . . Our final destination is the City of Freedom and we must not stop until we have entered the sublime and lofty Metropolis. . . .

Your servant in the cause of Christ and Freedom,

Martin Luther King, Jr.

October 6, 1958

---

companionship in the struggle. I know no other way to explain it. It is the fact that in the midst of external tension, God can give an inner peace.

As far as the repeated attacks on me and my family, I must say that here again God gives one the strength to adjust to such acts of violence. None of these attacks came as a total surprise to me, because I counted the cost early in the struggle. To believe in nonviolence does not mean that violence will not be inflicted upon you. The believer in nonviolence is the person who will willingly allow himself to be the victim of violence but will never inflict violence upon another. He lives by the conviction that through his suffering and cross bearing, the social situation may be redeemed.

The experience I had in New York gave me time to think. I became convinced that if the movement held to the spirit of nonviolence, our struggle and example would challenge and help redeem not only America but the world. It was my hope that we would remove from our souls the shackles of fear and the manacles of despair, and move on into the uncertain but promising future with the faith that the dawn of a new day was just around the horizon.

The pathetic aspect of the experience was not the injury to one individual. It demonstrated to me that a climate of hatred and bitterness so permeated areas of our nation that inevitably deeds of extreme violence must erupt. I saw its wider social significance. The lack of restraint upon violence in our society along with the defiance of law by men in high places cannot but result in an atmosphere which engenders desperate deeds.

I was intensely impatient to get back to continue the work we all knew had to be done regardless of the cost. So I rejoined the ranks of those who were working ceaselessly for the realization of the ideals of freedom and justice for all men. I did not have the slightest intention of turning back at that point.

13

◆

PILGRIMAGE TO
NONVIOLENCE

It was a marvelous experience to meet and talk with the great leaders of India, to meet and talk with and speak to thousands and thousands of people all over that vast country. These experiences will remain dear to me as long as the cords of memory shall lengthen.

FEBRUARY 3, 1959
The Kings, accompanied by Dr. L. D. Reddick, embark for India

FEBRUARY 10
After stay in Paris, King party arrives in India and has dinner with Prime Minister Nehru

MARCH 10
Departure from India to Jerusalem and Cairo

MARCH 18
Return to United States

For a long time I had wanted to take a trip to India. Even as a child, the entire Orient held a strange fascination for me—the elephants, the tigers, the temples, the snake charmers, and all the other storybook characters.

While the Montgomery boycott was going on, India's Gandhi was the guiding light of our technique of nonviolent social change. So as soon as our victory over bus segregation was won, some of my friends said: "Why don't you go to India and see for yourself what the Mahatma, whom you so admire, has wrought?"

In 1956 when Pandit Jawaharlal Nehru, India's prime minister, made a short visit to the United States, he was gracious enough to say that he wished that he and I had met. His diplomatic representatives made inquiries as to the possibility of my visiting his country some time. Our former American ambassador to India, Chester Bowles, wrote me along the same lines.

But every time that I was about to make the trip, something would interfere. At one time it was my visit by prior commitment to Ghana. At another time my publishers were pressing me to finish writing *Stride Toward Freedom*. Then along came Mrs. Izola Ware Curry. She not only knocked out the travel plans that I had but almost everything else as well.

After I recovered from this near-fatal encounter and was finally released by my doctors, it occurred to me that it might be better to get in the trip to India before plunging too deeply once again into the sea of the Southern segregation struggle.

I preferred not to take this long trip alone and asked my wife and my friend, Lawrence Reddick, to accompany me. Coretta was particularly interested in the women of India, and Dr. Reddick in the history and government of that great country. He had written my biography, *Crusader Without Violence*, and said that my true test would come when the people who knew Gandhi looked me over and passed judgment upon me and the Montgomery movement. The three of us made up a sort of three-headed team with six eyes and six ears for looking and listening.

And so on February 3, 1959, just before midnight, we left New York by plane. En route we stopped in Paris with Richard Wright, an old friend of Reddick's, who brought us up to date on European attitudes on the Negro question and gave us a taste of the best French cooking.

We missed our plane connection in Switzerland because of fog, and arrived in India after a roundabout route, two days late. But from the time we came down out of the clouds at Bombay on February 10, until March 10, when we waved good-bye at the New Delhi airport, we had one of the most concentrated and eye-opening experiences of our lives.

"We were looked upon as brothers"

We had a grand reception in India. The people showered upon us the most generous hospitality imaginable. Almost every door was open so that our party was able to see some of India's most important social experiments and talk with leaders in and out of government, ranging from Prime Minister Nehru, to village councilmen and Vinoba Bhave, the sainted leader of the land reform movement. Since our pictures were in the newspapers very often it was not unusual for us to be recognized by crowds in public places and on public conveyances. Occasionally I would take a morning walk in the large cities, and out of the most unexpected places someone would emerge and ask: "Are you Martin Luther King?"

We had hundreds of invitations that the limited time did not allow us to accept. We were looked upon as brothers, with the color of our skins as something of an asset. But the strongest bond of fraternity was the common cause of minority and colonial peoples in America, Africa, and Asia struggling to throw off racism and imperialism.

We had the opportunity to share our views with thousands of Indian people through endless conversations and numerous discussion sessions. I spoke before university groups and public meetings all over India. Because of the keen interest that the Indian people have in the race problem these meetings were usually packed. Occasionally interpreters were used, but on the whole I spoke to audiences that understood English.

The Indian people love to listen to the Negro spirituals. Therefore, Coretta ended up singing as much as I lectured. We discovered that autograph seekers are not confined to America. After appearances in public meetings and while visiting villages, we were often besieged for autographs. Even while riding planes, more than once pilots came into the cabin from the cockpit requesting our signatures. We got good press throughout our stay. Thanks to the Indian papers, the Montgomery bus boycott was already well known in that country. Indian publications perhaps gave a better continuity of our 381-day bus strike than did most of our papers in the United States.

We held press conferences in all of the larger cities—Delhi, Cal-

---

REFLECTIONS ON INDIA TRIP

How can one avoid being depressed when he discovers that of India's 400 million people, more than 365 million make an annual income of less than sixty dollars a year? Most of these people have never seen a doctor or a dentist.

As I looked at these conditions, I found myself saying that we in America cannot stand idly by and not be concerned. Then something within me cried out, "Oh, no, because the destiny of the United States is tied up with the destiny of India—with the destiny of every other nation." And I remembered that we spend more than a million dollars a day to store surplus food in this country. I said to myself, "I know where we can store that food free of charge—in the wrinkled stomachs of the millions of people who go to bed hungry at night." Maybe we spend too much of our national budget building military bases around the world rather than bases of genuine concern and understanding.

Address at Lincoln University, June 6, 1961

---

cutta, Madras, and Bombay—and talked with newspapermen almost everywhere we went. They asked sharp questions and at times appeared to be hostile, but that was just their way of bringing out the story that they were after. As reporters, they were scrupulously fair with us and in their editorials showed an amazing grasp of what was going on in America and other parts of the world.

"Crowded humanity"

India is a vast country with vast problems. We flew over the long stretches, from north to south, east to west; we took trains for shorter jumps and used automobiles and jeeps to get us into the less accessible places.

Everywhere we went we saw crowded humanity—on the roads, in the city streets and squares, even in the villages. Most of the people were poor and poorly dressed. In the city of Bombay, for example, over a half million people—mostly unattached, unemployed, or partially employed males—slept out of doors every night.

Great ills flowed from the poverty of India but strangely there was relatively little crime. This was another concrete manifestation of the wonderful spiritual quality of the Indian people. They were poor, jammed together, and half-starved, but they did not take it out on each other.

In contrast to the poverty-stricken, there were Indians who were rich, had luxurious homes, landed estates, fine clothes, and showed evidence of overeating. The bourgeoise—white, black, or brown— behaves about the same the world over.

India's leaders, in and out of government, were conscious of their country's other great problems and were heroically grappling with them. The country seemed to be divided. Some said that India should become Westernized and modernized as quickly as possible so that she might raise her standards of living. On the other hand, there were others—perhaps the majority—who said that Westernization would bring with it the evils of materialism, cutthroat competition, and rugged individualism. They said that India would lose her soul if she took to chasing Yankee dollars, and that the big machine would only raise the living standard of the comparatively few workers who got jobs, but the greater number of people would be displaced.

Prime Minister Nehru, at once an intellectual and a man charged with the practical responsibility of heading the government, seemed to steer a middle course between these extreme attitudes. In our talk with him he indicated that he felt that some industrialization was absolutely necessary; that there were some things that only big or heavy industry could do for the country but that if the state kept a watchful eye on the developments, most of the pitfalls might be avoided. At the same time, Mr. Nehru gave support to the movement that would encourage and expand the handicraft arts such as spinning and weaving in homes and villages and thus leave as much economic self-help and autonomy as possible to the local community.

That night we had dinner with Prime Minister Nehru; with us as a guest was Lady Mountbatten, the wife of Lord Mountbatten, who was viceroy of India when it received its independence. They were lasting friends only because Gandhi followed the way of love and nonviolence. The aftermath of nonviolence is the creation of the beloved community, so that when the battle is over, a new relationship comes into being between the oppressed and the oppressor.

"The Bhoodanists"

There was a great movement in India that is almost unknown in America. At its center was the campaign for land reform known as Bhoodan. It would solve India's great economic and social change by consent, not by force. The Bhoodanists were led by the sainted Vinoba Bhave and Jayaprakash Narayan, a highly sensitive intellectual who was trained in American colleges. Their ideal was the self-sufficient village. Their program envisioned persuading large landowners to give up some of their holdings to landless peasants; persuading small landowners to give up their individual ownership for common cooperative ownership by the villages; and encouraging farmers and villagers to spin and weave the cloth for their own clothes during their spare time from their agricultural pursuits. Since these measures would answer the questions of employment, food, and clothing, the village could then, through cooperative action, make just about everything that it would need or get it through barter or exchange from other villages. Accordingly, each village would be virtually self-sufficient and would thus free itself from the domination of the urban centers that were like evil loadstones drawing the people away from the rural areas, concentrating them in city slums, and debauching them with urban vices. At least this was the argument of the Bhoodanists and other Gandhians.

Such ideas sound strange and archaic to Western ears. However, the Indians have already achieved greater results than we Americans would ever expect. For example, millions of acres of land have been given up by rich landlords and additional millions of acres have been given up to cooperative management by small farmers. On the other hand, the Bhoodanists shrink from giving their movement the organization and drive that we in America would venture to guess that it must have in order to keep pace with the magnitude of the problems that everybody is trying to solve.

It would be a boon to democracy if one of the great nations of the world, with almost four hundred million people, proves that it is possible to provide a good living for everyone without surrendering to a dictatorship of either the "right" or "left." India is a tremendous force for peace and nonviolence, at home and abroad. It is a land where the idealist and the intellectual are yet respected. We should want to help India preserve her soul and thus help to save our own.

"The light that can shine through all the darkness"

On February 22, Mrs. King and I journeyed down to a city in India called Trivandrum. Then we went from Trivandrum down to a point known as Cape Comorin. This is where the mass of India ends and the vast rolling waters of the ocean have their beginning. It is one of the most beautiful parts of all the world. Three great bodies of water meet together in all of their majestic splendor: the Bay of Bengal, the Arabian Sea, and the Indian Ocean.

I remember how we went out there and looked at the big old rocks, a sight that was truly incredible, out into the waters, out into the ocean. Seated on a huge rock that slightly protruded into the ocean, we were enthralled by the vastness of the ocean and its terrifying immensities. We looked at the waves of those great bodies of water as they unfolded in almost rhythmic suspension. As the waves crashed against the base of the rock on which we were seated, an oceanic music brought sweetness to the ear. To the west we saw the magnificent sun, a red cosmic ball of fire, appear to sink into the very ocean itself. Just as it was almost lost from sight, Coretta touched me and said, "Look, Martin, isn't that beautiful!" I looked around and saw the moon, another ball of scintillating beauty. As the sun appeared to be sinking into the ocean, the moon appeared to be rising from the ocean. When the sun finally passed completely beyond sight, darkness engulfed the earth, but in the east the radiant light of the rising moon shone supreme. This was, as I said, one of the most beautiful parts in all the world, and that happened to be one of those days when the moon was full. This is one of the few points in all the world where you can see the setting of the sun and the rising of the moon simultaneously.

I looked at that and something came to my mind and I had to share it with Coretta, Dr. Reddick, and other people who were accompanying us around at that point. God has the light that can shine through all the darkness. We have experiences when the light of day vanishes, leaving us in some dark and desolate midnight—moments when our highest hopes are turned into shambles of de-

SERMON ON MAHATMA GANDHI

If you ask people in India why is it that Mahatma Gandhi was able to do what he did in India, they will say they followed him because of his absolute sincerity and his absolute dedication. Here was a man who achieved in his lifetime this bridging of the gulf between the ego and the id. Gandhi had the amazing capacity for self-criticism. This was true in individual life, in his family life, and was true in his people's life. Gandhi criticized himself when he needed it. And whenever he made a mistake, he confessed it publicly. Here was a man who would say to his people: I'm not perfect, I'm not infallible, I don't want you to start a religion around me, I'm not a god. And I'm convinced today that there would be a religion around Gandhi, if Gandhi had not insisted, all through his life: I don't want a religion around me because I'm too human, I'm too fallible, never think I'm infallible. And any time he made a mistake, even in his personal life, or even a decision that he made in the independence struggle, he came out in the public and said, "I made a mistake."

March 22, 1959, Montgomery

spair or when we are victims of some tragic injustice and some terrible exploitation. During such moments our spirits are almost overcome by gloom and despair, and we feel that there is no light anywhere. But ever and again, we look toward the east and discover that there is another light which shines even in the darkness, and "the spear of frustration" is transformed "into a shaft of light."

"Gandhians accepted us with open arms"

On March 1 we had the privilege of spending a day at the Amniabad ashram and stood there at the point where Gandhi started his walk of 218 miles to a place called Bambi. He started there walking with eight people. Gradually the number grew to millions and millions. Gandhi went on and reached down in the river and brought up a little salt in his hands to demonstrate and dramatize the fact that they were breaking this law in protest against the injustices they had faced over all the years with these salt laws. And Gandhi said to his people: "If you are hit, don't hit back; even if they shoot at you, don't shoot back. If they curse you, don't curse back. Just keep moving. Some of us might have to die before we get there. Some of us might be thrown in jail before we get there, but let's just keep moving." And they kept moving and walked and walked, and millions of them came together.

STATEMENT ON LEAVING INDIA

I wish to make a plea to the people and government of India. The issue of world peace is so critical that I feel compelled to offer a suggestion that came to me during the course of our conversations with Vinoba Bhave. The peace-loving peoples of the world have not yet succeeded in persuading my own country, America, and Soviet Russia to eliminate fear and disarm themselves. Unfortunately, as yet America and the Soviet Union have not shown the faith and moral courage to do this. Vinoba Bhave has said that India or any other nation that has the faith and moral courage could disarm itself tomorrow, even unilaterally. It may be that just as India had to take the lead and show the world that national independence could be achieved nonviolently, so India may have to take the lead and call for universal disarmament, and if no other nation will join her immediately, India should declare itself for disarmament unilaterally. Such an act of courage would be a great demonstration of the spirit of the Mahatma and would be the greatest stimulus to the rest of the world to do likewise.

March 9, 1959

Gandhi was able to mobilize and galvanize more people in his lifetime than any other person in the history of this world. And just with a little love and understanding goodwill and a refusal to cooperate with an evil law, he was able to break the backbone of the British Empire. This, I think, was one of the most significant things that ever happened in the history of the world. More than 390 million people achieved their freedom, and they achieved it nonviolently.

I was delighted that the Gandhians accepted us with open arms. They praised our experiment with the nonviolent resistance technique at Montgomery. They seemed to look upon it as an outstanding example of the possibilities of its use in Western civilization. To them, as to me, it also suggested that nonviolent resistance *when planned and positive in action* could work effectively even under totalitarian regimes.

We argued this point at some length with the groups of African students who were studying in India. They felt that nonviolent resistance could only work in a situation where the resisters had a potential ally in the conscience of the opponent. We soon discovered that they, like many others, tended to confuse passive resistance with nonresistance. This is completely wrong. True nonviolent resistance is not unrealistic submission to evil power. It is rather a courageous confrontation of evil by the power of love, in the faith that it is better to be the recipient of violence than the inflicter of it, since the latter only multiplies the existence of violence and bitterness in the universe, while the former may develop a sense of shame in the opponent, and thereby bring about a transformation and change of heart.

"The problem of the untouchables"

We went in some little villages, and in these villages, we saw hundreds of people sleeping on the ground; they didn't have any beds to sleep in. There was no running water there, nothing to wash with. We looked in these villages and we saw people there in their little huts and their little rooms, and their cows slept in the same room with them. If they had a few chickens—the chickens slept in the same room with them. We looked at these people. They had nothing that we would consider convenient, none of the comforts of life. Here they were, sleeping in the same room with the beasts of the field; this was all they had.

Pretty soon we discovered that these people were the untouchables. This caste system had existed for years. These were the people who worked hardest, and they were trampled over even by the Indian people themselves.

Gandhi looked at this system and couldn't stand it. He looked at his people and said, "Now you have selected me, and you've asked me to free you from the political domination and the economic exploitation inflicted upon you by Britain, and here you are, trampling over and exploiting seventy million of your brothers." And he decided that he would not ever adjust to that system, and that he would speak against it and stand up against it the rest of his life.

At age two, with sister Christine. (Courtesy of CSK Collection)

...ave a marvelous mother...father. I can hardly...ember a time that they ever...ed or had any great falling..." Martin Luther Sr. and...erta Williams King at...bration of their twenty-fifth...ding anniversary in 1951....urtesy of CSK Collection)

"It was in my senior year of college that I entered the ministry. I felt a sense of responsibility which I could not escape." With parents, brother A. D. King, sister Christine, and uncle Joel King, on Morehouse campus in 1948. (Courtesy of CSK Collecti

"My devoted wife has been a constant source of consolation to me through all the difficulties." At wedding party on June 18, 1953 (left to right) father-in-law Obadiah Sc Alberta Williams King, Bernice Scott, Alveda King, sister-in-law Edythe Scott, King Sr., Coretta Scott King, sister-in-law Naomi Barbert King, Betty Ann Hill, A. D. King, and Christine King. (Courtesy of CSK Collection)

began to think of the viciousness of people who would bomb my home. I could feel the ;er rising when I realized that my wife and baby could have been killed." With Coretta 1 Yolanda at the Dexter Avenue Baptist Church in 1956. (Photo by Dan Weiner – ırtesy Sandra Weiner)

"Ordinarily, a person leaving a courtroom with a conviction behind him would wear a somber face. But I left with a smile." Greeted by Coretta after conviction in antiboycott trial in March 1956. (AP/Wide World Photos)

Arrested for loitering while attempting to gain admittance to the trial of Ralph Abernathy in Montgomery, Alabama, on September 3, 1958, with Coretta nearb (Charles Moore/Black Star)

(opposite) "In 1960 an electrifying movement of Negro students shattered the pla surface of campuses and communities across the South." Attending a meeting w Atlanta student activists in 1960. (Howard Sochurek, *Life* Magazine © Time Ir

"After they transferred me to Reidsville, Harris Wofford and others strongly urged Mr. Kennedy to try to use his influence to do something about it, and he finally agreed." Greeted by family and friends after being released from Georgia State Prison at Reidsvi after serving time for a traffic violation in 1960. (AP/Wide World)

Darling, it is extremely difficult for me to think of being away from you and my Yoki
d Marty." Spending time with Martin III (age three), Yolanda (age five), and Coretta in
960. (Don Uhrbrock, *Life* Magazine © Time Inc.)

With the inspiring Jac
Robinson in the 1960
(AP/Wide World)

"I had used the phrase 'I have a dream' many
times before, and I just felt that I wanted to us
it here." At March on Washington for Jobs an
Freedom in August 1963. (Archive Photos)

"I met Malcolm X once in Washington,
but circumstances didn't enable me to
talk with him for more than a minute."
Encounter with Malcolm X in March
1964. (AP/Wide World)

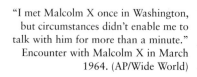

"I AM AN UNTOUCHABLE"

I remember when Mrs. King and I were in India, we journeyed down one afternoon to the southernmost part of India, the state of Kerala, the city of Trivandrum. That afternoon I was to speak in one of the schools, what we would call high schools in our country, and it was a school attended by and large by students who were the children of former untouchables. . . .

The principal introduced me and then as he came to the conclusion of his introduction, he says, "Young people, I would like to present to you a fellow untouchable from the United States of America." And for a moment I was a bit shocked and peeved that I would be referred to as an untouchable. . . .

I started thinking about the fact: twenty million of my brothers and sisters were still smothering in an airtight cage of poverty in an affluent society. I started thinking about the fact: these twenty million brothers and sisters were still by and large housed in rat-infested, unendurable slums in the big cities of our nation, still attending inadequate schools faced with improper recreational facilities. And I said to myself, "Yes, I am an untouchable, and every Negro in the United States of America is an untouchable."

From sermon at Ebenezer Baptist Church, July 4, 1965

The first thing he did was to adopt an untouchable girl as his daughter. His wife—a member of one of the high castes—thought he was going crazy. She said, "What in the world are you doing adopting an untouchable? We are not supposed to touch these people." And he said, "I am going to have this young lady as my daughter." He brought her into his ashram, and she lived there. He demonstrated in his own life that untouchability had to go.

One day Mahatma Gandhi stood before his people and said: "You are exploiting these untouchables. Even though we are fighting with all that we have of our bodies and our souls to break loose from the bondage of the British Empire, we are exploiting these people and we are taking from them their selfhood and their self-respect." He said, "I will refuse to eat until the leaders of the caste system will come to me with the leaders of the untouchables and say that there will be an end to untouchability and the Hindu temples of India will open their doors to the untouchables." And he refused to eat, and days passed. Finally when Gandhi was about to breathe his last breath, and his body was all but gone, a group from the untouchables and a group from the Brahmin caste came to him and signed a statement saying that they would no longer adhere to the caste system. The priest of the temple came to him and said, "Now the temples will be opened to the untouchables." That afternoon, untouchables from all over India went into the temples and all of these thousands and millions of people put their arms around the Brahmins and people of other castes. Hundreds of millions of people who had never touched each other for two thousand years were now singing and praising all together. This was a great contribution that Mahatma Gandhi brought about.

"Atoning for the injustices"

India appeared to be integrating its untouchables faster than the United States was integrating its Negro minority. Both countries had

---

SERMON ON GANDHI

The world doesn't like people like Gandhi. That's strange, isn't it? They don't like people like Christ; they don't like people like Lincoln. They killed him—this man who had done all of that for India, who gave his life and who mobilized and galvanized 400 million people for independence. . . . One of his own fellow Hindus felt that he was a little too favorable toward the Moslems, felt that he was giving in too much for the Moslems. . . . Here was the man of nonviolence, falling at the hands of a man of violence. Here was a man of love falling at the hands of a man with hate. This seems the way of history. And isn't it significant that he died on the same day that Christ died? It was on Friday. And this is the story of history, but thank God it never stopped here. Thank God Good Friday is never the end. The man who shot Gandhi only shot him into the hearts of humanity. Just as when Abraham Lincoln was shot, mark you, for the same reason that Mahatma Gandhi was shot— that is, the attempt to heal the wounds of the divided nation—when Abraham Lincoln was shot, Secretary Stanton stood by and said, "Now he belongs to the ages." The same thing could be said about Mahatma Gandhi now: He belongs to the ages.

March 22, 1959, in Montgomery

federal laws against discrimination, but in India the leaders of government, of religious, educational, and other institutions, had publicly endorsed the integration laws. The prime minister admitted to me that many Indians still harbored a prejudice against these long-oppressed people, but that it had become unpopular to exhibit this prejudice in any form. In part, this change in climate was created through the moral leadership of the late Mahatma Gandhi. In part, it was the result of the Indian Constitution, which specified that discrimination against the untouchables is a crime, punishable by imprisonment.

The Indian government spent millions of rupees annually developing housing and job opportunities in villages heavily inhabited by untouchables. Moreover, the prime minister said, if two applicants compete for entrance into a college or university, one of the applicants being an untouchable and the other of high caste, the school is required to accept the untouchable.

Professor Lawrence Reddick, who was with me during the interview, asked: "But isn't that discrimination?"

"Well, it may be," the prime minister answered. "But this is our way of atoning for the centuries of injustices we have inflicted upon these people."

From the prime minister down to the village councilmen, everybody declared publicly that untouchability is wrong. But in the United States some of our highest officials declined to render a moral judgment on segregation, and some from the South publicly boasted of their determination to maintain segregation. That would be unthinkable in India.

Although discrimination has not yet been eliminated in India, it is a crime to practice discrimination against an untouchable. But even without this coercion, so successfully has the government made the issue a matter of moral and ethical responsibility that no government figure or political leader on any level would dare defend discriminatory practices. One could wish that we here in the United States had reached this level of morality. America must seek its own ways of atoning for the injustices she has inflicted upon her Negro citizens.

The spirit of Gandhi was very much alive in India. Some of his disciples remembered the drama of the fight for national independence and, when they look around, find no one who comes near the stature of the Mahatma. But any objective observer must report that Gandhi is not only the greatest figure in India's history, but his influence is felt in almost every aspect of life and public policy.

The trip had a great impact upon me personally. It was wonderful to be in Gandhi's land, to talk with his son, his grandsons, his cousin, and other relatives; to share the reminiscences of his close comrades; to visit his ashram; to see the countless memorials for him; and, finally, to lay a wreath on his entombed ashes at Rajghat. We had learned a lot, but we were not rash enough to presume that we knew India—a vast subcontinent with all of its people, problems, contrasts, and achievements.

I left India more convinced than ever before that nonviolent resistance was the most potent weapon available to oppressed people in their struggle for freedom. It was a marvelous thing to see the amazing results of a nonviolent campaign. India won her independence, but without violence on the part of Indians. The aftermath of hatred and bitterness that usually follows a violent campaign was found nowhere in India. The way of acquiescence leads to moral and spiritual suicide. The way of violence leads to bitterness in the survivors and brutality in the destroyers. But the way of nonviolence leads to redemption and the creation of the beloved community.

I returned to America with a greater determination to achieve freedom for my people through nonviolent means. As a result of my visit to India, my understanding of nonviolence became greater and my commitment deeper.

14

THE SIT-IN MOVEMENT

A generation of young people has come out of decades of shadows to face naked state power; it has lost its fears, and experienced the majestic dignity of a direct struggle for its own liberation. These young people have connected up with their own history—the slave revolts, the incomplete revolution of the Civil War, the brotherhood of colonial colored men in Africa and Asia. They are an integral part of the history which is reshaping the world, replacing a dying order with modern democracy.

FEBRUARY 1, 1960
King moves with family to Atlanta; in Greensboro, North Carolina, lunch counter sit-in movement begins

FEBRUARY 17
Is arrested and charged with falsifying his 1956 and 1958 Alabama state income tax returns

APRIL 15
Speaks at founding conference of the Student Nonviolent Coordinating Committee (SNCC)

MAY 28
Is acquitted of tax evasion by an all-white jury in Montgomery

After four years as president of the Montgomery Improvement Association and five years as a resident of Montgomery, I decided to move from Montgomery to Atlanta. I would become co-pastor of the Ebenezer Baptist Church in Atlanta and thereby have more time and a better location to direct the Southwide campaigns of the SCLC.

For a year the Southern Christian Leadership Conference had been pleading with me to give it the maximum of my time, since the time was ripe for expanded militant action across the South. After giving the request serious and prayerful consideration, I came to the conclusion that I had a moral obligation to give more of my time and energy to the whole South. This was only possible by moving closer to the headquarters where transportation was more flexible and time hitherto consumed in longer travel could be saved and utilized for planning, directing, and supervising.

So I had the painful experience of having to leave Montgomery for Atlanta. It was not easy for me to decide to leave a community where bravery, resourcefulness, and determination had shattered the girders of the old order and weakened confidence of the rulers, despite their centuries of unchallenged rule. It was not easy to decide to leave a city whose Negroes resisted injustice magnificently and followed a method of nonviolent struggle that became one of the glowing epics of the twentieth century. I hated to leave Montgomery, but the people there realized that the call from the whole South was one that could not be denied.

This was the creative moment for a full-scale assault on the system of segregation. The time had come for a bold, broad advance of the Southern campaign for equality.

FAREWELL MESSAGE TO DEXTER CONGREGATION

Unknowingly and unexpectedly, I was catapulted into the leadership of the Montgomery Movement. At points I was unprepared for the symbolic role that history had thrust upon me. But there was no way out. I, like everybody in Montgomery, was pulled into the mainstream by the rolling tides of historical necessity. As a result of my leadership in the Montgomery movement, my duties and activities tripled. A multiplicity of new responsibilities poured in upon me in almost staggering torrents. So I ended up futilely attempting to be four or five men in one. One would have expected that many of these responsibilities would have tapered off after the boycott. But now, three years after the termination of the bus struggle, the same situation stands. At points the demands have increased.

November 29, 1959

I felt terribly frustrated over my inability to retreat, concentrate, and reflect. Even when I was writing *Stride Toward Freedom* I would only take off one or two weeks at a time. After returning from India I decided that I would take one day a week as a day of silence and meditation. This I attempted on several occasions, but things began to pile up so much that I found myself using that particular day as a time to catch up on so many things that had accumulated. I knew that I could not continue to live with such a tension-filled schedule. My whole life seemed to be centered around giving something out and only rarely taking something in. My failure to reflect would do harm not only to me as a person, but to the total movement. For that reason I felt a moral obligation to do it.

One of my reasons for moving to Atlanta was to meet this problem head-on. I felt that I would have more time to meditate and think through the total struggle ahead. Unfortunately, however, things happened which made my schedule more crowded in Atlanta than it was in Montgomery.

"The student demonstrations"

In 1960 an electrifying movement of Negro students shattered the placid surface of campuses and communities across the South. The young students of the South, through sit-ins and other demonstrations, gave America a glowing example of disciplined, dignified nonviolent action against the system of segregation. Though confronted in many places by hoodlums, police guns, tear gas, arrests, and jail sentences, the students tenaciously continued to sit down and demand equal service at variety store lunch counters, and they extended their protest from city to city. Spontaneously born, but guided by the theory of nonviolent resistance, the lunch counter sit-ins accomplished integration in hundreds of communities at the swiftest rate of change in the civil rights movement up to that time. In communities like Montgomery, Alabama, the whole student body rallied behind expelled students and staged a walkout while state government intimidation was unleashed with a display of military force appropriate to a wartime invasion. Nevertheless, the spirit of self-sacrifice and commitment remained firm, and the state governments found themselves dealing with students who had lost the fear of jail and physical injury.

The campuses of Negro colleges were infused with a dynamism of both action and philosophical discussion. Even in the thirties, when the college campus was alive with social thought, only a minority were involved in action. During the sit-in phase, when a few students were suspended or expelled, more than one college saw the total student body involved in a walkout protest. This was a change in student activity of profound significance. Seldom, if ever, in American history had a student movement engulfed the whole student body of a college.

Many of the students, when pressed to express their inner feelings, identified themselves with students in Africa, Asia, and South America. The liberation struggle in Africa was the great single international influence on American Negro students. Frequently, I heard them say that if their African brothers could break the bonds of colonialism, surely the American Negro could break Jim Crow.

I felt we had to continue to challenge the system of segregation, whether it was in the schools, public parks, churches, lunch counters, or public libraries. Segregation had to be removed from our

---

STATEMENT AT YOUTH MARCH FOR INTEGRATED SCHOOLS

As June approaches, with its graduation ceremonies and speeches, a thought suggests itself. You will hear much about careers, security, and prosperity. I will leave the discussion of such matters to your deans, your principals, and your valedictorians. But I do have a graduation thought to pass along to you. Whatever career you may choose for yourself—doctor, lawyer, teacher—let me propose an avocation to be pursued along with it. Become a dedicated fighter for civil rights. Make it a central part of your life.

It will make you a better doctor, a better lawyer, a better teacher. It will enrich your spirit as nothing else possibly can. It will give you that rare sense of nobility that can only spring from love and selflessly helping your fellow man. Make a career of humanity. Commit yourself to the noble struggle for equal rights. You will make a greater person of yourself, a greater nation of your country, and a finer world to live in.

April 18, 1959, Washington, D.C.

society. And Negroes had to be prepared to suffer, sacrifice, and even die to gain their goals. We could not rest until we had achieved the ideals of our democracy. I prayed much over our Southern situation, and I came to the conclusion that we were in for a season of suffering.

I urged students to continue the struggle on the highest level of dignity. They had rightly chosen to follow the path of nonviolence. Our ultimate aim was not to defeat or humiliate the white man but to win his friendship and understanding. We had a moral obligation to remind him that segregation is wrong. We protested with the ultimate aim of being reconciled with our white brothers.

A period began in which the emphasis shifted from the slow court process to direct action in the form of bus protests, economic boycotts, and mass marches to and demonstrations in the nation's capital and state capitals. The most significant aspect of this student movement was that the young people knocked some of the oldsters out of their state of apathy and complacency. What we saw was that segregation could not be maintained in the South without resultant chaos and social disintegration. One may wonder why the movement started with the lunch counters. The answer lay in the fact that there the Negro had suffered indignities and injustices that could not be justified or explained. Almost every Negro had experienced the tragic inconveniences of lunch counter segregation. He could not understand why he was welcomed with open arms at most counters in the store, but was denied service at a certain counter because it happened to be selling food and drink. In a real sense the "sit-in" represented more than a demand for service; it represented a demand for respect.

I was convinced that the student movement that was taking place all over the South in 1960 was one of the most significant developments in the whole civil rights struggle. It was no overstatement to characterize these events as historic. Never before in the United States had so large a body of students spread a struggle over so great an area in pursuit of a goal of human dignity and freedom. The student movement finally refuted the idea that the Negro was content with segregation. The students had taken the struggle for justice into their own hands. Negro freedom fighters revealed to the nation and the world their determination and courage. They were moving away from tactics which were suitable merely for gradual and long-term change. This was an era of offensive on the part of oppressed people. All peoples deprived of dignity and freedom marched on every continent throughout the world.

"A turning point in my life"

I can recall what may very well have been a turning point in my life as a participant in the Negro struggle in the South. It was the year 1960, in Montgomery, Alabama, when the glorious sit-ins at lunch

---

STATEMENT AT FOUNDING CONFERENCE OF STUDENT NONVIOLENT COORDINATING COMMITTEE

Today the leaders of the sit-in movement are assembled here from ten states and some forty communities to evaluate these recent sit-ins and to chart future goals. They realize that they must now evolve a strategy for victory. Some elements which suggest themselves for discussion are: (1) The need for some type of continuing organization. . . . (2) The students must consider calling for a nationwide campaign of "selective buying." . . . It is immoral to spend one's money where one cannot be treated with respect. (3) The students must seriously consider training a group of volunteers who will willingly go to jail rather than pay bail or fines. This courageous willingness to go to jail may well be the thing to awaken the dozing conscience of many of our white brothers. We are in an era in which a prison term for a freedom struggle is a badge of honor. (4) The youth must take the freedom struggle into every community in the South without exception. The struggle must be spread into every nook and cranny. Inevitably, this broadening of the struggle and the determination which it represents will arouse vocal and vigorous support and place pressure on the federal government that will compel its intervention. (5) The students will certainly want to delve deeper into the philosophy of nonviolence. It must be made palpably clear that resistance and nonviolence are not in themselves good. There is another element that must be present in our struggle that then makes our resistance and nonviolence truly meaningful. That element is reconciliation. Our ultimate end must be the creation of the beloved community.

April 15, 1960, in Raleigh, North Carolina

counters had seized the attention of all Americans. The white Southern power structure, in an attempt to blunt and divert that effort, indicted me for perjury and openly proclaimed that I would be imprisoned for at least ten years.

This case was tried before an all-white Southern jury. All of the State's witnesses were white. The judge and the prosecutor were white. The courtroom was segregated. Passions were inflamed. Feelings ran high. The press and other communications media were hostile. Defeat seemed certain, and we in the freedom struggle braced ourselves for the inevitable. There were two men among us who persevered with the conviction that it was possible, in this context, to marshal facts and law and thus win vindication. These men were our lawyers—Negro lawyers from the North: William Ming of Chicago and Hubert Delaney from New York.

They brought to the courtroom wisdom, courage, and a highly developed art of advocacy; but most important, they brought the lawyers' indomitable determination to win. After a trial of three days, by the sheer strength of their legal arsenal, they overcame the most vicious Southern taboos festering in a virulent and inflamed atmosphere and they persuaded an all-white jury to accept the word of a Negro over that of white men. The jury, after a few hours of deliberation, returned a verdict of acquittal.

I am frank to confess that on this occasion I learned that truth and conviction in the hands of a skillful advocate could make what started out as a bigoted, prejudiced jury, choose the path of justice. I cannot help but wish in my heart that the same kind of skill and devotion which Bill Ming and Hubert Delaney accorded to me could be available to thousands of civil rights workers, to thousands of ordinary Negroes, who are every day facing prejudiced courtrooms.

15

ATLANTA ARREST AND PRESIDENTIAL POLITICS

I fear that there is a dearth of vision in our government, a lack of a sense of history and genuine morality.

JUNE 23, 1960
King discusses civil rights with presidential candidate Senator John F. Kennedy

OCTOBER 19
Is arrested at Atlanta sit-in

OCTOBER 25
Charges are dropped for sit-in arrest but King is held for violating probation for earlier traffic offense and transferred to Reidsville State Prison

OCTOBER 26
Presidential candidate John F. Kennedy calls Coretta Scott King to express sympathy and offer assistance; Robert Kennedy calls Georgia governor S. Ernest Vandiver and Judge Oscar Mitchell seeking King's release on bail

OCTOBER 27
King's attorney Donald L. Hollowell arranges release from prison

NOVEMBER 1
King applauds Senator Kennedy for support

NOVEMBER 8
Kennedy wins close election, receiving strong support from black voters

M y first contact with John Kennedy was when he was a senator seeking the nomination for President. For several months, we had tried to work out a meeting and every time I could go he was away. Finally we worked out an engagement at his apartment in New York. That was June of 1960, about a month before the convention.

We talked for about an hour over the breakfast table. I was very frank about what I thought: that there was a need for a strong executive leadership and that we hadn't gotten this during the Eisenhower administration. If we didn't get it in the new administration, we would be set back even more. I was very impressed by the forthright and honest manner in which he discussed the civil rights question, and with his concern and his willingness to learn more about civil rights.

I specifically mentioned a need for an executive order outlawing discrimination in federally assisted housing. I also mentioned to him the need for strong civil rights legislation, and I stressed voting issues because we were deeply involved at that time in voter registration drives and had encountered a number of difficulties in states like Alabama and Mississippi.

As I recall, he agreed with all of these things. He agreed that there was a need for strong executive leadership and that this had not existed, and he felt if he received the nomination and was elected he could give this kind of leadership. He assured me also that he felt the whole question of the right to vote was a key and basic, and that this would be one of the immediate things that he would look into. He said that he had voted consistently for civil rights. I raised the question with him about 1957, when he voted against what we considered as a very important section of the civil rights bill. He said that since that time, if he had to face the issue again, he would reverse his position because many of the developments during the sit-in movement had pointed up the injustices and indignities that Negroes were facing all over the South, and for this reason he had reevaluated many of these things.

John Kennedy did not have the grasp and the comprehension of the depths of the problem at that time, as he later did. He knew that segregation was morally wrong and he certainly intellectually committed himself to integration, but I could see that he didn't have the emotional involvement then. He had not really been involved enough in and with the problem. He didn't know too many Negroes personally. He had never really had the personal experience of knowing the deep groans and passionate yearnings of the Negro for freedom, because he just didn't know Negroes generally and he hadn't had any experience in the civil rights struggle. So I felt that it was an intellectual commitment.

A few months later, after he had been nominated, I talked with him over at his house in Georgetown, and in that short period he had really learned a great deal about civil rights and had been advised rather well. I'd had little enthusiasm when he first announced his candidacy, but I had no doubt that he would do the right thing on the civil rights issue, if he were elected President.

He was very much concerned then about the election and possibly losing. Some of his friends were concerned about this and felt he had to do something dramatic to convince the nation of his commitment to civil rights. Some of the advisors thought that he should come South and make a civil rights speech right here in the South which would really convince people. They wanted him to come under my auspices to speak for a board meeting or a dinner sponsored by SCLC. I told him I just couldn't do that unless Mr. Nixon came, because we were a nonpartisan organization. I said, "Now Nixon may not come but I would have to invite him." But they felt, naturally, that it wouldn't work that way. So I kind of backed out on that idea because I thought it would be a mistake.

For many months during the election campaign, my close friends urged me to declare my support for John Kennedy. I spent many troubled hours searching for the responsible and fair decision. I was impressed by his qualities, by many elements in his record, and by his program. I had learned to enjoy and respect his charm and his incisive mind. But I made very clear to him that I did not endorse candidates publicly and that I could not come to the point that I would change my views on this.

"I didn't know where they were taking me"

Nevertheless, I was grateful to Senator Kennedy for the genuine concern he expressed about my arrest in October 1960 because of my participation in nonviolent efforts to integrate lunch counters in Atlanta, Georgia. I took part in the lunch counter sit-ins at Rich's department store as a follower, not a leader. I did not initiate the thing. It came into being with the students discussing the issues involved. They called me and asked me to join in. They wanted me to be in it, and I felt a moral obligation to be in it with them.

I was arrested along with some two hundred eighty students in a sit-in demonstration seeking to integrate lunch counters. I said when I went in Fulton County Jail that I could not in all good conscience post bail and that I would stay and serve the time if it was one year, five, or ten years. Of course the students agreed to stay also.

If, by chance, Your Honor, we are guilty of violating the law, please be assured that we did it to bring the whole issue of racial injustice under the scrutiny of the conscience of Atlanta. I must honestly say that we firmly believe that segregation is evil, and that our Southland will never reach its full potential and moral maturity until this cancerous disease is removed. We do not seek to remove this unjust system for ourselves alone but for our white brothers as well. The festering sore of segregation debilitates the white man as well as the Negro. So, if our actions in any way served to bring this issue to the forefront of the conscience of the community, they were not undertaken in vain.

And, sir, I know you have a legal obligation facing you at this hour. This judicial obligation may cause you to hand us over to another court rather than dismiss the charges. But, sir, I must say that I have a moral obligation facing me at this hour. This imperative drives me to say that if you find it necessary to set a bond, I cannot in all good conscience have anyone go buy my bail. I will choose jail rather than bail, even if it means remaining in jail a year or even ten years. Maybe it will take this type of self-suffering on the part of numerous Negroes to finally expose the moral defense of our white brothers who happen to be misguided and thusly awaken the dozing conscience of our community.

When they came to see after five or six days that we were not coming out and that the community was getting very much concerned, the merchants dropped the charges, which meant that everybody was released without bail immediately. But when I was released, they served me with papers stating that I had violated my probation and that I would be transferred to DeKalb jail and go on trial in the court there.

On the night of May 4, 1960, police stopped me in DeKalb County and discovered I still had an Alabama driver's license. Because of this, they gave me a ticket. I had gone to court, and I didn't even know it at the time but the lawyer pleaded guilty for me and they had fined me something like $25 or $50 and placed me on probation for I guess six months. I didn't even pay attention to the case, it was such a minor case; I didn't pay attention to it and never knew that the lawyer had really pleaded guilty. He had just told me, "I've got everything worked out." He made me think it was clear and all I needed to do was pay. Actually they later admitted in court

---

LETTER TO CORETTA

Reidsville, Georgia

Hello Darling,

Today I find myself a long way from you and the children. I am at the State Prison in Reidsville which is about 230 miles from Atlanta. They picked me up from the DeKalb jail about 4 o'clock this morning. I know this whole experience is very difficult for you to adjust to, especially in your condition of pregnancy, but as I said to you yesterday this is the cross that we must bear for the freedom of our people. So I urge you to be strong in faith, and this will in turn strengthen me. I can assure you that it is extremely difficult for me to think of being away from you and my Yoki and Marty for four months, but I am asking God hourly to give me the power of endurance. I have the faith to believe that this excessive suffering that is now coming to our family will in some little way serve to make Atlanta a better city, Georgia a better state, and America a better country. Just how I do not yet know, but I have faith to believe it will. If I am correct then our suffering is not in vain.

I understand that I can have visitors twice a month—the second and fourth Sunday. However, I understand that everybody—white and colored—can have visitors this coming Sunday. I hope you can find some way to come down. I know it will be a terrible inconvenience in your condition, but I want to see you and the children very badly.

Eternally Yours,
Martin

October 26, 1960

that they had never fined or arrested anybody on a charge like that, and they really had nothing on the statute to reveal how long you had to be in Atlanta before changing your license. So it was obviously a case of persecution.

I sat in the back of the courtroom while Mr. Charles M. Clayton, a Negro attorney who represented me, talked with the judge. We had this big trial and I had my lawyers arguing the case brilliantly and after all of that the judge said six months of hard labor, and this was not appealable.

So they took me back upstairs and put me in jail in the DeKalb County Jail. Then early in the morning, about three o'clock in the morning, they came and got me and took me to Reidsville. That was the state prison some two hundred and twenty miles from Atlanta. On the way, they dealt with me just like I was some hardened criminal. They had me chained all the way down to my legs, and they tied my legs to something in the floor so there would be no way for me to escape.

They talked with themselves. It was a long ride. I didn't know where they were taking me; but finally I assumed it must be to one of the state prisons after we had been gone so long. That kind of mental anguish is worse than dying, riding for mile after mile, hungry and thirsty, bound and helpless, waiting and not knowing what you're waiting for. And all over a traffic violation.

"Kennedy exhibited moral courage"

When people found out that they had taken me out in the wee hours of the morning and transferred me, there was real resentment all over. I think people had already started talking to both Nixon and Kennedy about doing something even when we were still in the Fulton County Jail—saying to them that they should make a statement about it. After they transferred me to Reidsville—in a segregated cell-block, a place where inmates who had attacked guards, psychotics, and other special cases were housed—Harris Wofford and others strongly urged Mr. Kennedy to try to use his influence to do something about it, and he finally agreed.

The first thing he did was call my wife. She was pregnant, and this was kind of a rough experience for her, so he called her and expressed his concern. He said that he would do whatever he could and that he would think this over with his brother and try to use his influence to get me released.

In the meantime, Robert Kennedy called the judge to find out about the bond. I understand Robert Kennedy was really angry about it, when they got it over to him and let him know all of the facts in the situation. In that spirit of anger, he called the judge. I don't know what he said in that conversation with the judge, but it was later revealed his main point was "Why can't he be bonded out?" I was released the next day. It was about two weeks before the election.

Senator Kennedy had served as a great force in making my release from Reidsville Prison possible. I was personally obligated to him and his brother for their intervention during my imprisonment. He did it because of his great concern and his humanitarian bent. I would like to feel that he made the call because he was concerned. He had come to know me as a person then. He had been in the debates and had done a good job when he talked about civil rights and what the Negro faces. Harris and others had really been talking with him about it. At the same time, I think he naturally had political considerations in mind. He was running for an office, and he needed to be elected, and I'm sure he felt the need for the Negro votes. So I think that he did something that expressed deep moral concern, but at the same time it was politically sound. It did take a little courage to do this; he didn't know it was politically sound.

I always felt that Nixon lost a real opportunity to express support of something much larger than an individual, because this expressed support for the movement for civil rights. It indicated the direction that this man would take, if he became president.

And I had known Nixon longer. He had been supposedly close to me, and he would call me frequently about things, seeking my advice. And yet, when this moment came, it was like he had never heard of me. So this is why I really considered him a moral coward and one who was really unwilling to take a courageous step and take a risk. And I am convinced that he lost the election because of that. Many Negroes were still on the fence, still undecided, and they were leaning toward Nixon.

◆

ON RICHARD NIXON

First, I must admit that I was strongly opposed to Vice President Nixon before meeting him personally. I went to him with an initial bias. I remembered his statements against Helen Gahegen Douglas and also the fact that he voted with the right wing of the Republican Party. These were almost unforgivable sins for me at that time. After meeting the vice president, however, I must admit that my impression somewhat changed. I have frankly come to feel that the position and the world contacts of the vice president have matured his person and judgment. Whether he can have experienced a complete conversion, I cannot say. But I do believe that he has grown a great deal and has changed many of his former opinions.

Since I am quite interested in civil rights, I might say just a word concerning his views at this point. I am coming to believe that Nixon is absolutely sincere about his views on this issue. His travels have revealed to him how the race problem is hurting America in international relations and it is altogether possible that he has no basic racial prejudice. Nixon happens to be a Quaker and there are very few Quakers who are prejudiced from a racial point of view. I also feel that Nixon would have done much more to meet the present crisis in race relations than President Eisenhower has done. . . .

Finally, I would say that Nixon has a genius for convincing one that he is sincere. When you are close to Nixon he almost disarms you with his apparent sincerity. You never get the impression that he is the same man who campaigned in California a few years ago, and who made a tear-jerking speech on television in the 1952 campaign to save himself from an obvious misdeed. And so I would conclude by saying that if Richard Nixon is not sincere, he is the most dangerous man in America.

Letter to Earl Mazo, September 2, 1958

◆

My father had endorsed Nixon until that call. He knew about my relations with Nixon, and I think he felt that Nixon would do a good job on the civil rights question. I guess deep down within there may have been a little of the religious feeling that a Catholic should not be president. I'm sure my father had been somewhat influenced by this, so that he had gone on record endorsing Nixon. After that call, he changed, and he made a very strong statement.

I was grateful to Senator Kennedy for the genuine concern he expressed in my arrest. After the call I made a statement to the press thanking him but not endorsing him. Very frankly, I did not feel at that time that there was much difference between Kennedy and Nixon. I could find some things in the background of both men that I didn't particularly agree with. Remembering what Nixon had done out in California to Helen Gahegen Douglas, I felt that he was an opportunist at many times who had no real grounding in basic convictions, and his voting record was not good. He improved when he became vice president, but, when he was a congressman and a senator, he didn't have a good voting record.

With Mr. Kennedy, after I looked over his voting record, I felt at points that he was so concerned about being president of the United States that he would compromise basic principles to become president. But I had to look at something else beyond the man—the people who surrounded him—and I felt that Kennedy was surrounded by better people. It was on that basis that I felt that Kennedy would make the best president.

I never came out with an endorsement. My father did, but I never made one. I took this position in order to maintain a nonpartisan posture, which I have followed all along in order to be able to look objectively at both parties at all times. As I said to him all along, I couldn't, and I never changed that even after he made the call during my arrest. I made a statement of thanks, and I expressed my gratitude for the call, but in the statement I made it clear that I did not endorse any candidate and that this was not to be interpreted as an endorsement.

I had to conclude that the then known facts about Kennedy were not adequate to make an unqualified judgment in his favor. I do feel that, as any man, he grew a great deal. After he became president I thought we really saw two Kennedys—a Kennedy the first two years and another Kennedy emerging in 1963. He was getting ready to throw off political considerations and see the real moral issues. Had President Kennedy lived, I would probably have endorsed him in 1964. But, back at that time, I concluded that there was something to be desired in both candidates.

16

THE ALBANY MOVEMENT

Why Albany? Because Albany symbolizes the bastions of segregation set upon by the compounded forces of morality and justice.

JANUARY 30, 1961
Kings' third child, Dexter Scott, is born

MAY 21
After the initial group of Freedom Riders seeking to integrate bus terminals are assaulted in Alabama, King addresses mass rally at mob-besieged Montgomery church

DECEMBER 15
King arrives in Albany in response to telegram from Dr. W. G. Anderson, head of the Albany Movement

DECEMBER 16
Is arrested with more than 700 Albany protesters

JULY 10, 1962
With Ralph Abernathy, is convicted of leading December protest; begins serving a 45-day sentence

JULY 12
Leaves jail after his fine is paid by unidentified person

JULY 25
After outbreak of racial violence in Albany, calls for Day of Penance to atone for violence

JULY 27
Albany city hall prayer vigil ends in arrest

AUGUST 10
Leaves jail and agrees to halt demonstrations

In 1961 the Kennedy administration waged an essentially cautious and defensive struggle for civil rights against an unyielding adversary. As the year unfolded, executive initiative became increasingly feeble, and the chilling prospect emerged of a general administration retreat.

Negroes had manifested their faith by racking up a substantial majority of their votes for President Kennedy. They had expected more of him than of the previous administration. His administration appeared to believe it was doing as much as was politically possible and had, by its positive deeds, earned enough credit to coast on civil rights. Politically, perhaps, this was not a surprising conclusion. How many people understood, during the first two years of the Kennedy administration, that the Negroes' "Now" was becoming as militant as the segregationists' "Never"?

Despite tormenting handicaps, Negroes moved from sporadic, limited actions to broadscale activities different in kind and degree from anything done in the past. A new spirit was manifest in the Negro's willingness to demonstrate in the streets of communities in which, by tradition, he was supposed to step aside when a white man strode toward him.

Areas such as Mississippi and rural Georgia, hitherto quiescent, were churned into turbulence by registration campaigns and freedom rides. The change in spirit was even more dramatically exemplified by the Negroes' willingness, in communities such as Albany, Georgia, to endure mass jailing.

Albany, Georgia, was a distillation of the tensions and conflicts straining the social fabric of the contemporary South. On one side were the segregationists who thought granite stubbornness was a policy. On the other side were Negroes marching forward utilizing nonviolence. Discrimination of all kinds had been simultaneously brought under our sights: school segregation, denial of voting rights, segregation in parks, libraries, restaurants, and buses.

The Negroes of Albany suffered in quiet silence. The throbbing pain of segregation could be felt but not seen. It scarred Negroes in every experience of their lives. They lived in segregation; they ate in segregation; they learned in segregation; they prayed, and rode and worked and died in segregation. And in silence. A corroding loss of self-respect rusted their moral fiber. Their discontent was turned inward on themselves. But an end came with the beginning of protest.

"I knew I had to stay"

As Rosa Parks triggered the Montgomery bus protest, so the arrival in December 1961 of eleven Freedom Riders had triggered the now historic nonviolent thrust in Albany. This Freedom Ride movement came into being to reveal the indignities and the injustices which Negro people faced as they attempted to do the simple thing of traveling through the South as interstate passengers. The Freedom Rides, which were begun by the young, grew to such proportion that they eventually encompassed people of all ages. As a result of this movement, many achievements had come into being. The Interstate Commerce Commission had said in substance that all bus terminals must be integrated. The dramatic Albany Movement was the climax to this psychological forward thrust.

The Albany Movement, headed by Dr. W. G. Anderson, was already functional and had developed a year-long history on the part of the Negro community to seek relief of their grievance. The presence of staff and personnel of variegated human relations fields gave rise to the notion that Albany had been made a target city, with the ominous decision having been made months before—probably in a "smoke-filled New York hotel room." The truth is, Albany had become a symbol of segregation's last stand almost by chance. The ferment of a hundred years' frustration had come to the fore. Sociologically, Albany had all the ingredients of a target city, but it could just as easily have been one of a hundred cities throughout the deep and mid South. Twenty-seven thousand Negroes lived in Albany, Georgia, but a hundred years of political, economic, and educational suppression had kept them hopelessly enslaved to a demonic, though sophisticated, system of segregation which sought desperately and ruthlessly to perpetuate these deprivations.

Negroes, wielding nonviolent protest in its most creative utilization to date, challenged discrimination in public places, denial of voting rights, school segregation, and the deprivation of free speech and assembly. On that broad front, the Albany Movement used all the methods of nonviolence: direct action expressed through mass demonstrations; jail-ins; sit-ins; wade-ins, and kneel-ins; political action; boycotts and legal actions. In no other city of the deep South had all those methods of nonviolence been simultaneously exercised.

The city authorities were wrestling with slippery contradictions, seeking to extend municipal growth and expansion while preserving customs suitable only in a backward and semi-feudal society. Confronted by the potency of the nonviolent protest movement, the city fathers sought to project an image of unyielding mastery. But in truth they staggered from blunder to blunder, losing their cocksureness and common sense as they built retaining walls of slippery sand to shore up a crumbling edifice of injustice.

The Southern Christian Leadership Conference gave full moral and financial support to the Albany Movement and the noble efforts of that community to realize justice, equal rights, and an end to second-class citizenship.

For us the first stage of victory required that Negroes break the barrier of silence and paralysis which for decades suppressed them and denied them the simplest of improvements. This victory was achieved when nonviolent protest aroused every element of the community: the youth, the elderly, men and women in the tens of thousands. Class distinctions were erased in the streets and in jail as domestics, professionals, workers, businessmen, teachers, and laundresses were united as cellmates, charged together with the crime of seeking human justice.

On December 16, 1961, the Negro community of that city made its stride toward freedom. Citizens from every quarter of the community made their moral witness against the system of segregation. They willingly went to jail to create an effective protest.

I too was jailed on charges of parading without a permit, disturbing the peace, and obstructing the sidewalk. I refused to pay the fine and had expected to spend Christmas in jail. I hoped thousands would join me. I didn't come to be arrested. I had planned to stay a day or so and return home after giving counsel. But after seeing negotiations break down, I knew I had to stay. My personal reason for being in Albany was to express a personal witness of a situation

I felt was very important to me. As I, accompanied by over one hundred spirited Negroes, voluntarily chose jail to bail, the city officials appeared so hardened to all appeals to conscience that the confidence of some of our supporters was shaken. They nervously counted heads and concluded too hastily that the movement was losing momentum.

I shall never forget the experience of seeing women over seventy, teenagers, and middle-aged adults—some with professional degrees in medicine, law, and education, some simple housekeepers and laborers—crowding the cells. This development was an indication that the Negro would not rest until all the barriers of segregation were broken down. The South had to decide whether it would comply with the law of the land or drift into chaos and social stagnation.

One must search for words in an attempt to describe the spirit of enthusiasm and majesty engendered in the next mass meeting, on that night when seven hundred Negro citizens were finally released from prison. Out from the jails came those men and women—doctors, ministers, housewives—all of whom had joined ranks with a gallant student leadership in an exemplary demonstration of nonviolent resistance to segregation.

Before long the merchants were urging a settlement upon the city officials and an agreement was finally wrung from their unwilling hands. That agreement was dishonored and violated by the city. It was inevitable that the sweep of events would see a resumption of the nonviolent movement, and when cases against the seven hundred odd prisoners were not dropped and when the city council refused to negotiate to end discrimination in public places, actions began again.

When the Albany Movement, true to its promise, resumed protest activity in July 1962, it invited the Southern Christian Leadership Conference to share leadership with it. As president of the SCLC, I marshaled our staff of personnel experienced in nonviolent action, voter registration, and law.

Ralph and I had been called to trial along with two other Albany citizens in February. Recorder's Court Judge A. N. Durden deferred judgment until Tuesday, July 10.

Jail Diary for July 10–July 11

Tuesday, July 10: *We left Atlanta in a party of seven via Southern Airlines to attend court trial in Albany, Georgia. The party included Juanita and Ralph Abernathy, Wyatt Walker, Ted Brown, Vincent Harding, Coretta, and myself. We left Atlanta around 7:45 A.M. and arrived in Albany promptly at 8:50. We were met at the airport by Andy Young, who had preceded us the night before, Dr. William Anderson, and the two detectives who had been assigned to us by the city. We proceeded directly to Dr. Anderson's residence. There we had breakfast and discussed our possible action in the event we were convicted. Dr. Anderson brought us up to date on the temper of the Negro community. He assured us that the people were generally enthusiastic and determined to stick with us to the end. He mentioned that several people had made it palpably clear that they would go to jail again and stay indefinitely. From all of these words we gradually concluded that we had no alternative but to serve the time if we were sentenced. Considering church and organizational responsibilities we concluded that we could not stay in more than three months. But if the sentence were three months or less we would serve the time. With this decision we left for court.*

At 10:00 A.M. Judge Durden called the court to order. He immediately began by reading a prepared statement. It said in short that he had found all four defendants guilty. The four defendants were Ralph Abernathy, Eddie Jackson, Solomon Walker, and myself. Ralph and I were given a fine of $178 or forty-five days on the streets. Jackson and Walker were given lesser fines and days, since, according to the judge, they were not the leaders.

Ralph and I immediately notified the court that we could not in all good conscience pay the fine, and thereby chose to serve the time. Eddie Jackson joined us in this decision. Mr. Walker decided to appeal.

After a brief press conference in the vestibule of the court we were brought immediately to the Albany City Jail which is in the basement of the same building which houses the court and the city hall. This jail is by far the worst I've ever been in. It is a dingy, dirty hole with nothing suggestive of civilized society. The cells are saturated with filth, and what mattresses there are for the bunks are as hard as solid rocks and as nasty as anything that one has ever seen. The companionship of

---

MESSAGE FROM JAIL

Our course of action was decided after very careful soul searching. There was the consideration of our wives and families, our respective pulpits, our official responsibility as chief officers of SCLC, and many long-standing commitments. However, in the face of all these, we were overwhelmed by some other primary concerns that could be resolved in no other way.

We chose to serve our time because we feel so deeply about the plight of more than seven hundred others who have yet to be tried. The fine and appeal for this number of people would make the cost astronomical. We have experienced the racist tactics of attempting to bankrupt the movement in the South through excessive bail and extended court fights. The time has now come when we must practice civil disobedience in a true sense or delay our freedom thrust for long years.

July 14, 1962

---

roaches and ants is not at all unusual. In several of the cells there are no mattresses at all. The occupants are compelled to sleep on the bare hard steel.

When we entered our cell—Ralph and I were placed together in a single cell—we found it as filthy as all the rest. However, conscious of the fact that he had some political prisoners on hand who could make these conditions known around the nation, the Chief immediately ordered the entire cell block to be cleaned. So with water, soap, and Lysol the boys got to work and gave the cleaning it so desperately needed.

The rest of the day was spent getting adjusted to our home for the next forty-five days. There is something inherently depressing about jail, especially when one is confined to his cell. We soon discovered that we would not be ordered to work on the streets because, according to the Chief, "it would not be safe." This, to me, was bad news. I wanted to work on the streets at least to give some attention to the daily round. Jail is depressing because it shuts off the world. It leaves one caught in the dull monotony of sameness. It is almost like being dead while one still lives. To adjust to such a meaningless existence is not easy. The only way that I adjust to it is to constantly remind myself that this self-imposed suffering is for a great cause and purpose. This realization takes a little of the agony and a little of the depression away. But, in spite of this, the painfulness of the experience remains. It is something like the mother giving birth to a child. While she is temporarily consoled by the fact that her pain is not just bare meaningless pain, she nevertheless experiences the pain. In spite of the fact that she realizes that beneath her pain is the emergence of life in a radiant infant, she experiences the agony right on. So is the jail experience. It is life without the singing of a bird, without the sight of the sun, moon, and stars, without the felt presence of the fresh air. In short, it is life without the beauties of life; it is bare existence—cold, cruel, and degenerating.

One of the things that takes the monotony out of jail is the visit of a relative or friend. About 1:30—three hours after we were arrested—our wives came by to see us. As usual Coretta was calm and sweet, encouraging me at every point. God blessed me with a great and wonderful wife. Without her love, understanding, and courage, I would have faltered long ago. I asked about the children. She told me that Yolanda cried when she discovered that her daddy was in jail. Somehow, I have never quite adjusted to bringing my children up under such inexplicable conditions. How do you explain to a little child why you have to go to jail? Coretta developed an answer. She told them that daddy has gone to jail to help the people.

The rest of the day was spent sleeping, adjusting to the unbearable heat, and talking with other friends—Wyatt, Dr. Anderson, Andy Young, Ted Brown, Vincent Harding, and Atty. King—who floated in. Around 11:00 P.M. I fell asleep. Never before have I slept under more miserable conditions. My bed was so hard, my back was so sore, and the jail was so ugly.

Wednesday, July 11: I awoke bright and early. It was around 6:00 to be exact. My back was still sore. Around 8:00 breakfast came. We had fasted all day Tuesday in order to prepare ourselves, spiritually, for the ordeals ahead. We broke the fast by eating breakfast. The food is generally good in this jail. This may be due to the fact that the food is cooked, not in the jail itself, but in a cafe, adjacent to the jail. For breakfast we had link sausage, eggs, and grits. I was pleasantly surprised when I discovered that the coffee had cream and sugar. In all the jails that I have inhabited we were not permitted to have sugar or cream in the coffee.

At 10:00 we had a visit from C. K. Steele, Andy Young, and Henry Elkins, my summer assistant pastor. He had brought me some articles that my wife sent from Atlanta. They told us about the mass meeting. It was lively and extremely well attended. They whispered to us that a group was planning to march to the city hall around noon.

Around noon the group did march. They were led by C. K. Steele. All were arrested—about fifty. They were first brought to the city jails. We heard them as they approached singing freedom songs. Naturally this was a big lift for us.

As the group neared the jail, two of the jailers came over and ordered Ralph and I to move over to what is known as the bull pen. This is a dark and desolate cell that holds nine persons. It is unbelievable that such a cell could exist in a supposedly civilized society.

About seven-thirty on the morning of July 13, we were called and notified that Chief Pritchett wanted to see us. They asked us to dress in our civilian clothes. We did that and went to see Chief Pritchett at about nine o'clock. At which time, the Chief said to us that we had been released, in other words that our fine had been paid. I said, "Well, Chief, we want to serve this time, we feel that we owe it to ourselves and the seven hundred and some-odd people of this community who still have these cases hanging over them." His only response then was, "God knows, Reverend, I don't want you in my jail." This was one time that I was out of jail and I was not happy to be out. Not that I particularly enjoyed the inconveniences and the discomforts of jail, but I did not appreciate the subtle and conniving tactics used to get us out of jail. We had witnessed persons being kicked off lunch counter stools during the sit-ins, ejected from churches during the kneel-ins, and thrown into jail during the Freedom Rides. But for the first time, we witnessed being kicked out of jail.

On July 24, officials unleashed force against our peaceful demonstration, brutally beating a pregnant woman and caning one of our lawyers. Some of the Negro onlookers, not our demonstrators, seething with resentment, hurled bottles and stones at the police. At that point, I temporarily halted mass demonstrations, and for several days, I visited homes, clubs, and pool rooms, urging that no retaliation be tolerated, and even the angriest of men acceded.

"Day of Penance"

While we are certain that neither the peaceful demonstrators nor persons active in the Albany Movement were involved in the violence that erupted last night, we abhor violence so much that when it occurs in the ranks of the Negro community, we assume part of the responsibility for it.

In order to demonstrate our commitment to nonviolence and our determination to keep our protest peaceful, we declare a "Day of Penance" beginning at 12 noon today. We are calling upon all members and supporters of the Albany Movement to pray for their brothers in the Negro community who have not yet found their way to the nonviolent discipline during this Day of Penance. We feel that as we observe this Day of Penance, the City Commission and white people of goodwill should seriously examine the problems and conditions existing in Albany. We must honestly say that the City Commission's arrogant refusal to talk with the leaders of the Albany Movement, the continued suppression of the Negro's aspiration for freedom, and the tragic attempt on the part of the Albany police officials to maintain segregation at any cost, all serve to create the atmosphere for violence and bitterness.

While we will preach and teach nonviolence to our people with every ounce of energy in our bodies, we fear that these admonitions will fall on some deaf ears if Albany does not engage in good-faith negotiations.

Albany city officials were quick to recognize that the watching and concerned millions across the nation would sense the moral righteousness of our conduct. Quickly, they became converted to nonviolence, and without embarrassment, Sheriff Pritchett declared to the press that he too was an advocate of nonviolence. An equilibrium, in which the external use of force was excluded, settled over the troubled city.

Jail Diary for July 27–August 10

Friday, July 27: *Ralph Abernathy and I were arrested again in Albany at 3:15 P.M. (for the second time in July and the third time since last December). We were accompanied by Dr. W. G. Anderson, Slater King,* the Rev. Ben Gay, and seven ladies. This group held a prayer vigil in front of City Hall, seeking to appeal to the City Commission to negotiate with leaders of the Albany Movement. When we arrived at the city hall, the press was on hand in large numbers and Police Chief Laurie Pritchett came directly over to us and invited us into his office. When we declined, he immediately ordered us arrested.

Around 9 P.M., one of the officers came to the cell and said Chief Pritchett wanted to see me in his office. I responded suspiciously, remembering that two weeks ago, we were summoned to Pritchett's office, only to discover that we were being tricked out of jail. (A mysterious donor paid the fine, $178 for each of us.) Today, we were determined that this would not happen again. So, I told the officer that Pritchett would have to step back to our cell. The officer reacted very bitterly, but he apparently got the message to Pritchett because the Chief came immediately and said: "Come on, Doctor. I am not trying to get you to leave. There is a long-distance call for you from a man named Spivak."

The call turned out to be Lawrence Spivak from the Meet the Press TV program. I was scheduled to be on the program, Sunday, July 29. He was very upset and literally begged me to come out on bond. I immediately called Atty. (C. B.) King and the Rev. Wyatt Walker, my assistant, to the jail and sought their advice. We all agreed that I should not leave and suggested that Dr. Anderson, president of the Albany Movement, get out on bond and substitute for me. Dr. Anderson agreed and I decided to remain in jail.

Saturday, July 28: I was able to arrange with Chief Pritchett for members of my staff to consult with me at any time. We held our staff meetings right there in jail. My wife, Coretta, also came to see me twice today before returning to Atlanta.

When Wyatt came to the jail, I emphasized that more demonstrations must be held with smaller numbers in front of the city hall instead of large marches because there is so much tension in the town.

A little while after I talked with Wyatt, fifteen more demonstrators were arrested as they appeared before City Hall and they all came in the jail singing loudly. This was a big lift for us. This group was immediately shipped out to another jail in the state.

Later that day. Pritchett came and asked me to leave jail for good. He said that someone had actually sent the cash money for my bond and technically he could make me leave. I told him I certainly did not want to be put in the position of being dragged out of jail, but that I had no intention of leaving because I wanted to serve my sentence.

Prichett told us: "You don't know how tense things are, do you? Do you know what happened?" When we said no, he replied: "Somebody almost busted C. B. King's head wide open." It sounded horrible and we became excited. I asked him who and he said calmly: "The sheriff over in the County Jail." I immediately sent for Wyatt and asked him to send a telegram to the President and to call Atty. Gen. Robert Kennedy and Burke Marshall of the Justice Dept. I told them I was very much concerned about this kind of brutality by law enforcement agencies and that something had to be done.

Sunday, July 29: *Everything was rather quiet this morning. We had our regular devotional services among all the prisoners. I read from the Book of Job. We hold services every morning and evening and sing whenever we feel like it. Since only Ralph and I are in a cell together, we can't see the other prisoners, but we can always hear them. Slater is two cells away. Marvin Rich, Ed Dickenson, and Earl Gorden (some white demonstrators) are across the hall in another cell block but they join us in services. After devotion, I started reading some of the books I had with me.*

They brought us the usual breakfast at 8 o'clock. It was one link sausage, one egg and some grits, two pieces of bread on a tin plate with a tin cup of coffee. We were astonished when the jailer returned at ten minutes after 10 this morning with a plate of hash, peas and rice and corn bread. He said it was supper and the last meal we were going to get that day because the cook was getting off early. Soon, the Rev. Mr. Walker came over with Dr. Roy C. Bell from Atlanta and Larry Still, a writer from Jet. Roy inspected Ralph's teeth and said he would arrange with Chief Pritchett to get us some "food packages." I told him this was needed because we would starve on the jail house food. The Albany Jail is dirty, filthy, and ill-equipped. I have been in many jails and it is really the worst I have ever seen.

Monday, July 30: *I spent most of the day reading and writing my book on Negro sermons before our hearing in federal court started. The heat was so unbearable, I could hardly get anything done. I think we had the hottest cell in the jail because it is back in a corner. There are* four bunks in our cell, but for some reason, they never put anybody in with us. Ralph says every time we go to the wash bowl we bump into each other. He is a wonderful friend and really keeps our spirits going. The food seemed to be worse than usual today. I could only drink the coffee.

I talked with Wyatt and he told me the demonstrations were still going as planned. We soon heard about them because they brought in about fifteen more they had arrested. We were then told to get ready to go to court to begin the hearing on the city's request for a federal injunction against the demonstrations. I was informed that Atty. Connie Motley was here from the New York office of the NAACP and I was very happy. Lawyers King and Donald L. Hollowell of Atlanta came to see me before the hearing started. We discussed how the Albany battle must be waged on all four fronts. A legal battle in the courts; with demonstrations and kneel-ins and sit-ins; with an economic boycott; and, finally, with an intense voter registration campaign. This is going to be a long summer.

Tuesday, July 31: I was very glad to get to court today because I had a chance to see my wife and my friends and associates who are keeping the Albany Movement going. I also had a chance to consult with Wyatt during the recesses. He told us demonstrations were going on while we were in court and that some of the youth groups led by the Student Nonviolent Coordinating Committee were testing places like drugstores and drive-ins and motels.

Later, my father came to me with the Rev. Allen Middleton, head of Atlanta's SCLC chapter. I was happy to hear that my mother has adjusted to my role in the Albany Movement. She understood that I still had to remain in jail as long as necessary. I told Dad to invite some preachers in to help him carry on the church, but he told me, "As long as you carry on in jail, I'll carry on outside."

Wednesday, August 1: My father and Dr. Middleton came to see me again this morning and told me they spoke at the mass meeting last night at Mt. Zion Baptist Church. The crowd was so large they overflowed into Shiloh Baptist across the street, where nightly mass meetings are usually held. Dad said he would remain through today's hearing and listen to Chief Pritchett's testimony about how he had to arrest Negroes to protect the white people from beating them. Dad said he told the people I didn't come to Albany on my own but I was invited there by the city officials to visit their jail.

Thursday, August 2: I learned about President Kennedy saying that the commissioners of Albany ought to talk to the Negro leaders. I felt this was a very forthright statement and immediately dictated a statement to the President commending him on his action.

Friday, August 3: They recessed the court hearing until Tuesday. I still have the feeling it is too long and drawn out and that the people should keep demonstrating no matter what happens.

Saturday, August 4: More demonstrators were arrested all day today and later on Pritchett came back and asked them to sing for him. "Sing that song about 'Ain't Going to Let Chief Pritchett Turn Me Around,'" he asked. I think he really enjoyed hearing it. The other jailers would just stare and listen.

Sunday, August 5: Today was a big day for me, because my children—Yolanda, Martin Luther III, and Dexter—came to see me. I had not seen them for five weeks. We had about twenty-five minutes together. They certainly gave me a lift.

Monday, August 6: I saw Coretta again before she left to take the children back to Atlanta. I devoted most of the day to reading newspapers and letters from all over the world. Some of them were just addressed to "Nation's No. 1 Troublemaker, Albany," without any state. I got a few bad ones like this, but most of them were good letters of encouragement from Negroes and whites. After dinner and devotional period I continued writing on my book. I had planned to finish it this summer, but I have only written eleven of the eighteen sermons to be

---

TELEGRAM TO PRESIDENT KENNEDY

DEAR MR PRESIDENT, GRATIFIED BY DIRECTNESS OF YOUR STATEMENT TO ALBANY CRISIS. REV ABERNATHY AND I EARNESTLY HOPE YOU WILL CONTINUE TO USE THE GREAT MORAL INFLUENCE OF YOUR OFFICE TO HELP THIS CRITICAL SITUATION.

August 2, 1962

included. I have written three sermons in jail. They all deal with how to make the Christian gospel relevant to the social and economic life of man. This means how the Christian should deal with race relations, war and peace, and economic injustices. They are all based on sermons I have preached. The sermons I wrote in jail are called "A Tender Heart and A Tough Mind," "Love in Action," and "Loving Your Enemies." I think I will name the book Loving Your Enemies.

Tuesday, August 7: *We went back to court today. As I listened to the testimony of the State's witnesses about how they were trying to prevent violence and protect the people, I told Ralph it was very depressing to see city officials make a farce of the court.*

Wednesday, August 8: *Today was the last day of the hearing and Ralph and I testified. Although the federal court hearing offered some relief from the hot jail, I was glad the hearings were over. It was always miserable going back to the hot cell from the air-conditioned courtroom. I was so exhausted and sick that Dr. Anderson had to come and treat me for the second time.*

Thursday, August 9: *Even though we decided to remain in jail, "We Woke Up This Morning with Our Mind on Freedom." Everyone appeared to be in good spirits and we had an exceptionally good devotional program and sang all of our freedom songs.*

Later, Wyatt and Dr. Anderson came and told me that two marches were being planned if Ralph and I were sentenced to jail tomorrow. All of the mothers of many prisoners agreed to join their families in jail including my wife, Mrs. Anderson, Wyatt's wife, Young's wife, Ralph's wife, and the wife of Atty. William Kunstler.

Friday, August 10: *The suspended sentence today did not come as a complete surprise to me. I still think the sentence was unjust and I want to appeal but our lawyers have not decided. Ralph and I agreed to call off the marches and return to our churches in Atlanta to give the Commission a chance to "save face" and demonstrate good faith with the Albany Movement.*

I thought the federal government could do more, because basic constitutional rights were being denied. The persons who were protesting in Albany, Georgia, were merely seeking to exercise constitu-

TERRIBLE COST OF THE BALLOT

Tears welled up in my heart and my eyes last week as I surveyed the shambles of what had been the Shady Grove Baptist Church of Lees-burg, Georgia. I had been awakened shortly after daybreak by my executive assistant, the Rev. Wyatt Tee Walker, who informed me that a SNCC staffer had just called and reported that the church where their organization had been holding voting clinics and registration classes had been destroyed by fire and/or dynamite. . . .

The naked truth is that whether the object of the Negro community's efforts are directed at lunch counters or interstate buses, First Amendment privileges or pilgrimages of prayer, school desegregation or the right to vote—he meets an implacable foe in the Southern white racist. No matter what it is we seek, if it has to do with full citizenship, self-respect, human dignity, and borders on changing the "Southern way of life," the Negro stands little chance, if any, of securing the approval, consent, or tolerance of the segregationist white South—Exhibit "A": the charred remains of Shady Grove Baptist Church, Lee County, Georgia. This is the terrible cost of the ballot in the deep South.

From newspaper column, September 1, 1962

TELEGRAM TO PRESIDENT KENNEDY

I HAVE LEARNED FROM AUTHENTIC SOURCES THAT NEGROES ARE ARMING THEMSELVES IN MANY QUARTERS WHERE THIS REIGN OF TERROR IS ALIVE. I WILL CONTINUE TO URGE MY PEOPLE TO BE NONVIOLENT IN THE FACE OF BITTEREST OPPOSITION, BUT I FEAR THAT MY COUNSEL WILL FALL ON DEAF EARS IF THE FEDERAL GOVERNMENT DOES NOT TAKE DECISIVE ACTION. IF NEGROES ARE TEMPTED TO TURN TO RETALIATORY VIOLENCE, WE SHALL SEE A DARK NIGHT OF RIOTING ALL OVER THE SOUTH.

September 11, 1962

tional rights through peaceful protest, nonviolent protest. I thought that the people in Albany were being denied their rights on the basis of the first amendment of the Constitution. I thought it would be a very good thing for the federal government to take a definite stand on that issue, even if it meant joining with Negro attorneys who were working on the situation.

"The people of Albany had straightened their backs"

Our movement aroused the Negro to a spirited pitch in which more than 5 percent of the Negro population voluntarily went to jail. At the same time, about 95 percent of the Negro population boycotted buses, and shops where humiliation, not service, was offered. Those boycotts were remarkably effective. The buses were off the streets and rusting in garages, and the line went out of business. Other merchants watched the sales of their goods decline week by week. National concerns even changed plans to open branches in Albany because the city was too unstable to encourage business to invest there. To thwart us, the opposition had closed parks and libraries, but in the process, they closed them for white people as well, thus they had made their modern city little better than a rural village without recreational and cultural facilities.

When months of demonstrations and jailings failed to accomplish the goals of the movement, reports in the press and elsewhere pronounced nonviolent resistance a dead issue.

There were weaknesses in Albany, and a share of the responsibility belongs to each of us who participated. There is no tactical theory so neat that a revolutionary struggle for a share of power can be won merely by pressing a row of buttons. Human beings with all their faults and strengths constitute the mechanism of a social movement. They must make mistakes and learn from them, make more mistakes and learn anew. They must taste defeat as well as success, and discover how to live with each. Looking back over it, I'm sorry I was bailed out. I didn't understand at the time what was happening. We lost an initiative that we never regained. We attacked the political power structure instead of the economic power structure. You don't win against a political power structure where you don't have the votes.

If I had that to do again, I would guide that community's Negro leadership differently than I did. The mistake I made there was to protest against segregation generally rather than against a single and distinct facet of it. Our protest was so vague that we got nothing, and the people were left very depressed and in despair. It would have been much better to have concentrated upon integrating the buses or the lunch counters. One victory of this kind would have been symbolic, would have galvanized support and boosted morale. But I don't mean that our work in Albany ended in failure. And what we learned from our mistakes in Albany helped our later campaigns in other cities to be more effective. We never since scattered our efforts in a general attack on segregation, but focused upon specific, symbolic objectives.

Yet, the repeal of Albany's segregation laws indicated clearly that the city fathers were realistically facing the legal death of segregation. After the "jail-ins," the City Commission repealed the entire section of the city code that carried segregation ordinances. The public library was opened on a thirty-day "trial" basis—integrated! To be sure, neither of these events could be measured as a full victory, but neither did they smack of defeat.

When we planned our strategy for Birmingham months later, we spent many hours assessing Albany and trying to learn from its errors. Our appraisals not only helped to make our subsequent tactics more effective, but revealed that Albany was far from an unqualified failure. Though lunch counters remained segregated, thousands of Negroes were added to the voting registration rolls. In the gubernatorial elections that followed our summer there, a moderate candidate confronted a rabid segregationist. By reason of the expanded Negro vote, the moderate defeated the segregationist in the city of Albany, which in turn contributed to his victory in the state. As a result, Georgia elected its first governor pledged to respect and enforce the law equally.

In short, our movement had taken the moral offensive, enriching our people with a spirit of strength to fight for equality and freedom even if the struggle is to be long and arduous. The people of Albany had straightened their backs, and, as Gandhi had said, no one can ride on the back of a man unless it is bent.

The atmosphere of despair and defeat was replaced by the surging sense of strength of people who had dared to defy tyrants, and had discovered that tyrants could be defeated. To the Negro in the South, staggering under a burden of centuries of inferiority, to have faced his oppressor squarely, absorbed his violence, filled the jails, driven his segregated buses off the streets, worshiped in a few white churches, rendered inoperative parks, libraries, and pools, shrunken his trade, revealed his inhumanity to the nation and the world, and sung, lectured, and prayed publicly for freedom and equality—these were the deeds of a giant. No one would silence him up again. That was the victory which could not be undone. Albany would never be the same again. We had won a partial victory in Albany, and a partial victory to us was not an end but a beginning.

17

THE BIRMINGHAM CAMPAIGN

In the entire country, there was no place to compare with Birmingham. The largest industrial city in the South, Birmingham had become, in the thirties, a symbol for bloodshed when trade unions sought to organize. It was a community in which human rights had been trampled on for so long that fear and oppression were as thick in its atmosphere as the smog from its factories. Its financial interests were interlocked with a power structure which spread throughout the South and radiated into the North. The challenge to nonviolent, direct action could not have been staged in a more appropriate arena.

MARCH 28, 1963
The Kings' fourth child, Bernice Albertine, is born

APRIL 2
Albert Boutwell wins runoff election over Police Commissioner Eugene "Bull" Connor for mayor of Birmingham, but Connor and other city commissioners refuse to leave office

APRIL 3
After delays in order to avoid interfering with election, SCLC and Alabama Christian Movement for Human Rights launch protest campaign in Birmingham

APRIL 12
After violating a state circuit court injunction against protests, King is arrested

APRIL 15
President Kennedy calls Coretta Scott King expressing concern for her jailed husband

I f you had visited Birmingham before the third of April in the one-hundredth-anniversary year of the Negro's emancipation, you might have come to a startling conclusion. You might have concluded that here was a city which had been trapped for decades in a Rip Van Winkle slumber; a city whose fathers had apparently never heard of Abraham Lincoln, Thomas Jefferson, the Bill of Rights, the Preamble to the Constitution, The Thirteenth, Fourteenth, and Fifteenth Amendments, or the 1954 decision of the United States Supreme Court outlawing segregation in the public schools.

If your powers of imagination are great enough to enable you to place yourself in the position of a Negro baby born and brought up to physical maturity in Birmingham, you would picture your life in the following manner:

You would be born in a Jim Crow hospital to parents who probably lived in a ghetto. You would attend a Jim Crow school. You would spend your childhood playing mainly in the streets because the "colored" parks were abysmally inadequate. When a federal court order banned park segregation, you would find that Birmingham closed down its parks and gave up its baseball team rather than integrate them.

If you went shopping with your mother or father, you would trudge along as they purchased at every counter except one, in the large or small stores. If you were hungry or thirsty, you would have to forget about it until you got back to the Negro section of town, for in your city it was a violation of the law to serve food to Negroes at the same counter with whites.

If your family attended church, you would go to a Negro church. If you attended your own Negro church and wanted to play safe, you might select a church that didn't have a pastor with a reputation for speaking out on civil rights. If you wanted to visit a church attended by white people, you would not be welcome. For although your white fellow citizens would insist that they were Christians, they practiced segregation as rigidly in the house of God as they did in the theater.

If you wanted to contribute to and be a part of the work of the National Association for the Advancement of Colored People, you would not have been able to join a local branch. In the state of

Alabama, segregationist authorities had been successful in enjoining the NAACP from performing its civil rights work by declaring it a "foreign corporation" and rendering its activities illegal.

If you wanted a job in this city—one of the greatest iron- and steel-producing centers in the nation—you had better settle on doing menial work as a porter or laborer. If you were fortunate enough to get a job, you could expect that promotions to a better status or more pay would come, not to you, but to a white employee regardless of your comparative talents.

If you believed your history books and thought of America as a country whose governing officials—whether city, state, or nation—are selected by the governed, you would be swiftly disillusioned when you tried to exercise your right to register and vote. Your race, constituting two-fifths of the city's population, would have made up one-eighth of its voting strength.

You would be living in a city where brutality directed against Negroes was an unquestioned and unchallenged reality. One of the city commissioners, a member of the body that ruled municipal affairs, would be Eugene "Bull" Connor, a racist who prided himself on knowing how to handle the Negro and keep him in his "place." As commissioner of public safety, Bull Connor, entrenched for many years in a key position in the Birmingham power structure, displayed as much contempt for the rights of the Negro as he did defiance for the authority of the federal government.

You would have found a general atmosphere of violence and brutality in Birmingham. Local racists intimidated, mobbed, and even killed Negroes with impunity. One of the more vivid examples of the terror of Birmingham was the castration of a Negro man, whose mutilated body had then been abandoned on a lonely road. No Negro home was protected from bombings and burnings. From the year 1957 through January 1963, while Birmingham was still claiming that its Negroes were "satisfied," seventeen unsolved bombings of Negro churches and homes of civil rights leaders occurred.

In Connor's Birmingham, the silent password was fear. It was a fear not only on the part of the black oppressed, but also in the hearts of the white oppressors. Certainly Birmingham had its white moderates who disapproved of Bull Connor's tactics. Certainly Birmingham had its decent white citizens who privately deplored the maltreatment of Negroes. But they remained publicly silent. It was a silence born of fear—fear of social, political, and economic reprisals. The ultimate tragedy of Birmingham was not the brutality of the bad people, but the silence of the good people.

In Birmingham, you would be living in a community where the white man's long-lived tyranny had cowed your people, led them to abandon hope, and developed in them a false sense of inferiority. You would be living in a city where the representatives of economic and political power refused to even discuss social justice with the leaders of your people.

You would be living in the largest city of a police state, presided over by a governor—George Wallace—whose inauguration vow had been a pledge of "segregation now, segregation tomorrow, segregation forever!" You would be living, in fact, in the most segregated city in America.

"Project C"

There was one threat to the reign of white supremacy in Birmingham. As an outgrowth of the Montgomery bus boycott, protest movements had sprung up in numerous cities across the South. In Birmingham, one of the nation's most courageous freedom fighters, the Reverend Fred Shuttlesworth, had organized the Alabama Christian Movement for Human Rights—ACHR—in the spring of 1956. Shuttlesworth, a wiry, energetic, and indomitable man, had set out to change Birmingham and to end for all time the terrorist, racist rule of Bull Connor.

When Shuttlesworth first formed his organization—which soon became one of the eighty-five affiliates of our Southern Christian Leadership Conference—Bull Connor doubtless regarded the group as just another bunch of troublesome "niggers." It soon became obvious even to Connor, however, that Shuttlesworth was in dead earnest. Back at Christmas 1956, Shuttlesworth's home was bombed and completely demolished. In the winter of 1956, his church, Bethel Baptist, was dynamited by racists, and later in 1957, Shuttlesworth and his wife were mobbed, beaten, and stabbed. They were also jailed eight times, four times during the Freedom Rides.

At the May 1962 board meeting of SCLC at Chattanooga, we decided to give serious consideration to joining Shuttlesworth and the ACHR in a massive direct action campaign to attack segregation in Birmingham. Along with Shuttlesworth, we believed that while a campaign in Birmingham would surely be the toughest fight of our civil rights careers, it could, if successful, break the back of segregation all over the nation. A victory there might well set forces in motion to change the entire course of the drive for freedom and justice. Because we were convinced of the significance of the job to be done in Birmingham, we decided that the most thorough planning and prayerful preparation must go into the effort. We began to prepare a top secret file which we called "Project C"—the "C" for Birmingham's *Confrontation* with the fight for justice and morality in race relations.

In preparation for our campaign, I called a three-day retreat and planning session with SCLC staff and board members at our training center near Savannah, Georgia. Here we sought to perfect a timetable and discuss every possible eventuality. In analyzing our campaign in Albany, Georgia, we decided that one of the principal mistakes we had made there was to scatter our efforts too widely. We had been so involved in attacking segregation in general that we had failed to direct our protest effectively to any one main facet. We concluded that in hard-core communities, a more effective battle could be waged if it was concentrated against one aspect of the evil and intricate system of segregation. We decided, therefore, to center the Birmingham struggle on the business community, for we knew that the Negro population had sufficient buying power so that its withdrawal could make the difference between profit and loss for many businesses.

Two weeks after the retreat, I went to Birmingham with my able executive assistant, the Reverend Wyatt Tee Walker, and my abiding friend and fellow campaigner from the days of Montgomery, the Reverend Ralph Abernathy, SCLC's treasurer. There we began to meet with the board of ACHR to assist in preparing the Negro community for what would surely be a difficult, prolonged, and dangerous campaign.

We met in the now famous Room 30 of the Gaston Motel. This room, which housed Ralph and myself, and served as the headquarters for all the strategy sessions in subsequent months, would later be the target of one of the bombs on the fateful and violent Saturday night of May 11, the eve of Mother's Day.

The first major decision we faced was setting the date for launching of "Project C." Since it was our aim to bring pressure to bear on the merchants, we felt that our campaign should be mounted around the Easter season—the second biggest shopping period of the year. If we started the first week of March, we would have six weeks to mobilize the community before Easter, which fell on April 14. But at this point we were reminded that a mayoralty election was to be held in Birmingham on March 5.

The leading candidates were Albert Boutwell, Eugene "Bull" Connor, and Tom King. All were segregationists, running on a platform to preserve the status quo. Yet both King and Boutwell were considered moderates in comparison to Connor. We were hopeful that Connor would be so thoroughly defeated that at least we would not have to deal with him. Since we did not want our campaign to be used as a political football, we decided to postpone it, planning to begin demonstrations two weeks after the election.

By March 1, 1963, the project was in high gear and the loose ends of organizational structure were being pulled together. Some 250 people had volunteered to participate in the initial demonstrations and had pledged to remain in jail at least five days.

At this point the results of the March 5 election intervened to pose a serious new problem. No candidate had won a clear victory. There would have to be a runoff vote, to be held the first week in April. The competing candidates were to be Boutwell and Connor.

Again we had to remap strategy. Had we moved in while Connor and Boutwell were electioneering, Connor would undoubtedly have capitalized on our presence by using it as an emotion-charged issue for his own political advantage, waging a vigorous campaign to persuade the white community that he, and he alone, could defend the city's official policies of segregation. We might actually have had the effect of helping Connor win. Reluctantly, we decided to postpone the demonstrations until the day after the runoff.

We left Birmingham sadly, realizing that after this second delay the intensive groundwork we had done in the Negro community might not bring the effective results we sought. We were leaving some 250 volunteers who had been willing to join our ranks and to go to jail. Now we might lose contact with these recruits for several weeks. Yet we dared not remain. It was agreed that no member of the SCLC staff would return to Birmingham until after the runoff.

In New York City, Harry Belafonte, an old friend and supporter of SCLC, agreed to call a meeting at his apartment. Approximately seventy-five leading New Yorkers were present. Fred Shuttlesworth and I spoke of the problems then existing in Birmingham and those we anticipated. We explained why we had delayed taking action until after the runoff, and why we felt it necessary to proceed with our plans whether Connor or Boutwell was the eventual victor. When we had finished, the most frequent question was: "What can we do to help?"

We answered that we were certain to need tremendous sums of money for bail bonds. We might need public meetings to organize more support. On the spot, Harry Belafonte organized a committee, and money was pledged that same night. For the next three weeks, Belafonte, who never did anything without getting totally involved, gave up his career to organize people and money. With these contacts established, the time had come to return to Birmingham. The runoff election was April 2. We flew in the same night. By word of mouth, we set about trying to make contact with our 250 volunteers for an unadvertised meeting. About sixty-five came out. The following day, with the modest task force, we launched the direct-action campaign in Birmingham.

"People came forward to join our army"

On Wednesday, April 3, 1963, the Birmingham *News* appeared on the stands, its front page bright with a color drawing showing a golden sun rising over the city. It was captioned: "New Day Dawns for Birmingham," and celebrated Albert Boutwell's victory in the runoff vote for mayor. The golden glow of racial harmony, the headline implied, could now be expected to descend on the city. As events were to show, it was indeed a new day for Birmingham; but not because Boutwell had won the election.

For all the optimism expressed in the press and elsewhere, we were convinced that Albert Boutwell was, in Fred Shuttlesworth's apt phrase, "just a dignified Bull Connor." We knew that the former state senator and lieutenant governor had been the principal author of Alabama's Pupil Placement Law, and was a consistent supporter of segregationist views. His statement a few days after election that "we citizens of Birmingham respect and understand one another" showed that he understood nothing about two-fifths of Birmingham's citizens, to whom even polite segregation was no respect.

Meanwhile, despite the results of the runoff, the city commissioners, including Bull Connor, had taken the position that they could not legally be removed from office until 1965. They would go into the courts to defend their position, and refused in the interim to move out of their City Hall offices. If they won in court they would remain in office for another two years. If they lost, their terms would still not expire until April 15, the day after Easter. In either case, we were committed to enter a situation in which a city was operating literally under two governments.

We had decided to limit the first few days' efforts to sit-ins. Being prepared for a long struggle, we felt it best to begin modestly, with a limited number of arrests each day. By rationing our energies in this manner, we would help toward the buildup and drama of a growing campaign. The first demonstrations were, accordingly, not spectacular, but they were well organized. After the first day we held a mass meeting, the first of sixty-five nightly meetings conducted at various churches in the Negro community. Through these meetings we were able to generate the power and depth which finally galvanized the entire Negro community. I spoke at the mass meetings nightly on the philosophy of nonviolence and its methods.

"The soul of the movement"

An important part of the mass meetings was the freedom songs. In a sense the freedom songs are the soul of the movement. They are more than just incantations of clever phrases designed to invigorate a campaign; they are as old as the history of the Negro in America. They are adaptations of songs the slaves sang—the sorrow songs, the shouts for joy, the battle hymns, and the anthems of our movement. I have heard people talk of their beat and rhythm, but we in the movement are as inspired by their words. "Woke Up This Morning with My Mind Stayed on Freedom" is a sentence that needs no music to make its point. We sing the freedom songs for the same reason the slaves sang them, because we too are in bondage and the songs add hope to our determination that "We shall overcome, Black and white together, We shall overcome someday." These songs bound us together, gave us courage together, helped us march together. We could walk toward any Gestapo force. We had cosmic companionship, for we were singing, "Come By Me, Lord, Come By Me."

With this music, a rich heritage from our ancestors who had the stamina and the moral fiber to be able to find beauty in broken fragments of music, whose illiterate minds were able to compose eloquently simple expressions of faith and hope and idealism, we can articulate our deepest groans and passionate yearnings—and end always on a note of hope that God is going to help us work it out, right here in the South where evil stalks the life of a Negro from the time he is placed in his cradle. Through this music, the Negro is able to dip down into wells of a deeply pessimistic situation and danger-fraught circumstances and to bring forth a marvelous, sparkling, fluid optimism. He knows it is still dark in his world, but somehow, he finds a ray of light.

Toward the end of the mass meetings, Abernathy or Shuttlesworth or I would extend an appeal for volunteers to serve in our nonviolent army. We made it clear that we would not send anyone out to demonstrate who had not convinced himself and us that he could accept and endure violence without retaliating. At the same time, we urged the volunteers to give up any possible weapons that they might have on their persons. Hundreds of people responded to this appeal. Some of those who carried penknives, Boy Scout knives—all kinds of knives—had them not because they wanted to use them against the police or other attackers, but because they wanted to defend themselves against Mr. Connor's dogs. We proved to them that we needed no weapons—not so much as a toothpick. We proved that we possessed the most formidable weapon of all—the conviction that we were right. We had the protection of our knowledge that we were more concerned about realizing our righteous aims than about saving our skins.

The invitational periods at the mass meetings, when we asked for volunteers, were much like those invitational periods that occur every Sunday morning in Negro churches, when the pastor projects the call to those present to join the church. By twenties and thirties and forties, people came forward to join our army. We did not hesitate to call our movement an army. It was a special army, with no supplies but its sincerity, no uniform but its determination, no arsenal except its faith, no currency but its conscience. It was an army that would move but not maul. It was an army that would sing but not slay.

We were seeking to bring about a great social change which could only be achieved through unified effort. Yet our community was divided. Our goals could never be attained in such an atmosphere. It was decided that we would conduct a whirlwind campaign of meetings with organizations and leaders in the Negro community, to seek to mobilize every key person and group behind our movement.

Along with members of my staff, I began addressing numerous groups representing a cross section of our people in Birmingham. I spoke to business and professional people, and I talked to a gathering of two hundred ministers. I met with many smaller groups, during a hectic one-week schedule. In most cases, the atmosphere when I entered was tense and chilly, and I was aware that there was a great deal of work to be done.

I went immediately to the point, explaining why we had been forced to proceed without letting them know the date in advance. I dealt with the argument of timing. To the ministers I stressed the need for a social gospel to supplement the gospel of individual salvation. I suggested that only a "dry as dust" religion prompts a minister to extol the glories of heaven while ignoring the social conditions that cause men an earthly hell. I pleaded for the projections of strong, firm leadership by the Negro minister, pointing out that he is freer, more independent, than any other person in the community.

I challenged those who had been persuaded that I was an "outsider." I pointed out that as president of SCLC, I had come in the interests of aiding an SCLC affiliate. I expounded on the weary and worn "outsider" charge, which we have faced in every community where we have gone to try to help. No Negro, in fact, no American, is an outsider when he goes to any community to aid the cause of freedom and justice. No Negro anywhere, regardless of his social standing, his financial status, his prestige and position, is an outsider so long as dignity and decency are denied to the humblest black child in Mississippi, Alabama, or Georgia.

Somehow God gave me the power to transform the resentments, the suspicions, the fears, and the misunderstanding I found that week into faith and enthusiasm. I spoke from my heart, and out of each meeting came firm endorsements and pledges of participation and support. With the new unity that developed, and now poured fresh blood into our protest, the foundations of the old order were doomed. A new order was destined to be born, and not all the powers of bigotry or Bull Connor could abort it.

"At the center of all that my life had brought me to be"

By the end of the first three days of lunch counter sit-ins, there had been thirty-five arrests. On Saturday, April 6, 1963, we began the next stage of our crusade with a march on City Hall. From then on, the daily demonstrations grew stronger. Our boycott of the downtown merchants was proving amazingly effective. A few days before Easter, a careful check showed less than twenty Negroes entering all the stores in the downtown area. Meanwhile, with the number of volunteers increasing daily, we were able to launch campaigns against a variety of additional objectives: kneel-ins at churches; sit-ins at the library; a march on the county building to mark the opening of a voter registration drive. And all the time the jails were slowly but steadily filling up.

Birmingham residents of both races were surprised at the restraint of Connor's men at the beginning of the campaign. True, police dogs and clubs made their debut on Palm Sunday, but their appearance that day was brief, and they quickly disappeared. What observers probably did not realize was that the commissioner was trying to take a leaf from the book of Police Chief Laurie Pritchett of Albany. Chief Pritchett felt that by directing his police to be nonviolent, he had discovered a new way to defeat the demonstrations. Mr. Connor, as it developed, was not to adhere to nonviolence long; the dogs were baying in kennels not far away; the hoses were primed.

A second reason Bull Connor had held off at first was that he thought he had found another way out. This became evident on April 10, when the city government obtained a court injunction directing us to cease our activities until our right to demonstrate had been argued in court. The time had now come for us to counter their legal maneuver with a strategy of our own. Two days later, we did an audacious thing, something we had never done in any other crusade. We disobeyed a court order.

I had intended to be one of the first to set the example of civil disobedience. Ten days after the demonstrations began, between four hundred and five hundred people had gone to jail; some had been released on bail, but about three hundred remained. Now that the job of unifying the Negro community had been accomplished, my time had come. We decided that, because of its symbolic significance, April 12, Good Friday, would be the day that Ralph Abernathy and I would present our bodies as personal witness in this crusade.

STATEMENT ON INJUNCTION

We cannot in all good conscience obey such an injunction which is an unjust, undemocratic, and unconstitutional misuse of the legal process.

We do this not out of any disrespect for the law but out of the highest respect for the law. This is not an attempt to evade or defy the law or engage in chaotic anarchy. Just as in all good conscience we cannot obey unjust laws, neither can we respect the unjust use of the courts.

We believe in a system of law based on justice and morality. Out of our great love for the Constitution of the U.S. and our desire to purify the judicial system of the state of Alabama, we risk this critical move with an awareness of the possible consequences involved.

April 11, 1963

Soon after we announced our intention to lead a demonstration on April 12 and submit to arrest, we received a message so distressing that it threatened to ruin the movement. Late Thursday night, the bondsman who had been furnishing bail for the demonstrators notified us that he would be unable to continue. The city notified him that his financial assets were insufficient. Obviously, this was another move on the part of the city to hurt our cause.

It was a serious blow. We had used up all the money we had on hand for cash bonds. We had a moral responsibility for our people in jail. Fifty more were to go in with Ralph and me. This would be the largest single group to be arrested to date. Without bail facilities, how could we guarantee their eventual release?

Good Friday morning, early, I sat in Room 30 of the Gaston Motel discussing this crisis with twenty-four key people. As we talked, a sense of doom began to pervade the room. I looked about me and saw that for the first time our most dedicated and devoted leaders were overwhelmed by a feeling of hopelessness. No one knew what to say, for no one knew what to do. Finally someone spoke up and, as he spoke, I could see that he was giving voice to what was on everyone's mind.

"Martin," he said, "this means you can't go to jail. We need money. We need a lot of money. We need it now. You are the only one who has the contacts to get it. If you go to jail, we are lost. The battle of Birmingham is lost."

I sat there, conscious of twenty-four pairs of eyes. I thought about the people in the jail. I thought about the Birmingham Negroes already lining the streets of the city, waiting to see me put into practice what I had so passionately preached. How could my failure now to submit to arrest be explained to the local community? What would be the verdict of the country about a man who had encouraged hundreds of people to make a stunning sacrifice and then excused himself?

Then my mind began to race in the opposite direction. Suppose I went to jail? What would happen to the three hundred? Where would the money come from to assure their release? What would happen to our campaign? Who would be willing to follow us into jail, not knowing when or whether he would ever walk out once more into the Birmingham sunshine?

I sat in the midst of the deepest quiet I have ever felt, with two dozen others in the room. There comes a time in the atmosphere of leadership when a man surrounded by loyal friends and allies realizes he has come face-to-face with himself and with ruthless reality. I was alone in that crowded room.

I walked to another room in the back of the suite, and I stood in the center of the floor. I thought I was standing at the center of all that my life had brought me to be. I thought of the twenty-four people, waiting in the next room. I thought of the three hundred, waiting in prison. I thought of the Birmingham Negro community, waiting. Then my tortured mind leaped beyond the Gaston Motel, past the city jail, past the city and state lines, and I thought of the twenty million black people who dreamed that someday they might be able to cross the Red Sea of injustice and find their way into the promised land of integration and freedom. There was no more room for doubt.

I whispered to myself, "I must go."

The doubt, the fear, the hesitation was gone. I pulled off my shirt and pants, got into work clothes, and went back to the other room.

"Friends," I said, "I've made my decision. I have to make a faith act. I don't know what will happen or what the outcome will be. I don't know where the money will come from."

I turned to Ralph Abernathy. "I know you have a need to be in your pulpit on Easter Sunday, Ralph. But I am asking you to take this faith act with me."

As Ralph stood up, unquestioningly, without hesitation, we all linked hands involuntarily, almost as if there had been some divine signal, and twenty-five voices in Room 30 at the Gaston Motel in Birmingham, Alabama, chanted the battle hymn of our movement, "We Shall Overcome."

"Held incommunicado, solitary confinement"

We rode from the motel to the Zion Hill church, where the march would begin. Many hundreds of Negroes had turned out to see us, and great hope grew within me as I saw those faces smiling approval as we passed. It seemed that every Birmingham police officer had been sent into the area. Leaving the church, where we were joined by the rest of our group of fifty, we started down the forbidden streets that lead to the downtown sector. It was a beautiful march. We were allowed to walk farther than the police had ever permitted before. We were singing, and occasionally the singing was interspersed with bursts of applause from the sidewalks.

As we neared the downtown area, Bull Connor ordered his men to arrest us, and somebody from the police force leaned over and reminded Mr. Connor, "Mr. Connor, we ain't got nowhere to put 'em." Ralph and I were hauled off by two muscular policemen, clutching the backs of our shirts in handfuls. All the others were promptly arrested. In jail Ralph and I were separated from everyone else and later from each other.

For more than twenty-four hours, I was held incommunicado, in solitary confinement. No one was permitted to visit me, not even my lawyers. Those were the longest, most frustrating and bewildering hours I have lived. Having no contact of any kind, I was besieged with worry. How was the movement faring? Where would Fred and the other leaders get the money to have our demonstrators released? What was happening to the morale in the Negro community?

I suffered no physical brutality at the hands of my jailers. Some of the prison personnel were surly and abusive, but that was to be expected in Southern prisons. Solitary confinement, however, was brutal enough. In the mornings the sun would rise, sending shafts of light through the window high in the narrow cell which was my home. You will never know the meaning of utter darkness until you have lain in such a dungeon, knowing that sunlight is streaming overhead and still seeing only darkness below. You might have thought I was in the grip of a fantasy brought on by worry. I did worry. But there was more to the blackness than a phenomenon conjured up by a worried mind. Whatever the cause, the fact remained that I could not see the light.

When I had left my Atlanta home some days before, my wife, Coretta, had just given birth to our fourth child. As happy as we were about the new little girl, Coretta was disappointed that her condition would not allow her to accompany me. She had been my strength and inspiration during the terror of Montgomery. She had been active in Albany, Georgia, and was preparing to go to jail with the wives of other civil rights leaders there, just before the campaign ended.

Now, not only was she confined to our home, but she was denied even the consolation of a telephone call from her husband. On the Sunday following our jailing, she decided she must do something. Remembering the call that John Kennedy had made to her when I was jailed in Georgia during the 1960 election campaign, she placed a call to the President. Within a few minutes, his brother, Attorney

General Robert Kennedy, phoned back. She told him that she had learned that I was in solitary confinement and was afraid for my safety. The attorney general promised to do everything he could to have my situation eased. A few hours later President Kennedy himself called Coretta from Palm Beach, and assured her that he would look into the matter immediately. Apparently the President and his brother placed calls to officials in Birmingham; for immediately after Coretta heard from them, my jailers asked if I wanted to call her. After the President's intervention, conditions changed considerably.

◆

TELEGRAM TO PRESIDENT KENNEDY

I AM DEEPLY GRATEFUL TO YOU FOR TAKING TIME OUT OF YOUR EASTER WEEKEND TO TELEPHONE MY WIFE CONCERNING THE BIRMINGHAM SITUATION. YOUR ENCOURAGING WORDS AND THOUGHTFUL CONCERN GAVE HER RENEWED STRENGTH TO FACE THE DIFFICULT MOMENTS THROUGH WHICH WE ARE NOW PASSING. SUCH MORAL SUPPORT GREATLY ENHANCES OUR HUMBLE EFFORTS TO MAKE THE AMERICAN DREAM A REALITY.

April 16, 1963

◆

Meanwhile, on Easter Sunday afternoon, two of our attorneys, Orzell Billingsley and Arthur Shores, had been allowed to visit me. They told me that Clarence B. Jones, my friend and lawyer, would be coming in from New York the following day. When they left, none of the questions tormenting me had been answered. When Clarence Jones arrived the next day, before I could even tell him how happy I was to see him, he said a few words that lifted a thousand pounds from my heart:

"Harry Belafonte has been able to raise fifty thousand dollars for bail bonds. It is available immediately. And he says that whatever else you need, he will raise it."

I found it hard to say what I felt. Jones's message had brought me more than relief from the immediate concern about money, more than gratitude for the loyalty of friends far away, more than confirmation that the life of the movement could not be snuffed out. What silenced me was a profound sense of awe. I was aware of a feeling that had been present all along below the surface of consciousness, pressed down under the weight of concern for the movement: I had never been truly in solitary confinement. God's companionship does not stop at the door of a jail cell. God had been my cellmate. When the decision came—in Room 30 on Good Friday—that we must commit a faith act, God was there. And he was also present in a Fifth Avenue, New York City, apartment where a dedicated young star had worked night and day, telephoning everyone he could think of to demand that they send him some money for bail bonds in Alabama. In the midst of deepest midnight, daybreak had come. I did not know whether the sun was shining at that moment. But I knew that once again I could see the light.

18

LETTER FROM BIRMINGHAM JAIL

*I remember saying in that letter that so often I have been disap-
pointed because we have not received the cooperation of the Church.
I remember saying that so often the Church in our struggle had been
a taillight, rather than a headlight. The Church had so often been
an echo, rather than a voice.*

APRIL 12, 1963
White Birmingham ministers write to King calling for end of
demonstrations

APRIL 16
King writes letter of response

I will never forget that one morning, I think the next morning after
I was placed in the cell in solitary confinement, a newspaper was
slipped in to me. I turned it over and found a kind of advertisement
that had been placed there, taken out by eight clergyman of all of
the major religious faiths in our nation. They were criticizing our
demonstrations. They were calling us extremists. They were calling
us law breakers and believers in anarchy and all of these things. And
when I read it, I became so concerned and even upset and at points
so righteously indignant that I decided to answer the letter.

My response to the published statement by eight fellow clergy-
men from Alabama (Bishop C.C.J. Carpenter, Bishop Joseph A.
Durick, Rabbi Hilton L. Grafman, Bishop Paul Hardin, Bishop
Holan B. Harmon, the Reverend George M. Murray, the Reverend

Edward V. Ramage, and the Reverend Earl Stallings) was composed under somewhat constricting circumstances. I didn't have anything at my disposal like a pad or writing paper. Begun on the margins of the newspaper in which the statement appeared, the letter was continued on scraps of writing paper supplied by a friendly Negro trusty, and concluded on a pad my attorneys were eventually permitted to leave me. I was able to slip it out of the jail to one of my assistants through the lawyer.

Although the text remains in substance unaltered, I have indulged in the author's prerogative of polishing it.

April 16, 1963

MY DEAR FELLOW CLERGYMEN:

While confined here in the Birmingham city jail, I came across your recent statement calling my present activities "unwise and untimely." Seldom do I pause to answer criticism of my work and ideas. If I sought to answer all the criticisms that cross my desk, my secretaries would have little time for anything other than such correspondence in the course of the day, and I would have no time for constructive work. But since I feel that you are men of genuine goodwill and that your criticisms are sincerely set forth, I want to try to answer your statements in what I hope will be patient and reasonable terms.

I think I should indicate why I am here in Birmingham, since you have been influenced by the view which argues against "outsiders coming in." I have the honor of serving as president of the Southern Christian Leadership Conference, an organization operating in every Southern state, with headquarters in Atlanta, Georgia. We have some eight-five affiliated organizations across the South, and one of them is the Alabama Christian Movement for Human Rights. Frequently we share staff, educational and financial resources with our affiliates. Several months ago the affiliate here in Birmingham asked us to be on call to engage in a nonviolent direct-action program if such were deemed necessary. We readily consented, and when the hour came we lived up to our promise. So I, along with several members of my staff, am here because I was invited here. I am here because I have organizational ties here.

But more basically, I am in Birmingham because injustice is here.

Just as the prophets of the eighth century B.C. left their villages and carried their "thus saith the Lord" far beyond the boundaries of their hometowns, and just as the Apostle Paul left his village of Tarsus and carried the gospel of Jesus Christ to the far corners of the Greco-Roman world, so am I compelled to carry the gospel of freedom beyond my own hometown. Like Paul, I must constantly respond to the Macedonian call for aid.

Moreover, I am cognizant of the interrelatedness of all communities and states. I cannot sit idly by in Atlanta and not be concerned about what happens in Birmingham. Injustice anywhere is a threat to justice everywhere. We are caught in an inescapable network of mutuality, tied in a single garment of destiny. Whatever affects one directly, affects all indirectly. Never again can we afford to live with the narrow, provincial "outside agitator" idea. Anyone who lives inside the United States can never be considered an outsider anywhere within its bounds.

You deplore the demonstrations taking place in Birmingham. But your statement, I am sorry to say, fails to express a similar concern for the conditions that brought about the demonstrations. I am sure that none of you would want to rest content with the superficial kind of social analysis that deals merely with effects and does not grapple with underlying causes. It is unfortunate that demonstrations are taking place in Birmingham, but it is even more unfortunate that the city's white power structure left the Negro community with no alternative.

In any nonviolent campaign there are four basic steps: collection of the facts to determine whether injustices exist; negotiation; self-purification; and direct action. We have gone through all these steps in Birmingham. There can be no gainsaying the fact that racial injustice engulfs this community. Birmingham is probably the most thoroughly segregated city in the United States. Its ugly record of brutality is widely known. Negroes have experienced grossly unjust treatment in the courts. There have been more unsolved bombings of Negro homes and churches in Birmingham than in any other city in the nation. These are the hard, brutal facts of the case. On the basis of these conditions, Negro leaders sought to negotiate with the city fathers. But the latter consistently refused to engage in good-faith negotiation.

Then, last September, came the opportunity to talk with leaders of Birmingham's economic community. In the course of the negotiations, certain promises were made by the merchants—for example, to remove the stores' humiliating racial signs. On the basis of these promises, the Reverend Fred Shuttlesworth and the leaders of the Alabama Christian Movement for Human Rights agreed to a moratorium on all demonstrations. As the weeks and months went by, we realized that we were the victims of a broken promise. A few signs, briefly removed, returned; the others remained.

As in so many past experiences, our hopes had been blasted, and the shadow of deep disappointment settled upon us. We had no alternative except to prepare for direct action, whereby we would present our very bodies as a means of laying our case before the conscience of the local and the national community. Mindful of the difficulties involved, we decided to undertake a process of self-purification. We began a series of workshops on nonviolence, and we repeatedly asked ourselves: "Are you able to accept blows without retaliating?" "Are you able to endure the ordeal of jail?" We decided to schedule our direct-action program for the Easter season, realizing that except for Christmas, this is the main shopping period of the year. Knowing that a strong economic-withdrawal program would be the by-product of direct action, we felt that this would be the best time to bring pressure to bear on the merchants for the needed change.

Then it occurred to us that Birmingham's mayoralty election was coming up in March, and we speedily decided to postpone action until after election day. When we discovered that the commissioner of public safety, Eugene "Bull" Connor, had piled up enough votes to be in the run-off, we decided again to postpone action until the day after the run-off so that the demonstrations could not be used to cloud the issues. Like many others, we waited to see Mr. Connor defeated, and to this end we endured postponement after postponement. Having aided in this community need, we felt that our direct-action program could be delayed no longer.

You may well ask: "Why direct action? Why sit-ins, marches, and so forth? Isn't negotiation a better path?" You are quite right in calling for negotiation. Indeed, this is the very purpose of direct action. Nonviolent direct action seeks to create such a crisis and foster such a tension that a community which has constantly refused to negotiate is forced to confront the issue. It seeks to dramatize the issue so that it can no longer be ignored. My citing the creation of tension as part of the work of the nonviolent resister may sound rather shocking. But I must confess that

I am not afraid of the word "tension." I have earnestly opposed violent tension, but there is a type of constructive, nonviolent tension which is necessary for growth. Just as Socrates felt that it was necessary to create a tension in the mind so that individuals could rise from the bondage of myths and half-truths to the unfettered realm of creative analysis and objective appraisal, so must we see the need for nonviolent gadflies to create the kind of tension in society that will help men rise from the dark depths of prejudice and racism to the majestic heights of understanding and brotherhood.

The purpose of our direct-action program is to create a situation so crisis-packed that it will inevitably open the door to negotiation. I therefore concur with you in your call for negotiation. Too long has our beloved Southland been bogged down in a tragic effort to live in monologue rather than dialogue.

One of the basic points in your statement is that the action that I and my associates have taken in Birmingham is untimely. Some have asked: "Why didn't you give the new city administration time to act?" The only answer that I can give to this query is that the new Birmingham administration must be prodded about as much as the outgoing one, before it will act. We are sadly mistaken if we feel that the election of Albert Boutwell as mayor will bring the millennium to Birmingham. While Mr. Boutwell is a much more gentle person than Mr. Connor, they are both segregationists, dedicated to maintenance of the status quo. I have hope that Mr. Boutwell will be reasonable enough to see the futility of massive resistance to desegregation. But he will not see this without pressure from devotees of civil rights. My friends, I must say to you that we have not made a single gain in civil rights without determined legal and nonviolent pressure. Lamentably, it is an historical fact that privileged groups seldom give up their privileges voluntarily. Individuals may see the moral light and voluntarily give up their unjust posture; but, as Reinhold Neibuhr has reminded us, groups tend to be more immoral than individuals.

We know through painful experience that freedom is never voluntarily given by the oppressor; it must be demanded by the oppressed. Frankly, I have yet to engage in a direct-action campaign that was "well timed" in the view of those who have not suffered unduly from the disease of segregation. For years now I have heard the word "Wait!" It rings in the ear of every Negro with piercing familiarity. This "Wait" has almost always meant "Never." We must come to see, with one of our distinguished jurists, that "justice too long delayed is justice denied."

We have waited for more than 340 years for our constitutional and God-given rights. The nations of Asia and Africa are moving with jet-like speed toward gaining political independence, but we still creep at horse-and-buggy pace toward gaining a cup of coffee at a lunch counter. Perhaps it is easy for those who have never felt the stinging darts of segregation to say, "Wait." But when you have seen vicious mobs lynch your mothers and fathers at will and drown your sisters and brothers at whim; when you have seen hate-filled policemen curse, kick, and even kill your black brothers and sisters; when you see the vast majority of your twenty million Negro brothers smothering in an airtight cage of poverty in the midst of an affluent society; when you suddenly find your tongue twisted and your speech stammering as you seek to explain to your six-year-old daughter why she can't go to the public amusement park that has just been advertised on television, and see tears welling up in her eyes when she is told that Funtown is closed to colored children, and see ominous clouds of inferiority beginning to form in her little mental sky, and see her beginning to distort her personality by developing an unconscious bitterness toward white people; when you have to concoct an answer for a five-year-old son who is asking: "Daddy, why do white people treat colored people so mean?"; when you take a cross-county drive and find it necessary to sleep night after night in the uncomfortable corners of your automobile because no motel will accept you; when you are humiliated day in and day out by nagging signs reading "white" and "colored"; when your first name becomes "nigger," your middle names becomes "boy" (however old you are), and your last name becomes "John," and your wife and mother are never given the respected title "Mrs."; when you are harried by day and haunted by night by the fact that you are a Negro, living constantly at tiptoe stance, never quite knowing what to expect next, and are plagued with inner fears and outer resentments; when you are forever fighting a degenerating sense of "nobodiness"—then you will understand why we find it difficult to wait. There comes a time when the cup of endurance runs over, and men are no longer willing to be plunged into the abyss of despair. I hope, sirs, you can understand our legitimate and unavoidable impatience.

You express a great deal of anxiety over our willingness to break laws. This is certainly a legitimate concern. Since we so diligently urge people to obey the Supreme Court's decision of 1954 outlawing segregation in the public schools, at first glance it may seem rather paradoxical for us consciously to break laws. One may well ask: "How can you advocate breaking some laws and obeying others?" The answer lies in the fact that there are two types of laws: just and unjust. I would be the first to advocate obeying just laws. One has not only a legal but a moral responsibility to obey just laws. Conversely, one has a moral responsibility to disobey unjust laws. I would agree with St. Augustine that "an unjust law is no law at all."

Now, what is the difference between the two? How does one determine whether a law is just or unjust? A just law is a man-made code that squares with the moral law or the law of God. An unjust law is a code that is out of harmony with the moral law. To put it in the terms of Saint Thomas Aquinas: an unjust law is a human law that is not rooted in eternal and natural law. Any law that uplifts human personality is just. Any law that degrades human personality is unjust. All segregation statutes are unjust because segregation distorts the soul and damages the personality. It gives the segregator a false sense of superiority and the segregated a false sense of inferiority. Segregation, to use the terminology of the Jewish philosopher Martin Buber, substitutes an "I-it" relationship for an "I-thou" relationship and ends up relegating persons to the status of things. Hence segregation is not only politically, economically, and sociologically unsound, it is morally wrong and sinful. Paul Tillich has said that sin is separation. Is not segregation an existential expression of man's tragic separation, his awful estrangement, his terrible sinfulness? Thus it is that I can urge men to obey the 1954 decision of the Supreme Court, for it is morally right; and I can urge them to disobey segregation ordinances, for they are morally wrong.

Let us consider a more concrete example of just and unjust laws. An unjust law is a code that a numerical or power majority group compels a minority group to obey but does not make binding on itself. This is difference made legal. By the same token, a just law is a code that a majority compels a minority to follow that it is willing to follow itself. This is sameness made legal.

Let me give another explanation. A law is unjust if it is inflicted on a minority that, as a result of being denied the right to vote, had no part in enacting or devising the law. Who can say that the legislature of Alabama which set up that state's segregation laws was democratically elected? Throughout Alabama all sorts of devious methods are used to prevent Negroes from becoming registered voters, and there are some counties in which, even though Negroes constitute a majority of the population, not a single Negro is registered. Can any law enacted under such circumstances be considered democratically structured?

Sometimes a law is just on its face and unjust in its application. For instance, I have been arrested on a charge of parading without a permit. Now, there is nothing wrong in having an ordinance which requires a permit for a parade. But such an ordinance becomes unjust when it is used to maintain segregation and to deny citizens the First Amendment privilege of peaceful assembly and protest.

I hope you are able to see the distinction I am trying to point out. In no sense do I advocate evading or defying the law, as would the rabid segregationist. That would lead to anarchy. One who breaks an unjust law must do so openly, lovingly, and with a willingness to accept the penalty. I submit that an individual who breaks a law that conscience tells him is unjust, and who willingly accepts the penalty of imprisonment in order to arouse the conscience of the community over its injustice, is in reality expressing the highest respect for law.

Of course, there is nothing new about this kind of civil disobedience. It was evidenced sublimely in the refusal of Shadrach, Meshach, and Abednego to obey the laws of Nebuchadnezzar, on the ground that a higher moral law was at stake. It was practiced superbly by the early Christians, who were willing to face hungry lions and the excruciating pain of chopping blocks rather than submit to certain unjust laws of the Roman Empire. To a degree, academic freedom is a reality today because Socrates practiced civil disobedience. In our own nation, the Boston Tea Party represented a massive act of civil disobedience.

We should never forget that everything Adolf Hitler did in Germany was "legal" and everything the Hungarian freedom fighters did in Hungary was "illegal." It was "illegal" to aid and comfort a Jew in Hitler's Germany. Even so, I am sure that, had I lived in Germany at the time, I would have aided and comforted my Jewish brothers. If today I lived in a Communist country where certain principles dear to the Christian faith are suppressed, I would openly advocate disobeying that country's antireligious laws.

I must make two honest confessions to you, my Christian and Jewish brothers. First, I must confess that over the past few years I have been gravely disappointed with the white moderate. I have almost reached the regrettable conclusion that the Negro's great stumbling block in his stride toward freedom is not the White Citizen's Counciler or the Ku Klux Klanner, but the white moderate, who is more devoted to "order" than to justice; who prefers a negative peace which is the absence of tension to a positive peace which is the presence of justice; who constantly says: "I agree with you in the goal you seek, but I cannot agree with your methods of direct action"; who paternalistically believes he can set the timetable for another man's freedom; who lives by a mythical concept of time and who constantly advises the Negro to wait for a "more convenient season." Shallow understanding from people of good will is more frustrating than absolute misunderstanding from people of ill will. Lukewarm acceptance is much more bewildering than outright rejection.

I had hoped that the white moderate would understand that law and order exist for the purpose of establishing justice and that when they fail in this purpose they become the dangerously structured dams that block the flow of social progress. I had hoped that the white moderate would understand that the present tension in the South is a necessary phase of the transition from an obnoxious negative peace, in which the Negro passively accepted his unjust plight, to a substantive and positive peace, in which all men will respect the dignity and worth of human personality. Actually, we who engage in nonviolent direct action are not the creators of tension. We merely bring to the surface the hidden tension that is already alive. We bring it out in the open, where it can be seen and dealt with. Like a boil that can never be cured so long as it is covered up but must be opened with all its ugliness to the natural medicines of air and light, injustice must be exposed, with all the tension its exposure creates, to the light of human conscience and the air of national opinion before it can be cured.

In your statement you assert that our actions, even though peaceful, must be condemned because they precipitate violence. But is this a logical assertion? Isn't this like condemning a robbed man because his possession of money precipitated the evil act of robbery? Isn't this like condemning Socrates because his unswerving commitment to truth and his philosophical inquiries precipitated the act by the misguided populace in which they made him drink hemlock? Isn't this like condemning Jesus because his unique God-consciousness and never-ceasing devotion to God's will precipitated the evil act of crucifixion? We must come to see that, as the federal courts have consistently affirmed, it is wrong to urge an individual to cease his efforts to gain his basic constitutional rights because the quest may precipitate violence. Society must protect the robbed and punish the robber.

I had also hoped that the white moderate would reject the myth concerning time in relation to the struggle for freedom. I have just received a letter from a white brother in Texas. He writes: "All Christians know that the colored people will receive equal rights eventually, but it is possible that you are in too great a religious hurry. It has taken Christianity almost two thousand years to accomplish what it has. The teachings of Christ take time to come to earth." Such an attitude stems from a tragic misconception of time, from the strangely irrational notion that there is something in the very flow of time that will inevitably cure all ills. Actually, time itself is neutral; it can be used either destructively or constructively. More and more I feel that the people of ill will have used time much more effectively than have the people of good will. We will have to repent in this generation not merely for the hateful words and actions of the bad people but for the appalling silence of the good people. Human progress never rolls in on wheels of inevitability; it comes through the tireless efforts of men willing to be co-workers with God, and without this hard work, time itself becomes an ally of the forces of social stagnation. We must use time creatively, in the knowledge that the time is always ripe to do right. Now is the time to make real the promise of democracy and transform our pending national elegy into a creative psalm of brotherhood. Now is the time to lift our national policy from the quicksand of racial injustice to the solid rock of human dignity.

You speak of our activity in Birmingham as extreme. At first I was rather disappointed that fellow clergymen would see my nonviolent efforts as those of an extremist. I began thinking about the fact that I stand in the middle of two opposing forces in the Negro community. One is a force of complacency, made up in part of Negroes who, as a result of long years of oppression, are so drained of self-respect and a sense of "somebodiness" that they have adjusted to segregation; and in part of a few middle-class Negroes who, because of a degree of academic and economic security and because in some ways they profit by segregation, have become insensitive to the problems of the masses. The other force is one of bitterness and hatred, and it comes perilously close to advocating violence. It is expressed in the various black nationalist groups that are springing up across the nation, the largest and best-known being Elijah Muhammad's Muslim movement. Nourished by the Negro's frustration over the continued existence of racial discrimination, this movement is made up of people who have lost faith in America, who have absolutely repudiated Christianity, and who have concluded that the white man is an incorrigible "devil."

I have tried to stand between these two forces, saying that we need emulate neither the "do-nothingism" of the complacent nor the hatred and despair of the black nationalist. For there is the more excellent way of love and nonviolent protest. I am grateful to God that, through the influence of the Negro church, the way of nonviolence became an integral part of our struggle.

If this philosophy had not emerged, by now many streets of the South would, I am convinced, be flowing with blood. And I am further convinced that if our white brothers dismiss as "rabble-rousers" and "outside agitators" those of us who employ nonviolent direct action, and if they refuse to support our nonviolent efforts, millions of Negroes will, out of frustration and despair, seek solace and security in black nationalist ideologies—a development that would inevitably lead to a frightening racial nightmare.

Oppressed people cannot remain oppressed forever. The yearning for freedom eventually manifests itself, and that is what has happened to the American Negro. Something within has reminded him of his birthright of freedom, and something without has reminded him that it can be gained. Consciously or unconsciously, he has been caught up by the Zeitgeist, and with his black brothers of Africa and his brown and yellow brothers of Asia, South America, and the Caribbean, the United States Negro is moving with a sense of great urgency toward the promised land of racial justice. If one recognizes this vital urge that has engulfed the Negro community, one should readily understand why public demonstrations are taking place. The Negro has many pent-up resentments and latent frustrations, and he must release them. So let him march; let him make prayer pilgrimages to the city hall; let him go on freedom rides—and try to understand why he must do so. If his repressed emotions are not released in nonviolent ways, they will seek expression through violence; this is not a threat but a fact of history. So I have not said to my people: "Get rid of your discontent." Rather, I have tried to say that this normal and healthy discontent can be channeled into the creative outlet of nonviolent direct action. And now this approach is being termed extremist.

But though I was initially disappointed at being categorized as an extremist, as I continued to think about the matter I gradually gained a measure of satisfaction from the label. Was not Jesus an extremist for love: "Love your enemies, bless them that curse you, do good to them that hate you, and pray for them which despitefully use you, and persecute you." Was not Amos an extremist for justice: "Let justice roll down like waters and righteousness like an ever-flowing stream." Was not Paul an extremist for the Christian gospel: "I bear in my body the marks of the Lord Jesus." Was not Martin Luther an extremist: "Here I stand; I cannot do otherwise, so help me God." And John Bunyan: "I will stay in jail to the end of my days before I make a butchery of my conscience." And Abraham Lincoln: "This nation cannot survive half slave and half free." And Thomas Jefferson: "We hold these truths to be self-evident, that all men are created equal . . ." So the question is not whether we will be extremists, but what kind of extremists we will be. Will we be extremists for hate or for love? Will we be extremists for the preservation of injustice or for the extension of justice? In that dramatic scene on Calvary's hill three men were crucified. We must never forget that all three were crucified for the same crime—the crime of extremism. Two were extremists for immorality, and thus fell below their environment. The other, Jesus Christ, was an extremist for love, truth, and goodness, and thereby rose above his environment. Perhaps the South, the nation, and the world are in dire need of creative extremists.

I had hoped that the white moderate would see this need. Perhaps I was too optimistic; perhaps I expected too much. I suppose I should have realized that few members of the oppressor race can understand the deep groans and passionate yearnings of the oppressed race, and still fewer have the vision to see that injustice must be rooted out by strong, persistent, and determined action. I am thankful, however, that *some of our white brothers in the South have grasped the meaning of this social revolution and committed themselves to it. They are still too few in quantity, but they are big in quality. Some—such as Ralph Mc-Gill, Lillian Smith, Harry Golden, James McBride Dabbs, Ann Braden, and Sarah Patton Boyle—have written about our struggle in eloquent and prophetic terms. Others have marched with us down nameless streets of the South. They have languished in filthy, roach-infested jails, suffering the abuse and brutality of policemen who view them as "dirty nigger lovers." Unlike so many of their moderate brothers and sisters, they have recognized the urgency of the moment and sensed the need for powerful "action" antidotes to combat the disease of segregation.*

Let me take note of my other major disappointment. I have been so greatly disappointed with the white church and its leadership. Of course, there are some notable exceptions. I am not unmindful of the fact that each of you has taken some significant stands on this issue. I commend you, Reverend Stallings, for your Christian stand on this past Sunday, in welcoming Negroes to your worship service on a nonsegregated basis. I commend the Catholic leaders of this state for integrating Spring Hill College several years ago.

But despite these notable exceptions, I must honestly reiterate that I have been disappointed with the Church. I do not say this as one of those negative critics who can always find something wrong with the Church. I say this as a minister of the gospel, who loves the Church; who was nurtured in its bosom; who has been sustained by its spiritual blessings and who will remain true to it as long as the cord of life shall lengthen.

When I was suddenly catapulted into the leadership of the bus protest in Montgomery, Alabama, a few years ago, I felt we would be supported by the white church. I felt that the white ministers, priests, and rabbis of the South would be among our strongest allies. Instead, some have been outright opponents, refusing to understand the freedom movement and misrepresenting its leaders; all too many others have been more cautious than courageous and have remained silent behind the anesthetizing security of stained-glass windows.

In spite of my shattered dreams, I came to Birmingham with the hope that the white religious leadership of this community would see the justice of our cause and, with deep moral concern, would serve as the channel through which our just grievances could reach the power structure. I had hoped that each of you would understand. But again I have been disappointed.

I have heard numerous Southern religious leaders admonish their worshipers to comply with a desegregation decision because it is the law, but I have longed to hear white ministers declare: "Follow this decree because integration is morally right and because the Negro is your brother." In the midst of blatant injustices inflicted upon the Negro, I have watched white churchmen stand on the sideline and mouth pious irrelevancies and sanctimonious trivialities. In the midst of a mighty struggle to rid our nation of racial and economic injustice, I have heard many ministers say: "Those are social issues, with which the gospel has no real concern." And I have watched many churches commit themselves to a completely otherworldly religion which makes a strange, un-Biblical distinction between body and soul, between the sacred and the secular.

I have traveled the length and breadth of Alabama, Mississippi, and all the other Southern states. On sweltering summer days and crisp autumn mornings I have looked at the South's beautiful churches with their lofty spires pointing heavenward. I have beheld the impressive outlines of her massive religious-education buildings. Over and over I have found myself asking: "What kind of people worship here? Who is their God? Where were their voices when the lips of Governor Barnett dripped with words of interposition and nullification? Where were they when Governor Wallace gave a clarion call for defiance and hatred? Where were their voices of support when bruised and weary Negro men and women decided to rise from the dark dungeons of complacency to the bright hills of creative protest?"

Yes, these questions are still in my mind. In deep disappointment I have wept over the laxity of the Church. But be assured that my tears have been tears of love. There can be no deep disappointment where there is not deep love. Yes, I love the Church. How could I do otherwise? I am in the rather unique position of being the son, the grandson, and the great-grandson of preachers. Yes, I see the Church as the body of Christ. But, oh! How we have blemished and scarred that body through social neglect and through fear of being nonconformists.

There was a time when the Church was very powerful—in the time when the early Christians rejoiced at being deemed worthy to suffer for what they believed. In those days the church was not merely a thermometer that recorded the ideas and principles of popular opinion; it was a thermostat that transformed the mores of society. Whenever the early Christians entered a town, the people in power became disturbed and immediately sought to convict the Christians for being "disturbers of the peace" and "outside agitators." But the Christians pressed on, in the conviction that they were "a colony of heaven," called to obey God rather than man. Small in number, they were big in commitment. They were too God-intoxicated to be "astronomically intimidated." By their effort and example they brought an end to such ancient evils as infanticide and gladiatorial contests.

Things are different now. So often the contemporary Church is a weak, ineffectual voice with an uncertain sound. So often it is an archdefender of the status quo. Far from being disturbed by the presence of the Church, the power structure of the average community is consoled by the Church's silent—and often even vocal—sanction of things as they are.

But the judgment of God is upon the Church as never before. If today's Church does not recapture the sacrificial spirit of the early Church, it will lose its authenticity, forfeit the loyalty of millions, and be dismissed as an irrelevant social club with no meaning for the twentieth century. Every day I meet young people whose disappointment with the Church has turned into outright disgust.

Perhaps I have once again been too optimistic. Is organized religion too inextricably bound to the status quo to save our nation and the world? Perhaps I must turn my faith to the inner spiritual church, the church within the church, as the true ecclesia and the hope of the world. But again I am thankful to God that some noble souls from the ranks of organized religion have broken loose from the paralyzing chains of conformity and joined us as active partners in the struggle for freedom. They have left their secure congregations and walked the streets of Albany, Georgia, with us. They have gone down the highways of the South on tortuous rides for freedom. Yes, they have gone to jail with us. Some have been dismissed from their churches, have lost the support of their bishops and fellow ministers. But they have acted in the faith that right defeated is stronger than evil triumphant. Their witness has been the spiritual salt that has preserved the true meaning of the gospel in these troubled times. They have carved a tunnel of hope through the dark mountain of disappointment.

I hope the Church as a whole will meet the challenge of this decisive hour. But even if the Church does not come to the aid of justice, I have no despair about the future. I have no fear about the outcome of our struggle in Birmingham, even if our motives are at present misunderstood. We will reach the goal of freedom in Birmingham and all over the nation, because the goal of America is freedom. Abused and scorned though we may be, our destiny is tied up with America's destiny. Before the pilgrims landed at Plymouth, we were here. Before the pen of Jefferson etched the majestic words of the Declaration of Independence across the pages of history, we were here. For more than two centuries our forebears labored in this country without wages; they made cotton king; they built the homes of their masters while suffering gross injustice and shameful humiliation—and yet out of a bottomless vitality they continued to thrive and develop. If the inexpressible cruelties of slavery could not stop us, the opposition we now face will surely fail. We will win our freedom because the sacred heritage of our nation and the eternal will of God are embodied in our echoing demands.

Before closing I feel impelled to mention one other point in your statement that has troubled me profoundly. You warmly commended the Birmingham police force for keeping "order" and "preventing violence." I doubt that you would have so warmly commended the police force if you had seen its dogs sinking their teeth into unarmed, nonviolent Negroes. I doubt that you would so quickly commend the policemen if you were to observe their ugly and inhumane treatment of Negroes here in the city jail; if you were to watch them push and curse old Negro women and young Negro girls; if you were to see them slap and kick old Negro men and young boys; if you were to observe them, as they did on two occasions, refuse to give us food because we wanted to sing our grace together. I cannot join you in your praise of the Birmingham police department.

It is true that the police have exercised a degree of discipline in handling the demonstrators. In this sense they have conducted themselves rather "nonviolently" in public. But for what purpose? To preserve the evil system of segregation. Over the past few years I have consistently preached that nonviolence demands that the means we use must be as pure as the ends we seek. I have tried to make clear that it is wrong to use immoral means to attain moral ends. But now I must affirm that it is just as wrong, or perhaps even more so, to use moral means to preserve immoral ends. Perhaps Mr. Connor and his police-men have been rather nonviolent in public, as was Chief Pritchett in Albany, Georgia, but they have used the moral means of nonviolence to maintain the immoral end of racial injustice. As T. S. Eliot has said: "The last temptation is the greatest treason: To do the right deed for the wrong reason."

I wish you had commended the Negro sit-inners and demonstrators of Birmingham for their sublime courage, their willingness to suffer, and their amazing discipline in the midst of great provocation. One day the South will recognize its real heros. They will be the James Merediths, with the noble sense of purpose that enables them to face jeering and hostile mobs, and with the agonizing loneliness that characterizes the life of the pioneer. They will be old, oppressed, battered Negro women, symbolized in a seventy-two-year-old woman in Montgomery, Ala-bama, who rose up with a sense of dignity and with her people decided not to ride segregated buses, and who responded with ungrammatical profundity to one who inquired about her weariness: "My feets is tired, but my soul is at rest." They will be the young high school and college students, the young ministers of the gospel and a host of their elders, courageously and nonviolently sitting in at lunch counters and willingly going to jail for conscience's sake. One day the South will know that when these disinherited children of God sat down at lunch counters, they were in reality standing up for what is best in the American dream and for the most sacred values in our Judeo-Christian heritage, thereby bringing our nation back to those great wells of democracy which were dug deep by the founding fathers in their formulation of the Constitu-tion and the Declaration of Independence.

Never before have I written so long a letter. I'm afraid it is much too long to take your precious time. I can assure you that it would have been much shorter if I had been writing from a comfortable desk, but what else can one do when he is alone in a narrow jail cell, other than write long letters, think long thoughts, and pray long prayers?

If I have said anything in this letter that overstates the truth and indicates an unreasonable impatience, I beg you to forgive me. If I have said anything that understates the truth and indicates my having a patience that allows me to settle for anything less than brotherhood, I beg God to forgive me.

I hope this letter finds you strong in the faith. I also hope that circumstances will soon make it possible for me to meet each of you, not as an integrationist or a civil rights leader but as a fellow clergyman and a Christian brother. Let us all hope that the dark clouds of racial prejudice will soon pass away and the deep fog of misunderstanding will be lifted from our fear-drenched communities, and in some not too distant tomorrow the radiant stars of love and brotherhood will shine over our great nation with all their scintillating beauty.

Yours for the cause of Peace and Brotherhood,

Martin Luther King, Jr.

19

FREEDOM NOW!

I have had many experiences in my relatively young life, but I have never in my life had an experience like I am having in Birmingham, Alabama. This is the most inspiring movement that has ever taken place in the United States of America.

APRIL 19, 1963
King and Ralph Abernathy are released on bond

MAY 2-7
Birmingham police use fire hoses and dogs against "Children's Crusade"; over 1,000 youngsters arrested

MAY 8
Protest leaders suspend mass demonstrations

MAY 11
After tentative settlement is reached, segregationists bomb the Gaston Motel where King was staying and the home of King's brother, the Reverend A. D. King

MAY 13
Federal troops arrive in Birmingham

After eight days of imprisonment, Ralph Abernathy and I accepted bond to come out of jail for two purposes. It was necessary for me to regain communication with the SCLC officers and our lawyers in order to map the strategy for the contempt cases that would be coming up shortly in the circuit court. Also, I had decided to put into operation a new phase of our campaign, which I felt would speed victory.

I called my staff together and repeated a conviction I had been voicing ever since the campaign began. If our drive was to be successful, we must involve the students of the community. Even though we realized that involving teenagers and high school students would bring down upon us a heavy fire of criticism, we felt that we needed this dramatic new dimension. Our people were demonstrating daily and going to jail in numbers, but we were still beating our heads against the brick wall of the city officials' stubborn resolve to maintain the status quo. Our fight, if won, would benefit people of all ages. But most of all we were inspired with the desire to give to our young a true sense of their own stake in freedom and justice. We believed they would have the courage to respond to our call.

"Children understood the stakes"

SCLC staff members James Bevel, Andy Young, Bernard Lee, and Dorothy Cotton began visiting colleges and high schools in the area. They invited students to attend after-school meetings at churches. The word spread fast, and the response from Birmingham's youngsters exceeded our fondest dreams. By the fifties and by the hundreds, these youngsters attended mass meetings and training sessions. They listened eagerly as we talked of bringing freedom to Birmingham, not in some distant time, but right now. We taught them the philosophy of nonviolence. We challenged them to bring their exuberance, their youthful creativity, into the disciplined dedication of the movement. We found them eager to belong, hungry for participation in a significant social effort. Looking back, it is clear that the introduction of Birmingham's children into the campaign was one of the wisest moves we made. It brought a new impact to the crusade, and the impetus that we needed to win the struggle.

Immediately, of course, a cry of protest went up. Although by the end of April the attitude of the national press had changed considerably, so that the major media were according us sympathetic coverage, yet many deplored our "using" our children in this fashion. Where had these writers been, we wondered, during the centuries when our segregated social system had been misusing and abusing Negro children? Where had they been with their protective words when, down through the years, Negro infants were born into ghettos, taking their first breath of life in a social atmosphere where the fresh air of freedom was crowded out by the stench of discrimination?

The children themselves had the answer to the misguided sympathies of the press. One of the most ringing replies came from a child of no more than eight who walked with her mother one day in a demonstration. An amused policeman leaned down to her and said with mock gruffness: "What do you want?"

The child looked into his eyes, unafraid, and gave her answer.

"F'eedom," she said.

She could not even pronounce the word, but no Gabriel trumpet could have sounded a truer note.

Even children too young to march requested and earned a place in our ranks. Once when we sent out a call for volunteers, six tiny youngsters responded. Andy Young told them that they were not old enough to go to jail but that they could go to the library. "You won't get arrested there," he said, "but you might learn something." So these six small children marched off to the building in the white district, where, up to two weeks before, they would have been turned away at the door. Shyly but doggedly, they went to the children's room and sat down, and soon they were lost in their books. In their own way, they had struck a blow for freedom.

The children understood the stakes they were fighting for. I think of one teenage boy whose father's devotion to the movement turned sour when he learned that his son had pledged himself to become a demonstrator. The father forbade his son to participate.

"Daddy," the boy said, "I don't want to disobey you, but I have made my pledge. If you try to keep me home, I will sneak off. If you think I deserve to be punished for that, I'll just have to take the punishment. For, you see, I'm not doing this only because I want to be free. I'm doing it also because I want freedom for you and Mama, and I want it to come before you die."

That father thought again, and gave his son his blessing.

The movement was blessed by the fire and excitement brought to it by young people such as these. And when Birmingham youngsters joined the march in numbers, a historic thing happened. For the first time in the civil rights movement, we were able to put into effect the Gandhian principle: "Fill up the jails."

Jim Bevel had the inspiration of setting a "D" Day, when the students would go to jail in historic numbers. When that day arrived, young people converged on the Sixteenth Street Baptist Church in wave after wave. Altogether on "D" Day, May 2, more than a thousand young people demonstrated and went to jail. At one school, the principal gave orders to lock the gates to keep the students in. The youngsters climbed over the gates and ran toward freedom. The assistant superintendent of schools threatened them with expulsion, and still they came, day after day. At the height of the campaign, by conservative estimates, there were 2,500 demonstrators in jail at one time, a large proportion of them young people.

Serious as they were about what they were doing, these teenagers had that marvelous humor that arms the unarmed in the face of danger. Under their leaders, they took delight in confusing the police. A small decoy group would gather at one exit of the church, bringing policemen streaming in cars and on motorcycles. Before the officers knew what was happening, other groups, by the scores, would pour out of other exits and move, two by two, toward our goal in the downtown section.

Many arrived at their destination before the police could confront and arrest them. They sang as they marched and as they were loaded into the paddy wagons. The police ran out of paddy wagons and had to press sheriff's cars and school buses into service.

Watching those youngsters in Birmingham, I could not help remembering an episode in Montgomery during the bus boycott. Someone had asked an elderly women why she was involved in our struggle.

"I'm doing it for my children and for my grandchildren," she had replied.

Seven years later, the children and grandchildren were doing it for themselves.

"The pride and the power of nonviolence"

With the jails filling up and the scorching glare of national disapproval focused on Birmingham, Bull Connor abandoned his posture of nonviolence. The result was an ugliness too well known to Americans and to people all over the world. The newspapers of May 4 carried pictures of prostrate women, and policemen bending over

STATEMENT AT SIXTEENTH STREET BAPTIST CHURCH

The reason I can't follow the old eye-for-an-eye philosophy is that it ends up leaving everybody blind. Somebody must have sense and somebody must have religion. I remember some years ago, my brother and I were driving from Atlanta to Chattanooga, Tennessee. And for some reason the drivers that night were very discourteous or they were forgetting to dim their lights. . . . And finally A.D. looked over at me and he said, "I'm tired of this now, and the next car that comes by here and refuses to dim the lights, I'm going to refuse to dim mine." I said, "Wait a minute, don't do that. Somebody has to have some sense on this highway and if somebody doesn't have sense enough to dim the lights, we'll all end up destroyed on this highway." And I'm saying the same thing for us here in Birmingham. We are moving up a mighty highway toward the city of Freedom. There will be meandering points. There will be curves and difficult moments, and we will be tempted to retaliate with the same kind of force that the opposition will use. But I'm going to say to you, "Wait a minute, Birmingham. Somebody's got to have some sense in Birmingham."

May 3, 1963

them with raised clubs; of children marching up to the bared fangs of police dogs; of the terrible force of pressure hoses sweeping bodies into the streets.

This was the time of our greatest stress, and the courage and conviction of those students and adults made it our finest hour. We did not fight back, but we did not turn back. We did not give way to bitterness. Some few spectators, who had not been trained in the discipline of nonviolence, reacted to the brutality of the policemen by throwing rocks and bottles. But the demonstrators remained nonviolent. In the face of this resolution and bravery, the moral conscience of the nation was deeply stirred and, all over the country, our fight became the fight of decent Americans of all races and creeds.

The moral indignation which was spreading throughout the land, the sympathy created by the children, the growing involvement of the Negro community—all these factors were mingling to create a certain atmosphere inside our movement. It was a pride in progress and a conviction that we were going to win. It was a mounting

◆

STATEMENT AT MASS MEETING

There are those who write history. There are those who make history. There are those who experience history. I don't know how many historians we have in Birmingham tonight. I don't know how many of you would be able to write a history book, but you are certainly making history and you are experiencing history. And you will make it possible for the historians of the future to write a marvelous chapter. Never in the history of this nation have so many people been arrested for the cause of freedom and human dignity.

May 5, 1963

◆

optimism which gave us the feeling that the implacable barriers that confronted us were doomed and already beginning to crumble. We were advised, in the utmost confidence, that the white business structure was weakening under the adverse publicity, the pressure of our boycott, and a parallel falling-off of white buying.

Strangely enough, the masses of white citizens in Birmingham were not fighting us. This was one of the most amazing aspects of the Birmingham crusade. Only a year or so ago, had we begun such a campaign, Bull Connor would have had his job done for him by murderously angry white citizens. Now, however, the majority were maintaining a strictly hands-off policy. I do not mean to insinuate that they were in sympathy with our cause or that they boycotted stores because we did. I simply suggest that it was powerfully symbolic of shifting attitudes in the South that the majority of the white citizens of Birmingham remained neutral through our campaign. This neutrality added force to our feeling that we were on the road to victory.

On one dramatic occasion even Bull Connor's men were shaken. It was a Sunday afternoon, when several hundred Birmingham Negroes had determined to hold a prayer meeting near the city jail. They gathered at the New Pilgrim Baptist Church and began an orderly march. Bull Connor ordered out the police dogs and fire hoses. When the marchers approached the border between the white and Negro areas, Connor ordered them to turn back. The Reverend Charles Billups, who was leading the march, politely refused. Enraged, Bull Connor whirled on his men and shouted: "Dammit. Turn on the hoses."

What happened in the next thirty seconds was one of the most fantastic events of the Birmingham story. Bull Connor's men stood facing the marchers. The marchers, many of them on their knees, ready to pit nothing but the power of their bodies and souls against Connor's police dogs, clubs, and fire hoses, stared back, unafraid and unmoving. Slowly the Negroes stood up and began to advance. Connor's men, as though hypnotized, fell back, their hoses sagging uselessly in their hands while several hundred Negroes marched past them, without further interference, and held their prayer meeting as planned. I felt there, for the first time, the pride and the power of nonviolence.

"The beginning of the end"

Even though pressure on Birmingham's business community was intense, there were stubborn men in its midst who seemed to feel they would rather see their own enterprises fail than sit across the table and negotiate with our leadership. However, when national pressure began to pile up on the White House, climaxing with the infamous day of May 3, the adminstration was forced to act. On

---

STATEMENT AT BIRMINGHAM MASS MEETING

Don't worry about your children, they're gonna be all right. Don't hold them back if they want to go to jail. For they are doing a job not only for themselves but for all of America and for all mankind. Somewhere we read, "A little child shall lead them." Remember there was another little child just twelve years old and he got involved in a discussion back in Jerusalem. . . . He said, "I must be about my father's business." These young people are about their fathers' business. And they are carving a tunnel of hope through the great mountain of despair. . . . We are going to see that they are treated right, don't worry about that . . . and go on and not only fill up the jails around here, but just fill up the jails all over the state of Alabama if necessary.

May 5, 1963

May 4, the attorney general dispatched Burke Marshall, his chief civil rights assistant, and Joseph F. Dolan, assistant deputy attorney general, to seek a truce in the tense racial situation. Though Marshall had no ultimate power to impose a solution, he had full authority to represent the President in the negotiations. It was one of the first times the federal government had taken so active a role in such circumstances.

I must confess that although I appreciated the fact that the administration had finally made a decisive move, I had some initial misgivings concerning Marshall's intentions. I was afraid that he had come to urge a "cooling off" period—to ask us to declare a one-sided truce as a condition to negotiations. To his credit, Marshall did not adopt such a position. Rather, he did an invaluable job of opening channels of communication between our leadership and the top people in the economic power structure. Said one staunch defender of segregation, after conferring with Marshall: "There is a man who listens. I had to listen back, and I guess I grew up a little."

With Burke Marshall as catalyst, we began to hold secret meetings with the Senior Citizens Committee. At these sessions, unpromising as they were at the outset, we laid the groundwork for the agreement that would eventually accord us all of our major demands.

Meanwhile, however, for several days violence swept through the streets of Birmingham. An armored car was added to Bull Connor's strange armament. And some Negroes, not trained in our nonviolent methods, again responded with bricks and bottles. On one of these days, when the pressure in Connor's hoses was so high that it peeled the bark off the trees, Fred Shuttlesworth was hurled by a blast of water against the side of a building. Suffering injuries in his chest, he was carried away in an ambulance. Connor, when told, responded in characteristic fashion. "I wish he'd been carried away in a hearse," he said. Fortunately, Shuttlesworth was resilient and though still in pain he was back at the conference table the next day.

Terrified by the very destructiveness brought on by their own acts, the city police appealed for state troopers to be brought into the area. Many of the white leaders now realized that something had to be done. Yet there were those among them who were still adamant. But one other incident was to occur that would transform recalcitrance into good faith. On Tuesday, May 7, the Senior Citizens Committee had assembled in a downtown building to discuss our demands. In the first hours of this meeting, they were so intransigent that Burke Marshall despaired of a pact. The atmosphere was charged with tension, and tempers were running high.

In this mood, these 125-odd business leaders adjourned for lunch. As they walked out on the street, an extraordinary sight met their eyes. On that day several thousand Negroes had marched on the town. The jails were so full that the police could only arrest a handful. There were Negroes on the sidewalks, in the streets, standing, sitting in the aisles of downtown stores. There were square blocks of Negroes, a veritable sea of black faces. They were committing no violence; they were just present and singing. Downtown Birmingham echoed to the strains of the freedom songs.

Astounded, these businessmen, key figures in a great city, suddenly realized that the movement could not be stopped. When they returned—from the lunch they were unable to get—one of the men who had been in the most determined opposition cleared his throat and said: "You know, I've been thinking this thing through. We ought to be able to work something out."

That admission marked the beginning of the end. Late that afternoon, Burke Marshall informed us that representatives from the business and industrial community wanted to meet with the movement leaders immediately to work out a settlement. After talking with these men for about three hours, we became convinced that they were negotiating in good faith. On the basis of this assurance we called a twenty-four-hour truce on Wednesday morning.

That day President Kennedy devoted the entire opening statement of his press conference to the Birmingham situation, emphasizing how vital it was that the problems be squarely faced and resolved and expressing encouragement that a dialogue now existed between the opposing sides. Even while the president spoke, the truce was briefly threatened when Ralph and I were suddenly clapped into jail on an old charge. Some of my associates, feeling that they had again been betrayed, put on their walking shoes and prepared to march. They were restrained, however; we were swiftly bailed out, and negotiations were resumed.

After talking all night Wednesday, and practically all day and night Thursday, we reached an accord. On Friday, May 10, this agreement was announced. It contained the following pledges:

1. The desegregation of lunch counters, rest rooms, fitting rooms, and drinking fountains, in planned stages within ninety days after signing.
2. The upgrading and hiring of Negroes on a nondiscriminatory basis throughout the industrial community of Birmingham, to include hiring of Negroes as clerks and salesmen within sixty days after signing of the agreement—and the immediate appointment of a committee of business, industrial, and professional leaders to implement an area-wide program for the acceleration of upgrading and employment of Negroes in job categories previously denied to them.
3. Official cooperation with the movement's legal representatives in working out the release of all jailed persons on bond or on their personal recognizance.
4. Through the Senior Citizens Committee or Chamber of Commerce, communications between Negro and white to be publicly established within two weeks after signing, in order to prevent the necessity of further demonstrations and protests.

I am happy to report to you this afternoon that we have commitments that the walls of segregation will crumble in Birmingham, and they will crumble soon. Now let nobody fool you. These walls are not crumbling just to be crumbling. They are breaking down and falling down, because in this community more people have been willing to stand up for freedom and to go to jail for that freedom than in any city at any time in the United States of America.

"Brutal answer to the pact"

Our troubles were not over. The announcement that a peace pact had been signed in Birmingham was flashed across the world by the hundred-odd foreign correspondents then covering the campaign on the crowded scene. It was headlined in the nation's press and heralded on network television. Segregationist forces within the city were consumed with fury. They vowed reprisals against the white businessmen who had "betrayed" them by capitulating to the cause of Negro equality.

On Saturday night, they gave their brutal answer to the pact. I had not gotten more than two hours' sleep a single night for the past four or five nights. I was about to close my eyes for an evening of good sleep, only to get a telephone call. Following a Ku Klux Klan meeting on the outskirts of town, the home of my brother, the Reverend A. D. King, was bombed. That same night a bomb was planted near the Gaston Motel, a bomb placed so as to kill or seriously wound anyone who might have been in Room 30—my room. Evidently the would-be assassins did not know I was in Atlanta that night.

The bombing had been well timed. The bars in the Negro district close at midnight, and the bombs exploded just as some of Birmingham's Saturday-night drinkers came out of the bars. Thousands of Negroes poured into the streets. Wyatt Walker, my brother, and others urged them to go home, but they were not under the discipline of the movement and were in no mood to listen to counsels of peace. Fighting began. Stones were hurled at the police. Cars were wrecked and fires started. Whoever planted the bombs had *wanted* the Negroes to riot. They wanted the pact upset.

Governor George Wallace's state police and "conservation men" sealed off the Negro area and moved in with their bullies and pistols. They beat numerous innocent Negroes; among their acts of chivalry was the clubbing of the diminutive Anne Walker, Wyatt's wife, as she was about to enter her husband's quarters at the partially bombed-out Gaston Motel. They further distinguished themselves by beating Wyatt when he was attempting to drive back home after seeing his wife to the hospital.

I shall never forget the phone call my brother placed to me in Atlanta that violent Saturday night. His home had just been destroyed. Several people had been injured at the motel. I listened as he described the erupting tumult and catastrophe in the streets of the city. Then, in the background as he talked, I heard a swelling burst of beautiful song. Feet planted in the rubble of debris, threatened by criminal violence and hatred, followers of the movement were singing "We Shall Overcome." I marveled that in a moment of such tragedy the Negro could still express himself with hope and with faith.

The following evening, a thoroughly aroused President told the nation that the federal government would not allow extremists to sabotage a fair and just pact. He ordered three thousand federal troops into position near Birmingham and made preparations to federalize the Alabama National Guard. This firm action stopped the troublemakers in their tracks.

Yet the segregationist diehards were to attempt still once more to destroy the peace. On May 20, the headlines announced that more than a thousand students who had participated in the demonstrations had been either suspended or expelled by the city's Board of Education. I was convinced that this was another attempt to drive the Negro community to an unwise and impulsive move. The plot might have worked; there were some people in our ranks who sincerely felt that, in retaliation, all the students of Birmingham should stay out of school and that demonstrations should be resumed.

I was out of the city at the time, but I rushed back to Birmingham to persuade the leaders that we must not fall into the trap. We decided to take the issue into the courts and did so, through the auspices of the NAACP Legal Defense and Educational Fund. On May 22, the local federal district court judge upheld the Birmingham Board of Education. But that same day, Judge Elbert P. Tuttle, of the Fifth Circuit Court of Appeals, not only reversed the decision of the district judge but strongly condemned the Board of Education for its action. In a time when the nation was trying to solve the problem of school dropouts, Judge Tuttle's ruling indicated, it was an act of irresponsibility to drive those youngsters from school in retaliation for having engaged in a legally permissible action to achieve their constitutional rights. The night this ruling was handed down, we had a great mass meeting. It was a jubilant moment, another victory in the titanic struggle.

The following day, in an appropriate postscript, the Alabama Supreme Court ruled Eugene "Bull" Connor and his fellow commissioners out of office, once and for all.

I could not close an account of events in Birmingham without noting the tremendous moral and financial support which poured in

upon us from all over the world during the six weeks of demonstrations and in the weeks and months to follow. Although we were so
preoccupied with the day-to-day crises of the campaign that we did
not have time to send out a formal plea for funds, letters of encouragement and donations ranging from pennies taken from piggy
banks to checks of impressive size flowed into our besieged command post at the Gaston Motel and our Atlanta headquarters.

One of the most gratifying developments was the unprecedented
show of unity that was displayed by the national Negro community
in support of our crusade. From all over the country came Negro
ministers, civil rights leaders, entertainers, star athletes, and ordinary
citizens, ready to speak at our meetings or join us in jail. The
NAACP Legal Defense and Educational Fund came to our aid several
times both with money and with resourceful legal talent. Many other
organizations and individuals contributed invaluable gifts of time,
money, and moral support.

The signing of the agreement was the climax of a long struggle
for justice, freedom, and human dignity. The millennium still had
not come, but Birmingham had made a fresh, bold step toward
equality.

*Birmingham is by no means miraculously desegregated. There is
still resistance and violence. The last-ditch struggle of a segregationist
governor still soils the pages of current events and it is still necessary for
a harried President to invoke his highest powers so that a Negro child
may go to school with a white child in Birmingham. But these factors
only serve to emphasize the truth that even the segregationists know:
The system to which they have been committed lies on its deathbed.
The only imponderable is the question of how costly they will make the
funeral.*

*I like to believe that Birmingham will one day become a model in
Southern race relations. I like to believe that the negative extremes of
Birmingham's past will resolve into the positive and utopian extreme of
her future; that the sins of a dark yesterday will be redeemed in the
achievements of a bright tomorrow. I have this hope because, once on a
summer day, a dream came true. The city of Birmingham discovered a
conscience.*

20

MARCH ON
WASHINGTON

There can be no doubt, even in the true depths of the most prejudiced minds, that the August 28 March on Washington was the most significant and moving demonstration for freedom and justice in all the history of this country.

JUNE 11, 1963
President Kennedy announces new civil rights proposal

JUNE 12
Assassin kills NAACP leader Medgar Evers

JUNE 22
King meets with Kennedy

AUGUST 28
Addresses the March on Washington for Jobs and Freedom

In the summer of 1963 a great shout for freedom reverberated across the land. It was a shout from the hearts of a people who had been too patient, too long. It was a shout which arose from the North and from the South. It was a shout which reached the ears of a President and stirred him to unprecedented statesmanship. It was a shout which reached the halls of Congress and brought back to the legislative chambers a resumption of the Great Debate. It was a shout which awoke the consciences of millions of white Americans and caused them to examine themselves and to consider the plight of twenty million black disinherited brothers. It was a shout which brought men of God down out of their pulpits, where they had been preaching only a Sunday kind of love, out into the streets to practice a Monday kind of militancy. Twenty million strong, militant, marching blacks, flanked by legions of white allies, were volunteers in an army which had a will and a purpose—the realization of a new and glorious freedom.

The shout burst into the open in Birmingham. The contagion of the will to be free, the spreading virus of the victory which was proven possible when black people stood and marched together with love in their hearts instead of hate, faith instead of fear—that virus spread from Birmingham across the land and a summer of blazing discontent gave promise of a glorious autumn of racial justice. The Negro revolution was at hand.

Birmingham had made it clear that the fight of the Negro could be won if he moved that fight out to the sidewalks and the streets, down to the city halls and the city jails and—if necessary—into the martyred heroism of a Medgar Evers. The Negro revolution in the South had come of age. It was mature. It was courageous. It was epic—and it was in the American tradition, a much delayed salute to the Bill of Rights, the Declaration of Independence, the Constitution, and the Emancipation Proclamation.

The Negro in the North came to the shocking realization that the subtle and hidden discrimination of the North was as humiliating and vicious as the obvious and overt sins of the South. In the South, the shout was being heard for public rights—nondiscrimination in hotels, motels, schools, parks. In the North, the shout was raised for private advancement—the elimination of de facto school segregation, the wiping out of housing and job discrimination. In Chicago, Illinois, intensified situations involving residential bias came to the fore.

Seen in perspective, the summer of 1963 was historic because it witnessed the first offensive in history launched by Negroes along a broad front. The heroic but spasmodic and isolated slave revolts of the antebellum South had fused, more than a century later, into a simultaneous, massive assault against segregation. And the virtues so long regarded as the exclusive property of the white South—gallantry, loyalty, and pride—had passed to the Negro demonstrators in the heat of the summer's battles.

In assessing the summer's events, some observers have tended to diminish the achievement by treating the demonstrations as an end in themselves. The heroism of the march, the drama of the confrontation, became in their minds the total accomplishment. It is true that these elements have meaning, but to ignore the concrete and specific gains in dismantling the structure of segregation is like noticing the beauty of the rain, but failing to see that it has enriched the soil. A social movement that only moves people is merely a revolt. A movement that changes both people and institutions is a revolution.

The summer of 1963 was a revolution because it changed the face of America. Freedom was contagious. Its fever boiled in nearly one thousand cities, and by the time it had passed its peak, many thousands of lunch counters, hotels, parks, and other places of public accommodation had become integrated.

The sound of the explosion in Birmingham reached all the way to Washington, where the Kennedy administration, which had firmly declared that civil rights legislation would have to be shelved for 1963, hastily reorganized its priorities and placed a strong civil rights bill at the top of the top of the Congressional calendar.

"Free in '63"

The thundering events of the summer required an appropriate climax. The dean of Negro leaders, A. Philip Randolph, whose gifts of imagination and tireless militancy had for decades dramatized the civil rights struggle, once again provided the uniquely suitable answer. He proposed a March on Washington to unite in one luminous action all of the forces along the far-flung front.

It took daring and boldness to embrace the idea. The Negro community was firmly united in demanding a redress of grievances, but it was divided on tactics. It had demonstrated its ability to organize skillfully in single communities, but there was no precedent for a convocation of national scope and gargantuan size. Complicating the situation were innumerable prophets of doom who feared that the slightest incidence of violence would alienate Congress and destroy all hope of legislation. Even without disturbances, they were afraid that inadequate support by Negroes would reveal weaknesses that were better concealed.

The debate on the proposal neatly polarized positions. Those with faith in the Negro's abilities, endurance, and discipline welcomed the challenge. On the other side were the timid, confused, and uncertain friends, along with those who had never believed in the Negro's capacity to organize anything of significance. The conclusion was never really in doubt, because the powerful momentum of the revolutionary summer had swept aside all opposition.

The shout had roared across America. It reached Washington, the nation's capital, on August 28 when more than two hundred thousand people, black and white, people of all faiths, people of every condition of life, stood together before the stone memorial to Abraham Lincoln. The enemies of racial justice had not wanted us to come. The enemies of civil rights legislation had warned us not to come. There were dire predictions of mass rioting and dark Southern hints of retaliation.

Even some friends of our cause had honest fears about our coming. The President of the United States publicly worried about the wisdom of such a project, and congressmen from states in which liberality supposedly prevailed broadly hinted that such a march would have no effect on their deliberative process. The sense of purpose which pervaded preparations for the march had an infectious quality that made liberal whites and leaders of great religious organizations realize that the oncoming march could not be stopped. Like some swelling chorus promising to burst into glorious song, the endorsement and pledges of participation began.

Just as Birmingham had caused President Kennedy to completely reverse his priorities with regard to seeking legislation, so the spirit behind the ensuing march caused him to become a strong ally on its execution. The President's reversal was characterized by a generous and handsome new interest not only in seeing the march take place but in the hope that it would have a solid impact on the Congress.

Washington is a city of spectacles. Every four years imposing Presidential inaugurations attract the great and the mighty. Kings, prime ministers, heroes, and celebrities of every description have been feted there for more than 150 years. But in its entire glittering history, Washington had never seen a spectacle of the size and grandeur that assembled there on August 28, 1963. Among the nearly 250,000 people who journeyed that day to the capital, there were many dignitaries and many celebrities, but the stirring emotion came from the mass of ordinary people who stood in majestic dignity as witnesses to their single-minded determination to achieve democracy in their time.

They came from almost every state in the union; they came in every form of transportation; they gave up from one to three days' pay plus the cost of transportation, which for many was a heavy financial sacrifice. They were good-humored and relaxed, yet disciplined and thoughtful. They applauded their leaders generously, but the leaders, in their own hearts, applauded their audience. Many a Negro speaker that day had his respect for his own people deepened as he felt the strength of their dedication. The enormous multitude was the living, beating heart of an indefinitely noble movement. It was an army without guns, but not without strength. It was an army into which no one had to be drafted. It was white, and Negro, and of all ages. It had adherents of every faith, members of every class, every profession, every political party, united by a single ideal. It was a fighting army, but no one could mistake that its most powerful weapon was love.

One significant element of the march was the participation of white churches. Never before had they been so fully, so enthusiastically, so directly involved. One writer observed that the march "brought the country's three major religious faiths closer than any other issue in the nation's peacetime history." I venture to say that no single factor which emerged in the summer of 1963 gave so much momentum to the on-rushing revolution and to its aim of touching the conscience of the nation as the decision of the religious leaders of this country to defy tradition and become an integral part of the quest of the Negro for his rights.

In unhappy contrast, the National Council of the AFL-CIO declined to support the march and adopted a position of neutrality. A number of international unions, however, independently declared their support, and were present in substantial numbers. In addition, hundreds of local unions threw their full weight into the effort.

We had strength because there were so many of us, representing so many more. We had dignity because we knew our cause was just. We had no anger, but we had a passion—a passion for freedom. So we stood there, facing Mr. Lincoln and facing ourselves and our own destiny and facing the future and facing God.

I prepared my speech partially in New York City and partially in Washington, D.C. The night of the twenty-seventh I got in to Washington about ten o'clock and went to the hotel. I thought through what I would say, and that took an hour or so. Then I put the outline together, and I guess I finished it about midnight. I did not finish the complete text of my speech until 4:00 A.M. on the morning of August 28.

Along with other participant speakers, I was requested by the national March on Washington Committee to furnish the press liaison with a summary or excerpts of my intended speech by the late afternoon or evening of August 27. But, inasmuch as I had not completed my speech by the evening before the march, I did not forward any portion of my remarks which I had prepared until the morning of August 28.

"I have a dream"

I started out reading the speech, and read it down to a point. The audience's response was wonderful that day, and all of a sudden this thing came to me. The previous June, following a peaceful assemblage of thousands of people through the streets of downtown Detroit, Michigan, I had delivered a speech in Cobo Hall, in which I used the phrase "I have a dream." I had used it many times before, and I just felt that I wanted to use it here. I don't know why. I hadn't thought about it before the speech. I used the phrase, and at that point I just turned aside from the manuscript altogether and didn't come back to it.

I am happy to join with you today in what will go down in history as the greatest demonstration for freedom in the history of our nation.

Five score years ago, a great American, in whose symbolic shadow we stand today, signed the Emancipation Proclamation. This momentous decree came as a great beacon light of hope to millions of Negro slaves, who had been seared in the flames of withering injustice. It came as a joyous daybreak to end the long night of their captivity.

But one hundred years later, the Negro still is not free. One hun-

dred years later, the life of the Negro is still sadly crippled by the mana-cles of segregation and the chains of discrimination. One hundred years later, the Negro lives on a lonely island of poverty in the midst of a vast ocean of material prosperity. One hundred years later, the Negro is still languished in the corners of American society and finds himself an exile in his own land.

And so we've come here today to dramatize a shameful condition. In a sense, we've come to our nation's capital to cash a check. When the architects of our republic wrote the magnificent words of the Consti-tution and the Declaration of Independence, they were signing a prom-issory note to which every American was to fall heir. This note was a promise that all men, yes, black men as well as white men, would be guaranteed the unalienable rights of "Life, Liberty and the pursuit of Happiness."

It is obvious today that America has defaulted on this promissory note insofar as her citizens of color are concerned. Instead of honoring this sacred obligation, America has given the Negro people a bad check, a check which has come back marked "insufficient funds." But we re-fuse to believe that the bank of justice is bankrupt. We refuse to believe that there are insufficient funds in the great vaults of opportunity of this nation. So we've come to cash this check, a check that will give us upon demand the riches of freedom and the security of justice.

We have also come to this hallowed spot to remind America of the fierce urgency of now. This is no time to engage in the luxury of cooling off or to take the tranquilizing drug of gradualism. Now is the time to make real the promises of democracy. Now is the time to rise from the dark and desolate valley of segregation to the sunlit path of racial jus-tice. Now is the time to lift our nation from the quicksands of racial injustice to the solid rock of brotherhood. Now is the time to make justice a reality for all of God's children.

It would be fatal for the nation to overlook the urgency of the mo-ment. This sweltering summer of the Negro's legitimate discontent will not pass until there is an invigorating autumn of freedom and equality. Nineteen sixty-three is not an end but a beginning. Those who hope that the Negro needed to blow off steam and will now be content will have a rude awakening if the nation returns to business as usual.

There will be neither rest nor tranquility in America until the Negro is granted his citizenship rights. The whirlwinds of revolt will continue *to shake the foundations of our nation until the bright day of justice emerges.*

But there is something that I must say to my people, who stand on the warm threshold which leads into the palace of justice: in the process of gaining our rightful place, we must not be guilty of wrongful deeds. Let us not seek to satisfy our thirst for freedom by drinking from the cup of bitterness and hatred. We must forever conduct our struggle on the high plane of dignity and discipline. We must not allow our creative protest to degenerate into physical violence. Again and again, we must rise to the majestic heights of meeting physical force with soul force.

The marvelous new militancy which has engulfed the Negro community must not lead us to a distrust of all white people, for many of our white brothers, as evidenced by their presence here today, have come to realize that their destiny is tied up with our destiny. They have come to realize that their freedom is inextricably bound to our freedom. We cannot walk alone. And as we walk, we must make the pledge that we shall always march ahead. We cannot turn back.

There are those who are asking the devotees of civil rights, "When will you be satisfied?" We can never be satisfied as long as the Negro is the victim of the unspeakable horrors of police brutality. We can never be satisfied as long as our bodies, heavy with the fatigue of travel, cannot gain lodging in the motels of the highways and the hotels of the cities. We cannot be satisfied as long as the Negro's basic mobility is from a smaller ghetto to a larger one. We can never be satisfied as long as our children are stripped of their selfhood and robbed of their dignity by signs stating "For Whites Only." We cannot be satisfied as long as a Negro in Mississippi cannot vote and a Negro in New York believes he has nothing for which to vote. No, no, we are not satisfied and we will not be satisfied until justice rolls down like waters and righteousness like a mighty stream.

I am not unmindful that some of you have come here out of great trials and tribulations. Some of you have come fresh from narrow jail cells. Some of you have come from areas where your quest for freedom left you battered by the storms of persecution and staggered by the winds of police brutality. You have been the veterans of creative suffering. Continue to work with the faith that unearned suffering is redemptive.

Go back to Mississippi, go back to Alabama, go back to South Caro-

lina, go back to Georgia, go back to Louisiana, go back to the slums and ghettos of our northern cities, knowing that somehow this situation can and will be changed.

Let us not wallow in the valley of despair. I say to you today, my friends: so even though we face the difficulties of today and tomorrow, I still have a dream. It is a dream deeply rooted in the American dream.

I have a dream that one day this nation will rise up and live out the true meaning of its creed—we hold these truths to be self-evident that all men are created equal.

I have a dream that one day on the red hills of Georgia the sons of former slaves and the sons of former slave owners will be able to sit down together at the table of brotherhood.

I have a dream that one day even the state of Mississippi, a state sweltering with the heat of injustice, sweltering with the heat of oppression, will be transformed into an oasis of freedom and justice.

I have a dream that my four little children will one day live in a nation where they will not be judged by the color of their skin but by the content of their character.

I have a dream today!

I have a dream that one day, down in Alabama, with its vicious racists, with its governor having his lips dripping with the words of interposition and nullification; one day right there in Alabama little black boys and black girls will be able to join hands with little white boys and white girls as sisters and brothers.

I have a dream today!

I have a dream that one day every valley shall be exalted, every hill and mountain shall be made low, the rough places will be made plain and the crooked places will be made straight and the glory of the Lord shall be revealed and all flesh shall see it together.

This is our hope. This is the faith that I will go back to the South with. With this faith we will be able to hew out of the mountain of despair a stone of hope.

With this faith we will be able to transform the jangling discords of our nation into a beautiful symphony of brotherhood. With this faith we will be able to work together, to pray together, to struggle together, to go to jail together, to stand up for freedom together, knowing that we will be free one day.

This will be the day, this will be the day when all of God's children

*will be able to sing with new meaning: "My country 'tis of thee, sweet
land of liberty, of thee I sing. Land where my fathers died, land of the
Pilgrim's pride, from every mountainside, let freedom ring!" And if
America is to be a great nation, this must become true.*

*And so let freedom ring from the prodigious hilltops of New Hamp-
shire.*

Let freedom ring from the mighty mountains of New York.

Let freedom ring from the heightening Alleghenies of Pennsylvania.

Let freedom ring from the snow-capped Rockies of Colorado.

Let freedom ring from the curvaceous slopes of California.

But not only that.

Let freedom ring from Stone Mountain of Georgia.

Let freedom ring from Lookout Mountain of Tennessee.

*Let freedom ring from every hill and molehill of Mississippi, from
every mountainside, let freedom ring!*

*And when this happens, when we allow freedom to ring, when we
let it ring from every village and every hamlet, from every state and
every city, we will be able to speed up that day when all of God's children, black men and white men, Jews and Gentiles, Protestants and
Catholics, will be able to join hands and sing in the words of the old
Negro spiritual, "Free at last, free at last. Thank God Almighty, we are
free at last."*

If anyone had questioned how deeply the summer's activities had
penetrated the consciousness of white America, the answer was evident in the treatment accorded the March on Washington by all the
media of communication. Normally Negro activities are the object
of attention in the press only when they are likely to lead to some
dramatic outbreak, or possess some bizarre quality. The march was
the first organized Negro operation that was accorded respect and
coverage commensurate with its importance. The millions who
viewed it on television were seeing an event historic not only because
of the subject but because it was being brought into their homes.

Millions or white Americans, for the first time, had a clear, long
look at Negroes engaged in a serious occupation. For the first time
millions listened to the informed and thoughtful words of Negro
spokesmen, from all walks of life. The stereotype of the Negro suffered a heavy blow. This was evident in some of the comments,

which reflected surprise at the dignity, the organization, and even the wearing apparel and friendly spirit of the participants. If the press had expected something akin to a minstrel show, or a brawl, or a comic display of odd clothes and bad manners, they were disappointed. A great deal has been said about a dialogue between Negro and white. Genuinely to achieve it requires that all the media of communications open their channels wide as they did on that radiant August day.

As television beamed the image of this extraordinary gathering across the border oceans, everyone who believed in man's capacity to better himself had a moment of inspiration and confidence in the future of the human race. And every dedicated American could be proud that a dynamic experience of democracy in the nation's capital had been made visible to the world.

21

◆

DEATH OF ILLUSIONS

Man's inhumanity to man is not only perpetrated by the vitriolic actions of those who are bad. It is also perpetrated by the vitiating inaction of those who are good.

SEPTEMBER 15, 1963
Dynamite blast kills four young black girls in Sunday school at Birmingham's Sixteenth Street Baptist Church

SEPTEMBER 19
King and other civil rights leaders meet with President John F. Kennedy

SEPTEMBER 22
Delivers eulogy for the four children

NOVEMBER 22
Assassination of President Kennedy; Lyndon B. Johnson becomes president

It would have been pleasant to relate that Birmingham settled down after the storm, and moved constructively to justify the hopes of the many who wished it well. It would have been pleasant, but it would not be true. After partial and grudging compliance with some of the settlement terms, the twentieth-century night riders had yet another bloodthirsty turn on the stage. On one horror-filled September morning they blasted the lives from four innocent girls, at Birmingham's Sixteenth Street Baptist Church: Addie Mae Collins, Denise McNair, Carole Robertson, and Cynthia Wesley. Police killed another child in the streets, and hate-filled white youths climaxed the day with the wanton murder of a Negro boy harmlessly riding his bicycle.

I shall never forget the grief and bitterness I felt on that terrible September morning. I think of how a woman cried out crunching through broken glass, "My God, we're not even safe in church!" I think of how that explosion blew the face of Jesus Christ from a stained glass window. I can remember thinking, was it all worth it? Was there any hope?

In Birmingham, which we had believed to be a city redeemed, a crucifixion had taken place. The children were the victims of a brutality which echoed around the world. Where was God in the midst of falling bombs?

In every battle for freedom there are martyrs whose lives are forfeited and whose sacrifice endorses the promise of liberty. The girls died as a result of the Holy Crusade of black men to be free. They were not civil rights leaders, as was Medgar Evers. They were not crusaders of justice, as was William Moore—a Baltimore postman who was gunned down as he sought to deliver the message of democracy to the citadel of injustice. They were youngsters—a tiny bit removed from baby food—and babies, we are told, are the latest news from heaven.

So, children are a glorious promise, and no one could tell what those children could have become—another Mary Bethune or Mahalia Jackson. But, they became the most glorious that they could have become. They became symbols of our crusade. They gave their lives to insure our liberty. They did not do this deliberately. They did it because something strange, something incomprehensible to man is reenacted in God's will, and they are home today with God.

"So they did not die in vain"

Perhaps the poverty of conscience of the white majority in Birmingham was most clearly illustrated at the funeral of the child martyrs. No white official attended. No white faces could be seen save for a pathetically few courageous ministers. More than children were buried that day; honor and decency were also interred.

Our tradition, our faith, our loyalty were taxed that day as we gazed upon the caskets which held the bodies of those children. Some of us could not understand why God permitted death and destruction to come to those who had done no man harm.

This afternoon we gather in the quiet of this sanctuary to pay our last tribute of respect to these beautiful children of God. They entered the stage of history just a few years ago, and in the brief years that they were privileged to act on this mortal stage, they played their parts exceedingly well. Now the curtain falls; they move through the exit; the drama of their earthly life comes to a close. They are now committed back to that eternity from which they came.

These children—unoffending, innocent, and beautiful—were the victims of one of the most vicious, heinous crimes ever perpetrated against humanity.

Yet they died nobly. They are the martyred heroines of a holy crusade for freedom and human dignity. So they have something to say to us in their death. They have something to say to every minister of the gospel who has remained silent behind the safe security of stained-glass windows. They have something to say to every politician who has fed his constitutents the stale bread of hatred and the spoiled meat of racism. They have something to say to a federal government that has compromised with the undemocratic practices of Southern Dixiecrats and the blatant hypocrisy of right-wing Northern Republicans. They have something to say to every Negro who passively accepts the evil system of segregation and stands on the sidelines in the midst of a mighty struggle for justice. They say to each of us, black and white alike, that we must substitute courage for caution. They say to us that we must be concerned not merely about who murdered them, but about the system, the way of life, and the philosophy which produced the murderers. Their death says to us that we must work passionately and unrelentingly to make the American dream a reality.

So they did not die in vain. God still has a way of wringing good out of evil. History has proven over and over again that unmerited suffering is redemptive. The innocent blood of these little girls may well serve as the redemptive force that will bring new light to this dark city. The holy Scripture says, "A little child shall lead them." The death of these little children may lead our whole Southland from the low road of man's inhumanity to man to the high road of peace and brother-hood. These tragic deaths may lead our nation to substitute an aristoc-racy of character for an aristocracy of color. The spilt blood of these innocent girls may cause the whole citizenry of Birmingham to trans-form the negative extremes of a dark past into the positive extremes of a bright future. Indeed, this tragic event may cause the white South to come to terms with its conscience.

So in spite of the darkness of this hour we must not despair. We must not become bitter; nor must we harbor the desire to retaliate with violence. We must not lose faith in our white brothers. Somehow we must believe that the most misguided among them can learn to respect the dignity and worth of all human personality.

May I now say a word to you, the members of the bereaved families. It is almost impossible to say anything that can console you at this difficult hour and remove the deep clouds of disappointment which are floating in your mental skies. But I hope you can find a little conso-lation from the universality of this experience. Death comes to every individual. There is an amazing democracy about death. It is not an aristocracy for some of the people, but a democracy for all of the people. Kings die and beggars die; rich men die and poor men die; old people die and young people die; death comes to the innocent and it comes to the guilty. Death is the irreducible common denominator of all men.

I hope you can find some consolation from Christianity's affirma-tion that death is not the end. Death is not a period that ends the great sentence of life, but a comma that punctuates it to more lofty signifi-cance. Death is not a blind alley that leads the human race into a state of nothingness, but an open door which leads man into life eternal. Let this daring faith, this great invincible surmise, be your sustaining power during these trying days.

"Accomplices to murder"

As did most citizens of the United States, I looked to the White House for solace in this moment of crisis. The White House could never restore the lives of these four unoffending children. But, in my mind and in my heart and in my soul, there was a dream and a hope that out of this unbelievable horror would come lasting good. When the President summoned me and leaders of the Birmingham movement to confer with him, this dream became more poignant and this hope more real.

We come to you today because we feel that the Birmingham situation is so serious that it threatens not only the life and stability of Birmingham and Alabama but our whole nation. The destiny of our nation is involved. We feel that Birmingham has reached a state of civil disorder. There are many things that would justify our coming to this conclusion.

The real problem that we face is this: the Negro community is about to reach a breaking point and a great deal of frustration is there and confusion. And there is a feeling of being alone and not being protected. If you walk the streets, you are not safe; if you stay at home, you are not safe; if you are in church, you are not safe. So that the Negro feels that everywhere he goes that if he remains stationary, he is in danger of some physical problem.

Now this presents a real problem for those of us who find ourselves in leadership positions, because we are preaching the philosophy and method of nonviolence. We have been consistent in standing up for nonviolence. But more and more we are faced with the problem of our people saying, "What's the use?" And we find it a little more difficult to get over nonviolence. And I am convinced that if something isn't done to give the Negro a new sense of hope and a sense of protection, there is a danger we will face the worse race riot we have ever seen in this country.

When I left the White House, I left with an almost audacious faith that, finally, something positive, something definitive, something real would be done by the leadership of this nation to redeem the community in which horror had come to make its home. I exercised what I believed to be a tremendous restraint. In doing so, I acted contrary to the wishes of those who had marched with me in the dangerous campaigns for freedom. I was certain that my silence and restraint were misunderstood by many who were loyal enough not to express their doubts. I did this because I was naive enough to believe that the proof of good faith would emerge.

It became obvious that this was a mistake. It began to become obvious when I realized that the mayor who had wept on television had not even had the common decency to come or to send an emissary to the funerals of these murdered innocents. I looked back and noted that the administration itself endorsed the pattern of segregation by having separate—and I wonder if they were equal—meetings with the white and colored leadership. The presidential envoys seemed to believe that, by meeting with white people at one hour and Negroes at another, they could bring about a redemptive understanding. This, we knew, they could not do. This, surely, the President must have understood, was impossible.

CHRISTMAS LETTER TO THE FAMILY OF DENISE MCNAIR

Dear Mr. and Mrs. McNair:

Here in the midst of the Christmas season my thoughts have turned to you. This has been a difficult year for you. The coming Christmas, when the family bonds are normally more closely knit, makes the loss you have sustained even more painful. Yet, with the sad memories there are the memories of the good days when Denise was with you and your family.

As you know, many of us are giving up our Christmas as a memorial for the great sacrifices made this year in the Freedom Struggle. I know there is nothing that can compensate for the vacant place in your family circle, but we did want to share a part of our sacrifice this year with you. Perhaps there is some small thing dear to your heart in which this gift can play a part.

We knew, when we went into Birmingham, that this was the test, the acid test of whether the Negro Revolution would succeed. If the forces of reaction which were seeking to nullify and cancel out all of the gains made in Birmingham were allowed to triumph, the day was lost in this battle for freedom. We were faced with an extreme situation, and our remedies had to be extreme.

I fear that, from the White House down to the crocodile-weeping city administration of Birmingham, the intent and the intensity of the Negro has been misunderstood. So, I must serve notice on this nation, I must serve notice on the White House. I must serve notice on the city administration of Birmingham. I must serve notice on the conscience of the American people. On August 28, we had marched on our capital. It was a peaceful march; it was a quiet march; it was a tranquil march. And I am afraid that some people, from the White House down, misunderstood the peace and the quiet and the tranquility of that march.

They must have believed that it meant that the Revolution was all over,
that its fires were quenched, that its marvelous militancy had died.
They could have made no greater error. Our passion to be free; our
determination to walk with dignity and justice have never abated. We
are more determined than ever before that nonviolence is the way. Let
them bring on their bombs. Let them sabotage us with the evil of coop-
eration with segregation. We intend to be free.

"Assassinated by a morally inclement climate"

Negroes tragically know political assassination well. In the life of
Negro civil rights leaders, the whine of the bullet from ambush,
the roar of the bomb have all too often broken the night's silence.
They have replaced lynching as a political weapon. More than a dec-
ade ago, sudden death came to Mr. and Mrs. Harry T. Moore,
NAACP leaders in Florida. The Reverend George Lee of Belzoni,
Mississippi, was shot to death on the steps of a rural courthouse.
The bombings multiplied. Nineteen sixty-three was a year of assassi-
nations. Medgar Evers in Jackson, Mississippi; William Moore in
Alabama; six Negro children in Birmingham—and who could doubt
that these too were political assassinations?

The unforgivable default of our society has been its failure to
apprehend the assassins. It is a harsh judgment, but undeniably true,
that the cause of the indifference was the identity of the victims.
Nearly all were Negroes. And so the plague spread until it claimed
the most eminent American, a warmly loved and respected President. The words of Jesus, "Inasmuch as ye have done it unto one of
the least of these my brethren, ye have done it unto me" were more
than a figurative expression; they were a literal prophecy.

Men everywhere were stunned into sober confusion at the news
of the assassination of President Jack Kennedy. We watched the
thirty-fifth President of our nation go down like a great cedar. The
personal loss was deep and crushing; the loss to the world was over-
powering. It is still difficult to believe that one so saturated with vim,
vitality, and vigor is no longer in our midst.

President Kennedy was a strongly contrasted personality. There
were in fact two John Kennedys. One presided in the first two years
under pressure of the uncertainty caused by his razor-thin margin

of victory. He vacillated, trying to sense the direction his leadership could travel while retaining and building support for his administration. However, in 1963, a new Kennedy had emerged. He had found that public opinion was not in a rigid mold. American political thought was not committed to conservatism, nor radicalism, nor moderation. It was above all fluid. As such it contained trends rather than hard lines, and affirmative leadership could guide it into constructive channels.

President Kennedy was not given to sentimental expressions of feeling. He had, however, a deep grasp of the dynamics of and the necessity for social change. His work for international amity was a bold effort on a world scale. His last speech on race relations was the most earnest, human, and profound appeal for understanding and justice that any President has uttered since the first days of the republic. Uniting his flair for leadership with a program of social progress, he was at his death undergoing a transformation from a hesitant leader with unsure goals to a strong figure with deeply appealing objectives.

The epitaph of John Kennedy reveals that he was a leader unafraid of change. He came to the presidency in one of the most turbulent and cataclysmic periods of human history, a time when the problems of the world were gigantic in intent and chaotic in detail. On the international scene there was the ominous threat of mankind being plunged into the abyss of nuclear annihilation. On the domestic scene the nation was reaping the harvest of its terrible injustice toward the Negro. John Kennedy met these problems with a depth of concern, a breath of intelligence, and a keen sense of history. He had the courage to be a friend of civil rights and a stalwart advocate of peace. The unmistakable cause of the sincere grief expressed by so many millions was more than simple emotion. It revealed that President Kennedy had become a symbol of people's yearnings for justice, economic well-being, and peace.

Our nation should do a great deal of soul-searching as a result of President Kennedy's assassination. The shot that came from the fifth-story building cannot be easily dismissed as the isolated act of a madman. Honesty impels us to look beyond the demented mind that executed this dastardly act. While the question "Who killed President

Kennedy?" is important, the question "What killed him?" is more important.

Our late President was assassinated by a morally inclement climate. It is a climate filled with heavy torrents of false accusation, jostling winds of hatred, and raging storms of violence.

It is a climate where men cannot disagree without being disagreeable, and where they express dissent through violence and murder. It is the same climate that murdered Medgar Evers in Mississippi and six innocent Negro children in Birmingham, Alabama.

So in a sense we are all participants in that horrible act that tarnished the image of our nation. By our silence, by our willingness to compromise principle, by our constant attempt to cure the cancer of racial injustice with the Vaseline of gradualism, by our readiness to allow arms to be purchased at will and fired at whim, by allowing our movie and television screens to teach our children that the hero is one who masters the art of shooting and the technique of killing, by allowing all these developments, we have created an atmosphere in which violence and hatred have become popular pastimes.

So President Kennedy has something important to say to each of us in his death. He has something to say to every politician who has fed his constituents the stale bread of racism and the spoiled meat of hatred. He has something to say to every clergyman who observed racial evils and remained silent behind the safe security of stained glass windows. He has something to say to the devotees of the extreme right who poured out venomous words against the Supreme Court and the United Nations, and branded everyone a communist with whom they disagree. He has something to say to a misguided philosophy of communism that would teach man that the end justifies the means, and that violence and the denial of basic freedom are justifiable methods to achieve the goal of a classless society.

He says to all of us that this virus of hate that has seeped into the veins of our nation, if unchecked, will lead inevitably to our moral and spiritual doom.

Thus the epitaph of John Kennedy's life illuminates profound truths that challenge us to set aside our grief of a season and move forward with more determination to rid our nation of the vestiges of racial segregation and discrimination.

The assassination of President Kennedy killed not only a man but a complex of illusions. It demolished the myth that hate and violence can be confined in an airtight chamber to be employed against but a few. Suddenly the truth was revealed that hate is a contagion; that it grows and spreads as a disease; that no society is so healthy that it can automatically maintain its immunity. If a smallpox epidemic had been raging in the South, President Kennedy would have been urged to avoid the area. There was a plague afflicting the South, but its perils were not perceived.

We were all involved in the death of John Kennedy. We tolerated hate; we tolerated the sick simulation of violence in all walks of life; and we tolerated the differential application of law, which said that a man's life was sacred only if we agreed with his views. This may explain the cascading grief that flooded the country in late November. We mourned a man who had become the pride of the nation, but we grieved as well for ourselves because we knew we were sick.

22

ST. AUGUSTINE

The bill now pending in Congress is the child of a storm, the product of the most turbulent motion the nation has ever known in peace-time.

FEBRUARY 9, 1964
Segregationist violence prompts St. Augustine, Florida, civil rights leader Robert Hayling to invite SCLC to join struggle

MAY 28
After the jailing of hundreds of demonstrators in St. Augustine, King appeals for outside assistance

JUNE 11
After King's arrest in St. Augustine, bi-racial committee is formed

JUNE
Why We Can't Wait is published

JULY 2
Attends the signing of Civil Rights Act of 1964

When 1963 came to a close, more than a few skeptical voices asked what substantial progress had been achieved through the demonstrations that had drawn more than a million Negroes into the streets. By the close of 1964, the pessimistic clamor was stilled by the music of major victories. Taken together, the two years marked a historical turning point for the civil rights movement; in the previous century no comparable change for the Negro had occurred. Now, even the most cynical acknowledged that at Birmingham, as at Concord, a shot had been fired that was heard around the world.

In the bursting mood that had overtaken the Negro, the words "compromise" and "retreat" were profane and pernicious. Our revolution was genuine because it was born from the same womb that always gives birth to massive social upheavals—the womb of intolerable conditions and unendurable situations. The Negro was determined to liberate himself. His cry for justice had hardened into a palpable, irresistible force. He was unwilling to retrogress or even mark time.

The mainstay of the SCLC program was still in the area of nonviolent direct action. Our feeling was that this method, more than any other, was the best way to raise the problems of the Negro people and the injustices of our social order before the court of world opinion, and to require action.

"Four Hundred Years of Bigotry and Hate"

St. Augustine, Florida, a beautiful town and our nation's oldest city, was the scene of raging tempers, flaring violence, and the most corrupt coalition of segregationist opposition outside of Mississippi. It was a stronghold of the Ku Klux Klan and the John Birch Society. There the Klan made a last-ditch stand against the nonviolent movement. They flocked to St. Augustine's Slave Market Plaza from all across north Florida, Georgia, and Alabama. Klansmen abducted four Negroes and beat them unconscious with clubs, ax handles, and pistol butts.

Florida responded out of a concern for its tourist trade. But when Governor Bryant realized that justice was the price to be paid for a good image, he resorted to the Old South line of attempting to crush those seeking their constitutional rights. Only Judge Bryan Simpson of the federal district court, a Republican appointee, proved to be free enough of the "system" to preserve constitutional rights for St. Augustine's Negroes.

SCLC came to St. Augustine at the request of the local unit which was seeking: (1) a bi-racial committee; (2) desegregation of public accommodations; (3) hiring of policemen, firemen, and office workers in municipal jobs; and (4) dropping of charges against persons peacefully protesting for their constitutional rights.

St. Augustine was a testing ground. Can the Deep South change?

Could southern states maintain law and order in the face of change? Could local citizens, black and white, work together to make democracy a reality throughout America? These were the questions the nonviolent movement sought to answer with a resounding: "Yes— God willing!"

Once in St. Augustine, SCLC uncovered a sore of hatred, violence, and ignorance which spread its venom throughout the business and political life of Florida and reached subtly into the White House. St. Augustine's 3,700 Negro citizens waged a heroic campaign in the midst of savage violence and brutality condoned and committed by police. We faced some lawlessness and violence that we hadn't faced before, even in Birmingham. Night after night, Negroes marched by the hundreds amidst showers of bricks, bottles, and insults. Day by day, Negroes confronted restaurants, beaches, and the Slave Market where they spoke and sang of their determination to be free.

After several months of raging violence in America's oldest city, in which more than three hundred SCLC-led demonstrators were arrested and scores of others injured by Klansmen wielding tire chains and other weapons, we were able to proclaim a relative victory in that rock-bound bastion of segregation and discrimination.

In combination with the local defense fund, we began to pave the way for compliance with the civil rights bill and rush through its passage. The legal and action strategies together had given us a body of precedent for dealing with hard-core communities who allowed vigilante mobs to preserve the Old South traditions.

We communicated with state and federal officials concerning conditions in St. Augustine. After tireless efforts, we succeeded in getting the governor of the state to persuade four distinguished citizens of St. Augustine to serve on a biracial committee to discuss ways to solve the racial problems of St. Augustine. In order to demonstrate our good faith, and show that we were not seeking to wreck St. Augustine, as some mistakenly believed, we agreed to call off demonstrations while the committee sought to work out a settlement. As the saying goes, "Every thousand-mile journey begins with the first step." This development was merely the first step in a long journey toward freedom and justice in St. Augustine, but it was an

important first step, for it at least opened the channels of communication—something that St. Augustine needed for so long.

When we left St. Augustine, we were about to get a civil rights
bill that would become the law of the land. The Civil Rights Act was
signed by President Lyndon Johnson two days before the Fourth of
July. The businessmen in St. Augustine said before we left that they
would comply with the civil rights bill, and we were very happy
about this. It represented a degree of progress, and I said to myself
maybe St. Augustine is now coming to terms with its conscience.

"A legislative achievement of rare quality"

Both houses of Congress approved a monumental, indeed, historic
affirmation of Jefferson's ringing truth that "all men are created
equal." First recommended and promoted by President Kennedy,
this bill was passed because of the overwhelming support and perse-
verance of millions of Americans, Negro and white. It came as a
bright interlude in the long and sometimes turbulent struggle for
civil rights: the beginning of a second emancipation proclamation
providing a comprehensive legal basis for equality of opportunity.
With the bill's passage, we stood at an auspicious position, a momentous time for thanksgiving and rededication, rather than intoxi-
cation and relaxation. The bill was born of the "blood, sweat, toil,
and tears" of countless congressmen of both major parties, legions
of amateur lobbyists, and great volumes of grassroots sentiment.
Supporters, black and white, did themselves honor as they sowed the
seeds of protest and political persuasion, reaping this glorious harvest in law. Furthermore, the bill's germination could be traced to
the Negro revolt of 1963, epitomized in Birmingham's fire hoses,
police dogs, and thousands of "not-to-be-denied" demonstrations;
to the massive militancy of the majestic March on Washington; to a
martyred President; to his successor, a Southern-sired President who
carried on and enhanced the Kennedy legacy; and to the memories
of bygone martyrs whose blood was shed so that America might find
remission for her sins of segregation.

I had been fortunate enough to meet Lyndon Johnson during his
tenure as vice president. He was not then a presidential aspirant, and
he was searching for his role under a man who not only had a four-

year term to complete but was confidently expected to serve out yet another term as chief executive. Therefore, the essential issues were easier to reach, and were unclouded by political considerations.

His approach to the problem of civil rights was not identical with mine—nor had I expected it to be. Yet his careful practicality was nonetheless clearly no mask to conceal indifference. His emotional and intellectual involvement were genuine and devoid of adornment. It was conspicuous that he was searching for a solution to a problem he knew to be a major shortcoming in American life. I came away strengthened in my conviction that an undifferentiated approach to white Southerners could be a grave error, all too easy for Negro leaders in the heat of bitterness. Later, it was Vice President Johnson I had in mind when I wrote in *The Nation* that the white South was splitting, and that progress could be furthered by driving a wedge between the rigid segregationists and the new white elements whose love of their land was stronger than the grip of old habits and customs.

The dimensions of Johnson's leadership spread from a region to a nation. His expressions, public and private, indicated that he had a comprehensive grasp of contemporary problems. He saw that poverty and unemployment were grave and growing catastrophes, and he was aware that those caught most fiercely in the grip of this economic holocaust were Negroes. Therefore, he had set the twin goal of a battle against discrimination within the war on poverty.

I had no doubt that we might continue to differ concerning the tempo and the tactical design required to combat the impending crisis. But I did not doubt that the President was approaching the solution with sincerity, with realism, and thus far with wisdom. I hoped his course would be straight and true. I would do everything in my power to make it so by outspoken agreement whenever proper, and determined opposition whenever necessary.

I had the good fortune of standing there with President Johnson when he signed that bill. Certainly one of the things that I will hold among my most cherished possessions is the pen that President Johnson used to sign this bill. It was a great moment. The legislature had joined the judiciary's long line of decisions invalidating state-compelled segregation, and the office of the President with its great tradition of executive actions, including Lincoln's Emancipation

Proclamation, Roosevelt's war decree banning employment discrimination, Truman's mandate ending segregated Armed Forces units, and Kennedy's order banning discrimination in federally aided housing.

"Legislation was first written in the streets"

Would the slower processes of legislation and law enforcement ultimately have accomplished greater results more painlessly? Demonstrations, experience has shown, are part of the process of stimulating legislation and law enforcement. The federal government reacts to events more quickly when a situation of conflict cries out for its intervention. Beyond this, demonstrations have a creative effect on the social and psychological climate that is not matched by the legislative process. Those who have lived under the corrosive humiliation of daily intimidation are imbued by demonstrations with a sense of courage and dignity that strengthen their personalities. Through demonstrations, Negroes learn that unity and militance have more force than bullets. They find that the bruises of clubs, electric cattle prods, and fists hurt less than the scars of submission. And segregationists learn from demonstrations that Negroes who have been taught to fear can also be taught to be fearless. Finally, the millions of Americans on the sidelines learn that inhumanity wears an official badge and wields the power of law in large areas of the democratic nation of their pride.

What specifically did we accomplish in 1963–64? The Civil Rights Act of 1964 is important even beyond its far-reaching provisions. It is historic because its enhancement was generated by a massive coalition of white and Negro forces. Congress was aroused from a century of slumber to a legislative achievement of rare quality. These multitudinous sponsors to its enactment explain why sections of the Civil Rights Act were complied with so hastily even in some hard-core centers of the South.

The Civil Rights Act was expected by many to suffer the fate of the Supreme Court decisions on school desegregation. In particular, it was thought that the issue of public accommodations would encounter massive defiance. But this pessimism overlooked a factor of supreme importance. The legislation was not a product of the charity of white America for a supine black America, nor was it the result of enlightened leadership by the judiciary. This legislation was first written in the streets. The epic thrust of the millions of Negroes who demonstrated in 1963 in hundreds of cities won strong white allies to the cause. Together they created a "coalition of conscience" which awoke a hitherto somnolent Congress. The legislation was polished and refined in the marble halls of Congress, but the vivid marks of its origin in the turmoil of mass meetings and marches were on it, and the vigor and momentum of its turbulent birth carried past the voting and insured substantial compliance.

Apart from its own provisions, the new law stimulated and focused attention on economic needs. An assault on poverty was planned. The fusing of economic measures with civil rights needs; the boldness to penetrate every region of the Old South; and the undergirding of the whole by the massive Negro vote, both North and South, all placed the freedom struggle on a new elevated level.

23

THE MISSISSIPPI
CHALLENGE

The future of the United States of America may well be determined here, in Mississippi, for it is here that Democracy faces its most serious challenge. Can we have government in Mississippi which represents all of the people? This is the question that must be answered in the affirmative if these United States are to continue to give moral leadership to the Free World.

JUNE 21, 1964
On the eve of the "Freedom Summer" campaign in Mississippi, three civil rights workers are reported missing after their arrest in Philadelphia, Mississippi

JULY 16
King asserts that nomination of Senator Barry Goldwater by Republicans will aid racists

JULY 20
Arrives in Mississippi to assist civil rights effort

AUGUST 4
The bodies of missing civil rights workers are discovered

AUGUST 22
Testifies at Democratic convention on behalf of Mississippi Freedom Democratic Party

In 1964 the meaning of so-called Negro revolution became clear for all to see and was given legislative recognition in the civil rights law. Yet, immediately following the passage of this law, a series of events shook the nation, compelling the grim realization that the revolution would continue inexorably until total slavery had been replaced by total freedom.

The new events to which I refer were: the Republican Convention held in San Francisco; the hideous triple lynchings in Mississippi; and the outbreak of riots in several Northern cities.

The Republican Party geared its appeal and program to racism, reaction, and extremism. All people of goodwill viewed with alarm and concern the frenzied wedding at the Cow Palace of the KKK with the radical right. The "best man" at this ceremony was a senator whose voting record, philosophy, and program were anathema to all the hard-won achievements of the past decade.

It was both unfortunate and disastrous that the Republican Party nominated Barry Goldwater as its candidate for President of the United States. In foreign policy Mr. Goldwater advocated a narrow nationalism, a crippling isolationism, and a trigger-happy attitude that could plunge the whole world into the dark abyss of annihilation. On social and economic issues, Mr. Goldwater represented an unrealistic conservatism that was totally out of touch with the realities of the twentieth century. The issue of poverty compelled the attention of all citizens of our country. Senator Goldwater had neither the concern nor the comprehension necessary to grapple with this problem of poverty in the fashion that the historical moment dictated. On the urgent issue of civil rights, Senator Goldwater represented a philosophy that was morally indefensible and socially suicidal. While not himself a racist, Mr. Goldwater articulated a philosophy which gave aid and comfort to the racist. His candidacy and philosophy would serve as an umbrella under which extremists of all stripes would stand. In the light of these facts and because of my love for America, I had no alternative but to urge every Negro and white person of goodwill to vote against Mr. Goldwater and to withdraw support from any Republican candidate that did not publicly disassociate himself from Senator Goldwater and his philosophy.

While I had followed a policy of not endorsing political candidates, I felt that the prospect of Senator Goldwater being President of the United States so threatened the health, morality, and survival of our nation, that I could not in good conscience fail to take a stand against what he represented.

The celebration of final enactment of the civil rights bill curdled and soured. Rejoicing was replaced by a deep and frightening concern that the counter-forces to Negro liberation could flagrantly nominate for the highest office in the land one who openly clasped the racist hand of Strom Thurmond. A cold fear touched the hearts of twenty million Negroes. They had only begun to come out of the dark land of Egypt where so many of their brothers were still in bondage—still denied elementary dignity. The forces to bar the freedom road, to drive us back to Egypt, seemed so formidable, so high in authority, and so determined.

"Mississippi's New Negroes"

A handsome young Negro, dressed in slacks and short-sleeve shirt, wiped his brow and addressed the police chief, "Now look here, chief, there's no need in trying to blow at us. Everybody scared of white folks has moved north, and you just as well realize that you've got to do right by the rest of us."

This comment by Aaron Henry of Clarksdale, Mississippi, was typical of Mississippi's New Negroes. And in spite of the threat of death, economic reprisals, and continuous intimidation, they were pressing hard toward the high call of freedom.

The remarkable thing was that the Negro in Mississippi had found for himself an effective way to deal with his problems and had organized efforts across the entire state. As part of SCLC's "people-to-people" program, several members of our staff and I had traveled the fertile and sometimes depressing Mississippi Delta country in 1962. That trip provided me with an opportunity to talk with thousands of people on a personal basis. I talked with them on the farms and in the village stores, on the city streets and in the city churches. I listened to their problems, learned of their fears, felt the yearnings of their hope.

There were some flesh-and-blood scenes that I can never dispel from my memory. One of our earliest stops was a Catholic school that included the elementary and high school grades. The sister in charge in each classroom asked the question, "Where are you going tonight?" The answer was chorused, "To the Baptist Church!" They were referring to the Baptist Church where I was to speak for the mass meeting. The sister had urged them to attend. How marvelous that the struggle for freedom and human dignity rose above the communions of Catholic and Protestant. This was a bit of the hope that I glimpsed in the Mississippi Delta. Then, of course, there was the pathos. How sobering it was to meet people who work only six months in the year and whose annual income averaged $500 to $600.

Along with the economic exploitation that the whole state of Mississippi inflicts upon the Negro, there was the ever-present problem of physical violence. As we rode along the dusty roads of the Delta country, our companions cited unbelievable cases of police brutality and incidents of Negroes being brutally murdered by white mobs.

In spite of this, there was a ray of hope. This ray of hope was seen in the new determination of the Negroes themselves to be free.

Under the leadership of Bob Moses, a team of more than a thousand Northern white students and local Negro citizens had instituted a program of voter registration and political action that was one of the most creative attempts I had seen to radically change the oppressive life of the Negro in that entire state and possibly the entire nation. The Negroes in Mississippi had begun to learn that change would come in that lawless, brutal police state only as Negroes reformed the political structure of the area. They had begun this reform in 1964 through the Freedom Democratic Party.

The enormity of the task was inescapable. We would have had to put the field staffs of SCLC, NAACP, CORE, SNCC, and a few other agencies to work in the Delta alone. However, no matter how big and difficult a task it was, we began. We encouraged our people in Mississippi to rise up by the hundreds and thousands and demand their freedom—now!

Nothing had inspired me so much for some time as my tour of Mississippi in July 1964 on behalf of the Mississippi Freedom Democratic Party. These were a great people who had survived a concentration camp existence by the sheer power of their souls. They had no money, no guns, very few votes and yet they were then the number-one power in the nation; for they were organized and moving by the thousands to rid the nation of its most violent racist element.

When I was about to visit Mississippi, I was told that a sort of guerrilla group was plotting to take my life during the visit. I was urged to cancel the trip, but I decided that I had no alternative but to go on into Mississippi, because I had a job to do. If I were constantly worried about death, I could not function. After a while, if your life is more or less constantly in peril, you come to a point where you accept the possibility of death philosophically.

We landed in Greenwood, the home of Byron de la Beckwith, indicted murderer of Medgar Evers. The sullen white crowd stood on one side of the gate and a cheering integrated crowd on the other. Two years ago this would not have been possible, for the first white persons to work in civil rights were thrown in jail for eating in a Negro restaurant.

We spent five days touring Jackson, Vicksburg, and Meridian. We walked the streets, preached on front porches, at mass meetings, or in the pool halls, and always God's children flocked by the thousands to learn of freedom. We stopped off in Philadelphia and visited the burned church which Andrew Goodman, James Chaney, and Michael Schwerner were investigating when they were so savagely murdered in June.

I was proud to be with the workers of the Council of Federated Organizations and students of the Summer Project, to work with them through the Freedom Democratic Party to make democracy a reality. Those young people made up a domestic Peace Corps. Our nation had sent our Peace Corps volunteers throughout the underdeveloped nations of the world and none of them had experienced the kind of brutality and savagery that the voter registration workers suffered in Mississippi.

The church burnings, harassment, and murders in this state were direct results of the fact that Negro citizens could not vote and participate in electing responsible public officials who would protect the rights of all the people. Many thousands had tried to register—in spite of violence, economic reprisals, and other forms of intimidation—yet in 1963 only 1,636 Negro persons were registered in the entire state.

The federal government had a choice of working toward the gradual political reform of Mississippi through the civil process and through representative institutions such as the Freedom Democratic Party, or to send federal troops anytime a constitutional issue arose. The Freedom Democratic Party hoped to unite all persons of good-will in the state of Mississippi under the platform and program of the National Democratic Party. We intended to send a delegation to Atlantic City and urge that they be seated. Our nation needed at least one party which was free of racism, and the National Democratic Party could make a significant step in this direction by recognizing the Mississippi Freedom Democratic Party as the official Mississippi delegation.

"Beacon light of hope"

Everyone expected the Democratic Convention to be very dull and routine. Lyndon Johnson would name his running mate personally, and there were no issues which loomed as controversial enough to stir the convention. But everyone underestimated the Mississippi Freedom Democratic Party. The group of sixty-eight Negroes from Mississippi descended on the convention with a display of power, which even Lyndon Johnson had difficulty coping with. Their power was the moral power on which this nation was built. They deliberately ignored the man-made rules of the convention and appealed directly to the heart and soul of America and her people. What we experienced in Atlantic City was a classical illustration of the power of nonviolence, in the political arena. Many Americans became aware of the facts for the first time as the Mississippi Freedom Democratic Party took its case before the nation and the credentials committee of the National Democratic Party.

The people of Mississippi knew they were in a police state. They realized that politics provided the avenue for educating their children, providing homes and jobs for their families, and literally making over the whole climate of the state of Mississippi. This is a lesson that all Americans needed to learn, especially those of us who had been deprived because of color.

Ladies and Gentlemen of the Credentials Committee, if you value the future of democratic government, you have no alternative but to recognize, with full voice and vote, the Mississippi Freedom Democratic Party.

This is in no way a threat. It is the most urgent moral appeal that I can make to you. The question cannot be decided by the splitting of legal hairs or by seemingly expedient political compromises. For what seems to be expedient today will certainly prove disastrous tomorrow, unless it is based on a sound moral foundation.

This is no empty moral admonition. The history of men and of nations has proven that failure to give men the right to vote, to govern themselves and to select their own representatives brings certain chaos to the social, economic, and political institution which allows such an injustice to prevail.

And finally this is no mean issue. The recognition of the Mississippi Freedom Democratic Party has assumed symbolic value for oppressed people the world over. Seating this delegation would become symbolic of the intention of this country to bring freedom and democracy to all people. It would be a declaration of political independence to under-privileged citizens long denied a voice in their own destinies. It would be a beacon light of hope for all the disenfranchised millions of this earth whether they be in Mississippi and Alabama, behind the Iron Curtain, floundering in the mire of South African apartheid, or freedom-seeking persons in Cuba. Recognition of the Freedom Democratic Party would say to them that somewhere in this world there is a nation that cares about justice, that lives in a democracy, and that insures the rights of the downtrodden.

The Freedom Democratic Party found itself immersed in the world of practical politics almost immediately. The strong moral appeal before the credentials committee had to be backed up with political support. The following days involved gaining enough persons on the committee to submit a minority report before the convention body, and then enough states to support us to demand a roll call vote which would make each state take sides openly. In general the sentiment of the convention was for the Freedom Party, but the fact that Lyndon Johnson had to run against Goldwater made everybody cautious, lest the entire South bolt the party with Mississippi.

Finally, a compromise emerged which required the regular party to take a loyalty oath, and granted delegate-at-large status to two of the Freedom Party. This was a significant step. It was not a great victory, but it was symbolic, and it involved the pledge of high party officials to work with the Freedom Party for the next four years to gain registered voters and political strength in Mississippi. But there was no compromise for these persons who had risked their lives to get this far. Had I been a member of the delegation, I would probably have advised them to accept this as an offer in good faith and attempted to work to strengthen their position. But life in Mississippi had involved too many compromises already, and too many promises had come from Washington for them to take these seriously; so their skepticism must be viewed sympathetically.

We will never forget Aaron Henry and Fannie Lou Hamer. Their testimony educated a nation and brought the political powers to their knees in repentance, for the convention voted never again to seat a delegation that was racially segregated. But the true test of their message would be whether or not Negroes in Northern cities heard them and would register and vote.

"Promising aspects of the elections"

In San Francisco, the Republican Party had taken a giant stride away from its Lincoln tradition, and the results of election day graphically illustrate how tragic this was for the two-party system in America. Those who sought to turn back the tide of history suffered a bitter defeat, and in the process degraded themselves and their party in a manner seldom witnessed on our national political scene. The forces of goodwill and progress dealt a telling blow to the fanaticism of the right, and Americans swallowed their prejudices in the interests of progress, prosperity, and world peace.

One of the more promising aspects of the election was that the grand alliance of labor, civil rights forces, intellectual and religious leaders was provided with its second major victory within a year. This was the coalition which had to continue to grow in depth and breadth, if we were to overcome the problems which confronted us.

President Johnson had the opportunity to complete the job which was started by Roosevelt and interrupted by the war. Our very survival as a nation depended on the success of several rather radical reforms. The key to progress was still to be found in the states which President Johnson lost to Goldwater. Until the Southern power block was broken and the committees of our Congress freed from the domination of racists and reactionaries within the Democratic Party, we could not expect the kind of imagination and creativity which this period in history demanded from our federal government.

The problems of poverty, urban life, unemployment, education, housing, medical care, and flexible foreign policy were dependent on positive and forthright action from the federal government. But so long as men like Senators Eastland, Russell, Byrd, and Ellender held the positions of power in our Congress, the entire progress of our nation was in as grave a danger as the election of Senator Goldwater might have produced. The battle was far from won. It had only begun. The main burden of reform would still be upon the Negro.

24

THE NOBEL
PEACE PRIZE

*Occasionally in life there are those moments of unutterable fulfill-
ment which cannot be completely explained by those symbols called
words. Their meaning can only be articulated by the inaudible language of the heart.*

DECEMBER 10, 1964
King receives Nobel Peace Prize in Oslo

DECEMBER 11
Delivers Nobel Lecture at University of Oslo

JANUARY 27, 1965
Integrated dinner in Atlanta honors King

After many months of exhausting activity in the civil rights movement, I had reluctantly checked into the hospital for a rest and
complete physical check-up. The following morning I was awakened
by a telephone call from my wife. She had received a call from a New
York television network. It had been announced in Oslo, Norway,
by the Norwegian Parliament that I was the recipient of the Nobel
Prize for Peace for 1964.

My eyes were hardly open, and I could not be sure whether this
was merely a dream or if I was hearing correctly. I was stunned at
first. I had known of my nomination for this honor, but in the rush
of responsibilities of a movement such as ours, one does not have
time to contemplate honors, so I was quite unprepared psychologically.

But then I realized that this was no mere recognition of the contribution of one man on the stage of history. It was a testimony to the magnificent drama of the civil rights movement and the thousands of actors who had played their roles extremely well. In truth, it is these "noble" people who had won this Nobel Prize.

"A reward for the ground crew"

Many friends, members of my congregation, staff members of the Southern Christian Leadership Conference—and just people in various cities—asked me the same question: "How does it feel to win the Nobel Peace Prize, the world's most coveted award? What does it mean to you?"

I felt so humbly grateful to have been selected for this distinguished honor that it was hard to form in my mind a lucid manner of expressing "what it meant to me." Sitting in my church study, plunged into one of those rare periods of solitude and contemplation, I found the answer.

I recalled that, some years ago, I was seated in a huge jet at O'Hare Field in Chicago. In a matter of moments, the mighty plane was to take off for Los Angeles. From the speaker we heard the announcement that there would be a delay in departure. There was some mechanical difficulty which would be repaired within a brief time. Looking out of the window, I saw half a dozen men approaching the plane. They were dressed in dirty, greasy overalls. They assembled around the plane and began to work. Someone told me this was the ground crew.

All during that flight, I am sure that there were some on the plane who were grateful for our competent pilot. Others were aware that there was an able co-pilot. The stewardesses were charming and gracious. I am sure that many of the passengers were conscious of the pilot, the co-pilot, and the stewardesses. But, in my mind, first and foremost, was the memory of the ground crew.

There are many wonderful pilots today, charting the sometimes rocky, sometimes smooth course of human progress; pilots like Roy Wilkins and Whitney Young and A. Philip Randolph. And yet, if it were not for the ground crew, the struggle for human dignity and social justice would not be in orbit.

That is why I thought of the Nobel Peace Prize as a prize, a reward, for the ground crew: fifty thousand Negro people in Montgomery, Alabama, who came to discover that it is better to walk in dignity than to ride in buses; the students all over this nation who, in sitting down in restaurants and department stores were actually standing up for the true American Dream; the Freedom Riders who knew that this nation cannot hope to conquer outer space until the hearts of its citizens have won inner peace; Medgar Evers, slain; the three Mississippi martyrs, slain; Americans, colored and white, who marched on Washington.

In the final analysis, it must be said that this Nobel Prize was won by a movement of great people, whose discipline, wise restraint, and majestic courage has led them down a nonviolent course in seeking to establish a reign of justice and a rule of love across this nation of ours: Herbert Lee, Fannie Lou Hamer, Medgar Evers, Chaney, Goodman and Schwerner, and the thousands of children in Birmingham, Albany, St. Augustine, and Savannah who had accepted physical blows and jail and had discovered that the power of the soul is greater than the might of violence. These unknown thousands had given this movement the international acclaim, which we received from the Norwegian Parliament.

Members of the ground crew would not win the Nobel Peace Prize. Their names would not go down in history. They were unknown soldiers in the second great American Revolution. Yet, when years have rolled past and when the blazing light of truth is focused on this marvelous age in which we are now living—men and women will know and children will be taught that we have a finer land, a better people, a more noble civilization—because of the ground crew which made possible the jet flight to the clear skies of brotherhood. On December 10 in Oslo, I would receive—for the ground crew—a significant symbol, which was not for me, really.

I was greatly humbled, yet tremendously gratified by the visit to Oslo for the Nobel Prize. The response to our cause in London, Stockholm, and Paris, as well as in Oslo, was far beyond even my imagination. These great world capitals looked upon racism in this nation with horror and revulsion, but also with a certain amount of hope that America could solve this problem and point the way to the rest of the world. I assured them that this was our intention in the civil rights movement and among those forces within the churches and the labor and intellectual communities who have pledged themselves to this challenge.

The Nobel Prize for Peace placed a new dimension in the civil rights struggle. It reminded us graphically that the tide of world opinion was in our favor. Though people of color are a minority here in America, there are billions of colored people who look to the United States and to her Negro population to demonstrate that color is no obstacle or burden in the modern world.

The nations of Northern Europe had proudly aligned themselves with our struggle and challenged the myths of race the world over. This was the promise of a strong international alliance for peace and brotherhood in the world. Northern Europe, Africa, and Latin America all indicated a willingness to confront the problem of racism in the world. This was the starting point of a peaceful world. The Negro had to look abroad also. Poverty and hunger were not peculiar to Harlem and the Mississippi Delta. India, Mexico, the Congo, and many other nations faced essentially the same problems that we faced.

From the moment it was announced that the Norwegian Parliament had chosen me as winner of the 1964 Prize, demands for my involvement in national and international affairs began to mushroom. En route to Oslo I had the opportunity to discuss racial matters with the lord chancellor of Britain and with members of the British Parliament. I also participated in the organization of a movement to bring together colored people in the London area. It included West Indians, Pakistanis, Indians, and Africans who, together, were fighting racial injustice in Britain.

In our struggle for freedom and justice in the U.S., which has also been so long and arduous, we feel a powerful sense of identification with those in the far more deadly struggle for freedom in South Africa. We know how Africans there, and their friends of other races, strove for half a century to win their freedom by nonviolent methods. We have honored Chief Lutuli for his leadership, and we know how this nonviolence was only met by increasing violence from the State, increasing repression, culminating in the shootings of Sharpeville and all that has happened since.

ying baseball with son Martin III in 1964. (© 1986 – Flip Schulke. All reproduction
l/or storage rights reserved)

Playing with youngest daughter Bernice. (© 1986 – Flip Schulke. All reproduction and/or storage rights reserved)

Eating Sunday supper with family, with photograph of Mahatma Gandhi overhead. (© 1986 – Flip Schulke. All reproduction and/or storage rights reserved)

With youngest son Dexter. (© 1986 – Flip Schulke. All reproduction and/or storage rights reserved)

"I fought hard to hold back the tears. My emotions were about to overflow." Displaying the Nobel Prize medallion after ceremony in December 1964. (AP/Wide World)

"I would rather die on the highways of Alabama than make a butchery of my conscience." Marching from Selm to Montgomery in 1965. (AP/Wide World)

gregation is on its deathbed in Alabama and the only thing uncertain about it is how
ly the segregationists and Wallace will make the funeral." Attacked while attempting to
ster at the Hotel Albert in Selma. (AP/Wide World)

1e same president who told me in his office that it was impossible to get a voting rights
was on television calling for the passage of a voting rights bill in Congress. And it did
s two months later." President Lyndon Johnson offering the pen with which he signed
law the Voting Rights Act of 1965. (Archive Photos)

"One young man said to me, 'We won!' I said, 'What do you mean, "We won"?'"
Speaking to residents of Watts after the riots in 1965. (Corbis)

th *(left to right)* Simone Signoret, Harry Belafonte, Yves Montand, Professor Jacques
onod, and Coretta at 1966 civil rights rally. (Agence France Presse/Archive Photos)

(overleaf)
"I am in Birmingham because injustice is here." Serving a five-day
prison sentence in 1967 for contempt of court, resulting from
Birmingham demonstrations of 1963. (Corbis)

Today great leaders—Nelson Mandela and Robert Sobukwé—are among the hundreds wasting away in Robben Island prison. Against the massively armed and ruthless State, which uses torture and sadistic forms of interrogation to crush human beings—even driving some to suicide—the militant opposition inside South Africa seems for the moment to be silenced.

It is in this situation, with the great mass of South Africans denied their humanity, denied their dignity, denied opportunity, denied all human rights; it is in this situation, with many of the bravest and best South Africans serving long years in prison, with some already executed; in this situation we in America and Britain have a unique responsibility. For it is we, through our investments, through our governments' failure to act decisively, who are guilty of bolstering up the South African tyranny.

Our responsibility presents us with a unique opportunity. We can join in the one form of nonviolent action that could bring freedom and justice to South Africa, the action which African leaders have appealed for: a massive movement for economic sanctions.

"I accept this award with an abiding faith"

This was, for most of us, our first trip to Scandinavia, and we looked forward to making many new friends. We felt we had much to learn from Scandinavia's democratic socialist tradition and from the manner in which they had overcome many of the social and economic problems that still plagued far more powerful and affluent nations. In both Norway and Sweden, whose economies are literally dwarfed by the size of our affluence and the extent of our technology, they have no unemployment and no slums. Their men, women, and children have long enjoyed free medical care and quality education. This contrast to the limited, halting steps taken by our rich nation deeply troubled me.

I brought greetings from many Americans of goodwill, Negro and white, who were committed to the struggle for brotherhood and to the crusade for world peace. On their behalf I had come to Oslo to accept the Nobel Peace Prize. It was indeed a privilege to receive the Nobel Prize on behalf of the nonviolent movement, and I pledged that the entire prize of approximately $54,000 would be used to further the movement.

I accept this award today with an abiding faith in America and an audacious faith in the future of mankind. I refuse to accept the idea that the "is-ness" of man's present nature makes him morally incapable of reaching up for the eternal "ought-ness" that forever confronts him. I refuse to accept the idea that man is mere flotsam and jetsam in the river of life which surrounds him. I refuse to accept the view that mankind is so tragically bound to the starless midnight of racism and war that the bright daybreak of peace and brotherhood can never become a reality. I believe that even amid today's mortar bursts and whining bullets, there is still hope for a brighter tomorrow. I believe that wounded justice, lying prostrate on the blood-flowing streets of our nations, can be lifted from this dust of shame to reign supreme among the children of men. I have the audacity to believe that peoples everywhere can have three meals a day for their bodies, education and culture for their minds, and dignity, equality, and freedom for their spirits. I believe that what self-centered men have torn down, other-centered men can build up. I still believe that one day mankind will bow down before the altars of God and be crowned triumphant over war and bloodshed, and nonviolent redemptive goodwill will proclaim the rule of the land. I still believe that we shall overcome. This faith can give us courage to face the uncertainties of the future. It will give our tired feet new strength as we continue our forward stride toward the City of Freedom.

Today I come to Oslo as a trustee, inspired and with renewed dedication to humanity. I accept this prize on behalf of all men who love peace and brotherhood.

I fought hard to hold back the tears. My emotions were about to overflow. Whatever I was, I owed to my family and to all those who struggled with me. But my biggest debt I owed to my wife. She was the one who gave my life meaning. All I could pledge to her, and to all those millions, was that I would do all I could to justify the faith that she, and they, had in me. I would try more than ever to make my life one of which she, and they, could be proud. I would do in private that which I knew my public responsibility demanded.

"What now?"

The Nobel Peace Prize was a proud honor, but not one with which we began a "season of satisfaction" in the civil rights movement. We returned from Oslo not with our heads in the clouds, congratulating ourselves for marvelous yesterdays and tempted to declare a holiday in our struggle, but with feet even more firmly on the ground, convictions strengthened and determinations driven by dreams of greater and brighter tomorrows.

In accepting the 1964 Nobel Peace Prize, I asked why such an honor had been awarded to a movement which remained beleaguered and committed to unrelenting struggle; to a movement which was surging forward with majestic scorn for risk and danger; to a movement which had not won the very peace and brotherhood which were the essence of Count Alfred Nobel's great legacy.

I suggested then that the prize was not given merely as recognition of past achievement, but also as recognition, a more profound recognition, that the nonviolent way, the American Negro's way, was the answer to the crucial political and moral question of our time: the need for man to overcome oppression and violence without resorting to violence and oppression.

In almost every press conference after my return from Oslo I was asked, "What now? In what direction is the civil rights movement headed?" I could not, of course, speak to for the entire civil rights movement. There were several pilots; I was but one, and the organization of which I was president, the Southern Christian Leadership

---

LECTURE AT UNIVERSITY OF OSLO

The time has come for an all-out world war against poverty. The rich nations must use their vast resources of wealth to develop the underdeveloped, school the unschooled, and feed the unfed. Ultimately a great nation is a compassionate nation. No individual or nation can be great if it does not have a concern for "the least of these." Deeply etched in the fiber of our religious tradition is the conviction that men are made in the image of God and that they are souls of infinite metaphysical value, the heirs of a legacy of dignity and worth. If we feel this as a profound moral fact, we cannot be content to see men hungry, to see men victimized with starvation and ill health when we have the means to help them. The wealthy nations must go all out to bridge the gulf between the rich minority and the poor majority.

December 11, 1964

Conference, was, mainly, a Southern organization seeking solutions to the peculiar problems of the South.

Pressure continued to build for SCLC to open offices in various cities of the North. We reached a decision on this after the "Jobs and Freedom Tour" of ten Northern cities that spring. Even though SCLC's main base of operations remained in the South, where we could most effectively assault the roots of racial evils, we became involved to a much greater extent with the problems of the urban North.

On another level, I now had to give a great deal of attention to the three problems which I considered as the largest of those that confront mankind: racial injustice around the world, poverty, and war. Though each appeared to be separate and isolated, all were interwoven into a single garment of man's destiny.

Whatever measure of influence I had as a result of the importance which the world attaches to the Nobel Peace Prize would have to be used to bring the philosophy of nonviolence to all the world's people who grapple with the age-old problem of racial injustice. I would have to somehow convince them of the effectiveness of this weapon that cuts without wounding, this weapon that ennobles the man who wields it.

I found myself thinking more and more about what I consider mankind's second great evil: the evil of poverty. This is an evil which exists in Indiana as well as in India; in New Orleans as well as in New Delhi.

Cannot we agree that the time has indeed come for an all-out war on poverty—not merely in President Johnson's "Great Society," but in every town and village of the world where this nagging evil exists? Poverty—especially that found among thirty-five million persons in the United States—is a tragic deficit of human will. We have, it seems, shut the poor out of our minds and driven them from the mainstream of our society. We have allowed the poor to become invisible, and we have become angry when they make their presence felt. But just as nonviolence has exposed the ugliness of racial injustice, we must now find ways to expose and heal the sickness of poverty—not just its symptoms, but its basic causes.

The third great evil confronting mankind was one about which I was deeply concerned. It was the evil of war. At Oslo I suggested that the philosophy and strategy of nonviolence become immediately a subject for study and serious experimentation in every field of human conflict, including relations between nations. This was not, I believed, an unrealistic suggestion.

World peace through nonviolent means is neither absurd nor unattainable. All other methods have failed. Thus we must begin anew. Nonviolence is a good starting point. Those of us who believe in this method can be voices of reason, sanity, and understanding amid the voices of violence, hatred, and emotion. We can very well set a mood of peace out of which a system of peace can be built.

Racial injustice around the world. Poverty. War. When man solves these three great problems he will have squared his moral progress with his scientific progress. And, more importantly, he will have learned the practical art of living in harmony.

The Nobel Peace Prize had given me even deeper personal faith that man would indeed rise to the occasion and give new direction to an age drifting rapidly to its doom.

Wherever I traveled abroad, I had been made aware that America's integrity in all of its world endeavors was being weighed on the scales of racial justice. This was dramatically and tragically evidenced when that travesty of lawlessness and callousness in Meridian, Mississippi, was headlined in Oslo on the very day of the Nobel Peace Prize ceremonies. On the same day the civil rights movement was receiving the Nobel Peace Prize, a U.S. commissioner in Mississippi dismissed charges against nineteen of the men arrested by the FBI in connection with the brutal slaying of three civil rights voter registration workers in Mississippi the previous summer. I was convinced that the whole national conscience must be mobilized to deal with the tragic situation of violence, terror, and blatant failure of justice in Mississippi. We considered calling for a nationwide boycott of Mississippi products.

Aside from the proposed boycott, however, there was a more immediate opportunity for Congress to speak out in a way that would remedy the root cause of Mississippi's injustices—the total denial of the right to vote to her Negro citizens. On Monday, January 4, 1965, the House of Representatives had the opportunity to challenge the seating of the entire Mississippi delegation in the

ADDRESS AT RECOGNITION DINNER IN ATLANTA

I must confess that I have enjoyed being on this mountaintop and I am tempted to want to stay here and retreat to a more quiet and serene life. But something within reminds me that the valley calls me in spite of all its agonies, dangers, and frustrating moments. I must return to the valley. Something tells me that the ultimate test of a man is not where he stands in moments of comfort and moments of convenience, but where he stands in moments of challenge and moments of controversy. So I must return to the valley—a valley filled with misguided bloodthirsty mobs, but a valley filled at the same time with little Negro boys and girls who grow up with ominous clouds of inferiority forming in their little mental skies; a valley filled with millions of people who, because of economic deprivation and social isolation, have lost hope, and see life as a long and desolate corridor with no exit sign. I must return to the valley—a valley filled with literally thousands of Negroes in Alabama and Mississippi who are brutalized, intimidated, and sometimes killed when they seek to register and vote. I must return to the valley all over the South and in the big cities of the North—a valley filled with millions of our white and Negro brothers who are smothering in an airtight cage of poverty in the midst of an affluent society.

January 27, 1965

House. Under the provisions of the Act of February 23, 1870, readmitting Mississippi to representation in the Congress, it was stipulated that the principal condition for readmission was that all citizens twenty-one years or older, who had resided in the state for six months or more and who were neither convicts nor insane, be allowed to vote freely. Mississippi had deliberately and repeatedly ignored this solemn pact with the nation for more than fifty years and maintained seats to which she was not entitled in an indifferent Congress. The conscience of America, troubled by the twin Mississippi tragedies of the presence of violence and the absence of law, could have expressed itself in supporting this moral challenge to immoral representation.

25

MALCOLM X

He was an eloquent spokesman for his point of view and no one can honestly doubt that Malcolm had a great concern for the problems that we face as a race. While we did not always see eye to eye on methods to solve the race problems, I always had a deep affection for Malcolm and felt that he had the great ability to put his finger on the existence and root of the problem.

MARCH 26, 1964
After press conference at U.S. Senate, King has brief encounter with Malcolm X

FEBRUARY 5, 1965
Coretta Scott King meets with Malcolm X in Selma, Alabama

FEBRUARY 21
Malcolm X is assassinated in Harlem

I met Malcolm X once in Washington, but circumstances didn't enable me to talk with him for more than a minute.

He is very articulate, but I totally disagree with many of his political and philosophical views—at least insofar as I understand where he now stands. I don't want to sound self-righteous, or absolutist, or that I think I have the only truth, the only way. Maybe he does have some of the answers. I know that I have often wished that he would talk less of violence, because violence is not going to solve our problem. And, in his litany of articulating the despair of the Negro without offering any positive, creative alternative, I feel that Malcolm has done himself and our

people a great disservice. Fiery, demagogic oratory in the black ghettos,
urging Negroes to arm themselves and prepare to engage in violence, as
he has done, can reap nothing but grief.

In the event of a violent revolution, we would be sorely outnum-
bered. And when it was all over, the Negro would face the same un-
changed conditions, the same squalor and deprivation—the only
difference being that his bitterness would be even more intense, his dis-
enchantment even more abject. Thus, in purely practical as well as
moral terms, the American Negro has no rational alternative to nonvio-
lence.

When they threw eggs at me in New York, I think that was really
a result of the Black Nationalist groups. They had heard all of these
things about my being soft, my talking about love, and they transferred that bitterness toward the white man to me. They began to
feel that I was saying to love this person that they had such a bitter
attitude toward. In fact, Malcolm X had a meeting the day before,
and he talked about me a great deal and told them that I would be
there the next night and said, "You ought to go over there and let
old King know what you think about him." And he had said a great
deal about nonviolence, criticizing nonviolence, and saying that I
approved of Negro men and women being bitten by dogs and the
firehoses. So I think this kind of response grew out of all of the talk
about my being a sort of polished Uncle Tom.

My feeling has always been that they have never understood
what I was saying. They did not see that there's a great deal of difference between nonresistance to evil and nonviolent resistance. Certainly I'm not saying that you sit down and patiently accept injustice.
I'm talking about a very strong force, where you stand up with all
your might against an evil system, and you're not a coward. You are
resisting, but you come to see that tactically as well as morally it is
better to be nonviolent. Even if one didn't want to deal with the
moral question, it would just be impractical for the Negro to talk
about making his struggle violent.

But I think one must understand that Malcolm X was a victim
of the despair that came into being as a result of a society that gives
so many Negroes the nagging sense of "nobody-ness." Just as one
condemns the philosophy, which I did constantly, one must be as

vigorous in condemning the continued existence in our society of the conditions of racist injustice, depression, and man's inhumanity to man.

"A product of the hate and violence"

The ghastly nightmare of violence and counter-violence is one of the most tragic blots to occur on the pages of the Negro's history in this country. In many ways, however, it is typical of the misplacement of aggressions which has occurred throughout the frustrated circumstances of our existence.

How often have the frustrations of second-class citizenship and humiliating status led us into blind outrage against each other and the real cause and course of our dilemma been ignored? It is sadly ironic that those who so clearly pointed to the white world as the seed of evil should now spend their energies in their own destruction.

Malcolm X came to the fore as a public figure partially as a result of a TV documentary entitled "The Hate That Hate Produced." That title points clearly to the nature of Malcolm's life and death. He was clearly a product of the hate and violence invested in the Negro's blighted existence in this nation. He, like so many of our number, was a victim of the despair that inevitably derives from the conditions of oppression, poverty, and injustice which engulf the masses of our race. But in his youth, there was no hope, no preaching, teaching, or movements of nonviolence. He was too young for the Garvey Movement, too poor to be a Communist—for the Communists geared their work to Negro intellectuals and labor without realizing that the masses of Negroes were unrelated to either—and yet he possessed a native intelligence and drive which demanded an outlet and means of expression. He turned first to the underworld, but this did not fulfill the quest for meaning which grips young minds. It was a testimony to Malcolm's personal depth and integrity that he could not become an underworld czar, but turned again and again to religion for meaning and destiny. Malcolm was still turning and growing at the time of his brutal and meaningless assassination.

* * *

I was in jail when he was in Selma, Alabama. I couldn't block his coming, but my philosophy was so antithetical to the philosophy of Malcolm X that I would never have invited Malcolm X to come to Selma when we were in the midst of a nonviolent demonstration. This says nothing about the personal respect I had for him.

During his visit to Selma, he spoke at length to my wife Coretta about his personal struggles and expressed an interest in working more closely with the nonviolent movement, but he was not yet able to renounce violence and overcome the bitterness which life had invested in him. There were also indications of an interest in politics as a way of dealing with the problems of the Negro. All of these were signs of a man of passion and zeal seeking for a program through which he could channel his talents.

But history would not have it so. A man who lived under the torment of knowledge of the rape of his grandmother and murder of his father under the conditions of the present social order, does not readily accept that social order or seek to integrate into it. And so Malcolm was forced to live and die as an outsider, a victim of the violence that spawned him, and which he courted through his brief but promising life.

The assassination of Malcolm X was an unfortunate tragedy. Let us learn from this tragic nightmare that violence and hate only breed violence and hate, and that Jesus' word still goes out to every potential Peter, "Put up thy sword." Certainly we will continue to disagree, but we must disagree without becoming violently disagreeable. We will still suffer the temptation to bitterness, but we must learn that hate is too great a burden to bear for a people moving on toward their date with destiny.

The American Negro cannot afford to destroy its leadership. Men of talent are too scarce to be destroyed by envy, greed, and tribal rivalry before they reach their full maturity. Like the murder of Patrice Lamumba in the Congo, the murder of Malcolm X deprived the world of a potentially great leader. I could not agree with either of these men, but I could see in them a capacity for leadership which I could respect and which was only beginning to mature in judgment and statesmanship.

I think it is even more unfortunate that this great tragedy occurred at a time when Malcolm X was reevaluating his own philosophical presuppositions and moving toward a greater understanding of the nonviolent movement and toward more tolerance of white people generally.

I think there is a lesson that we can all learn from this: that violence is impractical and that now, more than ever before, we must pursue the course of nonviolence to achieve a reign of justice and a rule of love in our society, and that hatred and violence must be cast into the unending limbo if we are to survive.

In a real sense, the growth of black nationalism was symptomatic of the deeper unrest, discontent, and frustration of many Negroes because of the continued existence of racial discrimination. Black nationalism was a way out of that dilemma. It was based on an unrealistic and sectional perspective that I condemned both publicly and privately. It substituted the tyranny of black supremacy for the tyranny of white supremacy. I always contended that we as a race must not seek to rise from a position of disadvantage to one of advantage, but to create a moral balance in society where democracy and brotherhood would be a reality for all men.

26

SELMA

In 1965 the issue is the right to vote and the place is Selma, Alabama. In Selma, we see a classic pattern of disenfranchisement typical of the Southern Black Belt areas where Negroes are in the majority.

FEBRUARY 1, 1965
King is jailed with more than two hundred others after voting rights march in Selma, Alabama

FEBRUARY 26
Jimmie Lee Jackson dies after being shot by police during demonstration in Marion, Alabama

MARCH 7
Voting rights marchers are beaten at Edmund Pettus Bridge

MARCH 11
Rev. James Reeb dies after beating by white racists

MARCH 25
Selma-to-Montgomery march concludes with address by King; hours afterward, Klan night riders kill Viola Gregg Liuzzo while she transports marchers back to Selma

When I was coming from Scandinavia in December 1964, I stopped by to see President Johnson and we talked about a lot of things, but finally we started talking about voting.

And he said, "Martin, you're right about that. I'm going to do it eventually, but I can't get a voting rights bill through in this session of Congress." He said, "Now, there's some other bills that I have here that I want to get through in my Great Society program, and I think in the long run they'll help Negroes more, as much as a voting rights bill. And let's get those through and then the other."

I said, "Well, you know, political reform is as necessary as anything if we're going to solve all these other problems."

"I can't get it through," he said, "because I need the votes of the Southern bloc to get these other things through. And if I present a voting rights bill, they will block the whole program. So it's just not the wise and the politically expedient thing to do."

I left simply saying, "Well, we'll just have to do the best we can."

I left the mountaintop of Oslo and the mountaintop of the White House, and two weeks later went on down to the valley of Selma, Alabama, with Ralph Abernathy and the others. Something happened down there. Three months later, the same President who told me in his office that it was impossible to get a voting rights bill was on television singing in speaking terms, "We Shall Overcome," and calling for the passage of a voting rights bill in Congress. And it did pass two months later.

The President said nothing could be done. But we started a movement.

"The ugly pattern of denial"

Selma, Alabama, was to 1965 what Birmingham was to 1963. The right to vote was the issue, replacing public accommodation as the mass concern of a people hungry for a place in the sun and a voice in their destiny.

In Selma, thousands of Negroes were courageously providing dramatic witness to the evil forces that bar our way to the all-important ballot box. They were laying bare for all the nation to see, for all the world to know, the nature of segregationist resistance. The ugly pattern of denial flourished with insignificant differences in thousands of Alabama, Louisiana, Mississippi, and other Southern communities.

The pattern of denial depended upon four main roadblocks.

First, there was the Gestapo-like control of county and local government by the likes of Sheriff Jim Clark of Selma, and Sheriff Rainey of Philadelphia, Mississippi. There was a carefully cultivated *mystique* behind the power and brutality of these men. The gun, the club, and the cattle prod produced the fear that was the main barrier to voting—a barrier erected by 345 years' exposure to the psychology and brutality of slavery and legal segregation. It was a fear rooted in feelings of inferiority.

Secondly, city ordinances were contrived to make it difficult for Negroes to move in concert. So-called parade ordinances and local laws making public meetings subject to surveillance and harassment by public officials were used to keep Negroes from working out a group plan of action against injustice. These laws deliberately ignored and defied the First Amendment of our Constitution.

After so many years of intimidation, the Negro community had learned that its only salvation was in united action. When one Negro stood up, he was run out of town; if a thousand stood up together, the situation was bound to be drastically overhauled.

The third link in the chain of slavery was the slow pace of the registrar and the limited number of days and hours during which the office was open. Out of 15,000 Negroes eligible to vote in Selma and the surrounding Dallas County, less than 350 were registered. This was the reason why the protest against the limited number of opportunities for registration had to continue.

The fourth link in the chain of disenfranchisement was the literacy test. This test was designed to be difficult, and the Justice Department had been able to establish that in a great many counties these tests were not administered fairly.

Clearly, the heart of the voting problem lay in the fact that the machinery for enforcing this basic right was in the hands of state-appointed officials answerable to the very people who believed they could continue to wield power in the South only so long as the Negro was disenfranchised. No matter how many loopholes were plugged, no matter how many irregularities were exposed, it was plain that the federal government must withdraw that control from the states or else set up machinery for policing it effectively.

The patchwork reforms brought about by the laws of 1957, 1960, and 1964 had helped, but the denial of suffrage had gone on too long, and had caused too deep a hurt for Negroes to wait out the time required by slow, piecemeal enforcement procedures. What was needed was the new voting rights legislation promised for the 1965 session of Congress.

Our Direct Action Department, under the direction of Rev. James Bevel, then decided to attack the very heart of the political structure of the state of Alabama and the Southland through a campaign for the right to vote. Planning for the voter registration project in Selma started around the seventeenth of December, 1964, but the actual project started on the second of January, 1965. Our affiliate organization, the Dallas County Voters League, invited us to aid and assist in getting more Negroes registered to vote. We planned to have Freedom Days, days of testing and challenge, to arouse people all over the community. We decided that on the days that the county and the state had designated as registration days, we would assemble at the Brown Chapel A.M.E. Church and walk together to the courthouse. More than three thousand were arrested in Selma and Marion together. I was arrested in one of those periods when we were seeking to go to the courthouse.

"Selma Jail"

When the king of Norway participated in awarding the Nobel Peace Prize to me he surely did not think that in less than sixty days I would be in jail. They were little aware of the unfinished business in the South. By jailing hundreds of Negroes, the city of Selma, Alabama, had revealed the persisting ugliness of segregation to the nation and the world.

When the Civil Rights Act of 1964 was passed, many decent Americans were lulled into complacency because they thought the day of difficult struggle was over. But apart from voting rights, merely to be a person in Selma was not easy. When reporters asked Sheriff Clark if a woman defendant was married, he replied, "She's a nigger woman and she hasn't got a Miss or a Mrs. in front of her name."

This was the U.S.A. in 1965. We were in jail simply because we could not tolerate these conditions for ourselves or our nation. There was a clear and urgent need for new and improved federal

INSTRUCTIONS FROM SELMA JAIL TO MOVEMENT ASSOCIATES

Do following to keep national attention focused on Selma:

1. *Joe Lowery:* Make a call to Florida Governor Leroy Collins and urge him to make a personal visit to Selma, to talk with city and county authorities concerning speedier registration and more days for registering.

2. *Walter Fauntroy:* Follow through on suggestion of having a congressional delegation to come in for personal investigation. They should also make an appearance at a mass meeting if they come.

3. *Lowery, via Lee White:* Make a personal call to President Johnson and urge him to intervene in some way (send a personal emissary to Selma, get the Justice Department involved, make a plea to Dallas and Selma officials in a press conference).

4. *Chuck Jones:* Urge lawyers to go to the 5th Circuit if Judge Thomas does not issue an immediate injunction against the continued arrests and speed up registration.

5. *Bernard Lafayette:* Keep some activity alive every day this week.

6. Consider a night march to the city jail protesting my arrest. Have another march to the courthouse to let Clark show true colors.

7. Stretch every point to get teachers to march.

8. *Clarence Jones:* Immediately post bond for staff members essential for mobilization who are arrested.

9. *Atlanta Office:* Call C. T. Vivian and have him return from California in case other staff is put out of circulation.

12. Local Selma editor sent a telegram to the President calling for a Congressional committee to come out and study the situation of Selma. We should join in calling for this. By all means, we cannot let them get the offensive. I feel they were trying to give the impression that they were orderly and that Selma was a good community because they integrated public accommodations. We have to insist that voting is the issue and here Selma has dirty hands. We should not be too soft. We have the offensive. We cannot let Baker control our movement. In a crisis, we needed a sense of drama.

13. Ralph to call Sammy Davis and ask him to do a Sunday benefit in Atlanta to raise money for the Alabama project. I find that all of these fellows respond better when I am in a jail or in a crisis.

February 1965

legislation and for expanded law enforcement measures to finally eliminate all barriers to the right to vote.

A brief statement I read to the press tried to interpret what we sought to do:

For the past month the Negro citizens of Selma and Dallas County have been attempting to register by the hundreds. To date only 57 persons have entered the registrar's office, while 280 have been jailed. Of the 57 who have attempted to register, none have received notice of successful registration, and we have no reason to hope that they will be registered. The registration test is so difficult and so ridiculous that even Chief Justice Warren might fail to answer some questions.

In the past year Negroes have been beaten by Sheriff Clark and his posse, they have been fired from their jobs, they have been victimized by the slow registration procedure and the difficult literacy test, all because they have attempted to vote.

Now we must call a halt to these injustices. Good men of the nation cannot sit idly by while the democratic process is defied and prostituted in the interests of racists. Our nation has declared war against totalitarianism around the world, and we call upon President Johnson, Governor Wallace, the Supreme Court, and the Congress of this great nation to declare war against oppression and totalitarianism within the shores of our country.

If Negroes could vote, there would be no Jim Clarks, there would be no oppressive poverty directed against Negroes. Our children would not be crippled by segregated schools, and the whole community might live together in harmony.

This is our intention: to declare war on the evils of demagoguery. The entire community will join in this protest, and we will not relent until there is a change in the voting process and the establishment of democracy.

When I left jail in Selma on Friday, February 5, I stated that I would fly to Washington. On Tuesday afternoon I met with Vice President Hubert H. Humphrey in his capacity as chairman of the newly created Council for Equal Opportunity and with Attorney General Nicholas Katzenbach. My colleagues and I made clear to the vice president and the attorney general our conviction that all citizens must be free to exercise their right and responsibility to vote without delays, harassment, economic intimidation, and police brutality.

I indicated that while there had been some progress in several Southern states in voter registration in previous years, in other states, new crippling legislation had been instituted since 1957 precisely to frustrate Negro registration. At a recent press conference President Johnson stated that another evil was the "slow pace of registration for Negroes." This snail's pace was clearly illustrated by the ugly events in Selma. Were this pace to continue, it would take another hundred years before all eligible Negro voters were registered.

There were many more Negroes in jail in Selma than there were Negroes registered to vote. This slow pace was not accidental. It was the result of a calculated and well-defined pattern which used many devices and tactics to maintain white political power in many areas of the South. I emphatically stated that the problem of securing voting rights could not be cured by patchwork or piecemeal legislation programs. We needed a basic legislative program to insure procedures for achieving the registration of Negroes in the South without delay or harassment. I expressed my conviction that the voting sections of the 1957, 1960, and 1964 Civil Rights Acts were inadequate to secure voting rights for Negroes in many key areas of the South.

I told Mr. Humphrey and General Katzenbach how pleased I was that the Department of Justice had under consideration legislation pertaining to voting which would implement President Johnson's State of the Union declaration, namely: "I propose we eliminate every remaining obstacle in the right and opportunity to vote."

I asked the attorney general to seek an injunction against the prosecution of the more than three thousand Negro citizens of Selma, who otherwise would face years of expensive and frustrating litigation before the exercise of their guaranteed right to vote was vindicated. Moreover, to the extent that existing laws were inadequate or doubtful to accomplish this all-important purpose, I asked the vice president and the attorney general to include in the administration's legislative program new procedures which would invest the attorney general and private citizens with the power to avoid the oppression and delays of spurious state court prosecution.

In a meeting with President Johnson, Vice President Humphrey,

Attorney General Katzenbach, and Florida Governor Leroy Collins, chairman of the newly created Community Relations Service, I urged the administration to offer a voting rights bill which would secure the right to vote without delay and harassment.

"Events leading to the confrontation"

During the course of our struggle to achieve voting rights for Negroes in Selma, Alabama, it was reported that a "delicate understanding" existed between myself, Alabama state officials, and the federal government to avoid the scheduled march to Montgomery on Tuesday, March 9.

On the basis of news reports of my testimony in support of our petition for an injunction against state officials, it was interpreted in some quarters that I worked with the federal government to throttle the indignation of white clergymen and Negroes. I was concerned about this perversion of the facts, and for the record would like to sketch in the background of the events leading to the confrontation of marchers and Alabama state troopers at Pettus Bridge in Selma, and our subsequent peaceful turning back.

The goal of the demonstrations in Selma, as elsewhere, was to dramatize the existence of injustice and to bring about the presence of justice by methods of nonviolence. Long years of experience indicated to us that Negroes could achieve this goal when four things occured:

1. nonviolent demonstrators go into the streets to exercise their constitutional rights;
2. racists resist by unleashing violence against them;
3. Americans of good conscience in the name of decency demand federal intervention and legislation;
4. the administration, under mass pressure, initiates measures of immediate intervention and supports remedial legislation.

The working out of this process has never been simple or tranquil. When nonviolent protests were countered by local authorities with harassment, intimidation, and brutality, the federal government always first asked the Negro to desist and leave the streets rather than bring pressure to bear on those who commit the criminal acts. We were always compelled to reject vigorously such federal requests and relied on our allies, the millions of Americans across the nation, to bring pressure on the federal government for protective action in our behalf. Our position always was that there is a wrong and right side to the questions of full freedom and equality for millions of Negro Americans and that the federal government did not belong in the middle on this issue.

During our nonviolent direct-action campaigns we were advised, and again we were so advised in Selma, that violence might ensue. Herein lay a dilemma: of course, there always was the likelihood that, because of the hostility to our demonstrations, acts of lawlessness may be precipitated. We realized that we had to exercise extreme caution so that the direct-action program would not be conducted in a manner that might be considered provocative or an invitation to violence. Accordingly, each situation had to be studied in detail: the strength and the temper of our adversaries had to be estimated and any change in any of these factors would affect the details of our strategy. Nevertheless, we had to begin a march without knowing when or where it would actually terminate.

How were these considerations applied to our plans for the march from Selma to Montgomery?

My associates and friends were constantly concerned about my personal safety, and in the light of recent threats of death, many of them urged me not to march that Sunday for the fear that my presence in the line would lead to assassination attempts. However, as a matter of conscience, I could not always respond to the wishes of my staff and associates; in this case, I made the decision to lead the march on Sunday and was prepared to do so in spite of any possible danger to my person.

In working out a time schedule, I had to consider my church responsibilities. Because I was so frequently out of my pulpit and because my life was so full of emergencies, I was always on the horns of a dilemma. I had been away for two straight Sundays and therefore felt that I owed it to my parishioners to be there. It was arranged that I take a chartered plane to Montgomery after the morning service and lead the march out of Selma, speak with a group for three or four hours, and take a chartered flight back in order to be on hand for the Sunday Communion Service at 7:30 P.M.

When Governor Wallace issued his ban on the march, it was my view and that of most of my associates that the state troopers would deal with the problem by arresting all of the people in the line. We never imagined that they would use the brutal methods to which they actually resorted to repress the march. I concluded that if I were arrested it would be impossible for me to get back to the evening service at Ebenezer to administer the Lord's Supper and baptism. Because of this situation, my staff urged me to stay in Atlanta and lead a march on Monday morning. This I agreed to do. I was prepared to go to jail on Monday but at the same time I would have met my church responsibilities. If I had had any idea that the state troopers would use the kind of brutality they did, I would have felt compelled to give up my church duties altogether to lead the line. It was one of those developments that none of us anticipated. We felt that the state troopers, who had been severely criticized over their terrible acts two weeks earlier even by conservative Alabama papers, would never again engage in that kind of violence.

I shall never forget my agony of conscience for not being there when I heard of the dastardly acts perpetrated against nonviolent demonstrators that Sunday, March 7. As a result, I felt that I had to lead a march on the following Tuesday and decided to spend Monday mobilizing for it.

The march on Tuesday, March 9, illustrated the dilemma we often face. Not to try to march again would have been unthinkable. However, whether we were marching to Montgomery or to a limited point within the city of Selma could not be determined in advance; the only certain thing was that we had to begin, so that a confrontation with injustice would take place in full view of the millions looking on throughout this nation.

The next question was whether the confrontation had to be a violent one; here the responsibility of weighing all factors and estimating the consequences rests heavily on the civil rights leaders. It is easy to decide on either extreme. To go forward recklessly can have terrible consequences in terms of human life and also can cause friends and supporters to lose confidence if they feel a lack of responsibility exists. On the other hand, it is ineffective to guarantee that no violence will occur by the device of not marching or undertaking token marches avoiding direct confrontation.

On Tuesday, March 9, Judge Frank M. Johnson of the federal district court in Montgomery issued an order enjoining me and the local Selma leadership of the nonviolent voting rights movement from peacefully marching to Montgomery. The issuance of Judge Johnson's order caused disappointment and bitterness to all of us. I felt that as a result of the order we had been put in a very difficult position. I felt that it was like condemning the robbed man for getting robbed. It was one of the most painful decisions I ever made—to try on the one hand to do what I felt was a practical matter of controlling a potentially explosive situation, and at the same time, not defy a federal court order. We had looked to the federal judiciary in Alabama to prevent the unlawful interference with our program to expand elective franchise for Negroes throughout the Black Belt.

I consulted with my lawyers and trusted advisors both in Selma and other parts of the country and discussed what course of action we should take. Information came in that troopers of the Alabama State Police and Sheriff James Clark's possemen would be arrayed in massive force across Highway 80 at the foot of Pettus Bridge in Selma. I reflected upon the role of the federal judiciary as a protector of the rights of Negroes. I also gave thoughtful consideration to the hundreds of clergymen and other persons of goodwill who had come to Selma to make a witness with me in the cause of justice by participating in our planned march to Montgomery. Taking all of this into consideration, I decided that our plans had to be carried out and that I would lead our march to a confrontation with injustice to make a witness to our countrymen and the world of our determination to vote and be free.

As my associates and I were spiritually preparing ourselves for the task ahead, Governor Collins of the Community Relations Service and John Doar, acting assistant attorney general, Civil Rights Division, came to see me to dissuade me from the course of action which we had painfully decided upon.

Governor Collins affirmed and restated the commitment of President Johnson to the achievement of full equality for all persons without regard to race, color, or creed, and his commitment to securing the right to vote for all persons eligible to do so. He mentioned the fact that the situation was explosive, and it would tarnish the image of our nation if the events of Sunday were repeated. He very strongly urged us not to march. I listened attentively to both Mr. Doar and Governor Collins. I said at that point, "I think instead of urging us not to march, you should urge the state troopers not to be brutal toward us if we do march, because we have got to march." I explained to them why, as a matter of conscience, I felt it was necessary to seek a confrontation with injustice on Highway 80. I felt that I had a moral obligation to the movement, to justice, to our nation, to the health of our democracy, and above all to the philosophy of nonviolence to keep the march peaceful. I felt that, if I had not done it, the pent-up emotions would have exploded into retaliatory violence. Governor Collins realized at this point that we were determined to march and left the room, saying that he would do what he could to prevent the state troopers from being violent.

I say to you this afternoon that I would rather die on the highways of Alabama than make a butchery of my conscience. I say to you, when we march, don't panic and remember that we must remain true to nonviolence. I'm asking everybody in the line, if you can't be nonviolent, don't get in here. If you can't accept blows without retaliating, don't get in the line. If you can accept it out of your commitment to nonviolence, you will somehow do something for this nation that may well save it. If you can accept it, you will leave those state troopers bloodied with their own barbarities. If you can accept it, you will do something that will transform conditions here in Alabama.

Just as we started to march, Governor Collins rushed to me and said that he felt everything would be all right. He gave me a small piece of paper indicating a route that I assumed Mr. Baker, public safety director of Selma, wanted us to follow. It was the same route that had been taken the previous Sunday. The press, reporting this detail, gave the impression that Governor Collins and I had sat down and worked out some compromise. There were no talks or agreement between Governor Collins and me beyond the discussions I have just described. I held on to my decision to march despite the fact that many people in the line were concerned about breaking the court injunction issued by one of the strongest and best judges in the South. I felt that we had to march at least to the point where the troopers had brutalized the people, even if it meant a recurrence of violence, arrest, or even death. As a nonviolent leader, I could not advocate breaking through a human wall set up by the policemen. While we desperately desired to proceed to Montgomery, we knew before we started our march that this human wall set up on Pettus Bridge would make it impossible for us to go beyond it. It was not that we didn't intend to go on to Montgomery, but that, in consideration of our commitment to nonviolent action, we knew we could not go under those conditions.

We sought to find a middle course. We marched until we faced the troopers in their solid line shoulder to shoulder across Highway 80. We did not disengage until they made it clear they were going to use force. We disengaged then because we felt we had made our point, we had revealed the continued presence of violence.

On March 11, I received the shocking information that the Reverend James Reeb had just passed away as a result of the dastardly act of brutality visited upon him in Selma. Those elements that had constantly harassed us and who did their cowardly work by night, went to the Walkers' Café and followed three clergymen and beat them brutally. Two of them were from Boston—the Reverend Miller and the Reverend Reeb—and Reverend Clark Olson was from Berkeley, California.

This murder, like so many others, is the direct consequence of the reign of terror in some parts of our nation. This unprovoked attack on the streets of an Alabama city cannot be considered an isolated incident in a smooth sea of tolerance and understanding. Rather, it is a result of a malignant sickness in our society that comes from the tolerance of organized hatred and violence. We must all confess that Reverend Reeb was murdered by a morally inclement climate—a climate filled with torrents of hatred and jostling winds of violence. He was murdered by an atmosphere of inhumanity in Alabama that tolerated the vicious murder of Jimmy Lee Jackson in Marion and the brutal beatings of Sunday in Selma. Had police not brutally beaten unarmed nonviolent persons desiring the right to vote on Sunday, it is doubtful whether this act of murder would have taken place on Tuesday. This is additional proof that segregation knows no color line. It attempts to control the movement and mind of white persons as well as Negroes. When it cannot dominate, it murders those that dissent.

"From Selma to Montgomery"

As soon as we had won legal affirmation on March 11 of our right to march to Montgomery, the next phase hinged on the successful completion of our mission to petition the governor to take meaningful measures to abolish voting restrictions, the poll tax, and police brutality. The President and federal judiciary had spoken affirmatively of the cause for which we struggled. All citizens had to make their personal witness. We could no longer accept the injustices that we had faced from Governor Wallace. We could no longer adjust to the evils that we had faced all of these years.

We made it very clear that this was a march of goodwill and to stimulate the Negro citizenry of Montgomery to make use of the new opportunity that had been provided through the federal court. We had a legal and constitutional right to march from Selma to Montgomery. We were very serious in saying that we planned to walk to Montgomery, and we went through a great deal of work and spent a lot of time planning the route, the stopping points, the tents and where they would be. We felt this would be a privilege that citizens could engage in as long as they didn't tie up traffic and walk out on the main highway but on the side of the road. Hosea Williams reported to me that there were three bridges, but that one could walk across these bridges single file rather than two or three abreast.

Things were shaping up beautifully. We had people coming in from all over the country. I suspected that we would have representatives from almost every state in the union, and naturally a large number from the state of Alabama. We hoped to see, and we planned to see, the greatest witness for freedom that had ever taken place on the steps of the capitol of any state in the South. And this whole march added drama to this total thrust. I think it will go down in American history on the same level as the March to the Sea did in Indian history.

Some of us started out on March 21 marching from Selma, Alabama. We walked through desolate valleys and across tiring hills. We walked on meandering highways and rested our bodies on rocky byways. Some of our faces were burnt from the outpourings of the sweltering sun. Some literally slept in the mud. We were drenched by the rain. Our bodies were tired. Our feet were sore. The thousands of pilgrims had marched across a route traveled by Sherman a hundred years before. But in contrast to a trail of destruction and bloodshed, they watered the red Alabama clay with tears of joy and love overflowing, even for those who taunted and jeered along the sidelines. Not a shot was fired. Not a stone displaced. Not a window broken. Not a person abused or insulted. This was certainly a triumphant entry into the "Cradle of the Confederacy." And an entry destined to put an end to that racist oligarchy once and for all.

It was with great optimism that we marched into Montgomery on March 25. The smell of victory was in the air. Voting rights legislation loomed as a certainty in the weeks ahead. Fifty thousand non-violent crusaders from every county in Alabama and practically every state in the union gathered in Montgomery on a balmy spring afternoon to petition Governor Wallace.

"How long? Not long"

So I stand before you this afternoon with the conviction that segregation is on its deathbed in Alabama and the only thing uncertain about it is how costly the segregationists and Wallace will make the funeral.

Our whole campaign in Alabama has been centered around the right to vote. In focusing the attention of the nation and the world today on the flagrant denial of the right to vote, we are exposing the very origin, the root cause, of racial segregation in the Southland.

The threat of the free exercise of the ballot by the Negro and the white masses alike resulted in the establishing of a segregated society. They segregated Southern money from the poor whites; they segregated Southern churches from Christianity; they segregated Southern minds from honest thinking; and they segregated the Negro from everything.

We have come a long way since that travesty of justice was perpetrated upon the American mind. Today I want to tell the city of Selma, today I want to tell the state of Alabama, today I want to say to the people of America and the nations of the world: We are not about to turn around. We are on the move now. Yes, we are on the move and no wave of racism can stop us.

We are on the move now. The burning of our churches will not deter us. We are on the move now. The bombing of our homes will not dissuade us. We are on the move now. The beating and killing of our clergymen and young people will not divert us. We are on the move now. The arrest and release of known murderers will not discourage us. We are on the move now.

Like an idea whose time has come, not even the marching of mighty armies can halt us. We are moving to the land of freedom.

Let us therefore continue our triumph and march to the realization of the American dream. Let us march on segregated housing until every ghetto of social and economic depression dissolves and Negroes and whites live side by side in decent, safe, and sanitary housing.

Let us march on segregated schools until every vestige of segregated and inferior education becomes a thing of the past and Negroes and whites study side by side in the socially healing context of the classroom.

Let us march on poverty until no American parent has to skip a meal so that their children may eat. March on poverty until no starved man walks the streets of our cities and towns in search of jobs that do not exist.

Let us march on ballot boxes, march on ballot boxes until race baiters disappear from the political arena. Let us march on ballot boxes until the Wallaces of our nation tremble away in silence.

Let us march on ballot boxes until we send to our city councils, state legislatures, and the United States Congress men who will not fear to do justice, love mercy, and walk humbly with their God. Let us march on ballot boxes until all over Alabama God's children will be able to walk the earth in decency and honor.

For all of us today the battle is in our hands. The road ahead is not altogether a smooth one. There are no broad highways to lead us easily and inevitably to quick solutions. We must keep going.

My people, my people, listen! The battle is in our hands. The battle is in our hands in Mississippi and Alabama, and all over the United States.

So as we go away this afternoon, let us go away more than ever before committed to the struggle and committed to nonviolence. I must admit to you there are still some difficulties ahead. We are still in for a season of suffering in many of the black belt counties of Alabama, many areas of Mississippi, many areas of Louisiana.

I must admit to you there are still jail cells waiting for us, dark and difficult moments. We will go on with the faith that nonviolence and its power transformed dark yesterdays into bright tomorrows. We will be able to change all of these conditions.

Our aim must never be to defeat or humiliate the white man but to win his friendship and understanding. We must come to see that the end we seek is a society at peace with itself, a society that can live with its conscience. That will be a day not of the white man, not of the black man. That will be the day of man as man.

I know you are asking today, "How long will it take?" I come to say to you this afternoon however difficult the moment, however frustrating the hour, it will not be long, because truth pressed to earth will rise again.

How long? Not long, because no lie can live forever.

How long? Not long, because you still reap what you sow.

How long? Not long. Because the arm of the moral universe is long, but it bends toward justice.

How long? Not long, because mine eyes have seen the glory of the coming of the Lord, trampling out the vintage where the grapes of wrath are stored. He has loosed the fateful lightning of his terrible swift sword. His truth is marching on.

He has sounded forth the trumpets that shall never call retreat. He is lifting up the hearts of men before His judgment seat. Oh, be swift, my soul, to answer Him. Be jubilant, my feet. Our God is marching on.

As the trains loaded and the busses embarked for their destinations, as the inspired throng returned to their homes to organize the final phase of political activity which would complete the revolution so eloquently proclaimed by the word and presence of the multitude in Montgomery, the scent of victory in the air gave way to the stench of death. We were reminded that this was not a march to the capital of a civilized nation, as was the March on Washington. We had marched through a swamp of poverty, ignorance, race hatred, and sadism.

We were reminded that the only reason that this march was possible was due to the presence of thousands of federalized troops,

marshals, and a federal court. We were reminded that the troops
would soon be going home, and that in the days to come we had to
renew our attempts to organize the very county in which Mrs. Viola
Liuzzo was murdered. If they murdered a white woman for standing
up for the Negro's right to vote, what would they do to Negroes who
attempted to register and vote?

Certainly it should not have been necessary for more of us to
die, to suffer jailings and beatings at the hands of sadistic savages in
uniforms. The Alabama voting project had been total in its commitment to nonviolence, and yet people were beginning to talk more
and more of arming themselves. The people who followed along the
fringe of the movement, who seldom came into the nonviolent
training sessions, were growing increasingly bitter and restless. But
we could not allow even the thought or spirit of violence to creep
into our movement.

When we marched from Selma to Montgomery, Alabama, I remember that we had one of the most magnificent expressions of the
ecumenical movement that I've ever seen. Protestants, Catholics,
and Jews joined together in a beautiful way to articulate the injustices and the indignities that Negroes were facing in the state of Alabama and all over the South on the question of the right to vote. I
had seen many clergymen come to the forefront who were not there
some years ago. The march gave new relevance to the gospel. Selma
brought into being the second great awakening of the church in
America. Long standing aside and giving tacit approval to the civil
rights struggle, the church finally marched forth like a mighty army
and stood beside God's children in distress.

Stalwart nonviolent activists within our ranks had brought about
a coalition of the nation's conscience on the infamous stretch of
highway between Selma and Montgomery. The awakening of the
church also brought a new vitality to the labor movement, and to
intellectuals across the country. A little known fact was that forty of
the nation's top historians took part in the march to Montgomery.

One can still hear the tramping feet and remember the glowing
eyes filled with determination and hope which said eloquently, "*We
must be free*," a sound which echoed throughout this nation, and
yes, even throughout the world. My mind still remembers vividly

the ecumenicity of the clergy, the combined forces of labor, civil rights organizations, and the academic community which joined our ranks and said in essence, "Your cause is morally right, and we are with you all the way."

After the march to Montgomery, there was a delay at the airport and several thousand demonstrators waited more than five hours, crowding together on the seats, the floors, and the stairways of the terminal building. As I stood with them and saw white and Negro, nuns and priests, housemaids and shop workers brimming with vitality and enjoying a rare comradeship, I knew I was seeing a microcosm of the mankind of the future in that moment of luminous and genuine brotherhood.

"Selma brought us a voting bill"

In his address to the joint session of Congress on March 15, 1965, President Johnson made one of the most eloquent, unequivocal, and passionate pleas for human rights ever made by a President of the United States. He revealed an amazing understanding of the depth and dimension of the problem of racial justice. His tone and his delivery were sincere. He rightly praised the courage of the Negro for awakening the conscience of the nation. He declared that the national government must by law insure every Negro his full rights as a citizen. When he signed the measure, the President announced that, "Today is a triumph for freedom as huge as any victory that's ever been won on any battlefield. Today we strike away the last major shackle of fierce and ancient bonds."

We were happy to know that our struggle in Selma had brought the whole issue of the right to vote to the attention of the nation. It was encouraging to know that we had the support of the President in calling for immediate relief of the problems of the disinherited people of our nation.

When SCLC went into Selma in January 1965, it had limited objectives. It sought primarily to correct wrongs existing in that small city. But our adversaries met us with such unrestrained brutality that they enlarged the issues to a national scale. The ironic and splendid result of the small Selma project was nothing less than the Voting Rights Act of 1965. For the aid Governor Wallace and Sheriff

Clark gave us in our legislative objectives, SCLC tendered them its warm appreciation.

In conclusion, Selma brought us a voting bill, and it also brought us the grand alliance of the children of light in this nation and made possible changes in our political and economic life heretofore undreamed of. With President Johnson, SCLC viewed the Voting Rights Act of 1965 as "one of the most monumental laws in the history of American freedom." We had a federal law which could be used, and use it we would. Where it fell short, we had our tradition of struggle and the method of nonviolent direct action, and these too we would use.

Let us not mark this great movement only by bloodshed and brutality. We certainly can never forget those who gave their lives in this struggle and who suffered in jail, but let us especially mark the sacrifices of Jimmie Lee Jackson, Rev. James Reeb, and Mrs. Viola Liuzzo as the martyrs of the faith. Cities that had been citadels of the status quo became the unwilling birthplace of a significant national legislation. Montgomery led to the Civil Rights Acts of 1957 and 1960; Birmingham inspired the Civil Rights Act of 1964; and Selma produced the Voting Rights Act of 1965.

When President Johnson declared that Selma, Alabama, is joined in American history with Lexington, Concord, and Appomattox, he honored not only our embattled Negroes, but the overwhelming majority of the nation, Negro and white. The victory in Selma is now being written in the Congress. Before long, more than a million Negroes will be new voters—and psychologically, new people. Selma is a shining moment in the conscience of man. If the worst in American life lurked in the dark streets of Selma, the best of American democratic instincts arose from across the nation to overcome it.

27

WATTS

As soon as we began to see our way clear in the South, the shock and horror of Northern riots exploded before our eyes and we saw that the problems of the Negro go far beyond mere racial segregation. The catastrophe in Los Angeles was a result of seething and rumbling tensions throughout our nation and, indeed, the world.

AUGUST 11–15, 1965
Widespread racial violence in Los Angeles results in more than 30 deaths

AUGUST 17
King arrives in Los Angeles at the invitation of local groups

As we entered the Watts area of Los Angeles, all seemed quiet, but there could still be sensed raging hostility which had erupted in volcanic force in the days previous. What had been an inferno of flame and smoke a few nights before was now an occupied territory. National Guardsmen in groups of three and four stood posted on each street corner. People, black and white, meandered through the charred remains of the Watts business district.

I had been warned not to visit. We were told that the people were in no mood to hear talk of nonviolence. There had been wild threats hurled at all Negro leaders and many were afraid to venture into the area. But I had visited Watts on many occasions and received the most generous of acclamations. One of the most responsive and enthusiastic gatherings I ever saw was our meeting in Watts during the "Get-Out-the-Vote" tour in 1964. So, despite the warn-ings, I was determined to hear firsthand from the people involved, just what the riot was all about.

Let me say first of all that I profoundly deplore the events that have occurred in Los Angeles in these last few tragic days. I believe and have said on many occasions that violence is not the answer to social conflict whether it is engaged in by white people in Alabama or by Negroes in Los Angeles. Violence is all the more regrettable in this period in light of the tremendous nonviolent sacrifices that both Negro and white people together have endured to bring justice to all men.

But it is equally clear, as President Johnson pointed out yesterday, that it is the job of all Americans "to right the wrong from which such violence and disorder spring." The criminal responses which led to the tragic outbreaks of violence in Los Angeles are environmental and not racial. The economic deprivation, racial isolation, inadequate housing, and general despair of thousands of Negroes teaming in Northern and Western ghettoes are the ready seeds which gave birth to tragic expressions of violence. By acts of commission and omission none of us in this great country has done enough to remove injustice. I therefore humbly suggest that all of us accept our share of responsibility for these past days of anguish.

"Stirring of a deprived people"

After visiting Watts and talking with hundreds of persons of all walks of life, it was my opinion that the riots grew out of the depths of despair which afflict a people who see no way out of their economic dilemma.

There were serious doubts that the white community was in any way concerned. There also was a growing disillusionment and resentment toward the Negro middle class and the leadership which it had produced. This ever-widening breach was a serious factor which led to a feeling on the part of ghetto-imprisoned Negroes that they were alone in their struggle and had to resort to any method to gain attention to their plight.

The nonviolent movement of the South meant little to them since we had been fighting for rights which theoretically were already theirs; therefore, I believed what happened in Los Angeles was of grave national significance. What we witnessed in the Watts area was the beginning of a stirring of a deprived people in a society who had been by-passed by the progress of the previous decade. I would minimize the racial significance and point to the fact that these were the rumblings of discontent from the "have nots" within the midst of an affluent society.

The issue of police brutality loomed as one of major significance. The slightest discourtesy on the part of an officer of the law was a deprivation of the dignity that most of the residents of Watts came west seeking. Whether it was true or not, the Negro of the ghetto was convinced that his dealings with the police denied him the dignity and respect to which he was entitled as a citizen and a human being. This produced a sullen, hostile attitude, which resulted in a spiral of hatred on the part of both the officer and the Negro. This whole reaction complex was often coupled with fear on the part of both parties. Every encounter between a Negro and the police in the hovering hostility of the ghetto was a potential outburst.

A misguided fire truck, a conflict in arrest, a sharp word between a store owner and customer—the slightest incident can trigger a riot in a community, but events converge in such a cataclysmic manner that often the situation seems to be the result of a planned organized attempt at insurrection. This was the term used by Mayor Sam Yorty—an insurrection staged by a group of organized criminals.

I am afraid that this was too superficial an explanation. Two separate and distinct forces were operating in Los Angeles. One was a hardened criminal element incapable of restraint by appeals to reason or discipline. This was a small number in contrast to the large number involved. The larger group of participants were not criminal elements. I was certain that the majority of the more than four thousand persons arrested in Los Angeles were being arrested for the first time. They were the disorganized, the frustrated, and the oppressed. Their looting was a form of social protest. Forgotten by society, taunted by the affluence around them, but effectively barred from its reach, they were acting out hostilities as a method of relief and to focus attention.

The objective of the people with whom I talked was consistently work and dignity. It was as though the speeches had been rehearsed, but on every corner the theme was the same. Unless some work could be found for the unemployed and underemployed, we would continually face the possibility of this kind of outbreak at every encounter with police authority. At a time when the Negro's aspirations were at a peak, his actual conditions of employment, education, and housing were worsening. The paramount problem is one of economic stability for this sector of our society. All other advances in education, family life, and the moral climate of the community were dependent upon the ability of the masses of Negroes to earn a living in this wealthy society of ours.

In the South there is something of shared poverty, Negro and white. In the North, white existence, only steps away, glares with conspicuous consumption. Even television becomes incendiary, when it beams pictures of affluent homes and multitudinous consumer products at the aching poor, living in wretched homes. In these terms, Los Angeles could have expected riots because it is the luminous symbol of luxurious living for whites. Watts is closer to it, and yet farther from it, than any other Negro community in the country. The looting in Watts was a form of social protest very common through the ages as a dramatic and destructive gesture of the poor toward symbols of their needs.

◆

ENCOUNTER IN WATTS

I was out in Watts during the riots. One young man said to me—and Andy Young, Bayard Rustin, and Bernard Lee, who were with me—"We won!" I said, "What do you mean, 'we won'? Thirty-some people dead—all but two are Negroes. You've destroyed your own. What do you mean, 'we won'?" And he said, "We made them pay attention to us."

When people are voiceless, they will have temper tantrums like a little child who has not been paid attention to. And riots are massive temper tantrums from a neglected and voiceless people.

July 1967

◆

There was joy among the rioters of Watts, not shame. They were completely oblivious to the destruction of property in their wake. They were destroying a physical and emotional jail; they had asserted themselves against a system which was quietly crushing them into oblivion and now they were "somebody." As one young man put it,

"We know that a riot is not the answer, but we've been down here suffering for a long time and nobody cared. Now at least they know we're here. A riot may not be *the* way, but it is *a* way." This was the new nationalist mood gripping a good many ghetto inhabitants. It rejected the alliance with white liberals as a means of social change. It affirms the fact that black men act alone in their own interest only, because nobody really cares.

Amazingly enough, and in spite of the inflammatory assertions to the contrary, these were not murderous mobs. They were destructive of property, but with all of the reports of thousands of violent people on the loose, very few people were killed, and almost all of them by the police. Certainly, had the intention of the mob been to murder, many more lives would have been lost.

What I emphasized is that, in spite of all of the hostility that some Negroes felt, and as violent and destructive as the mood temporarily became, it was not yet a blind and irredeemable condition. The people of Watts were hostile to nonviolence, but when we actually went to them and emphasized the dangers of hatred and violence, the same people cheered. Only minutes before the air had been thick with tension, but when they were reminded of the Rev. James Reeb and Viola Liuzzo, the martyrs of the Selma campaign, they cheered the thought that white people can and do cooperate with us in our search for jobs and dignity.

But let no one think that this is a defense of riots. The wake of destruction of property where many Negroes were employed and where many more were served consumer goods was one of the most tragic sights I ever witnessed. It was second only to the thought of thirty-seven persons dying needlessly in an uncontrolled tantrum of devastation and death. This was more human loss than had been suffered in ten years of nonviolent direct action, which produced the revolutionary social changes in the South.

Violence only serves to harden the resistance of the white reactionary and relieve the white liberal of guilt, which might motivate him to action and thereby leaves the condition unchanged and embittered. The backlash of violence is felt far beyond the borders of the community where it takes place. Whites are arming themselves in Selma and across Alabama in the expectation that rioting would spread South. In this kind of atmosphere a single drunken disorderly

Negro could set off the panic button that might result in the killing of many innocent Negroes.

However, a mere condemnation of violence is empty without understanding the daily violence that our society inflicts upon many of its members. The violence of poverty and humiliation hurts as intensely as the violence of the club. This is a situation that calls for statesmanship and creative leadership, of which I did not see evidence in Los Angeles. What we did find was a blind intransigence and ignorance of the tremendous social forces that were at work there. And so long as this stubborn attitude was maintained by responsible authorities, I could only see the situation worsening.

"A crisis for the nonviolent movement"

Los Angeles could have expected the holocaust when its officials tied up federal aid in political manipulation, when the rate of Negro unemployment soared above depression levels of the twenties, and when the population density of Watts became the worst in the nation. Yet even these tormenting physical conditions are less than the full sign. California in 1964 repealed its law forbidding racial discrimination in housing. It was the first major state in the country to take away gains Negroes had won at a time when progress was visible and substantial elsewhere, and especially in the South. California by that callous act voted for ghettos. The atrociousness of some deeds may be concealed by legal ritual, but the destructiveness is felt with bitter force by its victims. When all is finally entered into the annals of sociology; when philosophers, politicians, and preachers have all had their say, we must return to the fact that a person participates in this society primarily as an economic entity. At rock bottom we are neither poets, athletes, nor artists; our existence is centered in the fact that we are consumers, because we first must eat and have shelter to live. This is a difficult confession for a preacher to make, and it is a phenomenon against which I will continue to rebel, but it remains a fact that "consumption" of goods and services is the raison d'être of the vast majority of Americans. When persons are for some reason or other excluded from the consumer circle, there is discontent and unrest.

Watts was not only a crisis for Los Angeles and the Northern cities of our nation: It was a crisis for the nonviolent movement. I tried desperately to maintain a nonviolent atmosphere in which our nation could undergo the tremendous period of social change which confronts us, but this was mainly dependent on the obtaining of tangible progress and victories, if those of us who counsel reason and love were to maintain our leadership. However, the cause was not lost. In spite of pockets of hostility in ghetto areas such as Watts, there was still overwhelming acceptance of the ideal of nonviolence.

I was in touch with the White House on the matter and asked that the President do everything in his power to break the deadlock which had prevented the poverty program from entering Los Angeles. I also asked that the government's efforts be vastly increased toward obtaining full employment for both the Negro and white poor in our country. The President was sensitive to this problem and was prepared to give us the kind of leadership and vision which we needed in those turbulent times.

All in all, my visit to Watts was a tremendous help to me personally. I prayed that somehow leadership and statesmanship would emerge in the places of public office, the press, the business community, and among the Negro leadership and people of Watts, to avoid further conflict. Such a conflict would bring only bloodshed and shame to our entire nation's image abroad.

28

CHICAGO CAMPAIGN

It is reasonable to believe that if the problems of Chicago, the nation's second largest city, can be solved, they can be solved everywhere.

JULY 26, 1965
King leads march to Chicago City Hall and addresses a rally sponsored by Chicago's Coordinating Council of Community Organizations (CCCO)

JANUARY 7, 1966
Announces the start of the Chicago Campaign

JULY 10
At "Freedom Sunday" rally at Soldier's Field, launches drive to make Chicago an "open city" for housing

JULY 12–14
Racial rioting on Chicago's West Side results in two deaths and widespread destruction

AUGUST 5
Angry whites attack civil rights march through Chicago's southwest side

AUGUST 26
Arranges "Summit Agreement" with Mayor R. Daley and other Chicago leaders

In the early summer of 1965 we received invitations from Negro leaders in the city of Chicago to join with them in their fight for quality integrated education. We had watched this movement with interest, and members of the staff of the Southern Christian Leadership Conference had maintained constant communication with the leadership. As a result of meetings between members of my staff and leaders of Chicago civil rights organizations, I agreed to accept the invitation to spend some time in Chicago, beginning July 24.

Later in the year, after careful deliberation with my staff, the SCLC decided to begin a concentrated effort to create a broadly based, vibrant, nonviolent movement in the North. Our efforts would be directed at the social ills which plagued Chicago—the potentially explosive ghetto pathology of the Northern Negro.

My concern for the welfare of Negroes in the North was no less than that for Negroes in the South, and my conscience dictated that I should commit as much of my personal and organizational resources to their cause as was humanly possible. Our primary objective was to bring about the unconditional surrender of forces dedicated to the creation and maintenance of slums and ultimately to make slums a moral and financial liability upon the whole community. Chicago was not alone among cities with a slum problem, but certainly we knew that slum conditions there were the prototype of those chiefly responsible for the Northern urban race problem.

"Breaking down the infamous wall of segregation"

We worked under the Coordinating Council of Community Organizations, a coalition of local civil rights groups, convened by Al Raby, a former Chicago public school teacher. Our main concentration would be on the school issue—a fight for quality integrated education which had been waged in that city for more than five years. This did not mean that we would stop there, because it was painfully clear that the school issue was merely symptomatic of a system which relegated thousands of Negroes into economic and spiritual deprivation.

The only solution to breaking down the infamous wall of segregation in Chicago rested in our being able to mobilize both the white and black communities into a massive nonviolent movement, which would stop at nothing short of changing the ugly face of the black ghetto into a community of love and justice. Essentially it meant removing future generations from dilapidated tenements, opening the doors of job opportunities to all regardless of their color, and making the resources of all social institutions available for their up-lifting into the mainstream of American life.

No longer could we afford to isolate a major segment of our society in a ghetto prison and expect its spiritually crippled wards to accept the advanced social responsibilities of the world's leading na-tion. Birmingham, Alabama, once the most segregated city in the South, had been our target city for public accommodations, and our nonviolent movement there gave birth to the Civil Rights Bill of 1964. Selma, Alabama, had been our pilot city for the Voting Rights Bill of 1965, and I had faith that Chicago, considered one of the most segregated cities in the nation, could well become the metropo-lis where a meaningful nonviolent movement could arouse the con-science of this nation to deal realistically with the Northern ghetto.

We had no illusions that we could undertake alone such a mam-moth task; therefore, our advance SCLC team headed by the Rev. James Bevel laid the groundwork for our movement. We were con-fident that a convergence of many forces—religious, civic, political, and academic—would come about to demand a solution to Chica-go's problems.

It did not require an in-depth evaluation to determine what evils had to be eliminated from our society. Any efforts made to extend and prolong the suffering of Negroes imprisoned in the ghetto would be a flagrant attempt to perpetuate a social crisis capable of exploding in our faces and searing the very soul of this nation. In this regard, it was neither I, nor SCLC, that decided to go north, but rather, existing deplorable conditions and the conscience of good to the cause that summoned us.

"Lawndale was truly an island of poverty"

During 1966 I lived and worked in Chicago. The civil rights move-ment had too often been middle-class oriented and had not moved to the grassroots levels of our communities. So I thought the great challenge facing the civil rights movement was to move into these areas to organize and gain identity with ghetto dwellers and young people in the ghetto. This was one of the reasons why I felt that in moving to Chicago I would live in the very heart of the ghetto. I would not only experience what my brothers and sisters experience in living conditions, but I would be able to live with them.

In a big city like Chicago it is hard to do it overnight, but I thought that all of the civil rights organizations had to work more to organize the grassroots levels of our communities. There, the problems of poverty and despair were more than an academic exercise. The phone rang daily with stories of the most drastic forms of man's inhumanity to man and I found myself fighting a daily battle against the depression and hopelessness which the heart of our cities pumps into the spiritual bloodstream of our lives. The problems of poverty and despair were graphically illustrated. I remember a baby attacked by rats in a Chicago slum. I remember a young Negro murdered by a gang in Cicero, where he was looking for a job.

The slum of Lawndale was truly an island of poverty in the midst of an ocean of plenty. Chicago boasted the highest per capita income of any city in the world, but you would never believe it looking out of the windows of my apartment in the slum of Lawndale. From this vantage point you saw only hundreds of children playing in the streets. You saw the light of intelligence glowing in their beautiful dark eyes. Then you realized their overwhelming joy because someone had simply stopped to say hello; for they lived in a world where even their parents were often forced to ignore them. In the tight squeeze of economic pressure, their mothers and fathers both had to work; indeed, more often than not, the father will hold two jobs, one in the day and another at night. With the long distances ghetto parents had to travel to work and the emotional exhaustion that comes from the daily struggle to survive in a hostile world, they were left with too little time or energy to attend to the emotional needs of their growing children.

Too soon you began to see the effects of this emotional and environmental deprivation. The children's clothes were too skimpy to protect them from the Chicago wind, and a closer look revealed the mucus in the corners of their bright eyes, and you were reminded that vitamin pills and flu shots were luxuries which they could ill afford. The "runny noses" of ghetto children became a graphic symbol of medical neglect in a society which had mastered most of the diseases from which they will too soon die. There was something wrong in a society which allowed this to happen.

My neighbors paid more rent in the substandard slums of Lawndale than the whites paid for modern apartments in the suburbs. The situation was much the same for consumer goods, purchase prices of homes, and a variety of other services. This exploitation was possible because so many of the residents of the ghetto had no personal means of transportation. It was a vicious circle. You could not get a job because you were poorly educated, and you had to depend on welfare to feed your children; but if you received public aid in Chicago, you could not own property, not even an automobile, so you were condemned to the jobs and shops closest to your home. Once confined to this isolated community, one no longer participated in a free economy, but was subject to price fixing and wholesale robbery by many of the merchants of the area.

Finally, when a man was able to make his way through the maze of handicaps and get just one foot out of the jungle of poverty and exploitation, he was subject to the whims of the political and economic giants of the city, which moved in impersonally to crush the little flower of success that had just begun to bloom.

It is a psychological axiom that frustration generates aggression. Certainly, the Northern ghetto daily victimized its inhabitants. The Chicago West Side with its concentration of slums, the poor, and the young, represented in grotesque exaggeration the suppression that Negroes of all classes feel within the ghetto.

The Northern ghetto had become a type of colonial area. The colony was powerless because all important decisions affecting the community were made from the outside. Many of its inhabitants even had their daily lives dominated by the welfare worker and the policeman. The profits of landlord and merchant were removed and seldom if ever reinvested. The only positive thing the larger society saw in the slum was that it was a source of cheap surplus labor in times of economic boom. Otherwise, its inhabitants were blamed for their own victimization.

"An emotional pressure cooker"

This type of daily frustration was violence visited upon the slum inhabitants. Our society was only concerned that the aggressions thus generated did not burst outward. Therefore, our larger society had encouraged the hostility it created within slum dwellers to turn inward—to manifest itself in aggression toward one another or in self-destruction and apathy. The larger society was willing to let the frustrations born of racism's violence become internalized and consume its victims. America's horror was only expressed when the aggression turned outward, when the ghetto and its controls could no longer contain its destructiveness. In many a week as many Negro youngsters were killed in gang fights as were killed in the riots. Yet there was no citywide expression of horror.

Our own children lived with us in Lawndale, and it was only a few days before we became aware of the change in their behavior. Their tempers flared, and they sometimes reverted to almost infantile behavior. During the summer, I realized that the crowded flat in which we lived was about to produce an emotional explosion in my own family. It was just too hot, too crowded, too devoid of creative forms of recreation. There was just not space enough in the neighborhood to run off the energy of childhood without running into busy, traffic-laden streets. And I understood anew the conditions which make of the ghetto an emotional pressure cooker.

In all the speaking that I have done in the United States before varied audiences, including some hostile whites, the only time that I have ever been booed was one night in our regular weekly mass meeting by some angry young men of our movement. I went home that night with an ugly feeling. Selfishly, I thought of my sufferings and sacrifices over the last twelve years. Why would they boo one so close to them? But as I lay awake thinking, I finally came to myself, and I could not for the life of me have less than patience and understanding for those young people.

For twelve years I, and others like me, had held out radiant promises of progress. I had preached to them about my dream. I had lectured to them about the not too distant day when they would have freedom, "all, here and now." I had urged them to have faith in America and in white society. Their hopes had soared. They booed because they felt that we were unable to deliver on our promises, and because we had urged them to have faith in people who had too often proved to be unfaithful. They were hostile because they were watching the dream that they had so readily accepted turn into a frustrating nightmare.

When we first went to Chicago, there were those who were saying that the nonviolent movement couldn't work in the North, that problems were too complicated and that they were much different from the South and all that. I contended that nonviolence could work in the North.

This is no time to engage in the luxury of cooling off or to take the tranquilizing drug of gradualism. Now is the time to make real the promises of democracy, now is the time to open the doors of opportunity to all of God's children. Now is the time to end the long and desolate night of slumism. Now is the time to have a confrontation between the forces resisting change and the forces demanding change. Now is the time to let justice roll down like water and righteousness like a mighty stream.

We also come here today to affirm that we will no longer sit idly by in agonizing deprivation and wait on others to provide our freedom. We will be sadly mistaken if we think freedom is some lavish dish that the federal government and the white man will pass out on a silver platter while the Negro merely furnishes the appetite. Freedom is never voluntarily granted by the oppressor. It must be demanded by the oppressed.

"Resorting to violence against oppression"

The responsibility for the social eruption in July 1966 lay squarely upon the shoulders of those elected officials whose myopic social vision had been further blurred by political expedience rather than commitment to the betterment of living conditions and dedication to the eradication of slums and the forces which create and maintain slum communities. It must be remembered that genuine peace is not the absence of tension, but the presence of justice. Justice was not present on Chicago's West Side, or for that matter, in other slum communities.

Riots grow out of intolerable conditions. Violent revolts are generated by revolting conditions and there is nothing more dangerous than to build a society with a large segment of people who feel they have no stake in it, who feel they have nothing to lose. To the young victim of the slums, this society has so limited the alternatives of his life that the expression of his manhood is reduced to the ability to defend himself physically. No wonder it appears logical to him to strike out, resorting to violence against oppression. That is the only way he thinks he gets recognition.

After the riot in Chicago that summer, I was greatly discouraged. But we had trained a group of about two thousand disciplined devotees of nonviolence who were willing to take blows without retaliating. We started out engaging in constitutional privileges, marching before real estate offices in all-white communities. And that nonviolent, disciplined, determined force created such a crisis in the city of Chicago that the city had to do something to change conditions. We didn't have any Molotov cocktails, we didn't have any bricks, we didn't have any guns, we just had the power of our bodies and our souls. There was power there, and it was demonstrated once more.

I remember when the riot broke out that summer, some of the gang leaders and fellows were out there encouraging the riot. I'd been trying to talk to them, and I couldn't get to them. Then they sent the National Guard in, and that night I said, "Well, why aren't you all out there tonight? Now what you've got to do is join with us and let us get a movement that the National Guard can't stop. This is what we've got to do. I'm going on with nonviolence because I've tried it so long. I've come to see how far it has brought us. And I'm not going to turn my back on it now."

In the aftermath of the riot there were concerted attempts to discredit the nonviolent movement. Scare headlines announced paramilitary conspiracies—only to have the attorney general of the United States announce that these claims were totally unfounded. More seriously, there was a concerted attempt to place the responsibility for the riot upon the nonviolent Chicago Freedom Movement and upon myself. Both of these maneuvers were attempts to dodge the fundamental issue of racial subjugation. They represented an unwillingness to do anything more than put the lid back on the pot and a refusal to make fundamental structural changes required to right our racial wrongs.

The Chicago Freedom Movement would not be dampened by these phony accusations. We would not divert our energies into meaningless introspection. The best remedy we had to offer for riots was to press our nonviolent program even more vigorously. We stepped up our plans for nonviolent direct actions to make Chicago an open and just city.

"Demonstrations for open housing"

Mid-summer of 1966 saw the boil of Northern racism burst and spread its poisons throughout the streets of Chicago as thousands of Negro and white marchers began their demonstrations for open housing. When we were demonstrating around the whole issue of open housing, we were confronted with massive violence as we marched into certain areas. We suffered in the process of trying to dramatize the issue through our marches into all-white areas that denied us access to houses and where real estate agents would not allow us to see the listings.

Bottles and bricks were thrown at us; we were often beaten. Some of the people who had been brutalized in Selma and who were present at the Capitol ceremonies in Montgomery led marchers in the suburbs of Chicago amid a rain of rocks and bottles, among burning automobiles, to the thunder of jeering thousands, many of them waving Nazi flags. Swastikas bloomed in Chicago parks like misbegotten weeds. Our marchers were met by a hailstorm of bricks, bottles, and firecrackers. "White power" became the racist catcall, punctuated by the vilest of obscenities—most frequently directly at Catholic priests and nuns among the marchers. I've been in many demonstrations all across the South, but I can say that I had never seen, even in Mississippi, mobs as hostile and as hate-filled as in Chicago.

When we had our open housing marches many of our white liberal friends cried out in horror and dismay: "You are creating hatred and hostility in the white communities in which you are marching. You are only developing a white backlash." They failed to realize that the hatred and the hostilities were already latently or subconsciously present. Our marches merely brought them to the surface.

What insane logic it is to condemn the robbed man because his possession of money precipitates the evil act of robbery. Society must condemn the robber and never the robbed. What insane logic it is to condemn Socrates because his philosophical delving precipitated the evil act of making him drink the hemlock. What an insane logic it is to condemn Jesus Christ because his love for God and Truth precipitated the evil act of his crucifixion. We must condemn those who are perpetuating the violence, and not those individuals who engage in the pursuit of their constitutional rights.

We were the social physicians of Chicago revealing that there was a terrible cancer. We didn't cause it. This cancer was not in its terminal state, it was in its early stages and might be cured if we got at it. Not only were we the social physicians, in the physical sense, but we were the social psychiatrists, bringing out things that were in the subconscious all along. Those people probably had latent hostilities toward Negroes for many, many years. As long as the struggle was down in Alabama and Mississippi, they could look afar and think about it and say how terrible people are. When they discovered brotherhood had to be a reality in Chicago and that brotherhood extended to next door, then those latent hostilities came out.

Day after day during those Chicago marches, I never saw anyone retaliate with violence. There were lots of provocations, not only screaming white hoodlums lining the sidewalks, but also groups of Negro militants talking about guerrilla warfare. We had some gang leaders and members marching with us. I remember walking with the Blackstone Rangers while bottles were flying from the sidelines, and I saw their noses being broken and blood flowing from their wounds; and I saw them continue and not retaliate, not one of them, with violence. I am convinced that even violent temperaments can be channeled through nonviolent discipline, if they can act constructively and express through an effective channel their very legitimate anger.

In August, after being out a few days in Mississippi for the annual convention of the Southern Christian Leadership Conference, I was back in Chicago. The Board of Realtors of the Real Estate Board of the City of Chicago made certain statements concerning a willingness to do things that had not been done before. We wanted to see if they were serious about it. A meeting on August 17 lasted almost ten hours. It was a fruitful meeting, but we didn't get enough out of that meeting to merit calling off our demonstrations, so our demonstrations continued.

I just want to warn the city that it would be an act of folly, in the midst of seeking to negotiate a solution to this problem, to go seek an injunction, because if they don't know it, we are veteran jail-goers. And for us, jail cells are not dungeons of shame, they are havens of freedom and human dignity. I've been to jail in Alabama, I've been to jail in Florida, I've been to jail in Georgia, I've been to jail in Mississippi, I've been to jail in Virginia, and I'm ready to go to jail in Chicago. All I'm saying, my friends, is very simple: we sing a song in this movement, "Ain't Gonna Let Nobody Turn Me 'Round."

We had almost round-the-clock negotiations and hammered out what would probably stand out as the most significant and far-reaching victory that has ever come about in a Northern community on the whole question of open housing. For the first time in the city of Chicago, and probably any other city, the whole power structure was forced by the power of the nonviolent movement to sit down and negotiate and capitulate, and made concessions that had never been made before. Our nonviolent marches in Chicago of the summer brought about a housing agreement which, if implemented, would have been the strongest step toward open housing taken in any city in the nation.

"A drive to end slums"

When we first joined forces with the Coordinating Council of Community Organizations, we outlined a drive to end slums. We viewed slums and slumism as more than a problem of dilapidated, inadequate housing. We understood them as the end product of domestic colonialism: slum housing and slum schools, unemployment and underemployment, segregated and inadequate education, welfare dependency and political servitude. Because no single attack could hope to deal with this overwhelming problem, we established a series of concurrent projects aimed at each facet. Two significant programs were developed to this end.

We had a vigorous, turbulent campaign to make Chicago an open city. We knew that in spite of a marvelous open housing agreement on paper that we reached in Chicago, open housing was not going to be a reality in Chicago in the next year or two. We knew that it was going to take time to really open that city, and we could not neglect those who lived in the ghetto communities in the process.

At the same time Negro neighborhoods had to be made more hospitable for those who remained. Tenant unions, modeled after labor organizations, became the collective bargaining agents between landlord and resident. This program had remarkable success. In less than a year, unions were formed in three of the city's worst slum and ghetto areas. The collective bargaining contracts also included such measures as rent freezes and stabilization, daily janitorial and sanitation services, and immediate repairs of facilities that jeopardized health and safety. Twelve other smaller tenants unions also sprung up in various communities throughout the city. All met regularly in an informal federation.

Another phase of the housing thrust concerned neighborhood rehabilitation. The unique aspect of this program lay in the fact that the rehabilitated buildings would be turned over to housing cooperatives organized in each of the neighborhoods. The residents therefore gained their much-needed voice in management and administration of the properties. It was through such moves that we hoped to break the cycle of defeatism and psychological servitude that marked the mentality of slumism, achieving human as well as housing renewal.

The most spectacularly successful program in Chicago was Operation Breadbasket. Operation Breadbasket had a very simple program but a powerful one: "If you respect my dollar, you must respect my person." The philosophical undergirding of Operation Breadbasket rested in the belief that many retail business and consumer goods industries depleted the ghetto by selling to Negroes without returning to the community any of the profits through fair hiring practices. To reverse this pattern Operation Breadbasket committees selected a target industry, then obtained the employment statistics of individual companies within it. If the proportion of Negro employees was unsatisfactory, or if they were confined to the menial jobs, the company was approached to negotiate a more equitable employment practice. Leverage was applied where necessary through selective buying campaigns organized by the clergymen through their congregations and through the movement. They simply said, "We will no longer spend our money where we cannot get substantial jobs."

By 1967 SCLC had Operation Breadbasket functioning in some twelve cities, and the results were remarkable. In Chicago, Operation Breadbasket successfully completed negotiations with three major industries: milk, soft drinks, and chain grocery stores. Four of the companies involved concluded reasonable agreements only after short "don't buy" campaigns. Seven other companies were able to make the requested changes across the conference table, without necessitating a boycott. Two other companies, after providing their employment information to the ministers, were sent letters of commendation for their healthy equal-employment practices. The net results added up to approximately eight hundred new and upgraded jobs for Negro employees, worth a little over $7 million in new annual income for Negro families. We added a new dimension to Operation Breadbasket. Along with requesting new job opportunities, we requested that businesses with stores in the ghetto deposit the income for those establishments in Negro-owned banks, and that Negro-owned products be placed on the counters of all their stores.

"A special and unique relationship to Jews"

When we were working in Chicago, we had numerous rent strikes on the West Side, and it was unfortunately true that, in most instances, the persons we had to conduct these strikes against were Jewish landlords. There was a time when the West Side of Chicago was a Jewish ghetto, and when the Jewish community started moving out into other areas, they still owned the property there, and all of the problems of the landlord came into being.

We were living in a slum apartment owned by a Jew and a number of others, and we had to have a rent strike. We were paying $94 for four run-down, shabby rooms, and we would go out on our open housing marches on Gage Park and other places and we discovered that whites with five sanitary, nice, new rooms, apartments with five rooms, were paying only $78 a month. We were paying 20 percent tax.

The Negro ends up paying a color tax, and this has happened in instances where Negroes actually confronted Jews as the landlord or the storekeeper. The irrational statements that have been made are the result of these confrontations.

The limited degree of Negro anti-Semitism is substantially a Northern ghetto phenomenon; it virtually does not exist in the South. The urban Negro has a special and unique relationship to Jews. He meets them in two dissimilar roles. On the one hand, he is associated with Jews as some of his most committed and generous partners in the civil rights struggle. On the other hand, he meets them daily as some of his most direct exploiters in the ghetto as slum landlords and gouging shopkeepers. Jews have identified with Negroes voluntarily in the freedom movement, motivated by their religious and cultural commitment to justice. The other Jews who are engaged in commerce in the ghettos are remnants of older communities. A great number of Negro ghettos were formerly Jewish neighborhoods; some storekeepers and landlords remained as population changes occurred. They operate with the ethics of marginal business entrepreneurs, not Jewish ethics, but the distinction is lost on some Negroes who are maltreated by them. Such Negroes, caught in frustration and irrational anger, parrot racial epithets. They foolishly add to the social poison that injures themselves and their own people.

It would be a tragic and immoral mistake to identify the mass of Negroes with the very small number that succumb to cheap and dishonest slogans, just as it would be a serious error to identify all Jews with the few who exploit Negroes under their economic sway.

Negroes cannot irrationally expect honorable Jews to curb the few who are rapacious; they have no means of disciplining or suppressing them. We can only expect them to share our disgust and disdain. Negroes cannot be expected to curb and eliminate the few who are anti-Semitic, because they are subject to no controls we can exercise. We can, however, oppose them, and we have in concrete ways. There has never been a instance of articulated Negro anti-Semitism that was not swiftly condemned by virtually all Negro leaders with the support of the overwhelming majority. I have myself directly attacked it within the Negro community, because it is wrong. I will continue to oppose it, because it is immoral and self-destructive.

"A year of beginnings and of transition"

In March 1967 we announced my resumption of regular activities in Chicago on a schedule similar to that I maintained from January through November of the previous year. I took a brief leave of absence from our civil rights action program in order to write a book on the problems and progress of the movement during the past few years. I spent the months of January and February completing my book, entitled *Where Do We Go from Here, Chaos or Community?* In March I met with Al Raby and Chicago's other outstanding and committed civil rights leaders to evaluate the progress of our several ongoing programs and to lay plans for the next phase of our drive to end slums.

It was clear to me that city agencies had been inert in upholding their commitment to the open housing pact. I had to express our swelling disillusionment with the foot-dragging negative actions of agencies such as the Chicago Housing Authority, Department of Urban Renewal, and the Commission on Human Relations. It appeared that, for all intents and purposes, the public agencies had reneged on the agreement and had in fact given credence to the apostles of social disorder who proclaimed the housing agreement a sham and a batch of false promises. The city's inaction was not just a rebuff to the Chicago Freedom Movement or a courtship of the white backlash, but also another hot coal on the smoldering fires of discontent and despair that are rampant in our black communities. For more than a month during the marches we were told to come to the bargaining table, that compromise and negotiation were the only ways to solve the complex, multi-layered problems of open occupancy. We came, we sat, we negotiated. We reached the summit and then nearly seven months later we found that much of the ground had been cut out from beneath us.

I could not say that all was lost. There were many decent respected and sincere persons on the Leadership Council who had not broken faith. I pleaded with those responsible and responsive persons to take a good long hard look at the facts and act now in an effort to regain the spirit of good faith that existed when we began. It was not too late, even with the failures of yesterday to renew the effort and take some first steps toward the goals pledged last August.

Open housing had to become more than a meaningless scrap of paper. It had to become a reality if this city was to be saved. Our minds and our hearts were open for some real good faith reevaluation and determination to move on, but we also were ready to expose this evil. I had about reached the conclusion that it was going to be almost necessary to engage in massive demonstrations to deal with the problem.

We look back at 1966 as a year of beginnings and of transition. For those of us who came to Chicago from Georgia, Mississippi, and Alabama, it was a year of vital education. Our organization, carried out in conjunction with the very capable local leadership, experienced fits and starts, setbacks and positive progress. We found ourselves confronted by the hard realities of a social system in many ways more resistant to change than the rural South.

While we were under no illusions about Chicago, in all frankness we found the job greater than even we imagined. And yet on balance we believed that the combination of our organization and the wide-ranging forces of goodwill in Chicago produced the basis for changes.

I am thinking now of some teenage boys in Chicago. They have nicknames like "Tex," and "Pueblo," and "Goat" and "Teddy." They hail from the Negro slums. Forsaken by society, they once proudly fought and lived for street gangs like the Vice Lords, the Roman Saints, the Rangers. I met these boys and heard their stories in discussions we had on some long, cold nights at the slum apartment I rented in the West Side ghetto of Chicago.

I was shocked at the venom they poured out against the world. At times I shared their despair and felt a hopelessness that these young Americans could ever embrace the concept of nonviolence as the effective and powerful instrument of social reform. All their lives, boys like this have known life as a madhouse of violence and degradation. Some have never experienced a meaningful family life. Some have police records. Some dropped out of the incredibly bad slum schools, then were deprived of honorable work, then took to the streets.

But this year, they gave us all the gift of nonviolence, which is indeed the gift of love. The Freedom Movement has tried to bring a message to boys like Tex. First we explained that violence can be put down by armed might and police work, that physical force can never solve the underlying social problems. Second, we promised them we could prove, by example, that nonviolence works.

The young slum dweller has good reason to be suspicious of promises. But these young people in Chicago agreed last winter to give nonviolence a test. Then came the very long, very tense, hot summer of 1966, and the first test for many Chicago youngsters: the Freedom March through Mississippi. Gang members went there in carloads.

Those of us who had been in the movement for years were apprehensive about the behavior of the boys. Before the march ended, they were to be attacked by tear gas. They were to be called upon to protect women and children on the march, with no other weapon than their own bodies. To them, it would be a strange and possibly nonsensical way to respond to violence.

But they reacted splendidly! They learned in Mississippi, and returned to teach in Chicago, the beautiful lesson of acting against evil by renouncing force.

29

BLACK POWER

Negroes can still march down the path of nonviolence and interracial amity if white America will meet them with honest determination to rid society of its inequality and inhumanity.

JUNE 6, 1966
James Meredith, who integrated the University of Mississippi in 1962, is wounded by a sniper during his "March Against Fear" designed to encourage black voting in Mississippi; King and other civil rights leaders agree to continue the march

JUNE 16
Stokely Carmichael ignites controversy by using the "Black Power" slogan

J ames Meredith has been shot!"

It was about three o'clock in the afternoon on a Monday in June 1966, and I was presiding over the regular staff meeting of the Southern Christian Leadership Conference in our Atlanta headquarters. When we heard that Meredith had been shot in the back only a day after he had begun his Freedom March through Mississippi, there was a momentary hush of anger and dismay throughout the room. Our horror was compounded by the fact that the early reports announced that Meredith was dead. Soon the silence was broken, and from every corner of the room came expressions of outrage. The business of the meeting was forgotten in the shock of this latest evidence that a Negro's life is still worthless in many parts of his own country.

When order was finally restored, our executive staff immediately agreed that the march must continue. After all, we reasoned, Meredith began his lonely journey as a pilgrimage against fear. Wouldn't failure to continue only intensify the fears of the oppressed and deprived Negroes of Mississippi? Would this not be a setback for the whole civil rights movement and a blow to nonviolent discipline?

After several calls between Atlanta and Memphis, we learned that the earlier reports of Meredith's death were false and that he would recover. This news brought relief, but it did not alter our feeling that the civil rights movement had a moral obligation to continue along the path that Meredith had begun.

The next morning I was off to Memphis along with several members of my staff. Floyd McKissick, national director of CORE, flew in from New York and joined us on the flight from Atlanta to Memphis. After landing we went directly to the Municipal Hospital to visit Meredith. We were happy to find him resting well. After expressing our sympathy and gratitude for his courageous witness, Floyd and I shared our conviction with him that the march should continue in order to demonstrate to the nation and the world that Negroes would never again be intimidated by the terror of extremist white violence. Realizing that Meredith was often a loner and that he probably wanted to continue the march without a large group, we felt that it would take a great deal of persuasion to convince him that the issue involved the whole civil rights movement. Fortunately, he soon saw this and agreed that we should continue without him. We spent some time discussing the character and logistics of the march, and agreed that we would consult with him daily on every decision.

As we prepared to leave, the nurse came to the door and said, "Mr. Meredith, there is Mr. Carmichael in the lobby who would like to see you and Dr. King. Should I give him permission to come in?" Meredith consented. Stokely Carmichael entered with his associate, Cleveland Sellers, and immediately reached out for Meredith's hand. He expressed his concern and admiration and brought messages of sympathy from his colleagues in the Student Nonviolent Coordinating Committee. After a brief conversation we all agreed that James should get some rest and that we should not burden him with any additional talk. We left the room assuring him that we would conduct the march in his spirit and would seek as never before to expose the ugly racism that pervaded Mississippi and to arouse a new sense of dignity and manhood in every Negro who inhabited the bastion of man's inhumanity to man.

In a brief conference Floyd, Stokely and I agreed that the march would be jointly sponsored by CORE, SNCC, and SCLC, with the understanding that all other civil rights organizations would be invited to join. It was also agreed that we would issue a national call for support and participation.

One hour later, after making staff assignments and setting up headquarters at the Rev. James Lawson's church in Memphis, a group of us packed into four automobiles and made our way to that desolate spot on Highway 51 where James Meredith had been shot the day before. So began the second stage of the Meredith Mississippi Freedom March.

"Disappointment produces despair and despair produces bitterness"

As we walked down the meandering highway in the sweltering heat, there was much talk and many questions were raised.

"I'm not for that nonviolence stuff anymore," shouted one of the younger activists.

"If one of those damn white Mississippi crackers touches me, I'm gonna knock the hell out of him," shouted another.

Later on a discussion of the composition of the march came up.

"This should be an all-black march," said one marcher. "We don't need any more white phonies and liberals invading our movement. This is our march."

Once during the afternoon we stopped to sing, "We Shall Overcome." The voices rang out with all of the traditional fervor, the glad thunders and the gentle strength that had always characterized the singing of this noble song. But when we came to the stanza which speaks of "black and white together," the voices of a few of the marchers were muted. I asked them later why they refused to sing that verse. The retort was, "This is a new day, we don't sing those words anymore. In fact, the whole song should be discarded. Not 'We Shall Overcome,' but 'We Shall Overrun.'"

As I listened to all these comments, the words fell on my ears like strange music from a foreign land. My hearing was not attuned to the sound of such bitterness. I guess I should not have been surprised. I should have known that in an atmosphere where false promises are daily realities, where deferred dreams are nightly facts, where acts of unpunished violence toward Negroes are a way of life, nonviolence would eventually be seriously questioned. I should have been reminded that disappointment produces despair and despair produces bitterness, and that the one thing certain about bitterness is its blindness. Bitterness has not the capacity to make the distinction between some and *all*. When some members of the dominant group, particularly those in power, are racist in attitude and practice, bitterness accuses the whole group.

At the end of the march that first day we all went back to Memphis and spent the night in a Negro motel, since we had not yet secured the tents that would serve as shelter each of the following nights on our journey. The discussion continued at the motel. I decided that I would plead patiently with my brothers to remain true to the time-honored principle of our movement. I began with a plea for nonviolence. This immediately aroused some of our friends from the Deacons for Defense, who contended that self-defense was essential and that therefore nonviolence should not be a prerequisite for participation in the march. They were joined in this view by some of the activists from CORE and SNCC.

I tried to make it clear that besides opposing violence on principle, I could imagine nothing more impractical and disastrous than for any of us, through misguided judgment, to precipitate a violent confrontation in Mississippi. We had neither the resources nor the techniques to win. Furthermore, I asserted, many Mississippi whites, from the government on down, would enjoy nothing more than for us to turn to violence in order to use this as an excuse to wipe out scores of Negroes in and out of the march. Finally, I contended that the debate over the question of self-defense was unnecessary since few people suggested that Negroes should not defend themselves as individuals when attacked. The question was not whether one should use his gun when his home was attacked, but whether it was tactically wise to use a gun while participating in an organized demonstration. If they lowered the banner of nonviolence, I said, Mississippi injustice would not be exposed and the moral issues would be obscured.

Next the question of the participation of whites was raised. Stokely Carmichael contended that the inclusion of whites in the march should be de-emphasized and that the dominant appeal should be made for black participation. Others in the room agreed. As I listened to Stokely, I thought about the years that we had worked together in communities all across the South, and how joyously we had then welcomed and accepted our white allies in the movement. What accounted for this reversal in Stokely's philosophy?

I surmised that much of the change had its psychological roots in the experience of SNCC in Mississippi during the summer of 1964, when a large number of Northern white students had come down to help in that racially torn state. What the SNCC workers saw was the most articulate, powerful, and self-assured young white people coming to work with the poorest of the Negro people—and simply overwhelming them. That summer Stokely and others in SNCC had probably unconsciously concluded that this was no good for Negroes, for it simply increased their sense of their own inadequacies. Of course, the answer to this dilemma was not to give up, not to conclude that blacks must work with blacks in order for Negroes to gain a sense of their own meaning. The answer was only to be found in persistent trying, perpetual experimentation, persevering togetherness.

Like life, racial understanding is not something that we find but something that we must create. What we find when we enter these mortal plains is existence; but existence is the raw material out of which all life must be created. A productive and happy life is not something you find; it is something you make. And so the ability of Negroes and whites to work together, to understand each other, will not be found ready-made; it must be created by the fact of contact.

Along these lines, I implored everyone in the room to see the morality of making the march completely interracial. Consciences must be enlisted in our movement, I said, not merely racial groups. I reminded them of the dedicated whites who had suffered, bled, and died in the cause of racial justice, and suggested that to reject white participation now would be a shameful repudiation of all for which they had sacrificed.

Finally, I said that the formidable foe we now faced demanded more unity than ever before and that I would stretch every point to maintain this unity, but that I could not in good conscience agree to continue my personal involvement and that of SCLC in the march if it were not publicly affirmed that it was based on nonviolence and the participation of both black and white. After a few more minutes of discussion, Floyd and Stokely agreed that we could unite around these principles as far as the march was concerned. The next morning, we had a joint press conference affirming that the march was nonviolent and that whites were welcomed.

Now I've said all along and I still say it, that no individual in our movement can change Mississippi. No one organization in our movement can do the job in Mississippi alone. I have always contended that if all of us get together, we can change the face of Mississippi. This isn't any time for organizational conflicts, this isn't any time for ego battles over who's going to be the leader. We are all the leaders here in this struggle in Mississippi. You see, to change Mississippi we've got to be together. We aren't dealing with a force that has little power. We are dealing with powerful political dynasties, and somehow we must set out to be that David of Truth sent out against the Goliath of Injustice. And we can change this state. And I believe firmly that if we will stick together like this, we are going to do it.

"Black Power!"

As the day progressed, debates and discussions continued, but they were usually pushed to the background by the on-rush of enthusiasm engendered by the large crowds that turned out to greet us in every town. We had been marching for about ten days when we passed through Grenada on the way to Greenwood. Stokely did not conceal his growing eagerness to reach Greenwood. This was SNCC territory, in the sense that the organization had worked courageously there during that turbulent summer of 1964.

As we approached the city, large crowds of old friends and new turned out to welcome us. At a huge mass meeting that night, which was held in a city park, Stokely mounted the platform and after arousing the audience with a powerful attack on Mississippi justice, he proclaimed: "What we need is black power." Willie Ricks, the fiery orator of SNCC, leaped to the platform and shouted, "What do you want?" The crowd roared "Black Power." Again and again Ricks cried, "What do you want?" and the response "Black Power" grew louder and louder, until it had reached fever pitch.

So Greenwood turned out to be the arena for the birth of the Black Power slogan in the civil rights movement. The phrase had been used long before by Richard Wright and others, but never until that night had it been used as a slogan in the civil rights movement. For people who had been crushed so long by white power and who had been taught that black was degrading, this slogan had a ready appeal.

Immediately, however, I had reservations about its use. I had the deep feeling that it was an unfortunate choice of words for a slogan. Moreover, I saw it bringing about division within the ranks of the marchers. For a day or two there was fierce competition between those who were wedded to the Black Power slogan and those wedded to Freedom Now. Speakers on each side sought desperately to get the crowds to chant their slogan the loudest.

Now, there is a kind of concrete, real black power that I believe in. I don't believe in black separatism, I don't believe in black power that would have racist overtones, but certainly if black power means the amassing of political and economic power in order to gain our just and legitimate goals, then we all believe in that. And I think that all white people of goodwill believe in that.

We are 10 percent of the population of this nation and it would be foolish for me to stand up and tell you we are going to get our freedom by ourselves. There's going to have to be a coalition of conscience and we aren't going to be free here in Mississippi and anywhere in the United States until there is a committed empathy on the part of the white man of this country, and he comes to see along with us that segregation denigrates him as much as it does the Negro. I would be misleading you if I made you feel that we could win a violent campaign. It's impractical even to think about it. The minute we start, we will end up getting many people killed unnecessarily. Now, I'm ready to die myself. Many other committed people are ready to die. If you believe in something firmly, if you believe in it truly, if you believe it in your

heart, you are willing to die for it, but I'm not going to advocate a
method that brings about unnecessary death.

Sensing this widening split in our ranks, I asked Stokely and
Floyd McKissick to join me in a frank discussion of the problem. We
met the next morning, along with members of each of our staffs, in
a small Catholic parish house in Yazoo City. For five long hours I
pleaded with the group to abandon the Black Power slogan. It was
my contention that a leader has to be concerned about the problem
of semantics. Each word, I said, has a denotative meaning—its ex-
plicit and recognized sense—and a connotative meaning—its suggestive sense. While the concept of legitimate black power might
be denotatively sound, the slogan "Black Power" carried the wrong
connotations. I mentioned the implications of violence that the press
had already attached to the phrase. And I went on to say that some
of the rash statements on the part of a few marchers only reinforced
this impression.

Stokely replied by saying that the question of violence versus
nonviolence was irrelevant. The real question was the need for black
people to consolidate their political and economic resources to
achieve power. "Power," he said, "is the only thing respected in this
world, and we must get it at any cost." Then he looked me squarely
in the eye and said, "Martin, you know as well as I do that practically
every other ethnic group in America has done just this. The Jews,
the Irish, and the Italians did it, why can't we?"

"That is just the point," I answered. "No one has ever heard the
Jews publicly chant a slogan of Jewish power, but they have power.
Through group unity, determination, and creative endeavor, they
have gained it. The same thing is true of the Irish and Italians. Neither group has used a slogan of Irish or Italian power, but they have
worked hard to achieve it. This is exactly what we must do," I said.
"We must use every constructive means to amass economic and political power. This is the kind of legitimate power we need. We must
work to build racial pride and refute the notion that black is evil and
ugly. But this must come through a program, not merely through a
slogan."

Stokely and Floyd insisted that the slogan itself was important.
"How can you arouse people to unite around a program without a

slogan as a rallying cry? Didn't the labor movement have slogans? Haven't we had slogans all along in the freedom movement? What we need is a new slogan with 'black' in it."

I conceded the fact that we must have slogans. But why have one that would confuse our allies, isolate the Negro community, and give many prejudiced whites, who might otherwise be ashamed of their anti-Negro feeling, a ready excuse for self-justification?

Throughout the lengthy discussion, Stokely and Floyd remained adamant, and Stokely concluded by saying, with candor, "Martin, I deliberately decided to raise this issue on the march in order to give it a national forum, and force you to take a stand for Black Power."

I laughed. "I have been used before," I said to Stokely. "One more time won't hurt."

The meeting ended with the SCLC staff members still agreeing with me that the slogan was unfortunate and would only divert attention from the evils of Mississippi while most CORE and SNCC staff members joined Stokely and Floyd in insisting that it should be projected nationally. In a final attempt to maintain unity I suggested that we compromise by not chanting either "Black Power" or "Freedom Now" for the rest of the march. In this way, neither the people nor the press would be confused by the apparent conflict, and staff members would not appear to be at loggerheads. They all agreed with this compromise.

"A cry of disappointment"

But while the chant died out, the press kept the debate going. News stories now centered, not on the injustices of Mississippi, but on the apparent ideological division in the civil rights movement. Every revolutionary movement has its peaks of united activity and its valleys of debate and internal confusion. This debate might well have been little more than a healthy internal difference of opinion, but the press loves the sensational and it could not allow the issue to remain within the private domain of the movement. In every drama there has to be an antagonist and a protagonist, and if the antagonist is not there the press will find and build one.

So Black Power is now a part of the nomenclature of the national community. To some it is abhorrent, to others dynamic; to some it is repugnant, to others exhilarating; to some it is destructive, to others it is useful. Since Black Power means different things to different people and indeed, being essentially an emotional concept, can mean different things to the same person on differing occasions, it is impossible to attribute its ultimate meaning to any single individual or organization. One must look beyond personal styles, verbal flourishes, and the hysteria of the mass media to assess its values, its assets and liabilities honestly.

First, it is necessary to understand that Black Power is a cry of disappointment. The Black Power slogan did not spring full grown from the head of some philosophical Zeus. It was born from the wounds of despair and disappointment. It was a cry of daily hurt and persistent pain. For centuries the Negro has been caught in the tentacles of white power. Many Negroes have given up faith in the white majority because white power with total control has left them empty-handed. So in reality the call for Black Power is a reaction to the failure of white power.

Many of the young people proclaiming Black Power today were but yesterday the devotees of black-white cooperation and nonviolent direct action. With great sacrifice and dedication and a radiant faith in the future they labored courageously in the rural areas of the South; with idealism they accepted blows without retaliating; with dignity they allowed themselves to be plunged into filthy, stinking jail cells; with a majestic scorn for risk and danger they nonviolently confronted the Jim Clarks and the Bull Connors of the South, and exposed the disease of racism in the body politic. If they are America's angry children today, this anger is not congenital. It is a response to the feeling that a real solution is hopelessly distant because of the inconsistencies, resistance, and faintheartedness of those in power. If Stokely Carmichael now says that nonviolence is irrelevant, it is because he, as a dedicated veteran of many battles, has seen with his own eyes the most brutal white violence against Negroes and white civil rights workers, and he has seen it go unpunished.

Their frustration is further fed by the fact that even when blacks and whites die together in the cause of justice, the death of the white person gets more attention and concern than the death of the black person. Stokely and his colleagues from SNCC were with us in Alabama when Jimmy Lee Jackson, a brave young Negro man, was killed and when James Reeb, a committed Unitarian white minister, was fatally clubbed to the ground. They remembered how President Johnson sent flowers to the gallant Mrs. Reeb, and in his eloquent "We Shall Overcome" speech paused to mention that one person, James Reeb, had already died in the struggle. Somehow the President forgot to mention Jimmy, who died first. The parents and sister of Jimmy received no flowers from the President. The students felt this keenly. Not that they felt that the death of James Reeb was less than tragic, but because they felt that the failure to mention Jimmy Jackson only reinforced the impression that to white America the life of a Negro is insignificant and meaningless.

"Powerlessness into creative and positive power"

Second, Black Power, in its broad and positive meaning, was a call to black people to amass the political and economic strength to achieve their legitimate goals. No one could deny that the Negro was in dire need of this kind of legitimate power. Indeed, one of the great problems that the Negro confronted was his lack of power. From the old plantations of the South to the newer ghettos of the North, the Negro was confined to a life of voicelessness and powerlessness. Stripped of the right to make decisions concerning his life and destiny, he was subject to the authoritarian and sometimes whimsical decisions of the white power structure. The plantation and the ghetto were created by those who had power both to confine those who had no power and to perpetuate their powerlessness. The problem of transforming the ghetto was, therefore, a problem of power—a confrontation between the forces of power demanding change and the forces of power dedicated to preserving the status quo.

Power, properly understood, is the ability to achieve purpose. It is the strength required to bring about social, political, or economic changes. In this sense power is not only desirable but necessary in order to implement the demands of love and justice. One of the greatest problems of history is that the concepts of love and power are usually contrasted as polar opposites. Love is identified with a resignation of power and power with a denial of love. What is needed is a realization that power without love is reckless and abusive and that love without power is sentimental and anemic. Power at its best is love implementing the demands of justice. Justice at its best is love correcting everything that stands against love.

There is nothing essentially wrong with power. The problem is that in America power is unequally distributed. This has led Negro Americans in the past to seek their goals through love and moral suasion devoid of power and white Americans to seek their goals through power devoid of love and conscience. It has led a few extremists to advocate for Negroes the same destructive and conscienceless power that they justly abhorred in whites. It is precisely this collision of immoral power with powerless morality which constitutes the major crisis of our times.

"THE NECESSITY FOR TEMPORARY SEGREGATION"

There are points at which I see the necessity for temporary segregation in order to get to the integrated society. I can point to some cases. I've seen this in the South, in schools being integrated, and I've seen it with Teachers' Associations being integrated. Often when they merge, the Negro is integrated without power. . . . We don't want to be integrated out of power; we want to be integrated into power.

And this is why I think it is absolutely necessary to see integration in political terms, to see that there are some situations where separation may serve as a temporary way-station to the ultimate goal which we seek, which I think is the only answer in the final analysis to the problem of a truly integrated society.

March 25, 1968

In his struggle for racial justice, the Negro must seek to transform his condition of powerlessness into creative and positive power. To the extent that Black Power advocated the development of political awareness and strength in the Negro community, the election of blacks to key positions, and the use of the bloc vote to liberalize the political climate and achieve our just aspirations for freedom and human dignity, it was a positive and legitimate call to action.

Black Power was also a call for the pooling of black financial resources to achieve economic security. While the ultimate answer to the Negroes' economic dilemma was in a massive federal program for all the poor along the lines of A. Philip Randolph's Freedom Budget, a kind of Marshall Plan for the disadvantaged, there was something that the Negro himself could do to throw off the shackles of poverty.

Finally, Black Power was a psychological call to manhood. For years the Negro had been taught that he was nobody, that his color was a sign of his biological depravity, that his being was stamped with an indelible imprint of inferiority, that his whole history was soiled with the filth of worthlessness. All too few people realize how slavery and racial segregation scarred the soul and wounded the spirit of the black man. The whole dirty business of slavery was based on the premise that the Negro was a thing to be used, not a person to be respected. Black Power assumed that Negroes would be slaves unless there was a new power to counter the force of the men who are still determined to be masters rather than brothers.

Black Power was a psychological reaction to the psychological indoctrination that led to the creation of the perfect slave. While this reaction often led to negative and unrealistic responses and frequently brought about intemperate words and actions, one must not overlook the positive value in calling the Negro to a new sense of manhood, to a deep feeling of racial pride, and to an audacious appreciation of his heritage. The Negro had to be grasped by a new realization of his dignity and worth. He had to stand up amid a system that still oppresses him and develop an unassailable and majestic sense of his own value. He could no longer be ashamed of being black.

The job of arousing manhood within a people that had been taught for so many centuries that they were nobody is not easy. Even semantics conspire to make that which is black seem ugly and degrading. In Roget's *Thesaurus* there are some 120 synonyms for "blackness" and at least 60 of them are offensive—such words as "blot," "soot," "grime," "devil," and "foul." There are some 134 synonyms for "whiteness," and all are favorable, expressed in such words as "purity," "cleanliness," "chastity," and "innocence." A white lie is better than a black lie. The most degenerate member of a family is the "black sheep," not the "white sheep."

The history books, which had almost completely ignored the contribution of the Negro in American history, only served to intensify the Negroes' sense of worthlessness and to augment the anachronistic doctrine of white supremacy. All too many Negroes and whites are unaware of the fact that the first American to shed blood in the revolution which freed this country from British oppression was a black seaman named Crispus Attucks. Negroes and whites are almost totally oblivious of the fact that it was a Negro physician, Dr. Daniel Hale Williams, who performed the first successful operation on the heart in America. Another Negro physician, Dr. Charles Drew, was largely responsible for developing the method of separating blood plasma and storing it on a large scale, a process that saved thousands of lives in World War II and has made possible many of the important advances in postwar medicine. History books have virtually overlooked the many Negro scientists and inventors who have enriched American life. Although a few refer to George Washington Carver, whose research in agricultural products helped to revive the economy of the South when the throne of King Cotton began to totter, they ignore the contribution of Norbert Rillieux, whose invention of an evaporating pan revolutionized the process of sugar refining. How many people know that the multimillion-dollar United Shoe Machinery Company developed from the shoe-lasting machine invented in the last century by a Negro from Dutch Guiana, Jan Matzeliger; or that Granville T. Woods, an expert in electric motors, whose many patents speeded the growth and improvement of the railroads at the beginning of this century, was a Negro?

Even the Negroes' contribution to the music of America is sometimes overlooked in astonishing ways. In 1965 my oldest son and daughter entered an integrated school in Atlanta. A few months later my wife and I were invited to attend a program entitled "Music that has made America great." As the evening unfolded, we listened to the folk songs and melodies of the various immigrant groups. We were certain that the program would end with the most original of all American music, the Negro spiritual. But we were mistaken. Instead, all the students, including our children, ended the program by singing "Dixie."

As we rose to leave the hall, my wife and I looked at each other with a combination of indignation and amazement. All the students, black and white, all the parents present that night, and all the faculty members had been victimized by just another expression of America's penchant for ignoring the Negro, making him invisible and making his contributions insignificant. I wept within that night. I wept for my children and all black children who have been denied a knowledge of their heritage; I wept for all white children, who, through daily miseducation, are taught that the Negro is an irrelevant entity in American society; I wept for all the white parents and teachers who are forced to overlook the fact that the wealth of cultural and technological progress in America is a result of the commonwealth of inpouring contributions.

"A slogan that cannot be implemented into a program"

Nevertheless, in spite of the positive aspects of Black Power, which were compatible with what we have sought to do in the civil rights movement without the slogan, its negative values, I believed, prevented it from having the substance and program to become the basic strategy for the civil rights movement.

Beneath all the satisfaction of a gratifying slogan, Black Power was a nihilistic philosophy born out of the conviction that the Negro can't win. It was, at bottom, the view that American society is so hopelessly corrupt and enmeshed in evil that there is no possibility of salvation from within. Although this thinking is understandable as a response to a white power structure that never completely committed itself to true equality for the Negro, and a die-hard mentality that sought to shut all windows and doors against the winds of change, it nonetheless carried the seeds of its own doom.

Before this century, virtually all revolutions had been based on hope and hate. The hope was expressed in the rising expectation of freedom and justice. What was new about Mahatma Gandhi's movement in India was that he mounted a revolution on hope and love, hope and nonviolence. This same new emphasis characterized the civil rights movement in our country dating from the Montgomery bus boycott of 1956 to the Selma movement of 1965. We maintained the hope while transforming the hate of traditional revolutions into positive nonviolent power. As long as the hope was fulfilled there was little questioning of nonviolence. But when the hopes were blasted, when people came to see that in spite of progress their conditions were still insufferable, when they looked out and saw more poverty, more school segregation, and more slums, despair began to set in.

But revolution, though born of despair, cannot long be sustained by despair. This was the ultimate contradiction of the Black Power movement. It claimed to be the most revolutionary wing of the social revolution taking place in the United States. Yet it rejected the one thing that keeps the fire of revolutions burning: the ever-present flame of hope. When hope dies, a revolution degenerates into an undiscriminating catchall for evanescent and futile gestures. The Negro cannot entrust his destiny to a philosophy nourished solely on despair, to a slogan that cannot be implemented into a program.

Over cups of coffee in my home in Atlanta and my apartment in Chicago, I often talked late at night and over into the small hours of the morning with proponents of Black Power who argued passionately about the validity of violence and riots. They didn't quote Gandhi or Tolstoy. Their Bible was Frantz Fanon's *The Wretched of the Earth*. This black psychiatrist from Martinique, who went to Algeria to work with the National Liberation Front in its fight against the French, argued in his book—a well-written book, incidentally, with many penetrating insights—that violence is a psychologically healthy and tactically sound method for the oppressed. And so, realizing that they are a part of that vast company of the "wretched of the earth," young American Negroes, who were involved in the Black Power movement, often quoted Fanon's belief that violence is the only thing that will bring about liberation.

The plain, inexorable fact was that any attempt of the American Negro to overthrow his oppressor with violence would not work. We did not need President Johnson to tell us this by reminding Negro rioters that they were outnumbered ten to one. The courageous efforts of our own insurrectionist brothers, such as Denmark Vesey and Nat Turner, should be eternal reminders to us that violent rebellion is doomed from the start. Anyone leading a violent rebellion must be willing to make an honest assessment regarding the possible casualties to a minority population confronting a well-armed, wealthy majority with a fanatical right wing that would delight in exterminating thousands of black men, women, and children.

Occasionally Negroes contended that the 1965 Watts riot and

other riots in various cities represented effective civil rights action. But those who expressed this view always ended up with stumbling words when asked what concrete gains were won as a result. At best the riots produced a little additional anti-poverty money, allotted by frightened government officials, and a few water sprinklers to cool the children of the ghettos. Nowhere did the riots win any concrete improvement such as did the organized protest demonstrations.

When one tries to pin down advocates of violence as to what acts would be effective, the answers are blatantly illogical. Sometimes they talk of overthrowing racist state and local governments. They fail to see that no internal revolution has ever succeeded in overthrowing a government by violence unless the government had already lost the allegiance and effective control of its armed forces. Anyone in his right mind knows that this will not happen in the United States.

Nonviolence is power, but it is the right and good use of power. Constructively it can save the white man as well as the Negro. Racial segregation is buttressed by such irrational fears as loss of preferred economic privilege, altered social status, intermarriage, and adjustment to new situations. Through sleepless nights and haggard days, numerous white people struggled pitifully to combat these fears. By following the path of escape, some seek to ignore questions of race relations, and to close their minds to the issues involved. Others, placing their faith in legal maneuvers, counsel massive resistance. Still others hope to drown their fears by engaging in acts of meanness and violence toward their Negro brethren. But, how futile are all these remedies! Instead of eliminating fear, they instill deeper and more pathological fears. The white man, through his own efforts, through education and goodwill, through searching his conscience and through confronting the fact of integration, must do a great deal to free himself of these paralyzing fears. But to master fear he must also depend on the spirit the Negro generates toward him. Only through our adherence to nonviolence—which also means love in its strong and commanding sense—will the fear in the white community be mitigated.

"A genuine leader is not a searcher for consensus"

People have said to me, "Since violence is the new cry, isn't there a danger that you will lose touch with the people in the ghetto and be out of step with the times if you don't change your views on nonviolence?"

My answer is always the same. While I am convinced that the vast majority of Negroes reject violence, even if they did not I would not be interested in being a consensus leader. I refuse to determine what is right by taking a Gallup poll of the trends of the time. I imagine that there were leaders in Germany who sincerely opposed what Hitler was doing to the Jews. But they took their poll and discovered that anti-Semitism was the prevailing trend. In order to "be in step with the times," in order to "keep in touch," they yielded to one of the most ignominious evils that history has ever known.

Ultimately, a genuine leader is not a searcher for consensus but a molder of consensus. If every Negro in the United States turns to violence, I will choose to be that one lone voice preaching that this is the wrong way. Maybe this sounds like arrogance. But it is not intended that way. It is simply my way of saying that I would rather be a man of conviction than a man of conformity. Occasionally in life one develops a conviction so precious and meaningful that he will stand on it till the end. This is what I have found in nonviolence.

I cannot make myself believe that God wanted me to hate. I'm tired of violence, I've seen too much of it. I've seen such hate on the faces of too many sheriffs in the South. And I'm not going to let my oppressor dictate to me what method I must use. Our oppressors have used violence. Our oppressors have used hatred. Our oppressors have used rifles and guns. I'm not going to stoop down to their level. I want to rise to a higher level. We have a power that can't be found in Molotov cocktails.

One of the greatest paradoxes of the Black Power movement was that it talked unceasingly about not imitating the values of white society, but in advocating violence it was imitating the worst, the most brutal, and the most uncivilized value of American life. American Negroes had not been mass murderers. They had not murdered children in Sunday school, nor had they hung white men on trees bearing strange fruit. They had not been hooded perpetrators of violence, lynching human beings at will and drowning them at whim.

I am concerned that Negroes achieve full status as citizens and as human beings here in the United States. But I am also concerned about our moral uprightness and the health of our souls. Therefore I must oppose any attempt to gain our freedom by the methods of malice, hate, and violence that have characterized our oppressors.

Hate is just as injurious to the hater as it is to the hated. Like an unchecked cancer, hate corrodes the personality and eats away its vital unity. Many of our inner conflicts are rooted in hate. This is why the psychiatrists say, "Love or perish." Hate is too great a burden to bear.

Humanity is waiting for something other than blind imitation of the past. If we want truly to advance a step further, if we want to turn over a new leaf and really set a new man afoot, we must begin to turn mankind away from the long and desolate night of violence. May it not be that the new man the world needs is the nonviolent man? Longfellow said, "In this world a man must either be an anvil or a hammer." We must be hammers shaping a new society rather than anvils molded by the old. This not only will make us new men, but will give us a new kind of power. It will not be Lord Acton's image of power that tends to corrupt or absolute power that corrupts absolutely. It will be power infused with love and justice, that will change dark yesterdays into bright tomorrows, and lift us from the fatigue of despair to the buoyancy of hope. A dark, desperate, confused, and sin-sick world waits for this new kind of man and this new kind of power.

30

BEYOND VIETNAM

Today, young men of America are fighting, dying, and killing in Asian jungles in a war whose purposes are so ambiguous the whole nation seethes with dissent. They are told they are sacrificing for democracy, but the Saigon regime, their ally, is a mockery of democracy and the black American soldier has himself never experienced democracy.

AUGUST 12, 1965
King calls for halt to U.S. bombing of North Vietnam to encourage negotiated settlement of conflict

JANUARY 10, 1966
Backs Georgia State Senator-elect Julian Bond's right to oppose war

MAY 29
Urges halt to bombing on *Face the Nation* televised interview

APRIL 4, 1967
Delivers his first public antiwar speech at New York's Riverside Church

All my adult life I have deplored violence and war as instruments for achieving solutions to mankind's problems. I am firmly committed to the creative power of nonviolence as the force which is capable of winning lasting and meaningful brotherhood and peace. As a minister, a Nobel Prize holder, a civil rights leader, a Negro, a father, and above all as an American, I have wrestled with my conscience.

Despite this—whether right or wrong—in the summer and fall

of 1965, after President Johnson declared himself willing to negotiate, I believed that it was essential for all Americans to publicly avoid the debate on why we were waging war in the far-off lands of Vietnam. I believed that the crucial problem which faced Americans was how to move with great speed and without more bloodshed from the battlefield to the peace table. The issues of culpability and morality, while important, had to be subordinated lest they divert or divide. The President's strong declaration to negotiate, to talk peace, and thus end the death and destruction, had to be accepted, honored, and implemented.

Accepting this premise, my public statements, while condemning all militarism, were directed mainly to the mechanics for achieving an immediate cessation of hostilities. I did not march, I did not demonstrate, I did not rally. I petitioned in direct meetings with the President, and at his invitation with U.N. Ambassador Arthur Goldberg. In my meeting with Ambassador Goldberg, in September 1965, I urged that our efforts to seek peace by negotiations could be speeded by agreeing to negotiate directly with the National Liberation Front, by admitting Red China to the U.N., and by halting the bombing of North Vietnam.

For a while, knowing that my wife shares my passion for peace, I decided that I would leave it to her to take the stands and make the meetings on the peace issue and leave me to concentrate on civil rights. But as the hopeful days became disappointing months, I began the agonizing measurement of government promising words of peace against the baneful, escalating deeds of war. Doubts gnawed at my conscience. Uncertain, but still trusting, we watched setbacks in the search for peace and advances in the search for military advantage.

Some of my friends of both races and others who do not consider themselves my friends expressed disapproval because I had been voicing concern over the war in Vietnam. In newspaper columns and editorials, both in the Negro and general press, it was indicated that Martin King, Jr., is "getting out of his depth." I was chided, even by fellow civil rights leaders, members of Congress, and brothers of the cloth for "not sticking to the business of civil rights."

I agonized a great deal over this whole problem. I went away for two months to do a lot of thinking, but basically to write a book. I had a chance to reflect, to meditate, and to think. I thought about civil rights and I thought about the world situation and I thought about America.

Something said to me, "Martin, you have got to stand up on this. No matter what it means." I didn't rush into it. I didn't just decide to do it on a moment's notice. I had my own vacillations and I asked questions of whether on the one hand I should do it or whether I shouldn't.

As I went through this period one night I picked up an article entitled "The Children of Vietnam," and I read it. And after reading that article, I said to myself, "Never again will I be silent on an issue that is destroying the soul of our nation and destroying thousands and thousands of little children in Vietnam." I came to the conclusion that there is an existential moment in your life when you must decide to speak for yourself; nobody else can speak for you.

"I was a loud speaker but a quiet actor"

In February 1967, the slender cord which held me threatened to break as our government spurned the simple peace offer—conveyed by one no less than the authorized head of the Soviet Union—to halt our bombing of North Vietnam, not the bombing of all of Vietnam, in return for fully occupied seats at a peace table. We rejected it by demanding a military quid pro quo.

As I look back, I acknowledge that this end of faith was not sudden; it came like the ebbing of a tide. As I reviewed the events, I saw an orderly buildup of evil, an accumulation of inhumanities, each of which alone was sufficient to make men hide in shame. What was woeful, but true, was that my country was only talking peace but was bent on military victory. Inside the glove of peace was the clenched fist of war. I now stood naked with shame and guilt, as indeed every German should have when his government was using its military power to overwhelm other nations. Whether right or wrong, I had for too long allowed myself to be a silent onlooker. At best, I was a loud speaker but a quiet actor, while a charade was being performed.

So often I had castigated those who by silence or inaction condoned and thereby cooperated with the evils of racial injustice. Had

I not, again and again, said that the silent onlooker must bear the responsibility for the brutalities committed by the Bull Connors, or by the murderers of the innocent children in a Birmingham church? Had I not committed myself to the principle that looking away from evil is, in effect, a condoning of it? Those who lynch, pull the trigger, point the cattle prod, or open the fire hoses act in the name of the silent. I had to therefore speak out if I was to erase my name from the bombs which fall over North or South Vietnam, from the canisters of napalm. The time had come—indeed it was past due—when I had to disavow and dissociate myself from those who in the name of peace burn, maim, and kill.

More than that, I had to go from the pulpits and platforms. I had to return to the streets to mobilize men to assemble and petition, in the spirit of our own revolutionary history, for the immediate end of this bloody, immoral, obscene slaughter—for a cause which cries out for a solution before mankind itself is doomed. I could do no less for the salvation of my soul.

I had lived and worked in ghettos throughout the nation, and I traveled tens of thousands of miles each month into dozens of Northern and Southern Negro communities. My direct personal experience with Negroes in all walks of life convinced me that there was deep and widespread disenchantment with the war in Vietnam—first, because they were against war itself, and second, because they felt it has caused a significant and alarming diminishing of concern and attention to civil rights progress. I had held these views for a long time, but Negroes in so many circles urged me to articulate their concern and frustration. They felt civil rights was well on its way to becoming a neglected and forgotten issue long before it was even partially solved.

The great tragedy was that our government declared a war against poverty, and yet it only financed a skirmish against poverty. And this led to great despair. It led to great cynicism and discontent throughout the Negro community. I had lived in the ghettos of Chicago and Cleveland, and I knew the hurt and the cynicism and the discontent. And the fact was that every city in our country was sitting on a potential powderkeg.

* * *

As I moved to break the betrayal of my own silences and to speak from the burnings of my own heart—as I called for radical departures from the destruction of Vietnam—many persons questioned me about the wisdom of my path. At the heart of their concern, this query has often loomed large and loud: "Why are you speaking about the war, Dr. King? Why are you joining the voices of dissent?" "Peace and civil rights don't mix," they say. And when I hear them, though I often understand the source of their concern, I nevertheless am greatly saddened that such questions mean that the inquirers have not really known me, my commitment, or my calling. They seem to forget that before I was a civil rights leader, I answered a call, and when God speaks, who can but prophesy. I answered a call which left the spirit of the Lord upon me and anointed me to preach the gospel. And during the early days of my ministry, I read the Apostle Paul saying, "Be ye not conformed to this world, but be ye transformed by the renewing of minds." I decided then that I was going to tell the truth as God revealed it to me. No matter how many people disagreed with me, I decided that I was going to tell the truth.

I believe that the path from Dexter Avenue Baptist Church—the church in Montgomery, Alabama, where I began my pastorate—leads clearly to this sanctuary tonight.

There is . . . a very obvious and almost facile connection between the war in Vietnam and the struggle I and others have been waging in America. A few years ago there was a shining moment in that struggle. It seemed as if there was a real promise of hope for the poor—both black and white—through the poverty program. There were experiments, hopes, new beginnings. Then came the buildup in Vietnam, and I watched this program broken and eviscerated as if it were some idle political plaything of a society gone mad on war. And I knew that America would never invest the necessary funds or energies in rehabilitation of its poor so long as adventures like Vietnam continued to draw men and skills and money like some demonic, destructive suction tube. So I was increasingly compelled to see the war as an enemy of the poor and to attack it as such.

Perhaps a more tragic recognition of reality took place when it became clear to me that the war was doing far more than devastating the hopes of the poor at home. It was sending their sons and their brothers and their husbands to fight and to die in extraordinarily high proportions relative to the rest of the population. We were taking the black young men who had been crippled by our society and sending them eight thousand miles away to guarantee liberties in Southeast Asia which they had not found in southwest Georgia and East Harlem. So we have been repeatedly faced with the cruel irony of watching Negro and white boys on TV screens as they kill and die together for a nation that has been unable to seat them together in the same schools. So we watch them in brutal solidarity burning the huts of a poor village, but we realize that they would hardly live on the same block in Chicago. I could not be silent in the face of such cruel manipulation of the poor. . . .

As I have walked among the desperate, rejected, and angry young men, I have told them that Molotov cocktails and rifles would not solve their problems. I have tried to offer them my deepest compassion while maintaining my conviction that social change comes most meaningfully through nonviolent action. But they asked, and rightly so, "What about Vietnam?" They asked if our own nation wasn't using massive doses of violence to solve its problems, to bring about the changes it wanted. Their questions hit home, and I knew that I could never again raise my voice against the violence of the oppressed in the ghettos without having first spoken clearly to the greatest purveyor of violence in the world today: my own government. For the sake of those boys, for the sake of this government, for the sake of the hundreds of thousands trembling under our violence, I cannot be silent.

Now, it should be incandescently clear that no one who has any concern for the integrity and life of America today can ignore the present war. If America's soul becomes totally poisoned, part of the autopsy must read "Vietnam." It can never be saved so long as it destroys the deepest hopes of men the world over. So it is that those of us who are yet determined that "America will be" are led down the path of protest and dissent, working for the health of our land.

As if the weight of such a commitment to the life and health of America were not enough, another burden of responsibility was placed upon me in 1964; and I cannot forget that the Nobel Peace Prize was also a commission, a commission to work harder than I had ever worked before for the brotherhood of man. This is a calling that takes me beyond national allegiances.

But even if it were not present, I would yet have to live with the meaning of my commitment to the ministry of Jesus Christ. To me the relationship of this ministry to the making of peace is so obvious that I sometimes marvel at those who ask me why I am speaking against the war. Could it be that they do not know that the Good News was meant for all men—for communist and capitalist, for their children and ours, for black and for white, for revolutionary and conservative? Have they forgotten that my ministry is in obedience to the one who loved his enemies so fully that He died for them? What then can I say to the Vietcong or to Castro or to Mao as a faithful minister of this one? Can I threaten them with death or must I not share with them my life?

Finally, as I try to explain for you and for myself the road that leads from Montgomery to this place, I would have offered all that was most valid if I simply said that I must be true to my conviction that I share with all men the calling to be a son of the living God. Beyond the calling of race or nation or creed is this vocation of sonship and brotherhood. Because I believe that the Father is deeply concerned especially for His suffering and helpless and outcast children, I come tonight to speak for them. This I believe to be the privilege and the burden of all of us who deem ourselves bound by allegiances and loyalties which are broader and deeper than nationalism and which go beyond our nation's self-defined goals and positions. We are called to speak for the weak, for the voiceless, for the victims of our nation, for those it calls "enemy," for no document from human hands can make these humans any less our brothers. . . .

The war in Vietnam is but a symptom of a far deeper malady within the American spirit, and if we ignore this sobering reality, we will find ourselves organizing Clergy and Laymen Concerned committees for the next generation. They will be concerned about Guatemala and Peru. They will be concerned about Thailand and Cambodia. They will be concerned about Mozambique and South Africa. We will be marching for these and a dozen other names and attending rallies without end unless there is a significant and profound change in American life and policy. So such thoughts take us beyond Vietnam, but not beyond our calling as sons of the living God.

In 1957, a sensitive American official overseas said that it seemed to him that our nation was on the wrong side of a world revolution. During the past ten years we have seen emerge a pattern of suppression which has now justified the presence of U.S. military advisors in Venezuela. This need to maintain social stability for our investment accounts for the counter-revolutionary action of American forces in Guatemala. It tells why American helicopters are being used against guerrillas in Cambodia and why American napalm and Green Beret forces have already been active against rebels in Peru.

It is with such activity in mind that the words of the late John F. Kennedy come back to haunt us. Five years ago he said, "Those who make peaceful revolution impossible will make violent revolution inevitable." Increasingly, by choice or by accident, this is the role our nation has taken: the role of those who make peaceful revolution impossible by refusing to give up the privileges and the pleasures that come from the immense profits of overseas investments. I am convinced that if we are to get on the right side of the world revolution, we as a nation must undergo a radical revolution of values. We must rapidly begin the shift from a thing-oriented society to a person-oriented society. When machines and computers, profit motives and property rights, are considered more important than people, the giant triplets of racism, extreme materialism, and militarism are incapable of being conquered.

A true revolution of values will soon cause us to question the fairness and justice of many of our past and present policies. On the one hand we are called to play the Good Samaritan on life's roadside, but that will be only an initial act. One day we must come to see that the whole Jericho Road must be transformed so that men and women will not be constantly beaten and robbed as they make their journey on life's highway. True compassion is more than flinging a coin to a beggar. It comes to see that an edifice which produces beggars needs restructuring.

A true revolution of values will soon look uneasily on the glaring contrast of poverty and wealth. With righteous indignation, it will look across the seas and see individual capitalists of the West investing huge sums of money in Asia, Africa, and South America, only to take the profits out with no concern for the social betterment of the countries, and say: "This is not just." It will look at our alliance with the landed gentry of South America and say: "This is not just." The Western arrogance of feeling that it has everything to teach others and nothing to learn from them is not just.

A true revolution of values will lay hands on the world order and say of war: "This way of settling differences is not just." This business *of burning human beings with napalm, of filling our nation's homes with orphans and widows, of injecting poisonous drugs of hate into the veins of peoples normally humane, of sending men home from dark and bloody battlefields physically handicapped and psychologically deranged, cannot be reconciled with wisdom, justice, and love. A nation that continues year after year to spend more money on military defense than on programs of social uplift is approaching spiritual death.*

America, the richest and most powerful nation in the world, can well lead the way in this revolution of values. There is nothing except a tragic death wish to prevent us from reordering our priorities, so that the pursuit of peace will take precedence over the pursuit of war. There is nothing to keep us from molding a recalcitrant status quo with bruised hands until we have fashioned it into a brotherhood. . . .

These are revolutionary times. All over the globe men are revolting against old systems of exploitation and oppression, and, out of the wounds of a frail world, new systems of justice and equality are being born. The shirtless and barefoot people of the land are rising up as never before. The people who sat in darkness have seen a great light. We in the West must support these revolutions.

It is a sad fact that because of comfort, complacency, a morbid fear of communism, and our proneness to adjust to injustice, the Western nations that initiated so much of the revolutionary spirit of the modern world have now become the arch anti-revolutionaries. This has driven many to feel that only Marxism has a revolutionary spirit. Therefore, communism is a judgment against our failure to make democracy real and follow through on the revolutions that we initiated. Our only hope today lies in our ability to recapture the revolutionary spirit and go out into a sometimes hostile world declaring eternal hostility to poverty, racism, and militarism. With this powerful commitment we shall boldly challenge the status quo and unjust mores, and thereby speed the day when "every valley shall be exalted, and every mountain and hill shall be made low, the crooked shall be made straight, and the rough places plain."

A genuine revolution of values means in the final analysis that our loyalties must become ecumenical rather than sectional. Every nation must now develop an overriding loyalty to mankind as a whole in order to preserve the best in their individual societies. . . .

We must move past indecision to action. We must find new ways to speak for peace in Vietnam and justice throughout the developing world, a world that borders on our doors. If we do not act, we shall surely be dragged down the long, dark, and shameful corridors of time reserved for those who possess power without compassion, might without morality, and strength without sight.

Now let us begin. Now let us rededicate ourselves to the long and bitter, but beautiful, struggle for a new world. This is the calling of the sons of God, and our brothers wait eagerly for our response. Shall we say the odds are too great? Shall we tell them the struggle is too hard? Will our message be that the forces of American life militate against their arrival as full men, and we send our deepest regrets? Or will there be another message—of longing, of hope, of solidarity with their yearnings, of commitment to their cause, whatever the cost? The choice is ours, and though we might prefer it otherwise, we must choose in this crucial moment of human history.

When I first took my position against the war in Vietnam, almost every newspaper in the country criticized me. It was a low period in my life. I could hardly open a newspaper. It wasn't only white people either; it was Negroes. But then I remember a newsman coming to me one day and saying, "Dr. King, don't you think you're going to have to change your position now because so many people are criticizing you? And people who once had respect for you are going to lose respect for you. And you're going to hurt the budget, I understand, of the Southern Christian Leadership Conference; people have cut off support. And don't you think that you have to move now more in line with the administration's policy?" That was a good question, because he was asking me the question of whether I was going to think about what happens to me or what happens to truth and justice in this situation.

On some positions, Cowardice asks the question, "Is it safe?" Expediency asks the question, "Is it politic?" And Vanity comes along and asks the question, "Is it popular?" But Conscience asks the question, "Is it right?" And there comes a time when one must take a position that is neither safe, nor politic, nor popular, but he must do it because Conscience tells him it is right.

The ultimate measure of a man is not where he stands in moments of convenience, but where he stands in moments of challenge, moments of great crisis and controversy. And this is where I choose to cast my lot today. And this is why I wanted to go through with this, because I think this is where SCLC should be. There may be others who want to go another way, but when I took up the cross I recognized its meaning. It is not something that you merely put your hands on. It is not something that you wear. The cross is something that you bear and ultimately that you die on. The cross may mean the death of your popularity. It may mean the death of your bridge to the White House. It may mean the death of a foundation grant. It may cut your budget down a little, but take up your cross and just bear it. And that is the way I have decided to go. Come what may, it doesn't matter now.

A myth about my views on Vietnam credited me with advocating the fusion of the civil rights and peace movements, and I was criticized for such a "serious tactical mistake." I held no such view. In a formal public resolution, my organization, SCLC, and I explicitly declared that we had no intention of diverting or diminishing our activities in civil rights, and we outlined extensive programs for the immediate future in the South as well as in Chicago.

I was saddened that the board of directors of the NAACP, a fellow civil rights organization, would join in the perpetuation of the myth about my views. They challenged and repudiated a nonexistent proposition. SCLC and I expressed our view on the war and drew attention to its damaging effects on civil rights programs, a fact we believed to be incontrovertible and, therefore, mandatory to express in the interest of the struggle for equality. I challenged the NAACP and other critics of my position to take a forthright stand on the rightness or wrongness of this war, rather than going off creating a nonexistent issue.

I am a clergyman as well as a civil rights leader and the moral roots of our war policy are not unimportant to me. I do not believe our nation can be a moral leader of justice, equality, and democracy if it is trapped in the role of a self-appointed world policeman. Throughout my career in the civil rights movement I have been concerned about justice for all people. For instance, I strongly feel that we must end not merely poverty among Negroes but poverty among white people. Likewise, I have always insisted on justice for all the world over, because justice is indivisible. And injustice anywhere is a threat to justice everywhere. I will not stand idly by when I see an unjust war taking place

"SO PRECIOUS THAT YOU WILL DIE FOR IT"

I say to you, this morning, that if you have never found something so dear and so precious to you that you will die for it, then you aren't fit to live. You may be thirty-eight years old, as I happen to be, and one day, some great opportunity stands before you and calls upon you to stand up for some great principle, some great issue, some great cause. And you refuse to do it because you are afraid. You refuse to do it because you want to live longer. You're afraid that you will lose your job, or you are afraid that you will be criticized or that you will lose your popularity, or you're afraid that somebody will stab you or shoot at you or bomb your house. So you refuse to take the stand. Well, you may go on and live until you are ninety, but you are just as dead at thirty-eight as you would be at ninety. And the cessation of breathing in your life is but the belated announcement of an earlier death of the spirit. You died when you refused to stand up for right. You died when you refused to stand up for truth. You died when you refused to stand up for justice. . . .

Don't ever think that you're by yourself. Go on to jail if necessary, but you never go alone. Take a stand for that which is right, and the world may misunderstand you, and criticize you. But you never go alone, for somewhere I read that one with God is a majority. And God has a way of transforming a minority into a majority. Walk with him this morning and believe in him and do what is right, and He'll be with you even until the consummation of the ages. Yes, I've seen the lightning flash. I've heard the thunder roll. I've felt sin breakers dashing, trying to conquer my soul, but I heard the voice of Jesus saying, still to fight on. He promised never to leave me alone, never to leave me alone. No, never alone. No, never alone.

Sermon at Ebenezer, November 5, 1967

without in any way diminishing my activity in civil rights, just as millions of Negro and white people are doing day in and day out.

This war played havoc with the destiny of the entire world. It tore up the Geneva Agreement, seriously impaired the United Nations, exacerbated the hatreds between continents and, worse still, between races. It frustrated our development at home, telling our own underprivileged citizens that we place insatiable military demands above their most critical needs; it greatly contributed to the forces of reaction in America and strengthened the military-industrial complex against which even President Eisenhower solemnly warned us; it practically destroyed Vietnam and left thousands of American and Vietnamese youth maimed and mutilated; and it exposed the whole world to the risk of nuclear warfare.

The Johnson Administration seemed amazingly devoid of statesmanship, and when creative statesmanship wanes, irrational militarism increases. President Kennedy was a man who was big enough to admit when he was wrong—as he did after the Bay of Pigs incident. But Johnson seemed to be unable to make this kind of statesmanlike gesture in connection with Vietnam. Even when he could readily summon popular support to end the bombing in Vietnam, he persisted. Yet bombs in Vietnam also exploded at home; they destroyed the hopes and possibilities for a decent America.

I followed a policy of being very honest with President Johnson when he consulted me about civil rights. I went to the White House when he invited me. I made it very clear to him why I had taken a stand against the war in Vietnam. I had a long talk with him on the telephone about this and made it clear to him I would be standing up against it even more. I was not centering this on President Johnson. I thought there was collective guilt. Four Presidents participated in some way leading us to the war in Vietnam. So, I am not going to put it all on President Johnson. What I was concerned about was that we end the nightmarish war and free our souls.

There isn't a single official of our country that can go anywhere in the world without being stoned and eggs being thrown at him. It's because we have taken on to ourselves a kind of arrogance of power. We've ignored the mandates of justice and morality. And I don't know about you, but I wish I could make a witness more positive about this thing. I wish I was of draft age. I wish I did not have my ministerial exemption. I tell you this morning, I would not fight in the war in Vietnam. I'd go to jail before I'd do it. And I say to the federal government or anybody else: they can do to me what they did to Dr. Spock and William Sloan Coffin, my good friend, the chaplain of Yale. They can just as well get ready to convict me, because I'm going to continue to say to young men, that if you feel it in your heart that this war is wrong, unjust, and objectionable, don't go and fight in it. Follow the path of Jesus Christ.

31

THE POOR PEOPLE'S CAMPAIGN

We have moved into an era where we are called upon to raise certain basic questions about the whole society. We are still called upon to give aid to the beggar who finds himself in misery and agony on life's highway. But one day, we must ask the question of whether an edifice which produces beggars must not be restructured and refurbished. That is where we are now.

MAY 31, 1967
At an SCLC staff retreat King calls for a radical redistribution of economic and political power

DECEMBER 4
Launches the Poor People's Campaign

MARCH 18, 1968
Speaks to striking sanitation workers in Memphis

MARCH 28
Leads Memphis march that is disrupted by violence

I n November 1967 the staff of the Southern Christian Leadership Conference held one of the most important meetings we ever convened. We had intensive discussions and analyses of our work and of the challenges which confront us and our nation. At the end, we made a decision: the SCLC would lead waves of the nation's poor and disinherited to Washington, D.C., in the spring of 1968 to demand redress of their grievances by the United States government and to secure at least jobs or income for all.

We had learned from hard and bitter experience in our movement that our government did not move to correct a problem involving race until it was confronted directly and dramatically. It required a Selma before the fundamental right to vote was written into the federal statutes. It took a Birmingham before the government moved to open doors of public accommodations to all human beings. What we now needed was a new kind of Selma or Birmingham to dramatize the economic plight of the Negro, and compel the government to act.

We would go to Washington and demand to be heard, and we would stay until America responded. If this meant forcible repression of our movement, we would confront it, for we have done this before. If this meant scorn or ridicule, we embrace it for that is what America's poor now receive. If it meant jail, we accepted it willingly, for the millions of poor were already imprisoned by exploitation and discrimination. But we hoped, with growing confidence, that our campaign in Washington would receive a sympathetic understanding across our nation, followed by dramatic expansion of nonviolent demonstrations in Washington and simultaneous protests elsewhere. In short we would be petitioning our government for specific reforms, and we intended to build militant nonviolent actions until that government moves against poverty.

We intended to channel the smouldering rage and frustration of Negro people into an effective, militant, and nonviolent movement of massive proportions in Washington and other areas. Similarly, we would be calling on the swelling masses of young people in this country who were disenchanted with this materialistic society and asking them to join us in our new Washington movement. We also looked for participation by representatives of the millions of non-Negro poor—Indians, Mexican-Americans, Puerto Ricans, Appalachians, and others. And we welcomed assistance from all Americans of goodwill.

And so, we decided to go to Washington and to use any means of legitimate nonviolent protest necessary to move our nation and our government on a new course of social, economic, and political reform. In the final analysis, SCLC decided to go to Washington because, if we did not act, we would be abdicating our responsibilities as an organization committed to nonviolence and freedom. We were keeping that commitment, and we called on America to join us in our Washington campaign. In this way, we could work creatively against the despair and indifference that so often caused our nation to be immobilized during the cold winter and shaken profoundly in the hot summer.

"New tactics which do not count on government goodwill"

The policy of the federal government is to play Russian roulette with riots; it is prepared to gamble with another summer of disaster. Despite two consecutive summers of violence, not a single basic cause of riots has been corrected. All of the misery that stoked the flames of rage and rebellion remains undiminished. With unemployment, intolerable housing, and discriminatory education, a scourge in Negro ghettos, Congress and the administration still tinker with trivial, halfhearted measures.

Yet only a few years ago, there was discernible, if limited, progress through nonviolence. Each year, a wholesome, vibrant Negro self-confidence was taking shape. The fact is inescapable that the tactic of nonviolence, which had then dominated the thinking of the civil rights movement, has in the last two years not been playing its transforming role. Nonviolence was a creative doctrine in the South because it check-mated the rabid segregationists who were thirsting for an opportunity to physically crush Negroes. Nonviolent direct action enabled the Negro to take to the streets in active protest, but it muzzled the guns of the oppressor because even he could not shoot down in daylight unarmed men, women, and children. This is the reason there was less loss of life in ten years of Southern protest than in ten days of Northern riots. . . .

I agree with the President's National Advisory Commission on Civil Disorders that our nation is splitting into two hostile societies and that the chief destructive cutting edge is white racism. We need, above all, effective means to force Congress to act resolutely—but means that do not involve the use of violence.

The time has come for a return to mass nonviolent protest. Accordingly, we are planning a series of such demonstrations this spring and summer, to begin in Washington, D.C. They will have Negro and white participation, and they will seek to benefit the poor of both races.

◆

"A TESTAMENT OF HOPE"

The nation waited until the black man was explosive with fury before stirring itself even to partial concern. Confronted now with the interrelated problems of war, inflation, urban decay, white backlash, and a climate of violence, it is now *forced* to address itself to race relations and poverty, and it is tragically unprepared. What might once have been a series of separate problems now merge into a social crisis of almost stupefying complexity.

I am not sad that black Americans are rebelling; this was not only inevitable but eminently desirable. Without this magnificent ferment among Negroes, the old evasions and procrastinations would have continued indefinitely. Black men have slammed the door shut on a past of deadening passivity. Except for the Reconstruction years, they have never in their long history on American soil struggled with such creativity and courage for their freedom. These are our bright years of emergence; though they are painful ones, they cannot be avoided.

1968

◆

"Find a way to put pressure on them"

We know from past experience that Congress and the President wouldn't do anything until we developed a movement around which people of goodwill could find a way to put pressure on them, because it really meant breaking that coalition in Congress. It was still a coalition-dominated, rural-dominated, basically Southern Congress. There were Southerners there with committee chairmanships, and they were going to stand in the way of progress as long as they could. They got enough right-wing Midwestern or Northern Republicans to go along with them.

This really meant making the movement powerful enough, dramatic enough, morally appealing enough so that people of goodwill—the churches, labor, liberals, intellectuals, students, poor people themselves—began to put pressure on congressmen to the point that they could no longer elude our demands.

Our idea was to dramatize the whole economic problem of the poor. We felt there was a great deal that we needed to do to appeal to Congress itself. The early demonstrations would be more geared toward educational purposes—to educate the nation on the nature of the problem and the crucial aspects of it, the tragic conditions that we confront in the ghettos. After that, if we had not gotten a response from Congress, we would branch out. And we were honest enough to feel that we weren't going to get any instantaneous results from Congress, knowing its recalcitrant nature on this issue, and knowing that so many resources and energies were being used in Vietnam rather than on the domestic situation. So we didn't have any illusions about moving Congress in two or three weeks. But we did feel that, by starting in Washington, centering on Congress and departments of the government, we would be able to do a real educational job.

We called our demonstration a campaign for jobs and income because we felt that the economic question was the most crucial that black people, and poor people generally, were confronting. There was a literal depression in the Negro community. When you have mass unemployment in the Negro community, it's called a social problem; when you have mass unemployment in the white community, it's called a depression.

We would begin activity around Washington, but as that activity was beginning, some people would be talking to Washington. Some would be coming on mules to Washington. Some would be in their buggies being pulled by the mules. And we would have a mule train, all moving toward Washington, so that we would have forces moving out of the South—Mississippi joining forces with Alabama, Alabama joining with Georgia, Georgia joining with South Carolina, South Carolina with North Carolina with Virginia, and right on into Washington. Other forces would be coming up out of Chicago and Detroit and Cleveland and Milwaukee, others coming down from Boston, New York, Philadelphia, Baltimore—all moving toward Washington.

We would place the problems of the poor at the seat of government of the wealthiest nation in the history of mankind. If that power refused to acknowledge its debt to the poor, it would have failed to live up to its promise to insure "life, liberty, and the pursuit of happiness" to its citizens. If this society fails, I fear that we will hear very shortly that racism is a sickness unto death.

The American people are infected with racism—that is the peril.

Paradoxically, they are also infected with democratic ideals—that is the hope. While doing wrong, they have the potential to do right. But they do not have a millennium to make changes. Nor have they a choice of continuing in the old way. The future they are asked to inaugurate is not so unpalatable that it justifies the evils that beset the nation. To end poverty, to extirpate prejudice, to free a tormented conscience, to make a tomorrow of justice, fair play, and creativity—all these are worthy of the American ideal.

We have, through massive nonviolent action, an opportunity to avoid a national disaster and create a new spirit of class and racial harmony. We can write another luminous moral chapter in American history. All of us are on trial in this troubled hour, but time still permits us to meet the future with a clear conscience.

We have the power to change America and give a kind of new vitality to the religion of Jesus Christ. And we can get those young men and women who've lost faith in the church to see that Jesus was a serious man precisely because he dealt with the tang of the human amid the glow of the Divine and that he was concerned about their problems. He was concerned about bread; he opened and started Operation Breadbasket a long time ago. He initiated the first sit-in movement. The greatest revolutionary that history has ever known. And when people tell us when we stand up that we got our inspiration from this or that, go back and let them know where we got our inspiration.

I read Das Kapital *and* The Communist Manifesto *years ago when I was a student in college. And many of the revolutionary movements in the world came into being as a result of what Marx talked about.*

The great tragedy is that Christianity failed to see that it had the revolutionary edge. You don't have to go to Karl Marx to learn how to be a revolutionary. I didn't get my inspiration from Karl Marx; I got it from a man named Jesus, a Galilean saint who said he was anointed to heal the broken-hearted. He was anointed to deal with the problems of the poor. And that is where we get our inspiration. And we go out in a day when we have a message for the world, and we can change this world and we can change this nation.

"A great movement in Memphis"

During one week in March 1968 I made about thirty-five speeches. I started out on Thursday in Grosse Point, Michigan. I had to speak

RESOLUTIONS

And I'm simply saying this morning, that you should resolve that you will never become so secure in your thinking or your living that you forget the least of these. . . . In some sense, all of us are the least of these, but there are some who are least than the least of these. I try to get it over to my children early, morning after morning, when I get a chance. As we sit at the table, as we did this morning in morning devotions, I couldn't pray my prayer without saying, "God, help us, as we sit at this table to realize that there are those who are less fortunate than we are. And grant that we will never forget them, no matter where we are." And I said to my little children, "I'm going to work and do everything that I can do to see that you get a good education. I don't ever want you to forget that there are millions of God's children who will not and cannot get a good education, and I don't want you feeling that you are better than they are. For you will never be what you ought to be until they are what they ought to be."

From sermon on January 7, 1968

four times in Detroit on Friday. Saturday I went to Los Angeles. I had to speak five times. Then on Sunday I preached in three churches in Los Angeles. And I flew from there to Memphis.

As I came in to Memphis, I turned around and said to Ralph Abernathy, "They really have a great movement here in Memphis." The issue was the refusal of Memphis to be fair and honest in its dealings with its public servants, who happened to be sanitation workers. One thousand three hundred sanitation workers were on strike, and Memphis was not being fair to them. They were demonstrating something there that needed to be demonstrated all over our country. They were demonstrating that we can stick together and they were demonstrating that we are all tied in a single garment of destiny, and that if one black person suffers, if one black person is down, we are all down. The Negro "haves" must join hands with the Negro "have-nots." And armed with the compassionate traveler's check, they must journey into that other country of their brother's denial and hurt and exploitation. One day our society will come to respect the sanitation worker if it is to survive, for the person who picks up our garbage is in the final analysis as significant as the physician, for if he doesn't do his job, diseases are rampant. All labor has dignity.

Now let me say a word to those of you who are on strike. You have been out now for a number of days, but don't despair. Nothing worthwhile is gained without sacrifice. The thing for you to do is stay together and say to everybody in this community that you are going to stick it out to the end until every demand is met, and that you are going to say, "We ain't gonna let nobody turn us around." Let it be known everywhere that along with wages and all of the other securities that you are struggling for, you are also struggling for the right to organize and to be recognized.

We can all get more together than we can apart. And this is the way we gain power. Power is the ability to achieve purpose, power is the ability to affect change, and we need power. And I want you to stick it out so that you will be able to make Mayor Loeb and others say "Yes," even when they want to say "No."

Now the other thing is that nothing is gained without pressure. Don't let anybody tell you to go back on the job and paternalistically say, "Now you are my men and I'm going to do the right thing for you. Just come on back on the job." Don't go back on the job until the demands are met. Never forget that freedom is not something that is voluntarily given by the oppressor. It is something that must be demanded by the oppressed. Freedom is not some lavish dish that the power structure and the white forces in policy-making positions will voluntarily hand out on a silver platter while the Negro merely furnishes the appetite. If we are going to get equality, if we are going to get adequate wages, we are going to have to struggle for it. . . .

You know Jesus reminded us in a magnificent parable one day that a man went to hell because he didn't see the poor. His name was Dives. And there was a man by the name of Lazarus who came daily to his gate in need of the basic necessities of life and Dives didn't do anything about it. And he ended up going to hell. There is nothing in that parable which says that Dives went to hell because he was rich. Jesus never made a universal indictment against all wealth. It is true that one day a rich young ruler came to Him talking about eternal life and he advised him to sell all, but in that instance Jesus was prescribing individual surgery, not setting forth a universal diagnosis. If you will go on and read that parable in all of its dimensions and its symbolism you will remember that a conversation took place between heaven and hell. And on the other end of that long distance call between heaven and hell was Abraham in heaven talking to Dives in hell. It wasn't a millionaire in hell talking with a poor man in heaven, it was a little millionaire in hell talking with a multimillionaire in heaven. Dives didn't go to hell because he was rich. His wealth was his opportunity to bridge the gulf that separated him from his brother Lazarus. Dives went to hell because he allowed Lazarus to become invisible. Dives went to hell because he allowed the means by which he lived to outdistance the ends for which he lived. Dives went to hell because he sought to be a conscientious objector in the war against poverty.

And I come by here to say that America too is going to hell if she doesn't use her wealth. If America does not use her vast resources of wealth to end poverty and make it possible for all of God's children to have the basic necessities of life, she too will go to hell. I will hear America through her historians, years and generations to come, saying, "We built gigantic buildings to kiss the skies. We built gargantuan bridges to span the seas. Through our space ships we were able to carve highways through the stratosphere. Through our submarines we were able to penetrate oceanic depths." It seems that I can hear the God of the universe saying, "Even though you have done all of that, I was hungry and you fed me not. I was naked and you clothed me not. The children of my sons and daughters were in need of economic security and you didn't provide it for them. And so you cannot enter the kingdom of greatness." This may well be the indictment on America. And that same voice says in Memphis to the mayor, to the power structure, "If you do it unto the least of these of my children you do it unto me."

. . . Having to live under the threat of death every day, sometimes I feel discouraged. Having to take so much abuse and criticism, sometimes from my own people, sometimes I feel discouraged. Having to go to bed so often frustrated with the chilly winds of adversity about to stagger me, sometimes I feel discouraged and feel my work's in vain.

But then the holy spirit revives my soul again. In Gilead, there is *balm to make the wounded whole. If we will believe that, we will build a new Memphis. And bring about the day when every valley shall be exalted. Every mountain and hill will be made low. The rough places will be made plain, and the crooked places straight. And the glory of the Lord shall be revealed, and all flesh shall see it together.*

32

UNFULFILLED DREAMS

> **APRIL 3, 1968**
> Delivers final address at Bishop Charles J. Mason Temple in Memphis
>
> **APRIL 4**
> Is assassinated at Loraine Hotel

I guess one of the great agonies of life is that we are constantly trying to finish that which is unfinishable. We are commanded to do that. And so we, like David, find ourselves in so many instances having to face the fact that our dreams are not fulfilled.

Life is a continual story of shattered dreams. Mahatma Gandhi labored for years and years for the independence of his people. But Gandhi had to face the fact that he was assassinated and died with a broken heart, because that nation that he wanted to unite ended up being divided between India and Pakistan as a result of the conflict between the Hindus and the Moslems.

Woodrow Wilson dreamed a dream of a League of Nations, but he died before the promise was delivered.

The Apostle Paul talked one day about wanting to go to Spain. It was Paul's greatest dream to go to Spain, to carry the gospel there. Paul never got to Spain. He ended up in a prison cell in Rome. This is the story of life.

So many of our forebears used to sing about freedom. And they dreamed of the day that they would be able to get out of the bosom of slavery, the long night of injustice. And they used to sing little songs:

"Nobody knows de trouble I seen, nobody knows but Jesus." They thought about a better day as they dreamed their dream. And they would say, "I'm so glad the trouble don't last always. By and by, by and by I'm going to lay down my heavy load." And they used to sing it because of a powerful dream. But so many died without having the dream fulfilled.

And each of you in some way is building some kind of temple. The struggle is always there. It gets discouraging sometimes. It gets very disenchanting sometimes. Some of us are trying to build a temple of peace. We speak out against war, we protest, but it seems that your head is going against a concrete wall. It seems to mean nothing. And so often as you set out to build the temple of peace you are left lonesome; you are left discouraged; you are left bewildered.

Well, that is the story of life. And the thing that makes me happy is that I can hear a voice crying through the vista of time, saying: "It may not come today or it may not come tomorrow, but it is well that it is within thine heart. It's well that you are trying." You may not see it. The dream may not be fulfilled, but it's just good that you have a desire to bring it into reality. It's well that it's in thine heart.

Now let me bring out another point. Whenever you set out to build a creative temple, whatever it may be, you must face the fact that there is a tension at the heart of the universe between good and evil. Hinduism refers to this as a struggle between illusion and reality. Platonic philosophy used to refer to it as a tension between body and soul. Zoroastrianism, a religion of old, used to refer to it as a tension between the god of light and the god of darkness. Traditional Judaism and Christianity refer to it as a tension between God and Satan. Whatever you call it, there is a struggle in the universe between good and evil.

Now not only is that struggle structured out somewhere in the external forces of the universe, it's structured in our own lives. Psychologists have tried to grapple with it in their way, and so they say various things. Sigmund Freud used to say that this tension is a tension between what he called the id and the superego. Some of us feel that it's a tension between God and man. And in every one of us, there's a war going on. It's a civil war. I don't care who you are, I don't care where you live, there is a civil war going on in your life. And every time you set out to be good, there's something pulling on you, telling you to be evil. It's going on in your life. Every time you set out to love, something keeps pulling on you, trying to get you to hate. Every time you set out to be kind and say nice things about people, something is pulling on you to be jealous and envious and to spread evil gossip about them. There's a civil war going on. There is a schizophrenia, as the psychologists or the psychiatrists would call it, going on within all of us. And there are times that all of us know somehow that there is a Mr. Hyde and a Dr. Jekyll in us. And we end up having to cry out with Ovid, the Latin poet, "I see and approve the better things of life, but the evil things I do." We end up having to agree with Plato that the human personality is like a charioteer with two headstrong horses, wanting to go in different directions. Or sometimes we even have to end up crying out with Saint Augustine as he said in his Confessions, "Lord, make me pure, but not yet." We end up crying out with the Apostle Paul, "The good that I would I do not: And the evil that I would not, that I do." Or we end up having to say with Goethe that "there's enough stuff in me to make both a gentleman and a rogue." There's a tension at the heart of human nature. And whenever we set out to dream our dreams and to build our temples, we must be honest enough to recognize it.

In the final analysis, God does not judge us by the separate incidents or the separate mistakes that we make, but by the total bent of our lives. In the final analysis, God knows that his children are weak and they are frail. In the final analysis, what God requires is that your heart is right.

And the question I want to raise with you: is your heart right? If your heart isn't right, fix it up today; get God to fix it up. Get somebody to be able to say about you: "He may not have reached the highest height, he may not have realized all of his dreams, but he tried." Isn't that a wonderful thing for somebody to say about you? "He tried to be a good man. He tried to be a just man. He tried to be an honest man. His heart was in the right place." And I can hear a voice saying, crying out through the eternities, "I accept you. You are a recipient of my grace because it was in your heart. And it is so well that it was within thine heart."

I don't know about you, but I can make a testimony. You don't need to go out saying that Martin Luther King is a saint. Oh, no. I want you to know this morning that I'm a sinner like all of God's *children. But I want to be a good man. And I want to hear a voice saying to me one day, "I take you in and I bless you, because you tried. It is well that it was within thine heart."*

"I've been to the mountaintop"

And you know, if I were standing at the beginning of time with the possibility of taking a kind of general and panoramic view of the whole human history up to now, and the Almighty said to me, "Martin Luther King, which age would you like to live in?" I would take my mental flight by Egypt, and I would watch God's children in their magnificent trek from the dark dungeons of Egypt across the Red Sea, through the wilderness, on toward the promised land. And in spite of its magnificence, I wouldn't stop there.

I would move on by Greece, and take my mind to Mount Olympus. And I would see Plato, Aristotle, Socrates, Euripides, and Aristophanes assembled around the Parthenon, and I would watch them around the Parthenon as they discussed the great and eternal issues of reality. But I wouldn't stop there.

I would go on even to the great heyday of the Roman Empire and I would see developments around there, through various emperors and leaders. But I wouldn't stop there.

I would even come up to the day of the Renaissance, and get a quick picture of all that the Renaissance did for the cultural and aesthetic life of man. But I wouldn't stop there.

I would even go by the way that the man for whom I'm named had his habitat, and I would watch Martin Luther as he tacks his ninety-five theses on the door at the church in Wittenberg. But I wouldn't stop there.

I would come on up even to 1863 and watch a vacillating President by the name of Abraham Lincoln finally come to the conclusion that he had to sign the Emancipation Proclamation. But I wouldn't stop there.

I would even come up to the early thirties and see a man grappling with the problems of the bankruptcy of his nation, and come with an eloquent cry that "we have nothing to fear but fear itself." But I wouldn't stop there.

Strangely enough, I would turn to the Almighty and say, "If you allow me to live just a few years in the second half of the twentieth century, I will be happy."

Now that's a strange statement to make, because the world is all messed up. The nation is sick; trouble is in the land, confusion all around. That's a strange statement. But I know, somehow, that only when it is dark enough can you see the stars. And I see God working in this period of the twentieth century. Something is happening in our world. The masses of people are rising up. And wherever they are assembled today, whether they are in Johannesburg, South Africa; Nairobi, Kenya; Accra, Ghana; New York City; Atlanta, Georgia; Jackson, Mississippi; or Memphis, Tennessee, the cry is always the same: "We want to be free."

And another reason that I'm happy to live in this period is that we have been forced to a point where we are going to have to grapple with the problems that men have been trying to grapple with through history. Survival demands that we grapple with them. Men for years now have been talking about war and peace. But now, no longer can they just talk about it. It is no longer a choice between violence and nonviolence in this world; it's nonviolence or nonexistence. That is where we are today.

And also in the human rights revolution, if something isn't done, and done in a hurry, to bring the colored peoples of the world out of their long years of poverty, their long years of hurt and neglect, the whole world is doomed. Now, I'm just happy that God has allowed me to live in this period, to see what is unfolding. And I'm happy that he's allowed me to be in Memphis.

I can remember, I can remember when Negroes were just going around, as Ralph has said so often, scratching where they didn't itch and laughing when they were not tickled. But that day is all over. We mean business now and we are determined to gain our rightful place in God's world. And that's all this whole thing is about. We aren't engaged in any negative protest and in any negative arguments with anybody. We are saying that we are determined to be men. We are determined to be people. We are saying, we are saying that we are God's children. And if we are God's children, we don't have to live like we are forced to live.

Now, what does all of this mean in this great period of history? It means that we've got to stay together. We've got to stay together and maintain unity. You know, whenever Pharaoh wanted to prolong the period of slavery in Egypt, he had a favorite formula for doing it. What was that? He kept the slaves fighting among themselves. But whenever the slaves get together, something happens in Pharaoh's court, and he cannot hold the slaves in slavery. When the slaves get together, that's the beginning of getting out of slavery. Now let us maintain unity.

We aren't going to let any mace stop us. We are masters in our nonviolent movement in disarming police forces; they don't know what to do. I've seen them so often. I remember in Birmingham, Alabama, when we were in that majestic struggle there, we would move out of the Sixteenth Street Baptist Church day after day. By the hundreds we would move out, and Bull Connor would tell them to send the dogs forth, and they did come. But we just went before the dogs singing, "Ain't gonna let nobody turn me around." Bull Connor next would say, "Turn the firehoses on." And as I said to you the other night, Bull Connor didn't know history. He knew a kind of physics that somehow didn't relate to the transphysics that we knew about. And that was the fact that there was a certain kind of fire that no water could put out. And we went before the firehoses. We had known water. If we were Baptist or some other denomination, we had been immersed. If we were Methodist, and some others, we had been sprinkled—but we knew water. That couldn't stop us.

And we just went on before the dogs, and we would look at them; and we'd go on before the water hoses, and we would look at them. And we'd just go on singing, "Over my head, I see freedom in the air." And then we would be thrown in the paddy wagons, and sometimes we were stacked in there like sardines in a can. And they would throw us in, and old Bull would say, "Take 'em off." And they did, and we would just go on in the paddy wagon singing, "We shall overcome." And every now and then we'd get in jail, and we'd see the jailers looking through the windows being moved by our prayers and being moved by our words and our songs. And there was a power there which Bull Connor couldn't adjust to, and so we ended up transforming Bull into a steer, and we won our struggle in Birmingham.

We've got to give ourselves to this struggle until the end. Nothing would be more tragic than to stop at this point in Memphis. We've got to see it through. When we have our march, you need to be there. If it means leaving work, if it means leaving school, be there. Be concerned about your brother. You may not be on strike, but either we go up together or we go down together. Let us develop a kind of dangerous unselfishness.

One day a man came to Jesus and he wanted to raise some questions about some vital matters of life. At points he wanted to trick Jesus, and show him that he knew a little more than Jesus knew and throw him off base. Now that question could have easily ended up in a philosophical and theological debate. But Jesus immediately pulled that question from midair and placed it on a dangerous curve between Jerusalem and Jericho. And he talked about a certain man who fell among thieves. You remember that a Levite and a priest passed by on the other side—they didn't stop to help him. Finally, a man of another race came by. He got down from his beast, decided not to be compassionate by proxy. But he got down with him, administered first aid, and helped the man in need. Jesus ended up saying this was the good man, this was the great man, because he had the capacity to project the "I" into the "thou," and to be concerned about his brother.

Now you know, we use our imagination a great deal to try to determine why the priest and the Levite didn't stop. At times we say they were busy going to a church meeting, an ecclesiastical gathering, and they had to get on down to Jerusalem so they wouldn't be late for their meeting. At other times we would speculate that there was a religious law that one who was engaged in religious ceremonies was not to touch a human body twenty-four hours before the ceremony. And every now and then we begin to wonder whether maybe they were not going down to Jerusalem, or down to Jericho, rather, to organize a Jericho Road Improvement Association. That's a possibility. Maybe they felt it was better to deal with the problem from the causal root, rather than to get bogged down with an individual effect.

But I'm going to tell you what my imagination tells me. It's possible that those men were afraid. You see, the Jericho Road is a dangerous road. I remember when Mrs. King and I were first in Jerusalem. We rented a car and drove from Jerusalem down to Jericho. And as soon as we got on that road I said to my wife, "I can see why Jesus used this as a setting for his parable." It's a winding, meandering road. It's really conducive for ambushing. You start out in Jerusalem, which is about twelve hundred miles, or rather, twelve hundred feet above sea level.

And by the time you get down to Jericho, fifteen or twenty minutes later, you're about twenty-two hundred feet below sea level. That's a dangerous road. In the days of Jesus it came to be known as the "Bloody Pass." And you know, it's possible that the priest and the Levite looked over that man on the ground and wondered if the robbers were still around. Or it's possible that they felt that the man on the ground was merely faking. And he was acting like he had been robbed and hurt, in order to seize them over there, lure them there for quick and easy seizure. (Oh yeah.) And so the first question that the priest asked, the first question that the Levite asked was, "If I stop to help this man, what will happen to me?"

But then the Good Samaritan came by, and he reversed the question: "If I do not stop to help this man, what will happen to him?"

That's the question before you tonight. Not, "If I stop to help the sanitation workers, what will happen to my job?" Not, "If I stop to help the sanitation workers, what will happen to all of the hours that I usually spend in my office every day and every week as a pastor?" The question is not, "If I stop to help this man in need, what will happen to me?" The question is, "If I do not stop to help the sanitation workers, what will happen to them?" That's the question.

Let us rise up tonight with a greater readiness. Let us stand with a greater determination. And let us move on in these powerful days, these days of challenge, to make America what it ought to be. We have an opportunity to make America a better nation. And I want to thank God, once more, for allowing me to be here with you.

You know, several years ago I was in New York City autographing the first book that I had written. And while sitting there autographing books, a demented black woman came up. The only question I heard from her was, "Are you Martin Luther King?" And I was looking down writing and I said, "Yes."

And the next minute I felt something beating on my chest. Before I knew it I had been stabbed by this demented woman. I was rushed to Harlem Hospital. It was a dark Saturday afternoon. And that blade had gone through, and the X rays revealed that the tip of the blade was on the edge of my aorta, the main artery. And once that's punctured, you drown in your own blood; that's the end of you. It came out in the

New York Times *the next morning that if I had merely sneezed, I would have died.*

Well, about four days later, they allowed me, after the operation, after my chest had been opened and the blade had been taken out, to move around in the wheelchair in the hospital. They allowed me to read some of the mail that came in, and from all over the states and the world kind letters came in. I read a few, but one of them I will never forget. I had received one from the President and the Vice President; I've forgotten what those telegrams said. I'd received a visit and a letter from the governor of New York, but I've forgotten what the letter said.

But there was another letter that came from a little girl, a young girl who was a student at the White Plains High School. And I looked at the letter and I'll never forget it. It said simply, "Dear Dr. King: I am a ninth-grade student at the White Plains High School." She said, "While it should not matter, I would like to mention that I'm a white girl. I read in the paper of your misfortune and of your suffering. And I read that if you had sneezed, you would have died. And I'm simply writing to you to say that I'm so happy that you didn't sneeze."

I want to say that I too am happy that I didn't sneeze. Because if I had sneezed, I wouldn't have been around here in 1960, when students all over the South started sitting in at lunch counters. And I knew that as they were sitting in, they were really standing up for the best in the American Dream and taking the whole nation back to those great wells of democracy which were dug deep by the founding fathers in the Declaration of Independence and the Constitution.

If I had sneezed, I wouldn't have been around here in 1961, when we decided to take a ride for freedom and ended segregation in interstate travel.

If I had sneezed, I wouldn't have been around here in 1962, when Negroes in Albany, Georgia, decided to straighten their backs up. And whenever men and women straighten their backs up, they are going somewhere, because a man can't ride your back unless it is bent.

If I had sneezed, I wouldn't have been here in 1963, when the black people of Birmingham, Alabama, aroused the conscience of this nation and brought into being the Civil Rights Bill.

If I had sneezed, I wouldn't have had a chance later that year, in August, to try to tell America about a dream that I had had.

If I had sneezed, I wouldn't have been down in Selma, Alabama, to see the great movement there.

If I had sneezed, I wouldn't have been in Memphis to see a community rally around those brothers and sisters who are suffering. I'm so happy that I didn't sneeze.

I left Atlanta this morning, and as we got started on the plane—there were six of us—the pilot said over the public address system, "We are sorry for the delay, but we have Dr. Martin Luther King on the plane. And to be sure that all of the bags were checked and to be sure that nothing would be wrong on the plane, we had to check out everything carefully. And we've had the plane protected and guarded all night."

And then I got into Memphis. And some began to say the threats, or talk about the threats that were out, or what would happen to me from some of our sick white brothers.

Well, I don't know what will happen now; we've got some difficult days ahead. But it really doesn't matter with me now, because I've been to the mountaintop. And I don't mind. Like anybody, I would like to live a long life—longevity has its place. But I'm not concerned about that now. I just want to do God's will. And He's allowed me to go up to the mountain. And I've looked over, and I've seen the promised land. I may not get there with you. But I want you to know tonight, that we, as a people, will get to the promised land. And I'm happy tonight. I'm not worried about anything. I'm not fearing any man. Mine eyes have seen the glory of the coming of the Lord.

"A drum major for righteousness"

Every now and then I guess we all think realistically about that day when we will be victimized with what is life's final common denominator—that something we call death. We all think about it. And every now and then I think about my own death, and I think about my own funeral. And I don't think of it in a morbid sense. Every now and then I ask myself, "What is it that I would want said?" And I leave the word to you this morning.

I'd like somebody to mention that day, that Martin Luther King, Jr., tried to give his life serving others.

I'd like for somebody to say that day, that Martin Luther King, Jr., tried to love somebody.

I want you to say that day, that I tried to be right on the war question.

I want you to be able to say that day, that I did try to feed the hungry.

And I want you to be able to say that day, that I did try, in my life, to clothe those who were naked.

I want you to say, on that day, that I did try, in my life, to visit those who were in prison.

I want you to say that I tried to love and to serve humanity.

Yes, if you want to say that I was a drum major, say that I was a drum major for justice. Say that I was a drum major for peace. I was a drum major for righteousness. And all of the other shallow things will not matter. I won't have any money to leave behind. I won't have the fine and luxurious things of life to leave behind. But I just want to leave a committed life behind. And that's all I wanted to say.

If I can help somebody as I pass along, if I can cheer somebody with a word or song, if I can show somebody he's traveling wrong, then my living will not be in vain. If I can do my duty as a Christian ought, if I can bring salvation to a world once wrought, if I can spread the message as the master taught, then my living will not be in vain.

EDITOR'S
ACKNOWLEDGMENTS

◆

The Autobiography of Martin Luther King, Jr. is an outgrowth of discussions involving myself and members of the King family. In 1992 I proposed to the family several ideas for increasing public understanding of King's life and thought. As director of the Martin Luther King, Jr., Papers Project, I was aware of the enormous quantity of documents that existed regarding King; yet I also knew that these documents were available mainly to scholars who were able to travel to archives. Although the King Project's fourteen-volume edition of *The Papers of Martin Luther King, Jr.* was intended as a way to make these documents more widely available, this long-term effort will not be completed for many years. Designed as an essential foundation for future studies of King and his times, the project's annotated edition of King's writings and public statements has more often attracted the attention of researchers rather than casual readers, and many of the important revelations that have resulted from the King Project's research are not widely known outside the community of King scholars. Thus I urged the King family to join with me in developing innovative, popularly accessible ways to present the findings of the project.

The first result of these discussions was the development of a docudrama, *Passages of Martin Luther King.* With the assistance of Stanford drama professor Dr. Victor Leo Walker and Stanford undergraduate researcher Heather Williams, I explored ways of telling the story of King's life through his own words and the words of those who knew him best. After several dramatic readings at Stanford, *Passages* was produced by the Stanford drama department in April 1993. Revised versions were presented as dramatic readings at Dartmouth College and the University of Washington in January 1996 and 1998, respectively. I am grateful for the contributions of all of the individuals who participated in these presentations, which increased my familiarity with the documentary resources concerning King and prepared a foundation for this comprehensive autobiographical account of King's life.

Soon after Dexter King became the president and chief executive officer of the King Center in 1995, I found that we shared a common interest in facilitating the dissemination of King's ideas through various media. In association with Philip Jones, president and CEO of Intellectual Properties Management (IPM) and the manager of the King literary estate, Mr. King established a partnership with Warner Books that will result in increasing public awareness of King's ideas and achievements. I have greatly enjoyed the opportunity to work closely with Dexter and Philip to achieve our common goals, including the publication of this work. At every stage in the development of this work, their support and advice have been essential and available. Their energy and enthusiasm have been contagious.

My agent, Sandra Dijkstra, provided continuous encouragement for this project since its inception. Her expertise and that of her able staff made it possible for me to concentrate on research while they handled the financial and contractual matters. I especially appreciated the opportunity to work with a former student of mine, Rebecca Lowen, who is now with the Dijkstra Literary Agency.

Even before the book contract was signed, I became deeply involved in the task of searching for the source texts for the autobiography from the hundreds of thousands of King-related documents. My initial research assistant was Jennifer Marcus, a dedicated and talented researcher who helped produce the original prospectus for the autobiography and who remained involved in the project for most of her Stanford University undergraduate career.

Once I formally agreed to produce the autobiography in little more than a year, Randy Gellerman Mont-Reynaud became the principal researcher for the book. Randy examined thousands of documents and listened to hundreds of audio recordings to identify texts for possible inclusion and then assembled these texts in a preliminary chronological narrative. She brought to this difficult and daunting task considerable energy and enthusiasm—essential qualities for any effort of this scope.

The autobiography owes its completion to the extensive involvement of various members of the King Project staff. In particular, managing editor and archivist Susan Carson provided her unparalleled knowledge of the more than twenty thousand cataloged documents in the project's database. During the final stages of manuscript preparation, she and researcher Erin Wood contributed valuable suggestions for revision, supervised the effort to locate appropriate additional documents, and checked the manuscript for accuracy.

Other King Project staff also made this book possible. I wish to thank especially Adrienne Clay, Kerry Taylor, and Elizabeth Baez who, despite the other demands of the project's documentary edition, volunteered to read chapters and suggest necessary improvements. My assistant Vicki Brooks also contributed by proofreading chapters and by bringing a measure of organization to my office. Barbara Ifejika volunteered to help during the final stages of manuscript preparation.

Undergraduate and graduate student researchers have contributed to this work in a variety of ways. The following individuals have made significant contributions through the Martin Luther King, Jr., Research Fellowship summer internship program: Tenisha Armstrong (University of California, Santa Cruz), Brandi Brimmer (University of California, Los Angeles), Joy Clinkscales (American University), Andrew Davidson (Cornell University), Julian Davis (Brown University), Rashann Duvall (Yale University), Patrick Guarasci (Macalaster College), Lisa Marley (Brown University), and Maria-Theresa Robinson (Spelman College). Stanford students who worked on this volume include Stephanie Baca-Delancey, Joe Crespino, Elsa Cruz-Pearson, Nancy Farghalli, Hanan Hardy, Shaw-San Liu, Naila Moseley, Megan Thompkins, and Ali Zaidi.

I also appreciate the assistance of the following: Jeff Shram, Gail Westergard, and Christopher Carson.

Several others offered helpful comments on earlier versions of this manuscript. My editor at Warner Books, Rick Horgan, gave useful and tactful suggestions at various stages of manuscript preparation. I appreciate and benefited from the constructive criticisms of Candace Falk of the University of California, Berkeley, and of Michael Honey of the University of Washington, Tacoma. I am especially grateful for Coretta Scott King's willingness to read this manuscript with the painstaking care and sensitive understanding that only she could provide.

Finally, I appreciate the remarkable fact that Martin Luther King, Jr., had the foresight to create and leave behind the autobiographical documents on which this book is based.

SOURCE NOTES

Abbreviations of Collections and Repositories:

ABSP, DHU   Arthur B. Spingarn Papers, Howard University, Washington, D.C.

AC, InU-N   Audiotape Collection, Indiana University, Northwest Regional Campus, Gary, Indiana

ACA-ARC, LNT   American Committee on Africa Papers, Amistad Research Center, Tulane University, New Orleans, Louisiana

AFSCR, AFSCA   American Friends Service Committee Records, AFSC Archives, Philadelphia, Pennsylvania

CB, CtY   Chester Bowles Collection, Yale University, New Haven, Connecticut

CSKC, INP   Coretta Scott King Collection (in private hands)

DABCC, INP   Dexter Avenue King Memorial Baptist Church Collection (in private hands)

DCST, AB   Dallas County Sheriff's Department Surveillance Tape, Birmingham Public Library, Birminghan, Alabama

DHSTR, WHi   Donald H. Smith Tape Recordings, State Historical Society, Madison, Wisconsin

DJG, INP   David J. Garrow Collection (in private hands)

EMBC, INP   Etta Moten Barnett Collection (in private hands)

HG, GAMK   Hazel Gregory Papers, Martin Luther King, Jr., Center for Nonviolent Change, Inc., Atlanta, Georgia

JFKP, MWalk   John F. Kennedy Miscellaneous Papers, John F. Kennedy Library, Waltham, Massachusetts

JWWP, DHU   Julius Waties Waring Papers, Howard University, Washington, D.C.

MLKP, MBU	Martin Luther King, Jr., Papers, 1954–1968, Boston University, Boston, Massachusetts
MLKEC, INP	Martin Luther King Estate Collection (in private hands)
MLKJP, GAMK	Martin Luther King, Jr., Papers, 1954–1968, King Center, Atlanta, Georgia
MMFR, INP	Montgomery to Memphis Film Research Files (in private hands)
MVC, TMM	Mississippi Valley Collection, Memphis State University, Memphis, Tennessee
NAACPP, DLC	National Association for the Advancement of Colored People Papers, Library of Congress, Washington, D.C.
NBCC, NNNBC	National Broadcasting Company, Inc., Collection, NBC Library, New York, New York
NF, GEU	*Newsweek* File, Emory University Special Collections, Atlanta, Georgia
OGCP, MBU	Office of General Council Papers, Boston University, Boston, Massachusetts
PHBC, INP	Paul H. Brown Collection (in private hands)
SAVFC, WHi	Social Action Vertical File, State Historical Society, Madison, Wisconsin
SCLCT, INP	Southern Christian Leadership Conference Tapes (in private hands)
TWUC, NNU-T	Transport Workers Union Collection, Tamiment Library, New York University, New York, New York
UPWP, WHi	United Packinghouse Workers Union Papers, State Historical Society, Madison, Wisconsin
WAR, INP	William A. Robinson Miscellaneous Papers (in private hands)

1. EARLY YEARS

PRINCIPAL SOURCES:

"An Autobiography of Religious Development," November 1950, in Clayborne Carson, Ralph E. Luker, and Penny A. Russell, eds., *The Papers of Martin*

Luther King, Jr., Volume I: Called to Serve, January 1929–June 1951 (Berkeley: University of California Press, 1992), pp. 359–363.

Stride Toward Freedom: The Montgomery Story (New York: Harper and Row, 1958), chapter 1; "Family in Siege," drafts for *Stride Toward Freedom* (MLKP, MBU).

OTHER SOURCES:

"Facing the Challenge of the New Age," address at NAACP Emancipation Day Rally, Atlanta, January 1, 1957 (PHBC, INP).

"Why Jesus Called a Man a Fool," sermon at Mount Pisgah Missionary Baptist Church, Chicago, Autust 27, 1967, in Clayborne Carson and Peter Holloran, eds., *A Knock at Midnight: Inspiration from the Great Sermons of Reverend Martin Luther King, Jr.* (New York: IPM/Warner Books, 1998), pp. 145–164.

Interview with Edward T. Ladd on *Profile*, WAII-TV, at Emory University, Atlanta, April 12, 1964 (MLKEC, INP).

Interview with John Freeman on BBC's *Face to Face*, London, England, October 24, 1961 (MLKJP, GAMK).

Interview with Alex Haley, *Playboy* 12 (January 1965): 65–68, 70–74, 76–78.

Statement on Meredith March, Grenada, Mississippi, June 16, 1966 (MLKJP, GAMK).

Quoted in Ted Poston, "Fighting Pastor," *New York Post*, April 10, 1957.

"The Negro and the Constitution," May 1944, *Papers I*, pp. 110–111.

Letters to Alberta Williams King, June 11 and 18, 1944; Martin Luther King, Sr., June 15, 1944, *Papers I*, pp. 112–116.

2. MOREHOUSE COLLEGE

PRINCIPAL SOURCE:

"An Autobiography of Religious Development."

OTHER SOURCES:

Stride Toward Freedom, pp. 91, 145.

"A Legacy of Creative Protest," in *Massachusetts Review* 4 (September 1962): 43.

"Martin Luther King Explains Nonviolent Resistance," in William Katz, *The Negro in American History* (New York: Pitman, 1967), pp. 511–513.

"May 17—11 Years Later," *New York Amsterdam News*, May 22, 1965.

Interview with Edward T. Ladd.

Interview with John Freeman.

Quoted in Ted Poston, "Fighting Pastor" and "The Boycott and the 'New Dawn,'" *New York Post,* May 13, 1956.

Quoted in William Peters, "'Our Weapon Is Love,'" *Redbook* 107 (August 1956): 42–43, 71–73.

Quoted in L. D. Reddick, *Crusader Without Violence* (New York: Harper and Brothers, 1959), p. 74.

"Kick Up Dust," Letter to Editor, *Atlanta Constitution,* August 6, 1946, *Papers I,* p. 121.

3. CROZER SEMINARY

PRINCIPAL SOURCES:

Stride Toward Freedom, chapter 6.

"Pilgrimage to Nonviolence," *Christian Century* 77 (April 13, 1960): 439–441; "How my mind has changed," draft of *Christian Century* article (MLKP, MBU).

Strength to Love (New York: Harper and Row, 1963), chapter 17.

OTHER SOURCES:

"Autobiography of Religious Development."

"Preaching Ministry," 1949(?), course paper submitted at Crozer Theological Seminary, Chester, Pennsylvania (CSKC, INP).

"How Modern Christians Should Think of Man," 1949–50, *Papers I,* pp. 273–279.

"His Influence Speaks to World Conscience," *Hindustan Times,* January 30, 1958.

"The Theology of Reinhold Niebuhr," 1954(?), in Clayborne Carson, Ralph E. Luker, Penny A. Russell, and Peter Holloran, eds., *The Papers of Martin Luther King, Jr., Volume II: Rediscovering Precious Values, July 1951–November 1955* (Berkeley: University of California Press, 1994), pp. 269–279.

Fragment of Application to Boston University, December 1950(?), *Papers I,* p. 390.

Letter to Sankey L. Blanton, January 1951, *Papers I,* p. 391.

Letter to Alberta Williams King, October 1948, *Papers I,* p. 161.

Quoted in Peters, "'Our Weapon Is Love.'"

"The Significant Contributions of Jeremiah to Religious Thought," November 1948, *Papers I,* pp. 181–194.

"A Conception and Impression of Religion Drawn from Dr. Edgar S. Brightman's Book Entitled 'A Philosophy of Religion,'" March 28, 1951, *Papers I,* pp. 407–416.

4. BOSTON UNIVERSITY

PRINCIPAL SOURCE:

Stride Toward Freedom, chapter 6.

OTHER SOURCES:

"Rediscovering Lost Values," sermon at Second Baptist Church, Detroit, Michigan, February 28, 1954, *Papers II,* pp. 248–256.

Press conference on donation of papers to Boston University, Boston, Massachusetts, September 11, 1964 (OGCP, MBU).

Letter to George W. Davis, December 1, 1953, *Papers II,* pp. 223–224.

Abstract of "A Comparison of the Conceptions of God in the Thinking of Paul Tillich and Henry Nelson Wieman," April 15, 1955, *Papers II,* pp. 545–548.

"Memories of Housing Bias in Boston," *Boston Globe,* April 23, 1965.

5. CORETTA

PRINCIPAL SOURCES:

Stride Toward Freedom, chapter 1, and "Family in siege," unpublished draft.

Coretta Scott King, *My Life with Martin* (New York: Henry Holt, 1969, rev. 1993), chapter 3.

Interview with Edward T. Ladd.

Interview with Arnold Michaelis, *Martin Luther King, Jr.: A Personal Portrait* (videotape), December 1966 (MLKEC, INP).

OTHER SOURCES:

"Remarks in Acceptance of the NAACP Spingarn Medal," Detroit, Michigan, June 28, 1957 (ABSP, DHU).

Interview with Martin Agronsky, NBC's *Look Here,* Montgomery, October 27, 1957 (NBCC, NNNBC).

Interview with John Freeman.

Quoted in Poston, "Fighting Pastor."

Letter to Coretta Scott King, Atlanta, July 18, 1952; and letter to Coretta Scott King, Boston, July 23, 1954 (CSKC, INP).

6. DEXTER AVENUE BAPTIST CHURCH

PRINCIPAL SOURCE:

Stride Toward Freedom, chapters 1, and 2; and "Montgomery Before the Protest," unpublished draft of *Stride Toward Freedom* (MLKP, MBU).

OTHER SOURCES:

"Recommendations to the Dexter Avenue Baptist Church for the Fiscal Year 1954–
    55," September 5, 1954, *Papers II,* pp. 287–294.
Address to Dexter Avenue Baptist Church Congregation, Montgomery, May 2,
    1954 (CSKC, INP).
"The Three Dimensions of a Complete Life," sermon at Dexter Avenue Baptist
    Church, Montgomery, January 24, 1954 (CSKC, INP).
"Looking Beyond Your Circumstances," sermon at Dexter Avenue Baptist Church,
    September 18, 1955 (CSKC, INP).
Letter to Francis E. Stewart, July 26, 1954, *Papers II,* pp. 280–281.
Letter to Walter R. McCall, October 19, 1954, *Papers II,* pp. 301–302.
Letter to Ebenezer Baptist Church Members, November 6, 1954, *Papers II,*
    pp. 313–314.
Letter to Howard Thurman, October 31, 1955, *Papers II,* pp. 583–584.
Letter to John Thomas Porter, November 18, 1955, *Papers II,* p. 590.
Letter to L. Harold DeWolf, January 4, 1957 (MLKP, MBU).
Letter to Edward H. Whitaker, November 30, 1955, *Papers II,* p. 593.
Quoted in Poston, "The Boycott and the New Dawn."
Quoted in "My Life with Martin Luther King, Jr.," interview with Coretta Scott
    King, SCLC radio program, December 1969 (SCLCT, INP).

7. MONTGOMERY MOVEMENT BEGINS

PRINCIPAL SOURCES:

Stride Toward Freedom, chapters 1 and 2; and "The Decisive Arrest," unpublished
    draft of *Stride Toward Freedom,* May 1958 (MLKP, MBU).
"The Montgomery Story," address at Forty-seventh Annual NAACP Convention,
    San Francisco, California, June 27, 1956, in Clayborne Carson, Stewart Burns,
    Susan Carson, Peter Holloran, and Dana L. H. Powell, eds., *The Papers of
    Martin Luther King, Jr., Volume III: Birth of a New Age, December 1955–
    December 1956* (Berkeley: University of California Press, 1997), pp. 299–310.

OTHER SOURCES:

Address at Montgomery Improvement Association Mass Meeting at Holt Street
    Baptist Church, December 5, 1955, *Papers III,* pp. 71–79.
"Facing the Challenge of a New Age," address at First Institute for Nonviolence
    and Social Change, Atlanta, December 3, 1956, *Papers III,* pp. 451–463.
Quoted in Poston, "Fighting Pastor."

8. THE VIOLENCE OF DESPERATE MEN

PRINCIPAL SOURCE:

Stride Toward Freedom, chapters 5, 7, and 8; and "Family in Siege," draft.

OTHER SOURCES:

"Walk for Freedom," May 1956, *Papers III*, pp. 277–280.

"Why Jesus Called a Man a Fool."

"A Testament of Hope," *Playboy* 16 (January 1969): 175.

"Nonviolence: The Only Road to Freedom," *Ebony* 21 (October 1966): pp. 27–30.

Notes on MIA Executive Board Meeting, by Donald T. Ferron, January 30, 1956; and notes on MIA Mass Meeting at First Baptist Church, by Willie Mae Lee, January 30, 1956, *Papers III*, pp. 109–112, 113–114.

Interview with Martin Agronsky.

Quoted in Joe Azbell, "Blast Rocks Residence of Bus Boycott Leader," *Montgomery Advertiser*, Montgomery, January 31, 1956, *Papers III*, pp. 114–115.

Quoted in Wayne Phillips, "Negroes Pledge to Keep Boycott," *New York Times*, February 24, 1956. *Papers III*, pp. 135–136.

9. DESEGREGATION AT LAST

PRINCIPAL SOURCE:

Stride Toward Freedom, chapters 8 and 9; "Family in Siege," unpublished draft; and "The Violence of Desperate Men," unpublished draft (MLKP-MBU).

OTHER SOURCES:

Statement on ending the bus boycott, Montgomery, December 20, 1956, *Papers III*, pp. 485–487.

"Montgomery Sparked a Revolution," *Southern Courier*, December 11–12, 1965.

Reactions to Conviction, *Papers III*, pp. 198–199.

"A Knock at Midnight," in *Strength to Love*, chapter 6.

"The Montgomery Story."

Letter to Lillian Eugenia Smith, May 24, 1956, *Papers III*, pp. 273–274.

Letter to Sylvester S. Robinson, October 3, 1956, *Papers III*, pp. 391–393.

Interview with Joe Azbell, Montgomery, March 23, 1956, *Papers III*, pp. 202–203.

"Desegregation and the Future," address at annual luncheon of National Committee for Rural Schools, New York, December 15, 1956, *Papers III*, pp. 472–473.

Quoted in L. D. Reddick, *Crusader Without Violence*.

10. THE EXPANDING STRUGGLE

PRINCIPAL SOURCE:

Stride Toward Freedom, chapters 9–11.

OTHER SOURCES:

"Conquering Self-Centeredness," sermon at Dexter Avenue Baptist Church, Montgomery, August 11, 1957 (MLKJP, GAMK).

"The Future of Integration," address to the United Packinghouse Workers of America, AFL-CIO, Chicago, October 2, 1957 (UPWP, WHi).

"Facing the Challenge of a New Age," December 3, 1956.

"Facing the Challenge of a New Age," January 1, 1957.

"Give Us the Ballot," address at the Prayer Pilgrimage for Freedom, Washington, D.C., May 17, 1957 (MLKJP, GAMK).

"South-Wide Conference to Draft Final Plans for a Voting Rights Campaign," press release, Montgomery, October 30, 1957 (UPWP, WHi).

Letter to O. Clay Maxwell, November 20, 1958 (MLKP, MBU).

Letter to Frank J. Gregory, May 7, 1957 (MLKJP, GAMK).

Letter to Dwight D. Eisenhower, November 5, 1957 (NAACPP, DLC).

Letter to Fannie E. Scott, January 28, 1957 (MLKP, MBU).

Telegram to Coretta Scott King, New Orleans, February 14, 1957 (CSKC, INP).

Interview with Mike Wallace, "Does Desegregation Equal Integration?" *New York Post,* July 11, 1958.

Interview with Mike Wallace, "Self-Portrait of a Symbol: Martin Luther King," *New York Post,* February 15, 1961.

Interview with Martin Agronsky.

"The Consequences of Fame," *New York Post,* April 14, 1957.

Quoted in Poston, "Where Does He Go from Here?" *New York Post,* April 14, 1957.

11. BIRTH OF A NEW NATION

PRINCIPAL SOURCES:

"The Birth of a New Nation," sermon at Dexter Avenue Baptist Church, Montgomery, April 7, 1957 (MLKEC, INP).

Interview with Etta Moten Barnett, Accra, Ghana, March 6, 1957 (EMBC, INP).

OTHER SOURCES:

"Concerning Southern Civil Rights," address at Mississippi Freedom Party rally, Jackson, Mississippi, July 25, 1964 (MMFR, INP).

Why We Can't Wait (New York: New American Library, 1964), p. 21.

Annual Report, Dexter Avenue Baptist Church, Montgomery, November 1, 1956–October 31, 1957 (DABCC, INP).

12. BRUSH WITH DEATH

PRINCIPAL SOURCES:

Why We Can't Wait, p. 17

"I've Been to the Mountaintop," address at the Bishop Charles J. Mason Temple, Memphis, Tennessee, April 3, 1968 (MLKJP, GAMK).

"Advice for Living," *Ebony* 14 (December, 1958): 159.

OTHER SOURCES:

Annual Report, Dexter Avenue Baptist Church, Montgomery, November 1, 1957–November 30, 1958 (DABCC, INP).

Letter to the mass meeting of the Montgomery Improvement Association, October 6, 1958 (HG, GAMK).

Interview on assassination attempt by Izola Curry, New York, September 30, 1958 (MMFR, INP).

Statement issued from Harlem Hospital, New York, September 30, 1958 (MLKP, MBU).

Statement upon return to Montgomery, Montgomery, October 24, 1958 (MLKJP, GAMK).

13. PILGRIMAGE TO NONVIOLENCE

PRINCIPAL SOURCES:

"My Trip to the Land of Gandhi," *Ebony* 20 (July 1959): 84–86.

"Sermon on Mahatma Gandhi," at Dexter Avenue Baptist Church, Montgomery, March 22, 1959 (MLKJP, GAMK).

"A Walk Through the Holy Land," at Dexter Avenue Baptist Church, Montgomery, March 29, 1959 (MLKJP, GAMK).

"The Death of Evil upon the Seashore," in *Strength to Love,* chapter 8.

OTHER SOURCES:

"Remaining Awake Through a Great Revolution," sermon at National Cathedral, Washington, D.C., March 31, 1968 (MLKJP, GAMK).

"The American Dream," address at Lincoln University, Pennsylvania, June 6, 1961 (MLKP, MBU).

"The American Dream," sermon at Ebenezer Baptist Church, Atlanta, July 4, 1965 (MLKEC, INP).

"Equality Now: The President Has the Power," *Nation* 192 (February 4, 1961): 91–95.

Statement on leaving India, New Delhi, March 9, 1959 (MLKP, MBU).

Quoted in the Tour Diary of James Bristol, March 10, 1959 (AFSCR, AFSCA).

"Pilgrimage to Nonviolence."

Letter to G. Ramachandran, May 19, 1959 (MLKP, MBU).

Why We Can't Wait, p. 135.

14. THE SIT-IN MOVEMENT

PRINCIPAL SOURCES:

"The Burning Truth in the South," *Progressive* 24 (May 1960): 8–10.

Annual Address on the Fourth Anniversary of the Montgomery Improvement Association, December 3, 1959 (MLKJP, GAMK).

"Foreword," in William Kunstler, ed., *Deep in My Heart* (New York: William Morrow, 1966), pp. 21–26.

OTHER SOURCES:

"The Time for Freedom Has Come," *New York Times Magazine,* September 10, 1961. Copyright © 1961 by the New York Times Co. Reprinted by permission.

"A Creative Protest," address in Durham, North Carolina, February 16, 1960 (DJG, INP).

Why We Can't Wait, chapter 2.

Statement at Youth March for Integrated Schools, Washington, D.C., April 18, 1959 (MLKJP, GAMK).

Statement to press at beginning of the Youth Leadership Conference, Raleigh, North Carolina, April 15, 1960 (MLKP, MBU).

Farewell Message to Dexter Avenue Baptist Church Congregation, November 29, 1959 (MLKJP, GAMK).

Letter to Allan Knight Chalmers, April 18, 1960 (MLKP, MBU).

Letter to James W. Shaeffer, December 4, 1959 (MLKP, MBU).

Form letter to supporters, June 1960 (MLKP, MBU).

Letter to William Herbert Gray, April 6, 1960 (MLKP, MBU).

Quoted in "King Accepts Atlanta Job; Leaving City," *Montgomery Advertiser,* November 30, 1959.

15. ATLANTA ARREST AND PRESIDENTIAL POLITICS

PRINCIPAL SOURCE:

Interview with Berl I. Bernhard for John F. Kennedy Presidential Library, Atlanta, March 9, 1964 (MLKJP, GAMK).

OTHER SOURCES:

Why We Can't Wait, p. 147.

Why We Chose Jail, Not Bail: Statement to judge after the arrests at Rich's, Atlanta, October 19, 1960 (CSKC, INP).

"Out on Bond," *Atlanta Journal,* October 28, 1960.

Letter to Irl G. Whitchurch, August 6, 1959 (MLKP, MBU).

Letter to Chester Bowles, June 24, 1960 (CB, CtY).

Letter to Mrs. Frank Skeller, January 30, 1961 (MLKP, MBU).

Quoted in Andrew Young, *An Easy Burden* (New York: HarperCollins, 1996), p. 175.

16. THE ALBANY MOVEMENT

PRINCIPAL SOURCES:

Diary in Albany Jail, July 10–11, July 27–August 10, 1962 (CSKC, INP).

"Why It's Albany," *New York Amsterdam News,* August 18, 1962.

"Fumbling on the New Frontier," *Nation,* 194 (March 3, 1962): 190–193.

"Albany, Georgia—Tensions of the South," draft of article for *New York Times Magazine,* August 20, 1962 (MLKJP, GAMK).

Why We Can't Wait, chapters 1 and 2.

Address to District 65-AFL-CIO at Laurels Country Club, Monticello, New York, September 8, 1962 (MLKJP, GAMK).

OTHER SOURCES:

Letter to Earl Mazo, September 2, 1958 (MLKP, MBU).

Form letter to supporters, December 19, 1961 (JWWP, DHU).

"America's Great Crisis," address to Transport Workers Union Convention, New York, October 5, 1961 (TWUC, NNU-T).

"Solid Wall of Segregation Cracks at Albany," *SCLC Newsletter,* March, 1963 (MLKJP, GAMK).

Quoted in Vic Smith, "Peace Prevails," *Albany Herald,* December 18, 1961.

"Turning Point of Civil Rights," *New York Amsterdam News,* February 3, 1962.

"A Message from Jail," *New York Amsterdam News,* July 14, 1962.

"The Case against Tokenism," *New York Times Magazine,* August 5, 1962. Copyright © 1962 by the New York Times Co. Reprinted by permission.

"Terrible Cost of the Ballot," *New York Amsterdam News,* September 1, 1962 (MLKJP, GAMK).

Statement on release from jail, Albany, Georgia, July 13, 1962 (MLKJP, GAMK).

Address and responses to questions at National Press Club, Washington, D.C., July 19, 1962 (MLKP, MBU).

Statement on Violence in Albany, with W. G. Anderson, July 25, 1962 (CSKC, INP).

Telegram to John F. Kennedy, August 2, 1962 (JFKP, MWalK).

Telegram to John F. Kennedy, September 11, 1962 (JFKP, MWalK).

Interview with Alex Haley.

Quoted in *Time,* January 3, 1964, p. 15.

"Interview, Man of the Year," *Time* 83 (January 3, 1964): 13–16, 25–27.

17. THE BIRMINGHAM CAMPAIGN

PRINCIPAL SOURCE:

Why We Can't Wait, chapters 3 and 4; and draft of *Why We Can't Wait* (MLKP, MBU).

OTHER SOURCES:

Statement on Injunction, April 11, 1963, in Alan F. Westin and Barry Mahoney, *The Trial of Martin Luther King* (New York: Crowell, 1974), p. 79.

"Most Abused Man in Nation," *New York Amsterdam News,* March 31, 1962.

Address at Mass Meeting at St. Luke's Baptist Church, Birmingham, May 5, 1963 (MLKJP, GAMK).

Address at Mass Meeting, Yazoo City, Mississippi, June 21, 1966 (MLKJP, GAMK).

Telegram to John F. Kennedy, April 16, 1963 (JFKP, MWalK).

18. LETTER FROM BIRMINGHAM JAIL

PRINCIPAL SOURCE:

Why We Can't Wait, chapter 5.

OTHER SOURCES:

Address and press conference at St. John Baptist Church, Gary, Indiana, July 1, 1966 (AC, InU-N).

19. FREEDOM NOW!

PRINCIPAL SOURCE:

Why We Can't Wait, chapter 6.

OTHER SOURCES:

Statement at Sixteenth Street Baptist Church, Birmingham, May 3, 1963 (DCST, AB).

Statement at Mass Meeting at St. Luke's Baptist Church.

Statement at Mass Meeting, Birmingham, May 10, 1963 (MLKEC, INP).

"What a Mother Should Tell Her Child," sermon at Ebenezer Baptist Church, Atlanta, May 12, 1963 (MLKJP, GAMK).

Interview with Kenneth B. Clark, in *King, Malcolm, Baldwin: Three Interviews by Kenneth B. Clark* (Middletown, Connecticut, 1963), p. 27.

Interview with Alex Haley.

Press Conference USA, videotaped interview, Washington, D. C., July 5, 1963 (DJG, INP).

20. MARCH ON WASHINGTON

PRINCIPAL SOURCES:

Why We Can't Wait, chapter 7; and "A Summer of Discontent," draft for *Why We Can't Wait,* September 1963 (MLKP, MBU).

Address at March on Washington for Jobs and Freedom, Washington, D.C., August 28, 1963 (SCLCT, INP).

OTHER SOURCES:

Interview with Donald H. Smith, Altanta, November 29, 1963 (DHSTR, WHi).

Affidavit, Martin Luther King, Jr., vs. Mister Maestro, Inc. and Twentieth Century Fox Record Corporation, U.S. District Court, S.D. of New York, December 16, 1963 (MLKEC, INP).

21. DEATH OF ILLUSIONS

PRINCIPAL SOURCES:

Why We Can't Wait, chapter 8.

"Epitaph and Challenge," *SCLC Newsletter,* November–December 1963.

"Eulogy for the Martyred Children," Birmingham, September 18, 1963 (MLKJP, GAMK).

Meeting with John F. Kennedy and civil rights leaders, audio recording, Washington, D.C., September 19, 1963 (JFKP, MWalK).

OTHER SOURCES:

Annual Address to Seventh Annual Convention of SCLC, Virginia Union, Richmond, September 27, 1963 (MLKJP, GAMK).

Interview with Alex Haley.

Address on Three of the Children Killed at Sixteenth Street Baptist Church, Birmingham, September 18, 1963 (MLKP, MBU).

Handwritten Notes on John F. Kennedy assassination, November 1963 (MLKJP, GAMK).

"What Killed JFK?" *New York Amsterdam News,* December 21, 1963.

Christmas letter to the Family of Denise McNair, December 1963 (MLKJP, GAMK).

22. ST. AUGUSTINE

PRINCIPAL SOURCES:

Why We Can't Wait, chapter 8.

"Let Justice Roll Down," *Nation* 200 (March 15, 1965): 269–274. Copyright © 1965. Reprinted by permission.

"St. Augustine Florida, 400 Years of Bigotry and Hate," *SCLC Newsletter,* June 1964.

Statement on St. Augustine, Atlanta, June 17, 1964 (MLKJP, GAMK).

Annual Address to Eighth Annual Convention of SCLC, Savannah, Georgia, October 1, 1964 (SAVFC, WHi).

Passage of 1964 Civil Rights Act, Atlanta, July 2, 1964 (MLKJP, GAMK).

OTHER SOURCES:

"Hammer of Civil Rights," *Nation* 198 (March 9, 1964): 230–234.

Statement on Goldwater and St. Augustine, ABC interview, St. Augustine, Florida, July 16, 1964 (MLKJP, GAMK).

"Quest for Peace and Justice," Nobel Prize Lecture at University of Oslo, Oslo, Norway, December 11, 1964 (MLKJP, GAMK).

23. THE MISSISSIPPI CHALLENGE

PRINCIPAL SOURCES:

Statement in support of Freedom Democratic Party, Jackson, Mississippi, July 22, 1964 (MLKJP, GAMK).

Annual Address to Eighth Annual Convention of SCLC.

Address to Southern Association of Political Scientists, November 13, 1964 (MLKJP, GAMK).

"Ready in Mississippi," *New York Amsterdam News*, August 29, 1964.

"Pathos and Hope," *New York Amsterdam News*, March 3, 1962.

"People to People," *New York Amsterdam News*, September 1964.

OTHER SOURCES:

"Passage of 1964 Civil Rights Act," July 2, 1964.

Statement before the Credentials Committee, Democratic National Committee, Atlantic City, New Jersey, August 22, 1964 (MLKJP, GAMK).

24. THE NOBEL PEACE PRIZE

PRINCIPAL SOURCES:

"Mighty Army of Love," *New York Amsterdam News*, November 7, 1964.

"What the Nobel Prize Means to Me," *New York Amsterdam News*, November 28, 1964.

Acceptance Address at Nobel Peace Prize Ceremony, Oslo, Norway, December 10, 1964 (MLKJP, GAMK).

Statement Concerning Nobel Prize Money, Oslo, Norway, December 17, 1964 (MLKJP, GAMK).

"Dreams of Brighter Tomorrows," *Ebony* 20 (March 1965): 43.

OTHER SOURCES:

"Quest for Peace and Justice."

Address on South African Independence, London, England, December 7, 1964 (ACA-ARC, LNT).

Statement on the Nobel Peace Prize, Forneby, Norway, December 9, 1964 (MLKJP, GAMK).

Address upon Acceptance of the New York City Medallion, New York, December 17, 1964 (MLKJP, GAMK).

"The Nobel Prize," *Liberation* (January 1965): 28–29.

"Struggle for Racial Justice," address at Recognition Dinner, Atlanta, January 27, 1965 (NF, GEU).

"After the Nobel Ceremony, A Tender Moment Is Shared," *Ebony* 20 (March 1965): 38.

25. MALCOLM X

PRINCIPAL SOURCES:

Interview with Alex Haley.

"The Nightmare of Violence," *New York Amsterdam News,* February 25, 1965.

Press conference on the Death of Malcolm X, the Nation of Islam and Violence, Los Angeles, February 24, 1965 (MLKJP, GAMK).

OTHER SOURCES:

Telegram to Betty Shabazz, February 26, 1965 (MLKJP, GAMK).

Letter to Edward D. Ball, December 14, 1961 (MLKP, MBU).

Transcript, Testimony in *Williams v. Wallace,* March 11, 1965 (MLKJP, GAMK).

Interview with Robert Penn Warren, in *Who Speaks for the Negro?,* Robert Penn Warren, ed. (New York: Random House, 1965), pp. 203–221.

26. SELMA

PRINCIPAL SOURCES:

"Movement to Washington," Address at SCLC's Ministers Leadership Training Program, Miami, February 23, 1968 (MLKEC, INP).

"Selma—The Shame and the Promise," *Industrial Unions Department Agenda* 1 (March 1965): 18–21.

"Civil Rights No. 1—The Right to Vote," *New York Times Magazine,* March 14, 1965, p. 26. Copyright © 1965 by the New York Times Co. Reprinted by permission.

Transcript, Testimony in *Williams v. Wallace.*

Meeting scheduled with Hubert Humphrey, press release, Washington, D.C., February 7, 1965 (MLKJP, GAMK).

"Behind the Selma March," *Saturday Review* 48 (April 3, 1965): 16–17.

"After the March—An Open Letter to the American People," Atlanta, April 1, 1965 (MLKJP, GAMK).

Annual Address to Ninth Annual Convention of SCLC, Birmingham, Alabama, August 11, 1965 (MLKJP, GAMK).

OTHER SOURCES:

Address to rally prior to Selma March, Selma, Alabama, February 1, 1965 (MLKJP, GAMK).

"A Letter from Selma: Martin Luther King from a Selma, Alabama Jail," *New York Times*, February 5, 1965. Copyright © 1965 by the New York Times Co. Reprinted by permission.

Instructions from Selma Jail to movement associates, February 1965 (MLKJP, GAMK).

"Let Justice Roll Down," *The Nation*, March 15, 1965

Statement on brutal beating of three white ministers, March 10, 1965 (MLKJP, GAMK).

Handwritten draft of statement regarding death of James Reeb, March 11, 1965 (MLKJP, GAMK).

Statement announcing judge's permission to stage march to Selma, Montgomery, March 16, 1965 (MLKJP, GAMK).

Statement regarding the address made by Lyndon Baines Johnson on the situation in Selma, March 16, 1965 (MLKJP, GAMK).

Interview in Selma, Alabama, March 24, 1965 (MMFR, INP).

Address at St. Jude's, Montgomery, March 24, 1965 (MLKJP, GAMK).

Address at Selma to Montgomery March, March 25, 1965 (MLKJP, GAMK).

Address and Press Conference at St. John Baptist Church, Gary, Indiana, July 1, 1966.

Where Do We Go From Here: Chaos or Community? (New York: Harper and Row, 1967), pp. 1–2.

Form letter to supporters, June, 1965 (WAR, INP).

27. WATTS

PRINCIPAL SOURCES:

"A Cry of Hate or a Cry for Help?" Special to the *New York Times Magazine* draft (MLKJP, GAMK).

Statement on arrival in Los Angeles, August 17, 1965 (MLKJP, GAMK).

"Feeling Alone in the Struggle," *New York Amsterdam News*, August 28, 1965.

OTHER SOURCES:

"A Christian Movement in a Revolutionary Age," Rochester, New York, September 28, 1965 (CSKC, INP).

"Beyond the Los Angeles Riots, Next Stop: The North," *Saturday Review* 48 (November 13, 1965): 33–35.

"The Crisis in Civil Rights," Chicago, July 1967 (MLKJP, GAMK).

28. CHICAGO CAMPAIGN

PRINCIPAL SOURCES:

"Why Chicago Is the Target," *New York Amsterdam News*, September 11, 1965.
Where Do We Go from Here.
"The Good Samaritan," sermon at Ebenezer Baptist Church, Atlanta, August 28, 1966 (MLKJP, GAMK).
"One Year Later in Chicago," handwritten draft, February 1967 (SCLCR, GAMK).
Quoted in *Federal Role in Urban Affairs Hearings,* testimony before Subcommittee on Executive Reorganization, Committe on Government Operations, U.S. Senate, December 15, 1966.

OTHER SOURCES:

Statement to the press, Chicago, July 7, 1965 (MLKJP, GAMK).
The Chicago Plan, press release, Atlanta, January 7, 1966 (MLKJP, GAMK).
Address to Freedom Rally at Soldiers Field, Chicago, July 10, 1966 (MLKJP GAMK).
Statement on West Side Riots, Chicago, July 17, 1966 (MLKJP, GAMK).
"Why I Must March," address, Chicago, August 18, 1966 (MLKEC, INP).
Statement on nonviolence, Grenada, Mississippi, September 19, 1966 (MLKJP, GAMK).
"A Gift of Love," *McCalls* 94 (December 1966): 146–147.
Keynote address, National Conference for New Politics, Chicago, August 31, 1967 (MLKJP, GAMK).
Press conference, Liberty Baptist Church, Chicago, March 24, 1967 (MLKJP, GAMK).
"What Are Your New Year's Resolutions?" sermon at Ebenezer Baptist Church, Atlanta, January 7, 1968 (MLKJP, GAMK).
Interview with Merv Griffin, on *Merv Griffin Show,* July 6, 1967 (MLKEC, INP).
"Conversation with Martin Luther King," in James M. Washington, ed., *Testament of Hope* (San Francisco: Harper and Row, 1986; 1991 ed.), pp. 657–679.
Quoted in Flip Schulke, *King Remembered.*

29. BLACK POWER

PRINCIPAL SOURCE:

Where Do We Go from Here, chapter 2.

OTHER SOURCES:

Address during Meredith March, West Marks, Mississippi, June 12, 1966 (MLKJP, GAMK).

Address at mass meeting, Yazoo City, Mississippi, June 21, 1966 (MLKJP, GAMK).
"It Is Not Enough to Condemn Black Power," signed advertisement in *New York Times,* July 26, 1966.
Statement on Black Political Power, Grenada, Mississippi, June 16, 1966 (MLKJP, GAMK).
"Conversation with Martin Luther King."

30. BEYOND VIETNAM

PRINCIPAL SOURCES:

"Journey of Conscience," draft of address, 1967 (CSKC, INP).
"Beyond Vietnam," address at Riverside Church, New York City, April 4, 1967 (MLKJP, GAMK).
Press conference in Los Angeles, April 12, 1967 (DJG, INP).
"To Chart Our Course of the Future," Address at SCLC staff retreat at Penn Center, Frogmore, South Carolina, May 22, 1967 (MLKJP, GAMK).
Address at SCLC's Ministers Leadership Training Program.

OTHER SOURCES:

"My Dream—Peace: God's Man's Business," *New York Amsterdam News,* January 1, 1966.
Press conference, Los Angeles, California, April 12, 1967.
"Why I Am Opposed to the War in Vietnam," sermon at Ebenezer Baptist Church, Atlanta, April 30, 1967 (MLKJP, GAMK).
"To Serve the Present Age," sermon at Victory Baptist Church, Los Angeles, June 25, 1967 (MLKEC, INP).
Press conference on riots, Ebenezer Baptist Church, Atlanta, July 24, 1967 (MLKJP, GAMK).
Keynote address, National Conference for New Politics.
The Trumpet of Conscience (San Francisco: Harper and Row, 1967), p. 37.
Sermon at Ebenezer Baptist Church, Atlanta, November 5, 1967 (MLKEC, INP).
"What Are Your New Year's Resolutions?" sermon at Ebenezer Baptist Church, Atlanta, January 7, 1968 (MLKEC, INP).
"A Testament of Hope," *Playboy* 16 (January 1969): 175.

31. THE POOR PEOPLE'S CAMPAIGN

PRINCIPAL SOURCES:

Statement on Washington Campaign, Atlanta, December 4, 1967 (MLKJP, GAMK).

"Showdown for Non-Violence," *Look* 32 (April 16, 1968): 23–25.
"Movement to Washington."
Address in Memphis, Tennessee, March 18, 1968 (MVC, TMM and MLKJP, JMK).

OTHER SOURCES:

Address at SCLC staff retreat at Penn Center, May 22, 1967.
"What Are Your New Year's Resolutions?"
Address at mass meeting, Waycross, Georgia, March 22, 1968 (MLKJP, GAMK).
"A Testament of Hope," *Playboy.*

32. UNFULFILLED DREAMS

PRINCIPAL SOURCES:

"Unfulfilled Dreams," sermon at Ebenezer Baptist Church, Atlanta, March 3,
    1968, in *Knock at Midnight,* pp. 191–200.
"I've Been to the Mountaintop."
"The Drum Major Instinct," sermon at Ebenezer Baptist Church, Atlanta, Febru-
    ary 4, 1968, in *Knock at Midnight,* pp. 184–186.

INDEX

Now you can order superb titles directly from Abacus

☐ A Knock at Midnight   Clayborne Carson &
                                    Peter Holloran (eds)   £7.99

☐ Freedom in Exile: The
    Autobiography of the Dalai Lama   Dalai Lama   £9.99
☐ Ancient Wisdom, Modern World   Dalai Lama   £8.99
☐ Long Walk to Freedom   Nelson Mandela   £12.99

The prices shown above are correct at time of going to press. However, the publishers reserve the right to increase prices on covers from those previously advertised, without further notice.

──────────────── ⬭ABACUS⬭ ────────────────

Please allow for postage and packing: **Free UK delivery.**
Europe; add 25% of retail price; Rest of World; 45% of retail price.

To order any of the above or any other Abacus titles, please call our credit card orderline or fill in this coupon and send/fax it to:

Abacus, P.O. Box 121, Kettering, Northants NN14 4ZQ
Fax: 01832 733076   Tel: 01832 737526
Email: aspenhouse@FSBDial.co.uk

☐ I enclose a UK bank cheque made payable to Abacus for £ . . . .
☐ Please charge £ . . . . . . to my Visa, Delta, Maestro.

Expiry Date ☐☐☐☐   Maestro Issue No. ☐☐

NAME (BLOCK LETTERS please) . . . .

ADDRESS . . . .

. . . .

. . . .

Postcode . . . . Telephone . . . .

Signature . . . .

Please allow 28 days for delivery within the UK. Offer subject to price and availability.